Egypt, the Aegean and the Levant

Egypt, the Aegean and the Levant

Interconnections in the Second Millennium BC

Edited by
W. Vivian Davies and Louise Schofield

Published for the Trustees of the British Museum
by British Museum Press

© 1995 The Trustees of the British Museum
Published by British Museum Press
A division of British Museum Publications Ltd
46 Bloomsbury Street
London WC1B 3QQ

British Library Cataloguing in Publication Data
A catalogue record for this book is available from the British Library

ISBN 0-7141-0987-8

Front cover: Bull-leaper against the background
of a maze-pattern. Fragment of Minoan wall-painting
from Tell el-Dab'a. Drawing by Lyla Pinch-Brock.

Back cover: Ivory cosmetic box and bronze bowl
from a grave at Tell es-Sa'idiyeh.

Jacket and plate section designed by Andrew Shoolbred.

Printed in Great Britain by Henry Ling, Dorset.

CONTENTS

PREFACE

Egypt, the Aegean and the Levant publishes in expanded form the proceedings of a colloquium of the same name held at the British Museum in July 1992; it also includes a number of other relevant papers (Cline, Hankey, Stos-Gale et al., Davies) which have been subsequently offered or solicited. Broadly concerned with the subject of interconnections in the eastern Mediterranean world during the Middle and Late Bronze Ages, the volume pays special attention to the evidence from Tell el-Dab'a (Bietak, Morgan, Maguire, Philip, Weinstein, Warren in part), the site of ancient Avaris, the capital of the Hyksos rulers of Egypt during the Second Intermediate Period. Recent excavations at the site by an Austrian team led by Manfred Bietak have unearthed an unparalleled range and quantity of material bearing on Egypt's relations, cultural, economic and political, with the contemporary Mediterranean world - material which now includes, quite unexpectedly, a large collection of Minoan wall-paintings, the first such to be found on Egyptian soil, which have opened up an entirely new area of scholarly research (Bietak, Morgan). For the broader picture, there are contributions on Egypto-Minoan relations in general (Warren) and on cross-cultural evidence from various other key sites, from Amarna in Egypt (Hankey, Parkinson and Schofield, Stos-Gale et al.), from Mycenae on mainland Greece (Cline) and from Tell es-Sa'idiyeh in Jordan (Tubb). Several papers demonstrate the value of scientific analysis for recovering information which would probably not otherwise be retrievable (Philip, Stos-Gale, Davies).

In the editing and preparation of this volume we have received a great deal of practical assistance from various colleagues in the British Museum: from Christine Barratt, Claire Thorne, Helen Cole, Jenny May, Janet Peckham and, especially, Dr Jeffrey Spencer and Pat Terry. On the production side, the work has been seen very efficiently through to press by Joanna Champness and Susanna Friedman of British Museum Press. The costs of publication have been substantially defrayed by a generous grant from the Raymond and Beverly Sackler Foundation, to which the British Museum owes grateful thanks.

W Vivian Davies
Keeper of Egyptian Antiquities
British Museum

Louise Schofield
Curator
Department of Greek and Roman Antiquities
British Museum

AUTHORS' ADDRESSES

Manfred Bietak, Institut für Ägyptologie der Universität Wien, Frankgasse 1, A-1090, Vienna, Austria.

Eric H Cline, History Department, Xavier University, 3800 Victory Parkway, Cincinnati, Ohio 45207-4444, USA.

W Vivian Davies, Department of Egyptian Antiquities, British Museum, Great Russell Street, London WC1B 3DG.

Noel Gale, University of Oxford, Nuclear Physics Laboratory, Keble Road, Oxford OX1 3RH.

Vronwy Hankey, Hosey Croft, Westerham, Kent TN16 1TA.

Judy Houghton, University of Oxford, Nuclear Physics Laboratory, Keble Road, Oxford OX1 3RH.

Louise C Maguire, Department of Archaeology, University of Edinburgh, 16-20 George Square, Edinburgh EH8 9JZ.

Lyvia Morgan, History of Art Department, University of Manchester, Manchester M13 9PL.

Richard Parkinson, Department of Egyptian Antiquities, British Museum, Great Russell Street, London WC1B 3DG.

Graham Philip, Department of Archaeology, University of Durham, 46 Saddler Street, Durham DH1 3NU.

Louise Schofield, Department of Greek and Roman Antiquities, British Museum, Great Russell Street, London WC1B 3DG.

Zofia Stos-Gale, University of Oxford, Nuclear Physics Laboratory, Keble Road, Oxford OX1 3RH.

Jonathan N Tubb, Department of Western Asiatic Antiquities, British Museum, Great Russell Street, London WC1B 3DG.

Peter Warren, University of Bristol, Senate House, Tyndall Avenue, Bristol BS8 1TH.

James M Weinstein, Department of Classics, 120 Goldwin Smith Hall, Cornell University, Ithaca, New York 14850, USA.

MINOAN CRETE AND PHARAONIC EGYPT

Peter Warren

In memory of J D S Pendlebury (1904-1941)
who excavated in both countries and gave his life for one of them

Relationships between Egypt in the Pharaonic period and the contemporary Aegean world form a large and complex subject, supplied by a wealth of evidence. The complexity is increased because relationships were, it will be argued, both direct and influenced by intermediaries, the rulers, merchants and artists of the Levantine states

Our understanding has been formed through more than a dozen major studies and *corpora* by (in order of publication) A J Evans (1921-35), F Matz (1928), J D S Pendlebury (1930), H Kantor (1947), A Furumark (1950), H Groenewegen-Frankfort (1951), J Vercoutter (1956), W S Smith (1965), F Schachermeyr (1967), W Helck (1979), W Ward (1971), B J Kemp and R S Merrillees (1980), J Crowley (1989), and C Lambrou-Phillipson (1990). There are in addition scores of studies on specific topics, such as ivory, Ta-urt iconography or stone vessels. Recent studies specifically on New Kingdom-Aegean Late Bronze Age relationships have been published by S Wachsmann (1987), P Haider (1988a; 1988b; 1989; 1990), E Cline (1987; 1990-91; 1994; and this volume, 91-115), while the doctoral dissertation of J Phillips (1991a, to be published) massively updates Pendlebury's *Aegyptiaca* (1930) and also discusses Egyptianizing works in the Aegean. To be added to all these studies are the outstandingly important discoveries by M Bietak of the wall-paintings of Minoan form and subject at Tell el-Dab'a (Bietak, this volume, 19-28, **Plates 1-4**).

How, first, to review the evidence? This can be done in different ways, each with advantages and disadvantages. Broadly we can either examine the evidence for relationships chronologically, or by material categories, or by interpretative constructs of functional groupings such as gift exchange goods. Proceeding chronologically we retain a framework of historical development, but weaken any sense of categories or interpretative groupings. Discussion by categories and interpretations of material reverses the advantages and disadvantages; it fragments any sense of development, while emphasizing the distinctiveness of the categories. On balance it seems preferable to proceed chronologically, followed by proposed interpretative groupings, in order to try to advance understanding of the makers' and users' meanings and intentions in their material, that is the cognitive correlates of the incomplete, surviving products, Aegean and Aegeanizing in Egypt, Egyptian and Egyp-

tianizing in the Aegean. We end with a summary of the historical development of the exchanges.

Chronologically, contacts can be simplified into three stages: (1) the Cretan prepalatial Early Bronze Age and the Egyptian Early Dynastic, Old Kingdom and First Intermediate Period, c. 3000-1900 BC; (2) the Minoan Cretan Palace Period (Middle Minoan IB-Late Minoan IB) and the Egyptian Middle Kingdom and early New Kingdom down to Tuthmosis III, c. 1900-1425 BC; (3) the Mycenaean Period, beginning with Mycenaean Knossos, the contemporary Aegean and Amenophis III, and continuing with Mycenaean Mainland contacts with the later New Kingdom in the 14th and 13th centuries. This third stage is largely beyond the scope of the present study. It has been thoroughly discussed recently in the works of Cline and Haider.

1. Cretan Prepalatial Early Bronze Age - Early Dynastic, Old Kingdom and First Intermediate Period

Raw materials came in small quantities to Crete, probably but not certainly from Egypt: hippopotamus ivory (worked lower canine at Early Minoan IIA Knossos, c. 2600 BC [Krzyszkowska 1984]), carnelian and amethyst (for which stones see below, p. 6). Gold for jewellery may also have come from Egypt (see pp. 2 and 6); the strongest argument against a north-west Anatolian/north-east Aegean source, where gold was used quite plentifully at EBA Troy and Poliochni, or against north Aegean or Siphnian sources for the gold used in EM Crete, is its non-use in the intervening Cyclades. Not only did ivory come as raw material, but a few EM ivory seals have Egyptian shapes, like the squatting ape (Vandervondelen 1994) and perhaps the fly and the pyramid (Sakellarakis 1967, 276 and fig. 4; Sakellarakis and Sapouna-Sakellaraki 1991, 100 and figs. 69, 70, 76). There are also Egyptian designs such as the tête-bêche arrangement and that of back to back cynocephalus apes (Evans 1921, 119, 123-4; Matz 1928, 31, 33).

Stone vessels also arrived from Egypt (Warren 1969, 105-12). Several are known from Knossos, ranging in date from Predynastic to 6th Dynasty. Although only three are from early contexts (two at Knossos, one from the large tholos at Aghia Triadha [Warren 1980, 493-4; 1981; Warren and Hankey 1989, 125]), some fine bowls in unstratified or in later contexts (sometimes adapted into Minoan shapes at those later dates) may well have been very desirable heirlooms, which had reached Crete

1

at the time of their own *floruit* in Egypt, i.e. in the third millennium BC. In addition to acquiring Egyptian stone vessels the Minoans imitated some Egyptian forms in local Cretan stones, the miniature amphora and small cylindrical jar with everted rim and base (Warren and Hankey, 1989, 125-7, figs. 3-4 and pl. 2).

Tiny beads of faience, disk, globular and spherical, are found in Early Minoan round tombs in southern Crete (Xanthoudides 1924, 31, 124 and pls. xxvia, xxxii, lviii) and at Mochlos (Seager 1912, 55 and fig. 55, VI 35). Both the shape, simple though it is, and the technology are new in EM Crete, but had been used in Egypt since Predynastic times (Lucas and Harris 1962, 44-6). It may well be that the Minoans adopted both from Egypt for their own manufactures, as Evans also proposed (1921, 85, 488).

Egyptian scarabs of the First Intermediate Period and onwards reached Crete in Middle Minoan IA and, more importantly in terms of impact, encouraged the production of Minoan scarabs close to those of Egypt in shape, but with Minoan motifs (Warren 1980, 494-5; Yule 1980; 1981, 78-80; Warren and Hankey 1989, 129; Pini 1989).

A recently discovered object is of greater importance for our subject. This is the clay sistrum from the Middle Minoan IA funerary building 9 in the Arkhanes Phourni cemetery (Sakellarakis and Sapouna-Sakellaraki 1991, 121-2 and fig. 99) **(Plate 11,1)**. Hollow and light in weight to assist sound, this is very probably a Minoan piece (rather than an import), made in clear imitation of the Egyptian instrument (Hayes 1953, 248 for an example in blue faience from the pyramid of Amenemhat I [1963-1934 BC, Kitchen 1989, 153] at el-Lisht). The importance of the Arkhanes sistrum is that it surely implies knowledge of the use and purpose of the Egyptian instrument; in other words we observe symbolic transfer taking place.

A purely decorative transfer seems to have taken place in the opposite direction, since a heart-shaped spiraliform design found on the painted ceiling of the tomb of Hepzefa at Assiut (time of Sesostris I [1943-1898 BC, Kitchen 1989, 153]) is plausibly derived by M C Shaw from Minoan Crete (Shaw 1970; Barber 1991, 345-6 and fig. 15.23), building on the earlier work of H Kantor (1947, 29). Shaw also argues convincingly for a common denominator for the Cretan and Egyptian patterns, namely (exported) Minoan embroidered or woven patterned textiles (Shaw 1970, 28). Such exports of primary goods in MM IA, including fine pottery like the MM I vase from Qubbet el-Hawa tomb 88 (Warren and Hankey 1989, 130), could be the major economic reality behind the bric-à-brac or secondary material of the contemporary Egyptian scarabs in Crete, though the Arkhanes sistrum might reflect a more substantial exchange.

2. Cretan Palace Period - Middle Kingdom to Earlier New Kingdom (Tuthmosis III)

A. Cretan Protopalatial Period - Middle Kingdom, 1900-1700/1550 BC

Scarabs continue to reach Crete, of Middle Kingdom date and in Middle Minoan contexts (Warren and Hankey 1989, 134, 214), and to be both adapted and imitated (Evans 1921, 199-201. Also refs. above). Gold, used notably at Mallia on the hilts of daggers and swords and for the famous pendant with two conjoined insects, might have had an Egyptian source; it appears to have been little used north of Crete, in the Cyclades or on the Mainland, in the Middle Bronze Age. The extensive supplies and mining of gold in Egypt in Middle and earlier New Kingdom times are documented by Lucas and Harris (1962, 224-31) (see also p. 6).

Mallia has further clear Egyptian connections in Middle Minoan II, 18th century BC, namely the Egyptianizing terracotta plaques, notably that of a sphinx, from Quartier Mu, Building D room 4 (Poursat 1978; Poursat in Detournay, Poursat and Vandenabeele 1980, 116-24) **(Plate 11,2)**. We have here an entirely new level of evidence for relationship. Like the earlier Egyptian stone vessels and the Minoan sistrum the plaques are symbolic material but a major iconographical dimension is added. This may be analyzed in terms of the processes of iconographical transfer (Warren 1985a). What is involved is the transfer and modification of meaning between one culture and another. A series of steps may be postulated.

(1) Existing (Egyptian or Minoan) thought or belief.

(2) Transfer of thought, belief or ideology by an artist/craftsman (Egyptian or Minoan) into visual form, e.g. in relief carving, painting, metalwork, terracotta or jewellery, with consequent symbolic value.

(3) Viewing, or indirect perception through description or pattern books, of an (Egyptian) image or object by a (Minoan or Aegean) artist or by an (Aegean) intermediary, traveller or trader, communicating with an (Aegean) artist, or, vice versa, viewing of a Minoan image by an Egyptian.

(4) The relating by an (Aegean) artist of *his or her understanding* of the (Egyptian) image to the beliefs or ideology of his or her own (Aegean) world, and then the expression of this understanding and the now modified (Aegean) belief in the visual terms of (Aegean) iconography and its own structural principles, or vice versa by an Egyptian artist.

(5) Finally *our* understanding of what the Aegean/Egyptian artist was trying to convey, with an awareness that our structuring of reality may very well be different from that of the ancient Aegean or Egypt, just as the Aegean structuring may itself have been different from that of Pharaonic Egypt and vice versa. Herein lies one intellectual challenge within cognitive archaeology.

2

On the Mallia sphinx plaque (**Plate 11,2**), we observe a predominantly Egyptian sphinx, with Osirian beard and tail, while the head is purely Minoan. Here then is knowledge of Egyptian art and symbolism, perhaps adopted by the model stages just described as an Egyptianizing symbol of authority, possibly Minoan priestly authority, as has been argued on other grounds for the buildings of Quartier Mu. Minoan ceramic vessels with Egyptianizing appliqué decoration of a female with sagging breasts (*Gravidenflasche*-type [Brunner-Traut 1970]; for an actual imported Egyptian alabaster example from Katsamba, see Evans 1928, 255-8 and fig. 150), (**Plate 11,3-5**), and of cats, come from the same room in Building D (Poursat 1980 ibid.). Phillips has argued (1991b) that the cats are a purely indigenous creation, but the find context and the Egyptian parallels, even if not exact, suggest the Egyptianizing case should not be abandoned.

Another example of iconographical transfer in operation is seen in J Weingarten's detailed study (1991) of the Minoan adoption and adaptation of the Egyptian hippopotamus goddess Ta-urt (Taweret) into a Minoan fertility spirit or genius who waters vegetation and sacred stones. There happens to be a particularly fine example of the fully-fledged Minoan form in the genii carved in relief on an MM III-LMI serpentine triton shell rhyton from Mallia (Baurain and Darcque 1983).

At the same time, MM IB-II/12th Dynasty, there are Minoan links in Egypt. Fine polychrome pottery is well known from Qubbet el-Hawa, Kahun (also from here a very probably Minoan stone vase lid of serpentine, Kemp and Merrillees 1980, pl. 9 upper - excellent photograph), Harageh, Abydos and el-Lisht, while a recently found MM II cup from Tell el-Dab'a is in a 13th Dynasty context (Walberg 1991a), as is a probably Minoan gold pectoral with opposed dogs (Walberg 1991b and Bietak, this volume, 19-20, **Plate 14,1**).

The great treasure of 153 silver cups and bowls stored in four copper chests in the stone foundations of a temple at Tod has been much discussed. Two of the chests bore the name of Amenemhat II, third king of the 12th Dynasty (1901-1866 BC [Kitchen 1989, 153]). Some writers, notably E Davis (1977, 69-79) and B J Kemp and R S Merrillees (1980, 290-6), have argued against a link to Crete. R Laffineur (1988) and J Maran (1987) have argued for an Aegean link, but with the early Mycenaean, Shaft Grave, culture (16th century BC). The present writer and V Hankey have recently presented a detailed case, supported by new ceramic evidence from Knossos, that many of the Tod vessel forms have very close ceramic parallels in MM IB-II Crete, sufficient to indicate a Minoan origin or at least strong Minoan influence upon the silver vessels (Warren 1980, 495-7; Warren and Hankey 1989, 131-4 and pls. 5-11).

The diorite statuette of the traveller User (Evans 1921, 286-90; Edel 1990) (**Plate 12,1-4**), while it had no chronological context at Knossos, obviously did have some meaning when it first arrived there. E Uphill

(1984) showed how the statuette fitted into a wide distribution of similar Middle Kingdom statuettes of ambassadors, officials, merchants or craftsmen. Possibly User visited Knossos and left his statuette to mark his presence. Whether the reference to the goldcaster in the inscription of the statuette has any connection with any visit by User remains unknown (Edel 1990, 133), but we have already noted both the Egyptian connections and the extent of goldworking at Mallia in Middle Minoan II; in Cretan terms, this is the date of User.

The next connections widen the already remarkably varied range of materials. They come from the period of rule by the Hyksos, 1648-1540 BC. At Knossos there is the alabaster (calcite) lid inscribed with the cartouche of Khyan, the first Hyksos king; the reliability of its stated Middle Minoan III A context, in the 'Initiatory Area' of the North-West Lustral Basin of the palace, has been questioned but should be accepted (Evans 1921, 418-21; Hankey and Warren 1989, 136 with references, and pl. 14, A). Presumably its alabaster jar came with it, though it has not survived. Khyan sent named objects elsewhere outside Egypt, notably an obsidian vase to Bogazköy (Smith 1965, 28). The intention behind these royal objects may have been to cement or to advance trading exchanges of primary mass-produced goods, or they may have been gift exchange or not directly reciprocal diplomatic gifts in order to stabilize inter-state relationships; on occasion, a single royal gift could cover both functions, as when the Pharaoh sent more than a thousand alabaster jars of sweet oil to Babylonia (Amarna Letter 14, iii, 46; information from S. Dalley). Clearly assignment of an object to any of the above categories can be questioned on several grounds, not least the unknown quantitative factors involved in survival through time and in modern discovery. But where imported/exported objects have a highly distinctive or unique character, they can reasonably be understood as the material component of exchanges between rulers or high-ranking officials. By contrast a Hyksos period scarab from the city of Knossos (Warren 1980-81, 89 and fig. 47) continues the earlier instances of surely secondary material acquired by travellers or traders engaged with primary goods or official business.

That artistic connections existed between Crete and Egypt in the Hyksos period is evidenced by the well known jug from shaft tomb 879 at el-Lisht, decorated with birds and dolphins, the latter under Minoan inspiration (Kemp and Merrillees 1980, 220-5 and pls. 29-30; Warren and Hankey 1989, 135-6 and pl. 13). Had the decorator of the el-Lisht jug seen Minoan wall-paintings with dolphins or pithoi decorated with them, like those from Pachyammos? Iconographical transfer may have been complex, since the jug form itself is Syro-Palestinian MB II and birds occur on other pieces of Tell el-Yahudiyeh ware and its imitations in Cyprus.

Artistic and iconographical links in this period have now been raised to a new level by the discoveries of wall-paintings covering a wide range of Minoan subjects in Minoan styles and techniques at Tell el-Dab'a. Their fragmentary remains lay in the destruction debris of the Hyksos capital Avaris, over gardens beside the platform of a huge building (70m x 45m), which they are presumed to have decorated, in areas H/I and H/II of the 'Ezbet Helmi part of the site (Bietak 1992; 1993; this volume, 20-3, **Plates 15-17**). The destruction of the city by Ahmose is dated c. 1540 BC, some eleven years after he became the ruler of Egypt and founder of the 18th Dynasty in 1550 BC.

Some of the fragments have a red ground, in that respect like the 'Saffron Gatherer' fresco from Knossos, which is usually dated the earliest of the Minoan figural paintings. Subjects include bulls and bull-leapers, one astonishingly close to the well-known 'Taureador Fresco' from Knossos (Bietak 1992, 26, lower; this volume, 23, **Plate 2,1;** Hawkes 1968, pl. 9), one associated with a labyrinth pattern viewed from above (Bietak, 1992, 27, upper; this volume, 23, **Plate 1,1**), a scene with an acrobat beside a palm tree (Bietak, this volume, 24, **Plate 3,1**), the pose of the tumbler closely recalling the scene on a chalcedony sealstone from Knossos (Boardman 1970, 100 and pl. 60; 39, col. pl. 13); a leopard (Bietak this volume, 24, **Plate 4,2**); the Minoan flounced skirt of a large female figure; the arm and hand of a female with flowers resembling Cretan dittany (*Origanum dictamnus L.*); fragments of a large male figure with black hair and blue scalp like the shaved heads of Theran figures (Bietak, this volume, 24, **Plate 3,2**); a foot fragment with white boot like those of the acrobat; blue papyrus with brown stem like the depictions on the river scene of the miniature fresco from Thera Akrotiri, West House (room 5 east wall); part of a conical rhyton with handle; a possible river flowing diagonally across a labyrinth painting, and a fine fragment of a griffin's wing (Bietak, this volume, 24, **Plate 4,3**), its detail closely recalling the wing of the griffin supporting the seated goddess from the painting above the Lustral Basin of Ashlar Building 3 at Akrotiri (**Plate 4,4**).

Analysis of these astonishing discoveries has scarcely begun. Also to be taken into account are the newly discovered (1992) hundreds of fragments of paintings from an area some 200m distant from the paintings just described (Bietak, this volume, 23). But what is most striking about the paintings from beside the platform is the diversity of elements. Some of them could well have religious connections (griffin, rhyton, skirt of the large female figure), while the remarkable labyrinth depictions recall a closely similar fragment of labyrinth painting from the palace of Knossos (Evans, 1921, 356-7 and fig. 256) and another, part of a magnificent frieze, from the town site of Phaistos, Chalara, of MM III date (Levi 1967-8, 152 and n. 1., and fig. 108).

The Minoan connections are many and obvious, but whether Tell el-Dab'a derived the depictions from Crete (Knossos), or vice versa, is a matter for discussion, with major implications for our understanding of the development of Minoan painting. The Tell-el Dab'a paintings come from the destruction stratum preceding the stratum which in all probability corresponds in time to the eruption of Thera (p. 13). The paintings are, therefore, at least as early as, and probably a little earlier than, those at Thera.[1] They were from a great building destroyed in Ahmose's sack of Avaris, c. 1540 BC, and so existed in early LM IA in Cretan terms (Warren and Hankey 1989, 138-40). In order, therefore, to derive the Tell el-Dab'a paintings from Crete, we have to accept well-established figural and naturalistic frescoes in Crete by this date, or earlier, in MM III. But almost no naturalistic or figural painting in Crete can be dated any earlier or even so early, on stratigraphic grounds (Evans 1921, 536-7 and col. pl. VI for a lily fresco on a red-brown ground, possibly MM III), although the Saffron Gatherer was plausibly dated to MM III by Evans for stylistic reasons, notably its red ground and container vases decorated with white spots (Evans 1921, 265-6), and to MM IIIB/LM IA by Immerwahr (1990, 170). So the strength of the case for derivation from Knossos is (1) the extraordinary range and variety of the wholly Minoan subjects at Tell el-Dab'a, (2) the absence of any Egyptian background for the Dab'a paintings, in the subject matter, and the use of red ground and buon fresco technique for ground colours. Evans always postulated a strong MM III range of Minoan wall-paintings at Knossos (e.g. 1928, 680-2). This may then be the origin of the Tell el-Dab'a paintings (as also of those at Tell Kabri).

However, to derive paintings from a place for which the relevant evidence is no earlier, and is probably (the Saffron Gatherer and the Phaistos labyrinth perhaps excepted) a bit later, than the supposed derivations must leave some doubts, and certainly leaves the newness of figural and naturalistic painting in Crete unexplained. Evans himself did not derive Cretan monumental figure painting, which he assigned to MM III, from Egypt. He did derive the 'grandiose conception' of the later processional scheme from there, but at the LM IB stage and in relation to the Minoan processions in the Tombs of the Nobles (1935, 880-1). Immerwahr rightly points to the small size of these Egyptian representations (1990, 90), but does derive the monumentality of Minoan figural painting from Egypt, though on the basis of acquaintance with Middle Kingdom painting (1990, 50-3, 90, 159-60). At the same time she recognizes the difficulty for this proposal, that figural painting is unknown in the protopalatial period in Crete, contemporary with the Middle Kingdom (1990, 160). Indeed it is not known in Crete until another 150-200 years have elapsed.

It is therefore now worth airing an alternative view to that of the Knossian origin of the Tell el-Dab'a paintings, namely that the frescoes there are indeed Minoan, in subject, style, ground colour and technique (these last two with a long Minoan ancestry) and were painted at Avaris to Minoan order (it is not easy to imagine

4

otherwise), but were based on knowledge of Egyptian figural painting, and were *the first such Minoan frescoes to be painted*, providing a model for such work in Crete, to be taken up immediately in early LM IA.

Avaris was no Minoan trading post and no Minoan pottery or other finds are so far reported from the destruction period. Functional analysis of the adjacent large building whose platform alone survived (Bietak 1992, plan on p. 28; this volume, 20, **Plate 15,1-2**) and from which the paintings may have come will be critical. Bietak 1992 (and see this volume, 26) and V Hankey (1993) have already aired the possibility that the queen of one of the last Hyksos rulers was a Minoan.

Although technically of New Kingdom date, two further pieces must be mentioned here because of their close Hyksos connection. These are the axe of Ahmose, conqueror of Avaris and the Hyksos, and the dagger of his mother Ahhotep, both found in her tomb (Evans 1921, 550 and fig. 472; 714-5 and fig. 537; Kantor 1947, 63-4 [dagger]; Smith 1965, 155 and fig. 37; Morgan 1988, 53 and pl. 63; Hankey 1993). The griffin on the axe blade has wings decorated with the 'notched plume' motif. The Minoan origin of this proposed by Evans and with details noted by Morgan (1988, 53, 187, n. 112; this volume, 38) is now well confirmed by the notched plumed wings of the almost contemporary griffin guarding the seated goddess who presides over the crocus gatherers in the painting in Ashlar Building 3 at Akrotiri, Thera (Doumas 1992, pls. 122, 128; Bietak, this volume, **Plate 4,4**). The Aegean origin of a lion chasing a bull in a flying gallop position in a rocky setting on Ahhotep's dagger remains clear, again as proposed by Evans (cf. Kantor 1947, 63-4). Of less clear, though very possibly Aegean, origin is the flying gallop position of animals attacked by a human figure on the gold-plated hilt of the dagger of the Hyksos king Apophis (Evans 1921, 718-9 and fig. 540; Smith 1965, 155). The Egyptian works of the late Second Intermediate Period and earliest New Kingdom present a mirror image of the sphinx plaque at Mallia some 150 years earlier. The plaque showed Egyptian royal symbolism adopted and adapted in Crete; the axe shows a powerful symbol of Minoan religion adopted and adapted as a symbol of political power in Egypt (even though the griffin as such was earlier established in Syria and Egypt [Morgan 1988, 50]). The lion motif of the dagger, locally engraved, expresses the Aegean mode of symbolizing power and speed. Processes of iconographical transfer of ideology expressed in symbols are continuing between the two areas.

While the number and form of contacts throughout the Pharaonic period thus far brought undoubted benefits to both civilizations, they do not appear to have had profound effects on the civilizations as a whole. There are clear limits to Aegeanizing or Egyptianizing effects. But the Hyksos period and perhaps too the inception of the New Kingdom may have been different in this respect. One has the impression, greatly strength-

ened by the discoveries at Tell el-Dab'a, that contacts between Knossos and the Delta were more profound at this time than they had previously been or were to be even among the exchanges under Tuthmosis III.

B. Cretan Neopalatial Period (Late Minoan I) - earlier New Kingdom - 1550-1425 BC
Whereas symbolic and iconographic connections stand out in the Hyksos period and the reign of Ahmose, the following century (1525-1425 BC) yields a spate of essentially economic and political contacts at least as wide-ranging as those of the Middle Kingdom.

Raw materials reached Crete, for which Egyptian sources must be considered. Alabaster (calcite), used for Minoan vases (Warren 1969, 125-6, 143), certainly came from Egypt. Whether rock crystal (used for vases, gems, beads and inlays), amethyst (used for beads, occasionally for seals and for at least one vase, see below) and carnelian (for seals and jewellery) also did so needs discussion.

Small rock crystals occur in Crete (Marinatos 1931), but no Cretan crystal is known that is anywhere near as large as that from the palace of Zakros, which measures c. 8.4 x 7.0cm (Platon 1974, 206, fig. 121), or is large enough to have made the rhyton (height 16.5cm) from the same site (Platon 1974, 122 and fig. 71), or other rock crystal vases (Warren 1969, 136-7, 144), or the disk (10.8cm in diameter) from the Temple Repositories at Knossos (Evans 1921, 471 and fig. 337 G). On the other hand, there is a tantalizing find described to me (9/9/65) by the Cretan geologist M Dialinas of a vein of rock crystals, including ones large enough for the Zakros rhyton, among iron ores near Arolithi in the Rethymno province (Warren 1969, 137), though no such crystals have been collected. While there are occurrences of rock crystal in Egypt (Lucas and Harris 1962, 403) and there are large crystals in northern Yemen (Grohmann 1922, 180; Yule 1981, 197), its use throughout the Pharaonic period seems to have been mainly for small objects, including small vases (Lucas and Harris 1962, 403). Also to be noted is Anatolia, since several rock crystal objects are known from Troy (Schliemann 1880, 428, no. 547; Evans 1921, 471). But we must also not omit reference to the famous rock crystal bowl with reversed duck's head from Mycenae Grave Circle B, Tomb O (Mylonas 1973, 203-5 and pls. 183-5; Marinatos and Hirmer 1960, pl. 212 lower; Warren 1969, 104). While almost certainly a Minoan work, as G Mylonas and the writer independently argued, since neither Egyptians nor Mycenaeans were producing rock crystal vases in the 16th century BC, the bowl is equally clearly under Egyptian influence. Wooden bowls of very similar form, with reversed heads, are (or were in 1964) exhibited in the Egyptian Museum, Cairo, Room 34 Upper. Such vessels might have been copied by a Minoan lapidary in rock crystal, derived, like the shape, from Egypt.

Amethyst sources and uses are well documented in

Egypt, especially in the Middle Kingdom (Lucas and Harris 1962, 388-9; Shaw and Jameson 1993; Shaw 1994) and the raw material could well have come from there to the Aegean. The previously known amethyst vase fragment from the acropolis of Mycenae (Sakellarakis 1976, 181 and pl. VII, 20) has now been joined by a second piece, from the acropolis of Midea (K. Demakopoulou, Conference Lecture, Rewley House, Oxford, 16 April, 1994). The Midea fragment, found in 1991, was in a Late Helladic III B2 context. Both fragments are shown by Demakopoulou to be from the upper part, namely the lip, of a triton shell rhyton (Warren 1969, 91, type 35). It is even conceivable that they could be from one and the same vase, the fragments, still considered valuable as such, becoming separated and dispersed after breakage. But whether there was originally one vase or two, the original(s) must have been extraordinarily fine, valuable and precious. The shape is entirely Minoan (Warren ibid.; Baurain and Darcque 1983). The original(s) was (were) very probably Minoan work created from raw amethyst imported from Egypt in Late Minoan I, the vessel(s) being subsequently conveyed to the Argolid. It (or they) can thus be thought to stand in remarkably close relation to the rock crystal bowl from Mycenae, two (or three) of the finest lapidary productions of Late Minoan I. Carnelian was used quite frequently for jewellery and seals. Its abundant occurrence and frequent use in Egypt (Lucas and Harris 1962, 391) suggest the source of supply for the Aegean, where sources do not appear to be known.

Hippopotamus and elephant ivory were much used in neopalatial Crete (Krzyszkowska 1988), though where the raw material, dramatically evidenced by the tusks from the palace of Zakros (Platon 1974, fig. 25), came from is uncertain. L Hayward (1990) has drawn attention to Hatshepsut's acquisition of 700 tusks from Tjehenu, that is north-west Egypt/north-east Libya. She suggests that, together with Syria (at least by the time of the 14th century Ulu Burun shipwreck), this area is likely to have been a source of supply for the Aegean, rather than Pharaonic Egypt itself sending Sudanese or other southern ivory to Crete. Syrian or western Asiatic ivory also went to Egypt (Krzyszkowska 1988, 226-8).

Gold continued to be used. In neopalatial Crete it was a material for jewellery, seal fittings, objects in sheet form (Arkalokhori cave miniature axes), and was used as leaf covering on stone vessels carved in relief, likewise on seals, and as adjuncts and fittings to objects in other materials. How much it was used for vessels is unknown, at least in part because of the dearth of LM I tomb deposits. E Davis (1977) showed an apparent Minoan preference for silver, in contrast to early Mycenaean preference for gold, though at least one of the two Vapheio gold cups is surely Minoan. Where the metal came from is also unknown, but Egypt remains, as in the earlier periods, a distinct possibility

(Shaw 1994, 110 for mining areas in Egypt). Tuthmosis III's average annual income, at least during a certain part of his reign, was no less than 259kg (Vercoutter 1959). It should also be noted that analysis of Minoan gold pieces has shown them to align with a relatively restricted group of pieces from Syria-Palestine, Cyprus and Rhodes in being free of traces of tin or platinum, a freedom also characteristic of gold from Egyptian mines (Muhly 1983, 6-7, with references), though the correspondence does not prove derivation.

Logs of fine wood, African ebony (*Dalbergia melanoxylon*), were reaching the Aegean in the 14th century (Ulu Burun) (Knapp 1991, 34 for its sources), but whether they were so doing in earlier New Kingdom times is not known. Cedar of Lebanon was used for the shafts of two bronze double-axes (MM III - LMI) from the Arkalokhori cave (Netolitzky 1934), but will of course have come from Lebanon, not Egypt.

Ostrich eggs came to Crete in LM I, to be cleverly adapted into rhytons by the Minoans, who probably sent on the finished products found at Thera and Mycenae (Sakellarakis 1990). Marsa Matruh seems a likely exit port for the eggs (see p. 11), though the known Aegean pottery there is later, LM/LH III (Hulin 1989). A more exotic possible export from Egypt is the *Tridacna* shell. D Reese has discussed their origin - Red Sea, Persian Gulf, Indo-Pacific area - and Mediterranean distribution (1988; 1991). Part of one has been found in a Late Minoan IB (15th century BC) context at Knossos (Stratigraphical Museum excavations, directed by the writer, exc. no. 2025) and part of a remarkable work, an imitation tridacna in malachite, was found by Evans in the palace at Knossos (Evans 1935, 933 and fig. 905; Shackleton in Shackleton, Hood and Musgrave 1987, 286). The source of the malachite is not known and the mineral occurs in Crete itself (specimens from three places shown to the writer by M Dialinas, geologist, 9/9/65). But whether Cretan pieces could be extracted which were large enough to make the copy of the shell (even the fragment, which appears from Evans's illustration to be less than a quarter of the whole, measures about 4.8 x 3.4 cms) is uncertain. Malachite occurs quite widely in Sinai and was mined in Pharaonic times (Lucas and Harris 1962, 203-5, 461-2). It is doubtless found in other places in the Aegean and Near East. But the combination of finds and shape at Knossos, actual shell (very possibly from the Red Sea, the nearest source) and imitation shell in a mineral abundant in Egypt, suggests a possible Egyptian origin for both pieces. Moreover, the chronology of the distribution of unmodified tridacna shells carefully set out by Reese (1988, 40-1 and n. 58) allows us to suggest Tell el-Dab'a as a possible point of departure, though other coastal sites cannot be excluded.

Live animals appear to have been brought to the Aegean. The strongest case is that of monkeys, so carefully painted at Knossos (Cameron 1968, 3, 5) and Thera (Doumas 1992, pls. 85-9). Although the subject-matter of the panels with monkeys in the House of the Frescoes at Knossos is also found in Egyptian paintings (Evans 1928, 447; Cameron 1968, 19; N Marinatos 1987, 418 and figs. 1 and 6 [for the Egyptian type of column shown on the Theran fresco with monkeys]), the extraordinary variety of poses (Cameron ibid.) and anatomical details mastered by the Knossian and Theran painter(s) strongly suggests observation of actual animals, identified as *Cercopithecus aethiops aethiops* from Ethiopia or *C. aethiops tantalus* from south of the Sahara (Cameron 1968, 3, 5).

Antelopes, seen on the walls of Building Beta room 6 at Akrotiri (Doumas 1992, pls. 82-4) and probably on faience plaques from the Temple Repositories at Knossos (Warren 1975, col. pl. p. 97 and caption p. 96 for possibility of antelope), may well have come from Egypt. S Marinatos (1972b, 42-3) identified those in the Theran paintings as *Oryx beisa* from East Africa; the scimitar-horned oryx of North Africa (*O. dammah*) also seems possible, given its location and horns. Egyptian painting rather than live animals might have been the source for those in the Theran painting, and L Morgan has argued that the Theran antelopes include elements of the Cretan agrimi (wild goat) (1988, 59). Nevertheless, details of pose, liveliness and naturalism, as well as the considerable differences between the Theran and Knossian representations, suggest knowledge of actual oryxes.

An exotic bird, the Sudan crowned crane, *Balearica pavonina ceciliae*, may have reached Crete on its own or have been transported there in captivity from Egypt, if the carefully rendered bird with a distinct crested head on an LM I lentoid seal from Knossos is thus identified (Warren 1991a). Although this bird has not been documented north of Khartoum it may well have had more northerly habitats in the somewhat moister climate of the Bronze Age.

Aegean raw materials may have gone to Egypt. S Wachsmann has well argued that Egyptian composite bows were made from the imported horns of the Cretan agrimi, *Capra aegagrus cretensis*, based on the depictions of bows in the tombs of Puimre (Theban Tomb 39) and Menkheperreseneb (Th. T 86), i.e. under Tuthmosis III (1987, 78-92), an interpretation brilliantly anticipated by Evans (1935, 832-6). It may be added, again starting from Evans (1928, 537 and fig. 339), that the vase with goat's head protome depicted in the tomb of Rhekmire (Th. T 100) has LM I analogies in pottery in Crete (Evans 1928, fig. 341; Sackett and Popham 1970, 217, 238 [with refs.], fig. 9 left and pl. 57, a).

The Keftiu-bean is recorded in the Papyrus Ebers (Vercoutter 1956, 40). Whether this is the common *Vicia faba* (Broad bean), the smaller *V. faba equina* (Horse bean) or another bean, *Vigna sinensis* (Merrillees and Winter 1972, 112-5; Manniche 1989, 153-4), none of which need be Aegean, the fact of the name remains - Keftiu-bean. If Keftiu is accepted as Crete, some kind

of bean or pulse was presumably exported from there to Egypt, if only originally, before any local growth in Egypt. As for oil, Merrillees and Winter (1972, 114-5) argued that Cretan olive and sesame oils could be considered particularly suitable substances for trade with Egypt.

A further plant to be considered is the lichen or lichens found with burials of the 11th and late 12th/early 13th Dynasties (Merrillees and Winter 1972, 111-2) and in mummy abdomens of the 19th-21st Dynasties (Lucas and Harris 1962, 312; Merrillees and Winter 1972, 112). The lichen from the mummies was identified as *Parmelia furfuracea* (Lucas and Harris ibid.). While it seems that Syria or Asia Minor could have supplied this species to Egypt (where it is absent), no botanical identification in those areas is specifically documented by Merrillees; moreover, the species does occur in the Aegean, including Crete (Rechinger 1943a, 45; 1943b, 41). The fact that lichen has not been found in archaeological contexts in Crete is a weak argument against Bronze Age export to Egypt, since it is most unlikely to have survived in the soil of Crete. The island, therefore, can be considered a possible source, but it must be noted that species identification of the pre-19th Dynasty lichens does not appear to have been made, and more distant Aegean origins like Samos, where the species also occurs (Rechinger, 1943a, 45), cannot be ruled out (cf. Murray and Warren 1976, 50, n. 43).

Plants may have been involved if another likely form of contact took place, namely the communication of Cretan medical knowledge and practice (at least magical practice) to Egypt. Given the extensive attention to medicine by the Egyptians themselves (Dawson 1942; von Deines, Grapow and Westendorf 1954-73), it is all the more interesting that the London Medical Papyrus (British Museum EA 10059) contains a formula against the 'Asiatic disease' *in the language of the Keftiu* (Vercoutter 1956, 82-5; von Deines, Grapow and Westendorf 1958 (IV, 1) 258, (V) 440; Press 1978, 6). The Keftiu language must, therefore, have been understood, for medical purposes at least, in Egypt. Although the medicaments over which this formula was to be recited are not specified, they could well have been plants, so extensive was their use in Egypt (Manniche 1989, 58-167). It is also more likely that a Keftiu formula believed to have efficacy in Egypt was recited over Keftiu plants rather than, in this instance, Egyptian. The London Medical Papyrus is a copy from the end of the 18th Dynasty, deriving from an older original which is dated in the period from the end of the Second Intermediate Period to the time of Amenophis III (Vercoutter 1956, 82) or even from the end of the third millennium BC (Press ibid., citing von Deines, Grapow and Westendorf ibid.).

It was in the time of Tuthmosis III that the people and country of Keftiu were most frequently referred to in Egyptian records, although they had been known to the Egyptians since the end of the third millennium;

among numerous studies Vercoutter's remains fundamental (1956, 33-122, 369-95; for an excellent recent review, see Sakellarakis and Sakellarakis 1984). I follow these authors (and the great majority of scholars) in the view that the land of Keftiu was specifically Crete (Vercoutter's conclusion, 1956, 394-5). In relation to the foregoing discussion on the possible use of Keftiu, i.e. Cretan, medicinal plants in 18th Dynasty Egypt, we may recall that the island was the source *par excellence* of such plants throughout Greek and Roman antiquity.

While most of the raw materials, living creatures, exotic eggs and shells can be derived from, or argued to have been sent to, Egypt with only more or less probability, this is not the case with Egyptian finished products. These certainly came to Crete in the 16th and 15th centuries BC (MM III-LM I). The main evidence consists of alabaster (calcite) vases, brought perhaps along with the raw alabaster used to make Minoan vessels. While a majority of Egyptian vessels in Crete come from contexts in the next major historical period, Late Minoan II-IIIA/mainly Amenophis III, such as the superlative group in the 'Royal Tomb' at Isopata just north of Knossos (Evans 1906, 146-9 and fig. 125; Warren 1969, 112-3), it is possible that some of these arrived in Crete earlier in New Kingdom times and were there for a few decades before interment in LMII - IIIA1. One thinks especially of the small alabaster amphora with the cartouches of Tuthmosis III from the LM III A 1 tomb B at Katsamba (**Plate 13,3-4**) (Alexiou 1967, 46 and pl. 10; cf. the alabaster vase of Tuthmosis III in the tomb of his grandson Tuthmosis IV [Carter and Newberry 1904, 19 no. 46092, called aragonite]). Other alabaster vases certainly arrived in early New Kingdom times at Aghia Triadha, Knossos, Mallia (see below), Palaikastro and Zakros in Crete, while those in the Vapheio tholos and the Argive Heraion tholos probably came via Crete (Warren 1969, 112-4; 1989).

In addition to these New Kingdom alabaster vessels, there is a magnificent series of Egyptian stone vessels adapted into Minoan shapes in Crete, as well as others on the Greek Mainland which were very probably worked on in Crete and sent on from there (Warren 1969, 44 [Mycenae NM 3080], 103 [Mallia], 104 [Mycenae], 107 [for Shaft Grave I read V], 109 [Zakros, A3 A8]; 1992, 289 and n. 22 [Knossos: Isopata]; Phillips 1989; 1991a). While those from Knossos: Isopata and Zakros are Early Dynastic or Old Kingdom bowls, which could have been adapted at any time down to and including LM I-II (their context dates), the others, for example, from Mallia and Mycenae, started as New Kingdom alabastrons.

As well as adapting Egyptian stone vessels, the Minoans also copied Egyptian forms in local stones. This had begun already in the late prepalatial period (First Intermediate Period in Egyptian terms). Imitations subsequently came to be made in hard stones in Crete, probably already in the Middle Minoan period,

with the copying of beautiful carinated bowls of Chephren diorite (**Plate 13,1**) and in white-spotted obsidian (from Gyali) (**Plate 13,2**) (Evans 1921, 85-8 and figs. 54-5; Warren 1969, 75, 111). By MM III-LM I imitation seems to have reached its height, when a range of Cretan diorites and gabbros was used for high-shouldered bowls copying much older Egyptian forms (Warren 1969, 74-5). The main contribution made by the adapted Egyptian originals and by the Minoan copying in local and imported stones, over a long period, is to extend knowledge of the brilliant Minoan lapidary technology, inspired in these cases by Egyptian forms. In addition, the Egyptian alabaster originals, before adaptation, add to the numbers imported and to arguments based on those numbers.

Recent discoveries at the Minoan port town of Kommos have shown that another and quite different class of Egyptian object was being imported, namely pottery storage amphoras (and their contents, not known). Excellent publication by L V Watrous shows that the jars arrived from Late Minoan I times onwards, with most known from Late Minoan III A 1, the time of Amenophis III (Watrous 1992, 162-3, 172 [arrival in Middle Minoan thought likely], 175). Also imported from Egypt were bowls and pot stands of faience and blue frit, found at Knossos in LM IB and LM II contexts (15th century BC) (Cadogan 1976).

The early New Kingdom in turn received finished goods from the Aegean. Fine LM I and LH II A pottery and its probable contents have been much discussed (e.g. Evans 1928, 497-8, 507-10; 1935, 265-80; Furumark 1950, 203-15; Merrillees and Winter 1972, 101-5, 108-9, 115-7; Kemp and Merrillees 1980, 226-45; Warren and Hankey 1989, 137-44. See also Knapp 1991, 42-3, for a discussion of textual evidence for the ingredients of perfumed oils, summarizing earlier studies). Other valuable Aegean materials, vases of metal and perhaps stone, are documented in the mural decorations of the tombs of Senenmut (Th. T 71), Useramun (Th. T 131), Menkheperreseneb (Th. T 86) and Rhekmire (Th. T 100) at Thebes (Furumark 1950, 223-39; Vercoutter 1956; Wachsmann 1987; Matthäus 1991).

Although none survives, it is as good as certain that textiles with elaborately woven patterns were exported from Crete in the early 18th Dynasty. We have already noted the indirect evidence of the ceiling patterns in the tomb of the 12th Dynasty nomarch Hepzefa (p. 2). For the early 18th Dynasty (and on down to Amenophis III and Tutankhamun, although that does not concern us here) E Barber, building on Kantor (1947, 25, 29, 56-61), has produced a brilliant and detailed analysis (1991, 311-48, though without reference to a fundamental source book by Vilímková and Fortová-Sámalová [1963]). She demonstrates that a considerable number of painted motifs in tombs, notably those of Antef (Th. T 155), Amenemhet (scribe and chief steward of Useramun) (Th. T 82), Hapuseneb (Th. T 67), Amenmose (Th. T 251) and Menkheperreseneb (Th. T

86), will have been derived from Aegean textiles (including mats) and probably decorated leather. Textiles themselves are among the fine materials brought by the embassy (Minoan or from Mycenaean Knossos) depicted in the tomb of Menkheperreseneb. The Egyptians are also likely to have been stimulated by motifs on the kilts of the Cretan emissaries (Vercoutter 1956). Barber has considered too the immediate source of the Aegean textiles and has suggested that in the 12th Dynasty Aegean women weavers may have been resident at Kahun (1991, 351). This somewhat strengthens the previously rather slight case, based on pottery, for Minoan workers at Kahun and Harageh (discussed by David 1986, 186-9, 192-3). In the early 18th Dynasty Tuthmosis III brought back textiles and workers after the sack of Megiddo, whose products would have been added to imports from Crete. Dress patterns depicted on Late Minoan I and contemporary Theran frescoes leave no doubt about the quality and the extent of complex embroidered and woven garments in the earlier neopalatial period.

What of wooden chests for the textiles? Argument is unavoidably complicated, since it involves both Crete and Egypt, dating, the materials of objects and function. It is commonly and rightly accepted that Minoan terracotta larnakes of LM III A were based on wooden originals; in fact, the rectangular wooden coffin on four legs is found in LM II-III A 1 graves around Knossos (recently Watrous 1991, 286). Xanthoudides was the first to argue (long before remains of LM II-III A 1 wooden coffins were found) that the terracotta larnakes reproduced the wooden chests of household furniture (1904, 10-12; cf. Rutkowski 1968, 223). Evans, in accepting this argument, added that they derived from Egyptian wooden household furniture, known from its subsequent funerary use (1906, 9). Watrous, in a most useful study which builds on Evans's view with much additional evidence and illustration (1991, 287-8), argues that the Minoans are likely to have copied the Egyptian chests in LM I, the Mycenaeans of the Shaft Graves (LH I) deriving the form from contemporary Crete. A connection with Egyptian wooden linen chests seems convincing; although those with gabled lid from the tomb of Kha and Meryt cited by Watrous and used by Barber (1991, 345-6) are of early 14th century date, one, plain (plus a decorated miniature), from Sedment tomb 254, is from the time of Tuthmosis III (Merrillees 1968, 62-4, for a full discussion and dating of Sedment T 254). Barber's argument is that some of the painted patterns on the sides of the chests of Kha and Meryt (Watrous 1991, pl. 81, c-e) look like copies of textile patterns. But while accepting the Egyptian connection proposed by Evans and redeveloped by Watrous, one may ask which way round it was. Rutkowski (1968, 223) argued that the early LM wooden coffin (I would prefer to say simply wooden chest) was a combination of the older MM terracotta chest and new carpentry skills. Following Barber's argument, we may ask whether Minoan

wooden chests went to Egypt, containing exported Minoan textiles, such chests perhaps being imitated or independently paralleled (as in Sedment T 254) by Egyptian examples. As Barber says, linen chests would be most appropriately decorated with textile patterns. Original Cretan household chests in wood do not seem at all unlikely, as Xanthoudides and Rutkowski argued. Cretan chests of cypress wood were a notable export from the island in the 16th century AD (Moryson 1617, I, 256).

There remains symbolic material. Here too we find that the exchanges on this deeper level, begun already in the early Middle Kingdom and MM IA Crete, continue (in the Aegean at least) in neopalatial times. Three examples of iconographical transfer may be cited. The first is the depiction of large papyrus plants (Warren 1972, *pace* Doumas 1992, 34) in the House of the Ladies at Thera, argued by N Marinatos to be derived from the Egyptian iconographical form (1984, 92, 94, 96). The papyrus, often represented in triad form (and as such the hieroglyph for the Land of Lower Egypt), was a major symbol of fertility and regeneration in Egypt (J Yoyotte in Posener 1962, 206). While depiction of flowers and plants in triads is an obvious artistic or decorative device, the particular combination of papyrus and triad is likely to be based on a standard Egyptian form, as S Marinatos argued (1951, especially 109-10 and figs. 3-4).

The second example is the gold terminal of a large silver pin from Mycenae Shaft Grave III (Marinatos and Hirmer 1960, pl. 200, left; Hawkes 1968, col. pl. 44 [superb photograph]), very probably a Minoan work. It depicts the great goddess of Minoan religion with her papyrus-lily garland (Marinatos 1951; Warren 1985, 200-1). S Marinatos plausibly derived this representation from Egyptian symbolism, of which the verbal text would be, he argued, 'numerous years of joyful life', here seen as the Minoan goddess bringing continued fertility to the natural world. The Egyptian background of the *waz* or papyrus stalk in relation to the Minoan 'sacral ivy' motif had already been set out by Evans (1928, 480, 776). The *waz*-lily was a constant symbol in Minoan religion (Evans and Evans 1936, 93 s.v. *waz*) and the papyrus a sacred plant (Warren 1985, 201).

Thirdly, there are the tall poles fixed to the facades of Minoan shrine buildings, known from representations on stone vessels with relief scenes (Warren 1969, 174-81 and P 474, P 476, P 477; Platon 1974, figs. 76-7, 94), wall-paintings and sealings from rings engraved with cult scenes. The poles were interpreted as flagstaffs by St. Alexiou, who argued that they were derived from similar attachments to the exterior facades of Egyptian temple pylons, where they are shown with pennants flying (1963; 1969). A pennant in gold sheet from Phaistos, either a votive or an attachment for a model flagstaff, was published by Alexiou. The poles and their pennants may have been sun symbols in Egypt; their symbolic value in Crete was in general terms as in Egypt, namely as markers of sacred space, like the double-axes of sheet bronze set up on freestanding poles in Minoan shrines. They may well have had a more specific meaning too; K Kardara (1966) suggested they were means of summoning a thunder god and an earth goddess, although this view depends in part on the assumption that the upper section of the pole was of metal.

Interpretation and Conclusions

I. Sea Routes and Direction of Exchanges

A question of fundamental importance for understanding the relationships between Crete and Egypt is the direction of shipment of goods: were there direct exchanges, Crete-Egypt, Egypt-Crete, or were they indirect, conducted through intermediaries of the Levantine states and Cyprus? Minoan foreign connections were developed with Anatolia, Cyprus and the Near East as well as with Egypt, and among all these states of the Middle and Late Bronze Ages there were complex and multiple interconnections in the flow of goods, ideas and influences, as the works cited above (p. 1) demonstrate. Indeed the Minoan (and a little later the Mycenaean) palatial economy is the westernmost manifestation of a form which is essentially the same over the whole area of Anatolia, the Levant, Mesopotamia and Egypt. Each had its distinctive emphases (the Hittites and Mycenaeans military and religious, Egypt military and religious with an extraordinary range of technological competence, the Levantine states entrepreneurial, Crete a profound interaction of the aesthetic with the natural environment, through religion), though all were politically pyramidal, palace-centred, redistributive with varying degrees of mercantile interest and freedom, and all promoted interconnections. Within this complex international framework it is nevertheless worth considering whether there were direct Egypt-Crete relationships, since this bears upon the nature and depth of contact between the two civilizations.

Every writer on the subject from antiquity to the present has referred to the wind and sea circulation patterns of the eastern Mediterranean favouring direct sailing south-east from Crete to Egypt, given the prevailing north-westerly summer winds (e.g. recently McCaslin 1980, 88-90; Mantzourani and Theodorou 1991, especially figs. 6-8), and the consequent difficulty of passage north-west from Egypt to Crete (McCaslin 1980, 103-4, 107). In consequence, the anti-clockwise route from Egypt via the Levant coast, Cyprus and southern Anatolia to the Aegean is emphasized in most studies (e.g. Knapp 1991, 40, with references). The Ulu Burun wreck exemplifies such a voyage and its mixed cargo included African ebony. Egyptian goods could then have reached Crete this way. But what of direct passage from Egypt?

We know of direct voyages from Alexandria and Damietta (modern Dumyat) to Crete in the 17th century AD (Randolph [in Crete 1680] 1687, and reprint Athens 1983, 74-5; Triantaphyllidou-Baladié 1988, 207, 301), while in the 18th century the Crete-Alexandria route was the most common from the island (Triantaphyllidou-Baladié 1988, 95-6, 100-1). Since the products included snow exported from Crete (op. cit. 265) and butter brought to it (op. cit. 207), one may suppose that the shortest possible times were aimed at. L V Watrous has reported pre-World War I sailing caiques from Egypt and Libya trading along the south coast of Crete, though in Cretan products. He has also noted periods of the year when the prevailing wind is from the south (Watrous 1992, 177-8).

Perhaps the most instructive (and dramatic) account is that of the French traveller, Cl. Savary (1788). He sailed from Alexandria for Crete in September 1779. It may be observed first from his text that there appears to be nothing abnormal about such a voyage. He explains that with favourable winds he could have expected to complete it in not much more than five days (1788, 18). His wind was exactly that needed, from the south-east (op. cit. 7), but it was very light and after five days the Zakynthiot ship had completed scarcely half the journey. Despite their slowness, Savary estimated that if the light wind continued they would be in view of Rhodes next day, the sixth, and that from there to Crete the passage was not long (op. cit. 11). These details could easily be forgotten, since soon afterwards there was a dramatic change, contrary and strong winds set in, the *zéphir oriental* was gone, and it was to be two months before he landed in Herakleion (op. cit. 127), including eight days on Kasos, driven back there when actually making the final passage from the off-shore island of Dia into Herakleion harbour!

Given what we know of the substantial size of cargoes (Ulu Burun) and of ships (Thera Akrotiri, West House ships fresco, with crews of forty to fifty implied), and that climatic conditions do not appear to have changed much, if at all, since the Bronze Age (cf. Aiginetes 1954; McCaslin 1980, 88), there appears to be no inherent reason why direct voyages could not have taken place from Pharaonic Egypt to Minoan Crete, even if the Levantine-Cyprus-Anatolian route were the more common.

Whether direct voyages did take place can be posited only from the archaeological evidence. Several aspects of it are striking. Down through LM I there is a little Cypriot pottery in Crete and the Aegean (e.g. recently Mantzourani and Theodorou 1991; Watrous 1992, 172) and almost nothing Near Eastern. The Red Lustrous spindle bottle from Gournia may be Syrian, that from Kommos is Cypriot (Watrous ibid.). The Canaanite jar (and contents) from Thera and that from Kommos are Syrian (Watrous ibid.). There was cedar wood from Lebanon (p. 6), a little lapis lazuli and (in MM at least) tin coming to Crete through Syro-Palestinian ports. Invisibles such as spices may well have come too (Knapp 1991 for a detailed review of invisibles in LBA trade). Cretan goods also went to Cyprus and the Near East. At the same time there is a relative absence from Cyprus of the types of Egyptian objects found in Crete down to LM I-II (cf. Weinstein 1981, 14-20). The combination of these points - Egyptian material in Crete, Cretan links with Cyprus, relative absence of Egyptian material in Cyprus - strongly suggests that Cyprus was not, or not exclusively, on the route from Egypt to Crete. And it is almost inconceivable that ships travelling from the Syro-Palestinian coast to the Aegean, with or without goods from Egypt, would not have called at Cypriot ports *en route*.

To support this case against, or against the exclusivity of, the Levantine-Cyprus route as that for Egyptian materials in Crete, there is now the evidence of Egyptian storage amphoras at the south Cretan port of Kommos from at least Late Minoan I onwards (p. 8), to be added to the already striking quantity of Egyptian material and iconographical influences in Crete (and the Peloponnese, perhaps via Crete). Watrous has built the Kommos evidence into an entirely convincing case for a direct route from Egypt to Crete (1992, 172-3, 175-8). The links with Tell el-Dab'a in the 16th century strengthen the case yet further and indeed raise the connections themselves to an unsuspected level. It would, therefore, appear that there are good archaeological grounds, supported by climatic conditions and explicit sailing evidence from later periods, for accepting direct voyages from Crete to Egypt and vice versa, at least from the Middle Minoan period/Middle Kingdom onwards. This was the 'western route' argued by J Vercoutter some years ago (1954, 24-5) and later by W Helck (1979, 38 sqq.); E Cline too has argued in detail for direct communication (1991, 245-6, 255-6, 260-1; 1994).

A subsidiary matter is the point or points of departure from the Egyptian coast. Watrous supports a route due south from Crete (1992, figs. 10-11) to the Libyan coast (190 miles/305km), though this in turn would mean a long land route to and from Egypt. A port such as Marsa Matruh, nearer to the Pharaonic cities, must also be considered, lying as it does south of Karpathos and south-east of Crete. Any direct relationship between Crete and Marsa Matruh is not easy to argue. In favour are the following: Marsa Matruh is nearer to Crete than the Delta ports (250 miles/400km from Zakros as against 338 miles/540km Zakros to Alexandria); summer winds from the north-west would have been as favourable for voyages to Marsa Matruh as to the Delta and southerly winds, in September especially, would have been likewise for voyages back to Crete; it was a likely outlet port for ostrich eggs to reach Crete (many fragments having been excavated at Marsa Matruh [Conwell 1987]), and also for the Egyptian storage vessels at Kommos. Against, on the other hand, is the miniscule amount of Minoan pottery at the site (three fragments, with nothing pre-LM III) as opposed to substantial quantities of Cypriot and Egyptian and some

Mycenaean and Palestinian (Hulin 1989; White 1989); also against is the fact that the Egyptian pottery at Kommos could as easily have come from Delta ports. Direct linkage between Crete and Marsa Matruh thus remains unproven, though it could well have existed. Tell el-Dab'a, at least in Hyksos times, favours links through Delta ports.

II. Explanatory Hypotheses

How, then, may the Crete-Egypt connections be interpreted? So far we have considered them in terms of the material evidence (by no means every detail of it), and on a chronological basis. As a next step we take that evidence as a whole and suggest division of it into four categories, although there would certainly have been overlaps between them.

A. *Primary Exchanged or Traded Materials.* (1) Raw materials (e.g. from Egypt, fine and probably semi-precious stones, fine woods, perhaps gold, ostrich eggs and shells, animals and perhaps birds, probably ivory; from Crete, possibly goat horn, plants and plant products); (2) finished products (e.g. from Egypt, alabaster and faience vessels, pottery storage jars [and their contents - see Watrous 1992, 175 for a possible list]; from Crete, fine pottery [and its contents, probably fine oils] and very probably metal vessels and textiles); (3) organic goods (Knapp 1991) almost certainly formed a significant part of the exchanges. We know from textual evidence that Crete (Captara) exported grain, fermented beverage, oil, decorated weapons and clothing to Ugarit and Mari (Knapp 1991, 37-8, 42); there is no inherent reason why such items could not have gone to Egypt too. The surviving inorganic residues of the two regions are simply a partial representation of the actual or primary economic purpose of the exchanges.

B. *Political or Diplomatic Materials.* These take the form of gifts of individual, high-quality objects, personal (with names) or general, designed to cement or advance trading exchanges of primary goods or other forms of relationship such as royal visits or even dynastic connections. Fine Egyptian vessels in hard stones or alabaster vessels with royal cartouches or inscribed hard stone statuettes (User) may be so interpreted. Metal vessels (shown in the Tombs of the Nobles) and fine textiles could well have represented the Cretan contribution. No clear line can be drawn between such political gifts and primary economic exchanges (cf. Liverani 1983; Zaccagnini 1987); the latter too would have been under royal or partly-dependent merchant control. Note, for example, that on one occasion the Pharaoh sent to Babylonia more than a thousand stone vessels of 'sweet oil' together with stone vessels not containing oil (Amarna Letter 14, iii, 46).

C. *Symbolic Material.* This category comprises the evidence for political, religious or artistic influences by one country as seen on the products of the other, Aegeanizing in Egypt, Egyptianizing in Crete. The influences will have come about by processes of iconographical transfer such as the model proposed above. The Arkhanes sistrum, the Mallia plaque, the Minoan Ta-urt or genius, Ahmose's axe and Ahhotep's dagger, textile designs transferred to tomb decoration in Egypt, probably the Thera triadic papyrus fresco and the gold pin terminal, probably Minoan, from Mycenae, and the Minoan *waz*-lily motif comprise such symbolic material. Here too there is overlap with a political category, since there surely must be political and ideological content behind the Mallia and Ahmose/Ahhotep pieces. The paintings at Tell el-Dab'a appear to promote such symbolic evidence to a new level, very possibly providing visual expression of dynastic or religious connection between Hyksos kingship and Minoan Knossos. Finally, this symbolic material may be seen as more interesting and more significant than the exchange of primary goods, the economic category, since it penetrates, interlocks and modifies to a certain degree the beliefs, ideologies and thinking of each culture.

D. *Secondary Material Accompanying Primary Trade Goods.* To this category may be assigned scarabs and trinkets, brought back as personal talismans or mementos of those carrying out economic or political exchanges. The existence of such a category is supported by the later evidence of the Ulu Burun and Gelidonya shipwrecks, the contents of which can plausibly be divided into primary economic goods and personal possessions. Finally, it should be noted that this category too has overlap: Egyptian scarabs in Crete occasioned local scarabs or scaraboids with Egyptianizing Minoan motifs, and as such made a contribution to Minoan decoration.

III. Crete and Egypt. Historical Summary.
With the quadripartite model of the material evidence, the historical development of the interconnections may be summarized.

(1) The earliest evidence, not extensive, dates from at least Old Kingdom/Early Minoan IIA times, c. 2600 BC. It may have begun even earlier if the Predynastic-Archaic Period/Dynasties I-II stone vessels arrived in Crete around the time of their *floruit* in Egypt. The evidence itself belongs to categories A and B, that is raw materials (if the hippopotamus ivory, semi-precious stones and faience technology came from Egypt) and fine individual stone vessels, the obsidian vase and diorite bowl from Knossos and the pyxis of Chephren diorite from the Aghia Triadha large round tomb (EM II-/MMI/II context) (Warren and Hankey 1989, 125 and pl. 1).
This Egyptian material, because of its context-dates in Crete, poses an interesting question. The Crete-Egypt connections in the second millennium, from the Mid-

dle Minoan/Middle Kingdom period and onwards, are explicable as interchanges between Early State societies of some complexity, based on palatial centres and with socio-political hierarchies. But what was the corresponding socio-political framework of the preceding prepalatial Cretan Early Bronze Age of the third millennium? Egypt had by then developed full statehood and had built significant trade with rulers throughout the Syro-Palestinian region (Klengel 1984, 11-13). But to whom in Crete did Egyptian rulers of the Old Kingdom send fine stone vessels, either directly or by final decisions of Levantine intermediaries such as rulers of Byblos (Warren 1980, 493-4, for early Egyptian stone vessels in Near Eastern contexts)? Stone vessels and perhaps also, at this date, raw materials, such as ivory, look like prestige items; they presuppose demand and a sufficient level of social status and of organization in Crete to promote demand. Egypt, for its part, must have seen some economic *desideratum* in Crete, despite the apparent political imbalance. Knossos was probably the key. Not only does most of the evidence in Crete for third millennium contact come from there, but it was the one site in Crete that was at least proto-urban by the mid-third millennium (Warren 1981) and was presumably a place of sufficient size and importance for foreign rulers to have dealings with, in the form of raw materials and political gifts of high quality. Nothing is known of its political structure in Early Minoan IIA, c. 2600 BC, but, although it was 'prepalatial', some form of urban organization is probable, emerging from its previous four thousand year history. What may have gone in exchange to Egypt at this early date is also unknown, though textiles are one possibility.

(2) By the end of the third millennium and early in the second (First Intermediate Period and early Middle Kingdom, late pre-palatial in Crete), the continued supply of primary material to Crete is implied by secondary materials, the scarabs. At the same time, somewhat more complex relationships emerge with Minoan imitations of small Egyptian stone vessels and of locally made scarabs. If these were no more than artistic or decorational levels of transfer, there is also clear evidence of the transfer of more complex ideas and symbolism seen in the Minoan sistrum from Arkhanes, in a funerary context as in Egypt.

(3) In the Middle Kingdom, very fine decorated Cretan pottery appears in Egypt, as it does in the Near East. Some vessels, bridge-spouted and other jars, may have gone with scented oils as contents, though cups must have gone for their intrinsic ceramic value. These could have been primary traded goods rather than political or diplomatic gifts, appearing as they do at a number of sites. The Tod treasure appears to be a much more valuable consignment, perhaps a major gift to Amenemhat II, unless the silver vessels betoken a more complex situation of Minoan influence on metalwork of a third

region. In any case, the silver itself would have to have been imported into Crete in the first place. Meanwhile the statuette of User, if it arrived at the time of his *floruit*, suggests a diplomatic or commercial visit. The Mallia sphinx plaque is discussed under category C above.

(4) In the Hyksos or Second Intermediate Period, connections appear to have extended well beyond the economic or primary category to the political and symbolic. Most are noticed under C above - Apophis's dagger, Khyan's inscribed lid (and presumably the alabaster jar too) and the paintings of Tell el-Dab'a comprising the evidence, while a Hyksos period scarab from Knossos, probably 15th Dynasty, belongs to the class of secondary materials (Warren 1980-1, 89 and fig. 47; Lambrou-Phillipson 1990, 211, no. 68, and pl. 45, no. 68; Phillips 1991a no. 173).

(5) Despite the major change of dynasty with the inception of the New Kingdom, c. 1550 BC, and the destruction of the Hyksos capital, Avaris, c. 1540 BC, contacts continued in the early New Kingdom. The dagger of Ahhotep and the axe of Ahmose are decorated with Aegean symbolic information, while the axe motifs combine Egyptian conquest of the Hyksos through the medium of an Aegeanizing motif, the Minoan form of griffin. Connections with the reigns of the kings following Ahmose, that is Amenophis I, Tuthmosis I and II, are restricted to a fragment of a decorated Late Minoan I vase from Memphis, dated to the period of Ahmose-Amenophis I by J Bourriau (Warren and Hankey 1989, 139 [for RAT. 590 read RAT. 530]) and to Egyptian influences behind wall-painting at Late Cycladic I (=LM IA) Thera and on objects like the gold pin terminal from Mycenae. Pumice at Tell el-Dab'a in the building level of workmen's houses, which succeeded the city destroyed by Ahmose, provides a connection of a different sort. If the pumice is demonstrated chemically to be from the great Theran eruption, its stratified position and association with numerous royal name scarabs will place the eruption after the reign of Ahmose and before that of Tuthmosis III (i.e. within 1525-1479 BC) (Bietak 1992, 28; 1993; Rohl 1991-2, 75 and fig. left).

The reign of Tuthmosis III (1479-1425 BC), which coincides approximately with Late Minoan IB, appears to have been the next period of strong contact with Crete (cf. above pp. 7-8 on Keftiu). Primary traded goods in the form of raw materials (possibly including gold), finished products (alabaster, faience and pottery vases) and probably live animals came to Crete, and the reception and modification of Egyptian symbolic iconography is likely to have continued. Cretan raw materials and finished products, noted under category A above, went to Egypt, on the evidence of pottery finds, some of them Mycenaean (LH II A), and objects shown brought by Aegeans in the Tombs of the Nobles. Moreover, the reigns of Hatshepsut and Tuthmosis III are the only period in Egypt when contemporary visiting Minoan ambassadors are depicted, in the tombs of Senenmut, Antef, Useramun, Menkheperreseneb and Rhekmire. These depictions appear to mark at least three separate embassies from Crete (recently Wachsmann 1987; Barber 1991, 331-6). The purpose of the embassies was surely economic - to bring goods for exchange or to establish exchange contracts supported by diplomatic gifts such as fine textiles - and/or political, to arrange visits or even dynastic links.

The evidence for import of alabaster vessels to Knossos in particular, in the early New Kingdom and perhaps chiefly in the time of Tuthmosis III, also raises the question of the status of those bringing in the vessels. At Knossos the number of vessels, actual and estimated, and their wide distribution there are such as to suggest trade by independent or semi-independent merchants, alongside the clearly revealed palace-centred or 'royal' trade (Warren 1989; 1991b; for palace-controlled trade, Alexiou 1953-4; 1987; Kopcke 1987; Wiener 1991). E Cline has argued independently, and on the basis of the total range of known Late Bronze Age contacts between Egypt and Crete, for the same interpretation, a combination of royal and private commercial exchanges (1991, 251-3; cf. Zaccagnini 1987, 57), though he may be going too far in proposing that formal, ruler-to-ruler relations with the Aegean may have been initiated by Amenophis III, beyond earlier simple Crete-Egypt trading systems (Cline 1990-91; for an extended discussion of the opposite view, namely royal gradually giving place to mercantile, Sherratt and Sherratt 1991). Although the 'combination' interpretation is argued here, I do not think that distribution of alabaster vessels through the city of Knossos from the palace, the view of St. Alexiou, can yet be entirely ruled out.

Exchanges were to continue after the great destruction of the Minoan civilization in Late Minoan IB, down through the reigns of Amenophis II, Tuthmosis IV and Amenophis III, 1427-1342 BC (Late Minoan II-IIIA). Barber has emphasized textile-based design links between Aegean kilts and tomb decoration in the tomb of Menkheperreseneb (Th. T 86), on the one hand, and LM III A I pottery from Knossos on the other (1991, 348). Menkheperreseneb was active in the reign of Amenophis II (1427-1400 BC). Links may indeed have been even stronger, if the Kom el-Hetan base from the funerary temple of Amenophis III (Cline, this volume, **Plate 6,1**), with its list of Cretan and Aegean place-names, headed by names for the Greek Mainland and Crete, means that the great ruler actually visited the Aegean, as his inscribed faience plaques at Mycenae would confirm (recently, Hankey 1981; very useful update in Cline 1990-91 and this volume, 94, **Plate 6,3**). We referred earlier to overlap between the purely economic and the political definition of foreign goods. Might the magnificent collection of alabaster vessels in the 'Royal Tomb' at Isopata (p. 8) have been a gift sent or even brought to Knossos by Amenophis III? Finally, we may note too the famous ceiling fresco from his palace at Malkata, Thebes (Barber 1991, 348-9 and fig. 15, 24), showing bulls' heads (with a rosette between the horns) placed between rosette-centred spirals. This is perhaps the strongest of the building's Aegean decorative features. It could have been inspired by what he saw on his likely visit, if not by imported Aegean textiles or other media discussed by Barber.

In assessing the form and purpose of exchange between the economies of the Near East, Egypt and the Aegean, one can ask as we did for the third millennium contacts, *cui bono?* The evidence, certainly from the palace periods of each country, indicates a continuum of benefit from ruler and elite officials through merchants to producers and others. While ruler-benefit (royal trade) is always apparent, it is of interest to consider how far down the political, social or economic pyramid the receipt of prestige or other goods extended. For example, the four hundred bronze-smiths of the Mycenaean kingdom of Pylos clearly benefited (if only in the provision of work) from the import of copper and tin. As far as Egypt is concerned in respect of goods, materials and decorations imported from Minoan Crete, the impression is that benefit did not extend beyond ruler and elite (e.g. the owners of the various Tombs of the Nobles). As far as Crete is concerned, both the distribution of Egyptian goods, at Knossos anyway, and the range of imported raw materials suggest the benefits may have extended somewhat further, to include at least some producers.

Minoan civilization undoubtedly derived benefit from Egypt in the different forms we have examined. But those benefits, on the surviving evidence, appear to have formed only a small part in the totality of the Minoan achievement. There are, however, large unknowns among the raw materials, invisibles and perishable goods, including degrees of uncertainty as to whether many of them came from Egypt rather than the states of the Syro-Palestinian area. But some materials and objects certainly did come from Egypt.

Egyptian civilization docs not appear to have needed much from Crete, though Cretan pottery and its contents, probably metal vessels, bows and textiles and complex abstract design-motifs must have given pleasure as well as supplying functional requirements. Not needed much? Those words must now be heavily qualified by the discoveries at Tell el-Dab'a. But Avaris was Hyksos and Hyksos were intruders in the great Pharaonic traditions of Abydos, Memphis and Thebes.

Notes

1. It should be noted that the Theran paintings we see today were not the earliest there, earlier painted plaster having been covered over in at least one place in preparation of the surface for the existing frescoes (Marinatos 1972a, 37 and pls. 91,b-92,a). But the earlier Theran paintings have not shown evidence of figures or other naturalistic depictions.

References

Aiginetes, B 1954. Το κλιμα της Κρητης και ο σταθεροτης του κλιματος της Ελλαδος απο των μινωικων χρονων. *Πραγματειαι της Ακαδημιας Αθηνων* 18, 1-46.

Alexiou, S 1953-4. Ζητηματα του προιστορικου βιου. Κρητομυκηναικον εμποριον. *Αρχαιολογικη Εφημερις* (published 1961), 135-45.

Alexiou, S 1963. Μινωικοι ιστοι σημαιων. *Κρητικα Χρονικα* ΙΖ', 339-51.

Alexiou, S 1967. Υστερομινωικοι ταφοι λιμενος Κνωσου (Κατσαμπα), (*Βιβλιοθηκη της εν Αθηναις Αρχαιολογικης Εταιρειας* 56.) Athens.

Alexiou, S 1969. Ιστοι μινωικων ιερων και αιγυπτιακοι πυλωνες. *Athens Annals of Archaeology* 2, 84-8.

Alexiou, S 1987. Minoan palaces as centres of trade and manufacture. In R Hägg and N Marinatos (eds.), *The Function of the Minoan Palaces. Proceedings of the Fourth International Symposium at the Swedish Institute in Athens, 10-16 June 1984.* Skrifter utgivna av Svenska Institutet i Athen, 4⁰, XXXV, 251-3.

Barber, E J W 1991. *Prehistoric Textiles. The Development of Cloth in the Neolithic and Bronze Ages with Special Reference to the Aegean.* Princeton, Princeton University Press.

Baurain, C and Darcque, P 1983. Un triton en pierre à Malia. *Bulletin de Correspondance Hellénique* 107, 3-73.

Bietak, M 1992. Minoan wall-paintings unearthed at ancient Avaris. *Egyptian Archaeology. The Bulletin of the Egypt Exploration Society* 2, 26-8.

Bietak, M 1993. Avaris and the Minoan World: new excavation results from Tell el-Dab'a (Eastern Nile Delta). Lecture, University College London, 10 May 1993.

Boardman, J 1970. *Greek Gems and Finger Rings. Early Bronze Age to Late Classical.* London, Thames and Hudson.

Brunner-Traut, E 1970. Gravidenflasche. Das Salben des Mutterleibes. In A Kuschke and E Kutsch (eds.), *Archäologie und Alter Testament. Festschrift für Kurt Galling.* Tübingen, J C B Mohr, 35-48.

Cadogan, G 1976. Some faience, blue frit and glass from fifteenth century Knossos. *Temple University Aegean Symposium* 1, 18-19.

Cameron, M A S 1968. Unpublished paintings from the 'House of the Frescoes' at Knossos. *Annual of the British School at Athens* 63, 1-31.

Carter, H and Newberry, P E 1904. *Catalogue général des antiquités égyptiennes. The Tomb of Thoutmôsis IV.* London, Archibald Constable and Co.

Cline, E 1987. Amenhotep III and the Aegean: a reassessment of Egypto-Aegean relations in the 14th century BC. *Orientalia* 56/1, 1-36.

Cline, E 1990-91. Contact and trade or colonization? Egypt and the Aegean in the 14th - 13th centuries BC. *Minos* 25-6, 7-36.

Cline, E 1991. *Orientalia in the Late Bronze Age Aegean: A Catalogue and Analysis of Trade and Contact between the Aegean and Egypt, Anatolia and the Near East.* PhD dissertation UMI no. 9125617.

Cline, E 1994. *Sailing the Wine-Dark Sea. International Trade and the Late Bronze Age Aegean.* BAR International Series, 591. Oxford, Tempus Reparatum.

Conwell, D 1987. On ostrich eggs and Libyans. Traces of a Bronze Age people from Bates' Island, Egypt. *Expedition* 29/3, 25-34.

Crowley, J L 1989. *The Aegean and the East. An Investigation into the Transference of Artistic Motifs between the Aegean, Egypt and the Near East in the Bronze Age.* Studies in Mediterranean Archaeology and Literature Pocket-Book, 51. Jonsered, Paul Åströms Förlag.

David, A R 1986. *The Pyramid Builders of Ancient Egypt. A Modern Investigation of Pharaoh's Workforce.* London, Guild Publishing.

Davis, E N 1977. *The Vapheio Cups and Aegean Gold and Silver Ware.* New York and London, Garland Publishing, Inc.

Dawson, W R 1942. Medicine. In S R K Glanville (ed.), *The Legacy of Egypt.* Oxford, Oxford University Press, 179-97.

Deines, H von, Grapow, H and Westendorf, W 1954-73. *Grundriss der Medizin der alten Ägypter*, 9 vols. Berlin, Akademie-Verlag.

Detournay, B, Poursat, J-C and Vandenabeele, F 1980. *Fouilles exécutées à Mallia. Le quartier Mu* II. *Vases de pierres et de métal, vannerie, figurines et reliefs d'applique, éléments de parure et de décoration, armes, sceaux et empreintes.* Études crétoises, XXXVI. Paris, Paul Geuthner.

Doumas, C 1992. *The Wall-Paintings of Thera.* Athens, The Thera Foundation.

Edel, E 1990. Die hieroglyphische Inschrift auf der Dioritstatuette des User aus Knossos. In S Israelit-Groll (ed.), *Studies in Egyptology Presented to Miriam Lichtheim,* Vol. I. Jerusalem, The Hebrew University, 122-33.

Evans, A J 1906. *The Prehistoric Tombs of Knossos.* (= *Archaeologia* 59 [1905], 391-562). London, B Quaritch.

Evans, A J 1921-35. *The Palace of Minos at Knossos* I (1921), II (1928), III (1930), IV (1935). London, Macmillan.

Evans, J and Evans, A J 1936. *The Palace of Minos at Knossos.* Index Volume. London, Macmillan.

Furumark, A 1950. The settlement at Ialysos and Aegean history. *Opuscula Archaeologica* 6. Skrifter utgivna av Svenska Institutet i Rom, XV, 150-271.

Groenewegen-Frankfurt, H A 1951. *Arrest and Movement. An Essay on Space and Time in the Representational Art of the Ancient Near East.* London, Faber and Faber.

Grohmann, A 1922. *Südarabien als Wirtschaftsgebiet.* Vienna.

Haider, P 1988a. *Griechenland - Nordafrika.* Darmstadt.

Haider, P 1988b. Zu den ägyptisch-ägäischen Handelsbeziehungen zwischen ca. 1370 und 1200 v. Chr.: I Das Handelssystem. *Münstersche Beiträge zur Antiken Handelsgeschichte* 7, 12-26.

Haider, P 1989. Zu den ägyptisch-ägäischen Handelsbeziehungen zwischen ca. 1370 und 1200 v. Chr.: II Handelsgüter und Handelswege. *Münstersche Beiträge zur Antiken Handelsgeschichte* 8, 1-29.

Haider, P 1990. Ägäer in ägyptischen Diensten zwischen ca. 1550 und 1200 v. Chr. *Laverna* 1, 18-49.

Hankey, V 1981. The Aegean interest in El Amarna. *Journal of Mediterranean Anthropology and Archaeology* 1, 38-49.

Hankey, V 1993. A Theban 'battle axe'. *Minerva* 4/3, 13-14.

Hawkes, J 1968. *Dawn of the Gods.* New York, Random House.

Hayes, W C 1953. *The Scepter of Egypt. A Background for the Study of Egyptian Antiquities in the Metropolitan Museum of Art. Part I. From the Earliest Times to the End of the Middle Kingdom.* New York, Metropolitan Museum of Art.

Hayward, L G 1990. The origin of the raw elephant ivory used in Greece and the Aegean during the Late Bronze Age. *Antiquity* 64, 103-9.

Helck, W 1979. *Die Beziehungen Ägyptens und Vorderasiens zur Ägäis bis ins 7. Jahrhundert v. Chr.* Erträge der Forschung, 120. Darmstadt, Wissenschaftliche Buchgesellschaft.

Hulin, L 1989. Marsa Matruh 1987, preliminary ceramic report. *Journal of the American Research Center in Egypt* 26, 115-26.

Immerwahr, S A 1990. *Aegean Painting in the Bronze Age.* University Park and London, The Pennsylvania State University Press,

Kantor, H 1947. The Aegean and the Orient in the second millennium BC. *American Journal of Archaeology* 51, 1-103.

Kardara, Kh. 1966. Υπαιθριοι στυλοι και δενδρα ως μεσα επιφανειας του θεου του κεραυνου. *Αρχαιολογικη Εφημερις*, 149-200.

Kemp, B J and Merrillees, R S 1980. *Minoan Pottery in Second Millennium Egypt.* Mainz am Rhein, Philipp von Zabern.

Kitchen, K A 1987. The Basics of Egyptian Chronology in Relation to the Bronze Age. In P Åström (ed.), *High, Middle or Low? Acts of an International Colloquium on Absolute Chronology held at the University of Gothenburg 20th-22nd August 1987,* Part 1. Gothenburg, Paul Åströms Förlag, 37-55.

Kitchen, K A 1989. Supplementary notes on 'The Basics of Egyptian Chronology'. In P Åström (ed.), *High, Middle or Low? Acts of an International Colloquium on Absolute Chronology held at the University of Gothenburg 20th-22nd August 1987*, Part 3. Gothenburg, Paul Åströms Förlag, 152-9.

Klengel, H 1984. Near Eastern trade and the emergence of interaction with Crete in the third millennium BC. *Studi Micenei ed Egeo-Anatolici* 24, 7-19.

Knapp, A B 1991. Spice, drugs, grain and grog: organic goods in Bronze Age East Mediterranean trade. In N H Gale (ed.), *Bronze Age Trade in the Mediterranean. Papers presented at the Conference held at Rewley House, Oxford, in December 1989.* Studies in Mediterranean Archaeology, XC. Jonsered, Paul Åströms Förlag, 21-68.

Kopcke, G 1987. The Cretan palaces and trade. In R Hägg and N Marinatos (eds.), *The Function of the Minoan Palaces*. Skrifter utgivna av Svenska Institutet i Athen, 4°, XXXV, 255-60.

Krzyszkowska, O 1984. Ivory from hippopotamus tusk in the Aegean Bronze Age. *Antiquity* 58, 123-5.

Krzyszkowska, O 1988. Ivory in the Aegean Bronze Age: elephant tusk or hippopotamus ivory? *Annual of the British School at Athens* 83, 209-34.

Laffineur, R 1988. Réflections sur le Trésor de Tod. *Aegaeum* 2, 17-30.

Lambrou-Phillipson, C 1990. *Hellenorientalia. The Near Eastern Presence in the Bronze Age Aegean, ca. 3000-1100 BC. Interconnections Based on the Material Record and Written Evidence plus Orientalia: A Catalogue of Egyptian, Mesopotamian, Mitannian, Syro-Palestinian, Cypriot and Asia Minor Objects from the Bronze Age Aegean.* Studies in Mediterranean Archaeology and Literature Pocket-book, 95. Göteborg, Paul Åströms Förlag.

Levi, D 1967-8. L'abitato di Festòs in località Chálara. *Annuario della Scuola Archeologica di Atene* 45-46, 55-166.

Liverani, M 1983. Political lexicon and political ideologics in the Amarna letters. *Berytus* 31, 41-56.

Lucas, A and Harris, J R 1962. *Ancient Egyptian Materials and Industries.* London, Edward Arnold.

Manniche, L 1989. *An Ancient Egyptian Herbal.* London, British Museum Publications.

Mantzourani, E K and Theodorou, A J 1991. An attempt to delineate the sea routes between Crete and Cyprus during the Bronze Age. In V Karageorghis (ed.), *Proceedings of an International Symposium 'The Civilizations of the Aegean and their Diffusion in Cyprus and the Eastern Mediterranean 2000-600 BC', 18-24 September 1989*, 38-56. Cyprus, Department of Antiquities.

Maran, J 1987. Die Silbergefässe von eṭ-Tôd und die Schachtgräberzeit auf dem griechischen Festland. *Praehistorische Zeitschrift* 62, 221-7.

Marinatos, N 1984. *Art and Religion in Thera. Reconstructing a Bronze Age Society.* Athens, D & I Mathioulakis.

Marinatos, N 1987. The monkey in the shrine: a fresco fragment from Thera. In *ΕΙΛΑΠΙΝΗ. Τομος τιμητικος για τον Καθηγητη Νικολαο Πλατωνα*, 417-21. Heraklion, Βικελαια Βιβλιοτηκι.

Marinatos, S 1931. Η ορεια κρυσταλλος. *Εφημερεις Αρχαιολογικη*, 158-60.

Marinatos, S 1951. 'Numerous years of joyful life' from Mycenae. *Annual of the British School of Athens* 46, 102-16.

Marinatos, S 1972a. *Excavations at Thera V (1971 Season)*. Athens, Βιβλιοθηκη της εν Αθηναις Αρχαιολογικης Εταιρειας, 64.

Marinatos, S 1972b. *Treasures of Thera.* Athens, Commercial Bank of Greece.

Marinatos, S and Hirmer, M 1960. *Crete and Mycenae.* London, Thames and Hudson.

Matthäus, H 1991. Die absolute Chronologie der Periode SM II/SH II B. Il Congresso internazionale di Micenologia, Roma - Napoli, 14-20 Ottobre 1991.

Matz, F 1928. *Die frühkretischen Siegel.* Berlin/Leipzig, Walter de Gruyter.

McCaslin, D E 1980. *Stone Anchors in Antiquity: Coastal Settlements and Maritime Trade-routes in the Eastern Mediterranean ca. 1600-1050 BC.* Studies in Mediterranean Archaeology, LXI. Göteborg, Paul Åströms Förlag.

Merrillees, R S 1968 *The Cypriote Bronze Age Pottery found in Egypt.* Studies in Mediterranean Archaeology, XVIII. Lund, Paul Åströms Förlag.

Merrillees, R S and Winter, J 1972. Bronze Age trade between the Aegean and Egypt. Minoan and Mycenaean pottery from Egypt in the Brooklyn Museum. *Miscellanea Wilbouriana* 1. New York, The Brooklyn Museum, 101-33.

Morgan, L 1988. *The Miniature Wall Paintings of Thera. A Study in Aegean Culture and Iconography.* Cambridge, Cambridge University Press.

Muhly, J 1983. Gold analysis and the sources of gold in the Aegean. *Temple University Aegean Symposium* 8, 1-14.

Murray, C and Warren, P M 1976. *PO-NI-KI-JO* among the dye-plants of Minoan Crete. *Kadmos* 15, 40-60.

Mylonas, G 1973. *Ο ταφικος κυκλος Β των Μυκηνων.* Athens, Βιβλιοθηκη της εν Αθηναις Αρχαιολογικης Εταιρειας, 73.

Netolitzky, F 1934. Pflanzliche Nahrungsmittel und Hölzer aus dem prähistorischen Kreta und Kephallonia. *Buletinul Facultăţii de Ştiinţe din Cernăuţi* 8, 172-8.

Pendlebury, J D S 1930. *Aegyptiaca. A Catalogue of Egyptian Objects in the Aegean Area.* Cambridge, Cambridge University Press.

Phillips, J 1989. The minoanization of Aegyptiaca. Colloquium paper. *Recent Research on the Inter-*

national Trade of the Late Bronze Age in the Mediterranean. American Schools of Oriental Research, Meeting, Anaheim, California, 17-21 November, 1989.

Phillips, J 1991a. *The Impact and the Implications of the Egyptian and Egyptianizing Objects Found in Bronze Age Crete ca. 3000-1100 BC.* Ph.D. dissertation, Toronto.

Phillips, J 1991b. The Minoan origin of some so-called 'Egyptianizing' features, *Z' (7th) International Cretological Congress, Rethymno 25-31 August 1991. Abstracts,* 75.

Pini, I 1989. Zehn frühkretische Skarabäen. In T Hackens (ed.), *Technologie et analyse des gemmes anciennes/Technology and Analysis of Ancient Gemstones.* PACT 23, 99-111.

Platon, N 1974. Ζακρος. Το νεον μινωικον ανακτορον.

Posener, G 1962. *A Dictionary of Egyptian Civilization.* London, Methuen and Co.

Poursat, J-C 1978. Le sphinx minoen: un nouveau document. *Antichità Cretesi. Studi in onore di Doro Levi* I, 111-4.

Press, L 1978. The worship of healing divinities and the oracle in the 2nd millennium BC from a study in Aegean glyptic art. *Archeologia* (Warsaw) 29, 1-15.

Randolph, B 1687. *The Present State of the Islands in the Archipelago (or Arches), Sea of Constantinople and Gulph of Smyrna; with the Islands of Candia, and Rhodes* (also reprint, Βιβλιοθηκη Ιστορικων Μελετων 181, Athens 1983).

Rechinger, K H 1943a. Flora Aegaea. Flora des Inseln und Halbinseln des ägäischen Meeres. *Denkschriften der Akademie der Wissenschaften in Wien. Mathematisch-naturwissen-schaftliche Klasse* 105/1, 1-924.

Rechinger, K H 1943b. Neue Beiträge zur Flora von Kreta. *Denkschriften der Akademie der Wissenschaften in Wien. Mathematisch-naturwissenschaftliche Klasse* 105/2, 1-184.

Reese, D S 1988. A new engraved Tridacna shell from Kish. *Journal of Near Eastern Studies* 47/1, 35-41.

Reese, D S 1991. The trade in Indo-Pacific shells into the Mediterranean basin and Europe. *Oxford Journal of Archaeology* 10, 159-96.

Rohl, D 1991-2. *Journal of the Ancient Chronology Forum* 5, 75 (caption) and photo left (pumice).

Rutkowski, B 1968. The origin of the Minoan coffin. *Annual of the British School at Athens* 63, 219-27.

Sackett, L H and Popham, M R 1970. Excavations at Palaikastro, VII. *Annual of the British School at Athens* 65, 203-42.

Sakellarakis, E and Sakellarakis, Y 1984. The Keftiu and the Minoan thalassocracy. In R Hägg and N Marinatos (eds.), *The Minoan Thalassocracy. Myth and Reality. Proceedings of the Third International Symposium at the Swedish Institute in Athens, 31*

May - 5 June 1982. Skrifter utgivna av Svenska Institutet i Athen, 4°, XXXII, 192-203.

Sakellarakis, J A 1967. Minoan cemeteries at Arkhanes. *Archaeology* 20/4, 276-81.

Sakellarakis, J A 1976. Mycenaean stone vases. *Studi Micenei ed Egeo-Anatolici* 17, 173-87.

Sakellarakis, J A 1990. The fashioning of ostrich-egg rhyta in the Creto-Mycenaean Aegean. In D A Hardy, C G Doumas, J A Sakellarakis and P M Warren (eds.), *Thera and the Aegean World III,* I. Archaeology. Athens, The Thera Foundation, 285-308.

Sakellarakis, J A and Sapouna-Sakellaraki E, 1991. *Archanes.* Athens, Ekdotike Athenon S. A.

Savary, Cl. 1788. *Lettres sur la Grèce, faisant suite des celles sur l'Égypte.* Paris, Onfroi.

Schachermeyr, F 1967. *Ägäis und Orient.* Österreichische Akademie der Wissenschaften, Philosophisch-historische Klasse, Denkschriften, 93.

Schliemann, H 1880. *Ilios. City and Country of the Trojans.* London, J Murray.

Seager, R B 1912. *Explorations in the Island of Mochlos.* Boston and New York, American School of Classical Studies at Athens.

Shackleton, J, Hood, S and Musgrave, J H 1987. The Ashmolean shell plaque, AM 1938.537. *Annual of the British School at Athens* 82, 283-95.

Shaw, I 1994. Pharaonic quarrying and mining: settlement and procurement in Egypt's marginal regions. *Antiquity* 68, 108-19.

Shaw, I and Jameson, R 1993. Amethyst mining in the Eastern Desert: a preliminary survey at Wadi el-Hudi. *Journal of Egyptian Archaeology* 79, 81-97.

Shaw, M C 1970. Ceiling patterns from the tomb of Hepzefa. *American Journal of Archaeology* 74, 25-30.

Sherratt, A and Sherratt, S 1991. From luxuries to commodities: the nature of Mediterranean Bronze Age trading systems. In N H Gale (ed.), *Bronze Age Trade in the Mediterranean. Papers presented at the Conference held at Rewley House, Oxford, in December 1989.* Studies in Mediterranean Archaeology, XC. Göteborg, Paul Åströms Förlag, 351-98.

Smith, W S 1965. *Interconnections in the Ancient Near East.* New Haven and London, Yale University Press.

Triantaphyllidou-Baladié, G 1988. *Το εμποριο και η οικονομια της Κρητης απο της αρχες της Οθωμανικης Κυριαρχιας εως το τελος του 18ου αιωνα (1669-1795).*

Uphill, E 1984. User and his place in Egypto-Minoan history. *Bulletin of the Institute of Classical Studies* 31, 213.

Vandervondelen, M 1994. Singes accroupis. Étude de quelques statuettes de la période prépalatiale crétoise. *Studia Varia Bruxellensia ad Orbem*

Graeco-Latinum Pertinentia 3, 175-83.

Vercoutter, J 1954. *Essai sur les relations entre Egyptiens et Préhellènes.* L'Orient Ancien Illustré, 6. Paris.

Vercoutter, J 1956. *L'Égypte et le monde égéen préhellénique.* Étude critique des sources égyptiennes. Cairo, IFAO.

Vercoutter, J 1959. The gold of Kush. Two gold-washing stations at Faras East. *Kush* 7, 120-53.

Vilímková, M and Foŕtová-Šámalová, P 1963. *Egyptian Ornament.* London, Allan Wingate.

Wachsmann, S 1987. *Aegeans in the Theban Tombs.* Orientalia Lovaniensia Analecta, 20. Leuven, Peeters.

Walberg, G 1991a. The finds at Tell el-Dab'a and Middle Minoan chronology. *Ägypten und Levante* 2, 115-8.

Walberg, G 1991b. A gold pendant from Tell el-Dab'a. *Ägypten und Levante* 2, 111-3.

Ward, W 1971. *Egypt and the East Mediterranean World 2200-1900 BC.* Beirut, American University in Beirut.

Warren, P M 1969. *Minoan Stone Vases.* Cambridge, Cambridge University Press.

Warren, P M 1975. *The Aegean Civilizations.* Oxford, Phaidon.

Warren, P M 1980. Problems of chronology in Crete and the Aegean in the third and earlier second millennium BC. *American Journal of Archaeology* 84, 487-99.

Warren, P M 1980-81. Knossos: Stratigraphical Museum excavations 1978-80. Part I. *Archaeological Reports for 1980-1,* 27, 73-92.

Warren, P M 1981. Knossos and its foreign relations in the Early Bronze Age. *Πεπραγμενα του ΔΠ Διεθνους Κρητολογικου Συνεδριου. Ηρακλειο, 29 Αυγουστου – 3 Σεπτεμβριου 1976* Α', 628-37. Athens, University of Crete.

Warren, P M 1985a. The Aegean and Egypt: matters for research. *Discussions in Egyptology* 2, 61-4.

Warren, P M 1985b. The fresco of the garlands from Knossos. In P Darcque and J-C Poursat (eds.), *L'iconographie minoenne. Actes de la Table Ronde d'Athènes (21-22 avril 1983).* Bulletin de Correspondance Hellénique Supplément, XI, 188-208.

Warren, P M 1989. Egyptian stone vessels from the city of Knossos: contributions towards Minoan economic and social structure. *APIAΔNH* 5 *(Αφιερωμα στον Στυλιανο Αλεξιου),* 1-9.

Warren, P M 1991a. Realism and naturalism in Minoan art - *partes pro toto.* Z' *(7th) International Cretological Congress, Rethymno, 25-31 August 1991.* Abstracts, 97. Rethymno.

Warren, P M 1991b. A merchant class in Bronze Age Crete? The evidence of Egyptian stone vases from the city of Knossos. In N H Gale (ed.), *Bronze Age Trade in the Mediterranean. Papers presented at the Conference held at Rewley House, Oxford, in December 1989.* Studies in Mediterranean Archaeology, XC. Göteborg, Paul Åströms Förlag, 295-301.

Warren, P M 1992. Lapis lacedaemonius. In J M Sanders (ed.), *ΦΙΛΟΛΑΚΩΝ. Lakonian Studies in Honour of Hector Catling.* Oxford, Oxbow and British School at Athens, 285-96.

Warren, P M and Hankey, V 1989. *Aegean Bronze Age Chronology.* Bristol, Bristol Classical Press.

Watrous, L V 1991. The origins and iconography of the Late Minoan painted larnax. *Hesperia* 60, 285-307.

Watrous, L V 1992. *Kommos,* III *The Late Bronze Age Pottery.* Princeton, Princeton University Press.

Weingarten, J 1991. *The Transformation of Egyptian Taweret into the Minoan Genius. A Study in Cultural Transmission in the Middle Bronze Age.* Studies in Mediterranean Archaeology, LXXXVIII. Göteborg, Paul Åströms Förlag.

Weinstein, J 1981. The Egyptian empire in Palestine: a reassessment. *Bulletin of the American Schools of Oriental Research* 241, 1-28.

White, D 1989. The third season of Marsa Matruh, the site of a Late Bronze Age trading station on the northwest coast of Egypt. *American Journal of Archaeology Abstracts* 13, 34-5.

Wiener, M H 1991. The nature and control of Minoan foreign trade. In N H Gale (ed.), *Bronze Age Trade in the Mediterranean. Papers presented at the Conference held at Rewley House, Oxford, in December 1989.* Studies in Mediterranean Archaeology, XC, 325-50.

Xanthoudides, S 1904. Εκ Κρητης. *Αρχαιολογικον Δελτιον* 3, 1-56.

Xanthoudides, S 1924. *The Vaulted Tombs of Mesará.* Liverpool and London, University Press of Liverpool and Hodder and Stoughton.

Yule, P 1980. Native Cretan scarabs and scarboids and Aegean chronology. Paper to *The Fifth International Colloquium on Aegean Prehistory. University of Sheffield 16-19 April 1980.* (Colloquium not yet published).

Yule, P 1981. *Early Cretan Seals: a Study of Chronology.* Marburger Studien zu Vor- und Frühgeschichte, 4 (1980).

Zaccagnini, C 1987. Aspects of ceremonial exchange in the Near East during the second millennium BC. In M Rowlands, M T Larsen and K Kristiansen (eds.), *Centre and Periphery in the Ancient World.* Cambridge, Cambridge University Press, 57-65.

CONNECTIONS BETWEEN EGYPT AND THE MINOAN WORLD
NEW RESULTS FROM TELL EL-DAB'A/AVARIS

Manfred Bietak

Early Connections

Contacts between Egypt and the Minoan world as represented within the stratigraphic sequence at Tell el-Dab'a have appeared within two very definite periods **(Fig. 1)**. The first in the time of the early 13th Dynasty (c. first half of the 18th century BC), the second during the period comprising the end of the Hyksos period and the early 18th Dynasty (c. second half of the 16th century BC). There is no proof for any contact in between.

Evidence for the early contacts has been identified within a 13th Dynasty palatial complex, which is situated in the centre of the ancient settlement of Tell el-Dab'a. Within the overall stratigraphy of Tell el-Dab'a, this is str. G/4. Tell el-Dab'a was at this period a specialized settlement near the north-eastern border of Egypt, with land and sea connections to the Levant and the Sinai. The main purpose of this settlement seems to have been to serve as a base for trading with Canaan, Syria and, as it now transpires, with the Aegean during the time of the late Middle Kingdom.[1] As excavations at Tell el-Dab'a have shown, the main bulk of the inhabitants were Canaanites, who were carriers of the Syro-Palestinian Middle Bronze Age culture. To judge from the archaeological evidence, they were in Egyptian service during this period as soldiers, seamen, shipbuilders, trading agents and probably as mining specialists.[2] The officials who controlled the foreign trade from this base for the Egyptian crown had their official seat in a palace of the early 13th Dynasty, uncovered at Tell el-Dab'a in area F/I. It has emerged from the investigation of the cemetery to the south of this palace that even these officials were of Canaanite origin. This is shown by their burial customs and by the objects in their tombs.[3] Their official title was probably *imy-r ḫ3swt*, 'overseer of foreign countries'.[4]

Within the earlier stratum of the gardens of this palace, fragments of Kamares Ware were found.[5] They are from cups belonging to the so-called Classical Kamares style.[6] It is the first time that Middle Minoan pottery has appeared in contexts of stratified Egyptian material culture. The earlier finds of Kamares Ware were all from disputable contexts.[7]

In addition to the Kamares sherds of MM IIA-IIIA (relative dating), a post-Kamares sherd[8] of MM IIIA/B was discovered within the palace compound of the 13th Dynasty. It was retrieved, however, from a Ramesside tree-pit and its stratigraphic origin is, there-fore, doubtful. Nevertheless, it seems highly likely to me that this sherd too was deposited in the palace compound during its late occupation, as Middle Minoan sherds do not occur at Tell el-Dab'a outside this palace area. Only the inhabitants of this official palace had access to foreign luxuries. In the living compounds of the lower classes not a single Minoan sherd has been found. This post-Kamares sherd seems to me, therefore, to have a special significance.

It is no coincidence that the palace tombs also reveal contacts with the Aegean. The plundered tomb F/I-p/17-no.14 contained, besides other jewellery, a golden pendant[9] **(Plate 14,1)**, which measures 3.6 x 3.8cm and has a thickness of 0.12cm. The pendant was produced in repoussé technique and was sealed at the back with a gold sheet. The motif of the pendant shows two antithetical beasts, most probably dogs, in heraldic arrangement, with muzzles joined, and each raising one paw. Their tails are curled. Around each of their necks is a rope, which is twisted around their bodies and fastened onto their tails. They stand on individual bases, which look like sledges or inverted columns, ending in volutes. One front paw and one hind leg of each rest on the volutes. The second hind leg of both animals rests on a ball in the centre of the base. By comparison with the 'Master of the Animals' from the Aegina Treasure[10] the base can be identified as a field out of which lotus-flowers grow. Our pendant gives a simplified version with the petals missing, although the buds are still shown.

The size of the paws and a suggestion of a mane on the neck give the impression of a feline beast, a lion. However, the pointed nose and curled tail make the identification of the animal as a dog more plausible. It should also be noted that the bodies of the animals are shown as very well muscled. The ears have the shape of a heart or an ivy leaf. On top of the heads tangential spirals meet in the central axis of the pendant. On top of the spirals a loop allows the pendant to be attached to a chain. This necklace probably contained other beads, which have indeed been found in this tomb, albeit in a displaced position. The beads were globular amethysts most probably mounted between golden tunnel-beads.

In toto, this is a magnificent piece of jewellery, foreign to Egypt, as indicated by the technique and by the individual features, such as the lotus fields at the base and the antithetical composition of the beasts. It has been identified by Gisela Walberg as Minoan or at least Aegean.[11]

I would like to add some further observations and notes. Antithetical beasts, such as lions or dogs, are known not only from Minoan glyptic art but also from much earlier Ancient Near Eastern representations. They are normally shown with the 'Master of the Animals', who is placed between the two beasts. Most probably this motif came to the Aegean world from the Ancient Near East, as did other themes.

On our pendant the 'Master' is missing, but probably the carrier of the pendant was to be regarded as symbolically taking his place. The animals are at his disposal. The rope around their necks, bodies and curled tails renders them tame. At the same time the two beasts offer a symbolic protection to the carrier of the pendant.

Two dogs with very similar feline features (e.g. a mane) with ropes around their necks and forming a very similar composition to our pendant are known from the ivory handle of the Gebel el-Araq knife.[12] The lotus-flowers and the curled tails of the beasts of our pendant could be seen as an indication of Egyptian influence,[13] as was also recognized by R Higgins in a study of the pendant of the 'Master of the Animals' from the Aegina Treasure.[14]

Another artefact from the same stratum which displays at least some Minoan influence is a dagger (Reg. No. 7323) from the palace tomb F/I-m/18-no. 3 (**Plate 14,2**, and Philip, this volume, **Fig. 2,2**).[15] The basic shape of the blade is that of an MB IIA-type of veined dagger. What is unique, besides the cast handle in combination with an ivory hilt and pommel, is the motif of the tangential interlocked spirals, which are connected with the veins at the base of the blade. This unique piece shows Near Eastern Middle Bronze Age II A and Minoan syncretic features. It is no coincidence that this dagger appears in a stratum from which we also have the above-mentioned pendant and six Kamares sherds. Most probably, this dagger was produced in coastal Syria, a meeting place of the Minoan and Canaanite worlds. In glyptic art, we have evidence of Minoan and Aegean influence on northern Syrian seals from the 17th century BC onwards.[16]

The Context of the Minoan Wall-Paintings at Tell el-Dab'a/'Ezbet Helmi[17]

Dating from two hundred years after the palace of the early 13th Dynasty, there is evidence of further intensive contact between Egypt and the Minoan world, from the time of the late Hyksos period and the early 18th Dynasty. Within the western edge of the settlement of Tell el-Dab'a, which is now generally identified with the capital of the Hyksos, Avaris, and Piramesse, excavations at 'Ezbet Helmi have revealed an enormous compound, which should be identified as the citadel of Avaris during the late Hyksos period (**Fig. 2**).[18]

The citadel (area H/I-IV) was fortified along the riv-

erside of the Pelusiac branch of the Nile with a massive enclosure wall incorporating buttresses. It comprised an area of more than 50,000 square metres. Within this enormous area, several major buildings were found, which had been decorated with wall-paintings of Minoan style. The find-circumstances are still partly obscure, because of agricultural levelling and extensive modern building in what is a growing rural village.

Of special interest is a platform-construction (area H/I) (**Plate 15,1-2**), measuring about 120 x 90 cubits. It consists of massive mud-brick walls, enclosing compartments which had been filled up to the top of the platform. The top is no longer preserved. The platform cut into an enclosure wall with buttresses, which has been left intact. To the north of this platform, H/I, was a garden (**Plate 16,1-2**). The pottery found under the platform dates it to the late Hyksos period (str. D/2).

A few words about the construction are in order here. The layout of the building on top of the platform can be deduced from the articulation of the walls within it. We can thus tell that the building is typical of Egyptian palatial architecture, such as is found in other palatial constructions at Deir el-Ballas.[19]

From the same platform we also discovered, among the debris, chips of limestone, bases of columns and a roof slab of limestone belonging to a kiosk with cornice. There were fragments of royal statues of quartzite and calcite, deliberately smashed into pieces, and fragments of palatial pottery. It is also likely that the famous doorway of the 12th Dynasty, found to the north of the platform, was reused by the Hyksos within this construction.[20] The finds thus confirm the palatial character of the building.

On top of the garden, and to the east and south of the platform, there were found many thousands of fragments of painted wall-plaster (**Plate 17,1-2**). The most feasible explanation of this context is that the wall-paintings came from the palatial building of the Hyksos period built on top of the platform and that the debris with the paintings was partly disposed of here during the sacking and partial destruction of the building after the end of the Hyksos period. The majority of paintings seem, however, to have stayed on the walls and were removed only later together with building material from the platform. A second and more substantial demolition occurred after the first half of the 18th Dynasty.

In support of this explanation, it is necessary to elaborate a little on some details of the stratigraphic situation of the wall-paintings. The debris on top of the gardens of the Hyksos period, including some of the wall-paintings, is covered by a stratigraphy of the early 18th Dynasty dated by numerous scarabs, among them many royal ones from the times of Ahmose and Amenhotep II. During this building activity of the 18th Dynasty, debris and wall-paintings were either trans-

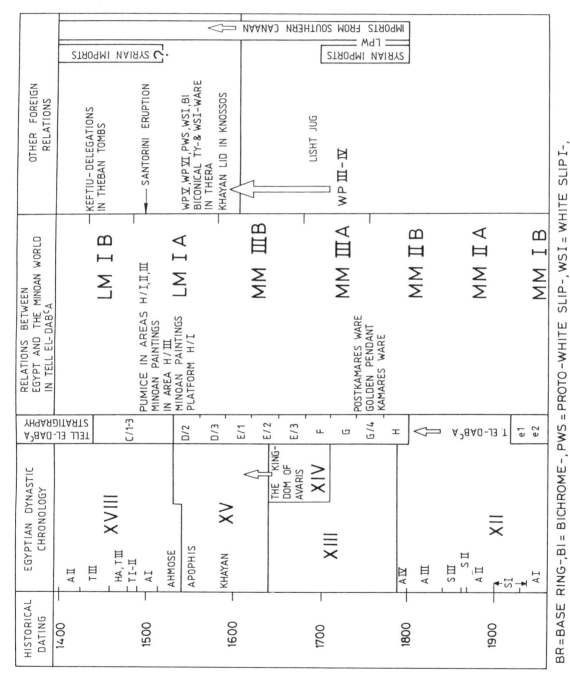

Fig. 1.   Contacts between Egypt and the Minoan world
as suggested by the archaeological evidence at Tell el-Dab'a.

BR=BASE RING-, BI= BICHROME-, PWS = PROTO-WHITE SLIP-, WSI = WHITE SLIP I-,
WP=WHITE PAINTED-, LPW= LEVANTINE PAINTED WARE

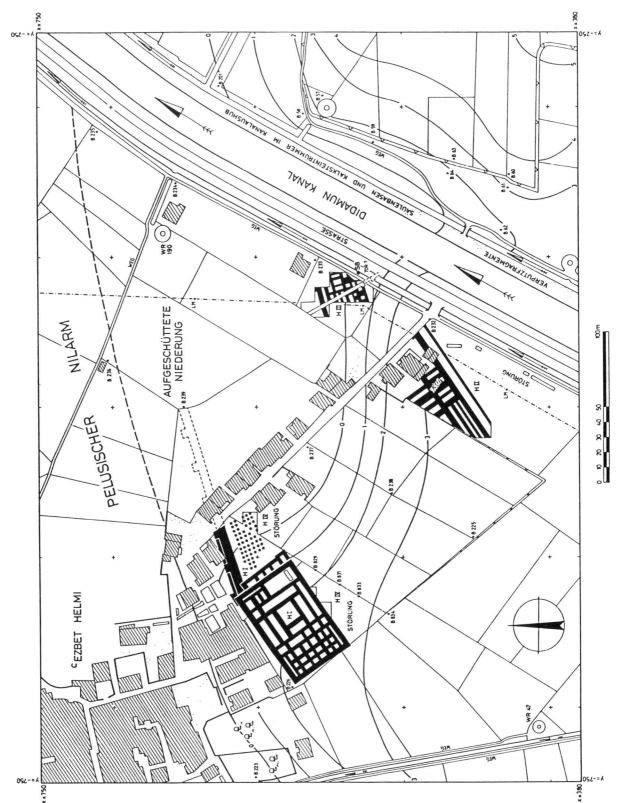

Fig. 2.   Plan of the Hyksos and early 18th Dynasty citadel at Tell el-Dab'a /
'Ezbet Helmi (after Josef Dorner 1993).

ported upwards or removed in due course from the platform or another building nearby. More wall-paintings in debris were found also on top of the early 18th Dynasty stratigraphy, but it is important to note that there are remains of Minoan wall-paintings under the earliest 18th Dynasty buildings.[21]

Two hundred metres towards the south, there is a second major building complex from the late Hyksos period, named by us 'area H/II'. It was dismantled during the early 18th Dynasty, when a new major construction was built, most probably by Ahmose. Fragments of wall-paintings were also found in H/II; these could, therefore, date from the early 18th Dynasty. Another possibility is that they might have been dispersed from the nearby area, H/III, of the early 18th Dynasty, where additional Minoan paintings have now been found along an enclosure wall.[22]

To sum up, we have a series of Minoan paintings dating to the late Hyksos period and also a second series dating to the early 18th Dynasty. In this paper I shall deal primarily with the paintings of the Hyksos period.

**Description and Interpretation
of the Wall-Paintings**[23]
1. *General Observations*
It will be recalled that we can reconstruct a palatial building of the late Hyksos period on top of a massive platform. The mud-brick walls of the building were coated with lime-plaster in two or three layers. The surface was smoothed with a stone float. While the surface was still wet, strings were applied in order to prepare the borders and the geometric patterns of the paintings. The ground colour, mostly ochre or red, was painted on the wet surface. On top of the ground colour, executed in fresco, features such as plants, figures and anatomical details were painted in tempera (secco). Sometimes the figural motifs themselves were executed partly in fresco. There is thus a mixed technique, fresco and secco, to be found in the execution of the wall-paintings.

The outlining and sketching of the figures were done in red or black paint; later, these preliminary drawings were covered by the final overpaint. In some cases there was further outlining of details, especially of the eyes and of the head and limbs.

As well as large tableaux, which include major surfaces devoted to ornamental patterns (e.g. the maze), there are also floral and figural motifs. We have mainly two sizes: frieze-size (but not true miniature) and large, slightly under life-size. Tableaux are very occasionally bordered by multi-coloured stripes. There are dadoes, imitating stone.

The choice of colours was limited. In addition to black and white, there is yellow ochre, red and blue (Egyptian blue). Yellow and blue were sometimes made lighter by an admixture of white. Sometimes blue was changed to a greenish blue. In such cases the ochre ground-colour was only thinly covered with blue. This combination produced a greenish hue. The blue pigment was revealed by observation with a binocular microscope.

Besides the mural paintings on lime-plaster, there were also stucco reliefs. Fragments were found in area H/I, including bull representations, and in H/II, these including over life-size figural representations. The combined technique of fresco and secco on lime-plaster is typical for Minoan painting, while it is unknown in Ancient Egypt and the Ancient Near East.[24] In the Levant, fresco-technique only appears in combination with paintings where it may be suspected that Minoan artists have been at work, as at Alalakh[25] and Kabri.[26] The choice of colours - white, yellow, red, blue, grey and black - is in absolute accordance with the colours used in Minoan paintings. Of special interest is the use of blue for plants and as a substitute for grey.[27] For human skin, red and white are used, representing males and females respectively. As at Knossos, the colour code may not be invariable. There seems to be some other colour convention in operation in the case of the bull-leapers. I would not wish to enter into the discussion about the popular interpretation of white bull-leapers as females in this context. Suffice it to say at present that, as at Knossos, we have representations of light-coloured bull-leapers, some white, some light yellow.[28] For the yellow skin of one of our bull-leapers (**Plate 1,1**) we have a parallel: a young boy from Thera,[29] while older boys are rendered in red. For the use of white colour for male figures, see the famous 'plumed prince' in stucco relief at Knossos.[30]

In addition to the technique and the colour conventions, the themes of the paintings also belong absolutely to Minoan art. Especially striking are the numerous bull-leaping themes.

2. *Bulls and Bull-Leapers*
The leapers all wear Minoan kilts, belts and boots (**Plate 2,1**). Typical also are the curls, which are normally represented in several strands together, whereas the scalp of the head is partly shaved and represented in blue, a convention for pre-adolescent youth representations on the paintings from Thera.[31]

It is certain that two of our scenes (frieze-size) belong to a series and form a sequence. A good parallel is the Taureador series from the palace of Knossos as reconstructed by M Cameron. Of special significance is a defeated bull, broken down on his knees (**Plate 2,2**). He was probably the subject of the final panel. He is faced by a bull-teaser, while another acrobat probably grasps the bull's head and rests his chin on it. Of this latter acrobat only the head is preserved.

Extraordinary is the representation of a bull-leaper against the background of a maze-pattern (**Plate 1,1**). The leaper clasps the bull's neck. The upper body of the acrobat is not preserved, but it was probably swinging upwards. The bull's head is shown *en face*.

Representations of bulls *en face* are not unknown in

Minoan art. They are seen, for instance, on the Vapheio cups and on a seal impression from Sklavokambos.[32] The combination of the maze-pattern (labyrinth) with the bull-leaper is associated by L Morgan and M Shaw with the palace of Knossos. It should be mentioned in this connection that the base of the fresco is framed by a triglyph/semi-rosette frieze - a typical symbol of palatial architecture, well represented at Knossos.

The maze-pattern itself was formed by triple grid lines, impressed by strings into the still wet plaster surface. A similar but more elaborate maze-pattern was found by Sir Arthur Evans at the palace of Knossos (**Fig. 3**).[33]

In addition to the bull and leaper, there is also a fragment with a blue rectangle, which is most probably the upper border of the semi-rosette frieze (**Plate 1,2**). As evidenced by other fragments, the upper border of the maze-pattern is framed by a landscape scene showing palms and perhaps hills against a red background.

This composition, fragmentary as it is (it is now in the process of restoration), revolutionizes our understanding of the meaning of the maze. What is important to stress here is its connection not only with bull-leaping but also with a landscape.

There are also large-scale bulls at Tell el-Dab'a, which show a connection with Knossian representations. We have a large-scale bull-hide and a bull's heel in relief.

3. *Acrobats*
At least three fragments showing acrobats standing on their hands have been found at Tell el-Dab'a. They are performing next to palm trees (**Plate 3,1**). One wears a plumed head-dress or pin ending in a *waz*-lily (more correctly 'wadj-lily'). They have typical Minoan kilts and boots. Similar representations are known from a Knossian and a mainland seal where the acrobats flank papyrus (**Fig. 4**).[34] There may also be a parallel among the paintings. N Marinatos has recently reconstructed the head of a male figure from Thera (the so-called 'African') as an acrobat. He too is performing next to a palm tree and has a plumed head-dress.[35]

The acrobats of Tell el-Dab'a are not heraldically disposed like those on the seals. They are arranged rather in a paratactic fashion separated by palms; they are in a palm grove. The context for their performance may have been a religious festival.[36]

4. *Large-scale Human Figures*
Of particular interest is an almost life-size human head of a male with a beard and curls on his forehead (**Plate 3,2**). We know such representations from seals found on both Crete and the mainland. Bearded men normally wear long robes in Minoan art (**Fig. 5**),[37] although there are exceptions. They are often identified as priestly figures.[38] Beards, however, also occur on some of the eminent figures on the ships seen on the miniature south-wall frieze of the West House, Thera - in particular, the leader of the fleet and a helmsman.[39] The alternative interpretation that they have pointed chins seems

unconvincing to me.

Matching the size of our bearded man are fragments of an arm and torso; they are, however, painted in a cruder style. Evidence of full-size female representations exists in the form of skirts very similar to those worn by the women on the Theran frescoes.[40]

5. *Landscapes and Animals*
Very prominent among our frescoes are landscapes with rivers and aquatic plants: reeds, papyrus, waz-lilies and possibly myrtle. Patches of terrain are sometimes punctuated with gravel or pebbles, some rendered in the 'easter egg' style. Hills against a red background also occur. What we are lacking are the craggy rocks, so typical of the Minoan landscape. It seems that we are also missing typical Minoan flowers like crocuses, whereas lilies have recently been identified.

The animals of the Tell el-Dab'a frescoes fit the landscape of the Delta. A hunting scene with grey antelopes is of particular interest (**Plate 4,1**). The legs of the antelopes are outlined in black; their heads are not preserved. They are in galloping pose, fleeing from dogs, whose red collars indicate domestication. In another composition, a man is accompanied by a dog in flying-gallop pose. He is probably a hunter.

There are also representations of felines, such as leopards, in flying-gallop pose against a red background surrounded by blue vegetation (**Plate 4,2**). Lions in the act of hunting are seen against a background of reeds. The felines are executed by masterly artists, who have made very fine use of colours. The leopard, for example, has white fur, executed by very fine strokes on the inside of his hind legs and the tail. The representation is very naturalistic.

The display of nature and its hierarchy, so typical of Minoan art,[41] is manifest also at Tell el-Dab'a. Griffins, who can be said to be at the top of the hierarchical scale because of their divine nature, are represented by two examples. First, a small-scale griffin's wing and head; the griffin may have been hunting, as on the Nilotic scene on the miniature east-wall frieze of the West House, Thera.[42] Noteworthy is the design of hanging spirals, painted in black with red central spots, which is typical of the wings of griffins (**Plate 4,3**). The upper border of the wings is framed by blue. Black pigment is used to indicate the feather texture of the wings. The similarity to the Theran griffin next to the goddess of nature from Xeste 3, Thera (**Plate 4,4**), is indeed striking.[43] Second, we have the remains of a wing of a large-scale griffin. This one also displays striking similarities to his Theran counterpart. In size, he is similar to, perhaps even larger than, the one from the Throne Room of the palace of Knossos. The wing of our griffin was painted against a background of aquatic plants, just as at Knossos. It is, therefore, conceivable that he formed part of a similar composition. Perhaps the griffin of Tell el-Dab'a was also shown flanking a throne, goddess or a queen.[44]

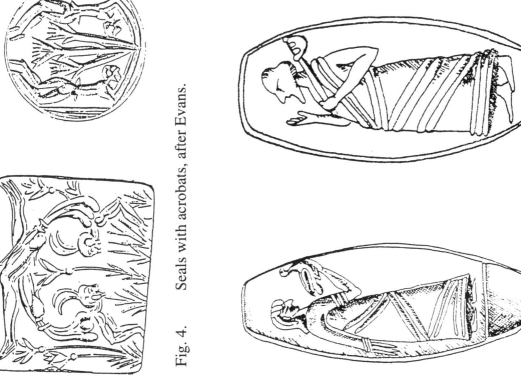

Fig. 4.   Seals with acrobats, after Evans.

Fig. 5.   Seals of bearded men identified as priests, after Evans.

Fig. 3.   Maze-pattern from Knossos, after Evans.

General Conclusions

The themes, technique and style of the paintings can be proven to be Minoan.[45] Features that typify Minoan painting, such as the mixed technique of fresco and secco, the planning of the borders by the device of pressing strings into the wet plaster, and the outlining of figures for heightened effect (compare with the so-called 'Parisienne' at Knossos) are all present at Tell el-Dab'a. Even the convention of using blue colour to indicate partially shaved heads (well known from the Theran frescoes)[46] is attested on one bull-leaper at Tell el-Dab'a. The quality of the paintings is very high, as is evident from the fine lines and vivacity of style, not to mention the polishing of the surfaces. This is no provincial art.

The similarities to Theran art are indeed striking but should not be over-interpreted. We need not assume that the artists came from Thera rather than from Crete. The similarities are due to chronology. The Theran frescoes are the ones closest to the Tell el-Dab'a examples chronologically[47] (LMI A), whereas most of the preserved Knossos frescoes date to later times. Close parallels for our themes in Minoan iconography can, however, be found in glyptic art.[48]

Finally, some thoughts about the reason for the presence of Minoan wall-paintings in the Hyksos residence of the eastern Nile Delta. W D Niemeier has tried to explain the same phenomenon in relation to the appearance of Minoan paintings in the Levant, at Tell Kabri, Alalakh, and probably Qatna.[49] According to him, the technique and iconography of the paintings can be best explained as resulting from the importation of artists from the Minoan world to different courts of the Ancient Near East. Niemeier's hypothesis is logical as far as it goes, but it does not quite explain the ritual aspect of the paintings.[50] Acrobats performing in palm-groves, bull-leaping scenes framed by half-rosette triglyph friezes, the typical display of natural hierarchy with felines and griffins would have had a special meaning, which Minoans alone could have fully understood and appreciated.

I have proposed very cautiously, as a working hypothesis, the possibility of an inter-dynastic marriage between the Hyksos and a Minoan princess.[51] This idea has received strong support from V Hankey.[52] It has to be stressed, however, that we cannot prove this hypothesis. It gains some plausibility from the presence of the large griffin which, as noted above, can be associated with queenship in Minoan Crete. In theory, this could be an explanation for the presence of Minoan paintings in the Levant, i.e. it is the result of inter-dynastic links existing throughout the eastern Mediterranean.

It should be mentioned again that in our most recent campaign Minoan paintings have also been found in an 18th Dynasty level at Avaris within a compound of palatial character. Two explanations for the continued presence of Minoan wall-paintings are possible.

First, there could have been trade interests, or links, between Avaris and Crete, not yet established on archaeological grounds. These might have survived a dynastic change and might have carried on into the 18th Dynasty, even after the fall of the Hyksos. Second, the 17th Dynasty, from which the 18th Dynasty originated, could have had its own independent relations with the Aegean even under the Hyksos.[53]

It is especially important to note the intimate connection between the courts of Knossos and Avaris as displayed by certain motifs, such as the maze-pattern and the half-rosette triglyphic frieze and the bull-leaping scenes.[54] Was there a special relationship between the two courts?[55] And were the influences mutual? How can we explain typical Egyptian subjects, such as the Nilotic landscape with its reeds, papyri and palms and the monkeys picking flowers, on Knossian and Theran frescoes?[56] Were the motifs transported to Crete and Thera by Minoan artists working in Avaris? Was Avaris a meeting point for artistic exchanges?

We cannot answer these questions at present. But the Minoan presence in Avaris, elusive as it is, will have considerable historical consequences, to be explored, it is hoped, in future research.

Notes

1. For an almost up-to-date bibliography on the excavation of Tell el-Dab'a, see M Bietak, *Tell el-Dab'a*, V, Part 1, Vienna, 1991, 17-18.

2. See recently on this subject M Bietak, *Ägypten und Levante* 2 (1991), 64-72.

3. Ibid.

4. Ibid.

5. G Walberg, *Ägypten und Levante* 2 (1991), 115-8.

6. G Walberg, *Kamares. A Study of the Character of Palatial Middle Minoan Pottery*, Uppsala, 1976.

7. B J Kemp and R S Merrillees, *Minoan Pottery in Second Millennium Egypt*, with a chapter by Elmar Edel, Mainz, 1980.

8. M Bietak, *Anzeiger der Phil.-hist. Klasse der Österreichischen Akademie der Wissenschaften* 121 (1984), 330, fig. 7.

9. G Walberg, *Ägypten und Levante* 2 (1991), 111-4 and frontispiece.

10. R A Higgins, *The Aegina Treasure*, London, 1979, 22-8.

11. *Ägypten und Levante* 2 (1991), 111-2.

12. H Asselberg, *Chaos en Beheersing*, Leiden, 1961, Abb. 56, 57; latest treatment, R M Boehmer, *MDAIK* 47, 1991, 51-60.

13. As suggested to me by Nanno Marinatos.

14. *Supra,* n.10.

15. M Bietak, *Ägypten und Levante* 3 (1991) 67, pl. 22,C and 23,B.

16. Latest treatment, D Collon, *Ägypten und Levante* 4 (1994), 81-8; see also M Bietak, ibid.

17. Preliminary report by M Bietak, J Dorner, I Hein and P Jánosi, *Ägypten und Levante* 4 (1994), 9-80. The excavation area was under the supervision of Josef Dorner and Peter Jánosi.

18. On the identification of Tell el-Dab'a with Avaris and Piramesse, see L Habachi, *ASAE* 52 (1954), 443-559; J van Seters, *The Hyksos. A New Investigation*, New Haven and London, 1966; M Bietak, *Tell el-Dab'a,* II. *Der Fundort in Rahmen einer archäologisch-geographischen Untersuchung über das ägyptische Ostdelta*, Vienna, 1975; and Avaris and Piramesse. Archaeological Exploration in the Eastern Nile Delta. *Proc. of the British Academy* 65, 1979, 225-90 (also issued as a separate publication, Oxford, 1981, second revised edition, 1986).

19. W S Smith, *The Art and Architecture of Ancient Egypt*, The Pelican History of Art, Baltimore, 1958, 156-9, figs. 51-2; P Lacovara, *Deir el-Ballas. Preliminary Report on the Deir el-Ballas Expedition 1980-1986*, ARCE Reports 12, Winona Lake, 1990, 2-5, fig. 1,5-6, and 14. The South Palace especially has features similar to our platform H/I, while the North Palace shares similarities with our structure H/II. An interpretation of the former as an observation post (Lacovara, op.cit. 5) is unconvincing when we take into consideration the archaeological context with the paintings and the architectural pieces at Tell el-Dab'a.

20. Cf. P Jánosi, *Ägypten und Levante* 4 (1994), 20-38.

21. A detailed report on the stratigraphy of the wall-paintings by Peter Jánosi and Josef Dorner is in preparation for the next preliminary report of the Tell el-Dab'a excavations in *Ägypten und Levante* 5 forthcoming.

22. This new excavation, conducted in 1993, will not be considered in this article.

23. For preliminary reports, see M Bietak, *Egyptian Archaeology* 2 (1992), 26-8, and *Ägypten und Levante* 4 (1994), 44-58. I would like to thank those colleagues who have given valuable advice on various aspects of the Minoan paintings at Tell el-Dab'a, namely Ellen Davis, Sinclair Hood, Nanno Marinatos, Lyvia Morgan and Maria Shaw.

24. W D Niemeier, *Aegeum* 7 (1991), 197; M A S Cameron, R E Jones and S E Philipakis, *BSA* 72 (1977), 121-84; W Noll, L Born and R Holm, *Die Natur-wissenschaften* 62 (1975), 87-94.

25. L Woolley, *Alalakh, An Account of the Excavations at Tell Atchana in the Hatay 1937-1949*, London, 1955, 28ff. and 233ff; W D Niemeier, *Aegeum* 7 (1991), 197.

26. W D Niemeier, loc. cit.

27. C Doumas in *L'iconographie minoenne. Actes de la table ronde d'Athènes (21-22 Avril 1983)*, ed. by P Darque and J-C Poursat, *Bulletin de Correspondance Hellénique*, Supplement XI, Paris, 1985 (I owe this reference to N Marinatos).

28. See S Damiani-Indelicato, *Cretan Studies* 1 (1988), 39-47, and N Marinatos, *Ägypten und Levante* 4 (1994), 89-93.

29. C Doumas, *The Wall Paintings of Thera*, Athens, 1992, nos. 109, 112.

30. See the more recent reconstruction of this figure by W D Niemeier, *AM* 102 (1987), 65-97.

31. E N Davis, *AJA* 90 (1986), 399-406.

32. E N Davis, *The Vapheio Cups and Aegean Gold and Silver Ware*, New York, 1973; A Evans, *Palace of Minos,* II, fig. 150, and cf. also fig. 137; J H Betts, *Kadmos* 6 (1967), fig. 12,A.

33. A Evans, *Palace of Minos*, I, fig. 256 (= Morgan, this volume, fig. 11).

34. A Evans, *Palace of Minos*, IV, figs. 443-4. See also N Marinatos forthcoming.

35. See C Doumas, *The Wall Paintings of Thera*, Athens, 1992, fig. 148.

36. N Marinatos, Acrobats in Minoan Art, forthcoming.

37. A Evans, *Palace of Minos*, IV, figs. 336 and 343.

38. Most recently, N Marinatos, *Minoan Religion*, Columbia S.C., 1993, 128, figs. 88-90 (with bibliography).

39. See L Morgan, *The Miniature Wall-Paintings of Thera*, Cambridge, 1989, pls. 126-8, 174-5. Cf. also C Doumas, op. cit. 31, figs. 40, 36-8.

40. C Doumas, op. cit. 11, 12, 120.

41. N Marinatos, op. cit. 196-9.

42. C Doumas, op. cit. 30-1.

43. C Doumas, op cit. figs. 122, 128.

44. H Reusch, Zum Wandschmuck des Thronsaales im Knossos in *Minoica*, Festschrift J Sundwall, Berlin, 1958, 334ff.; cf. also N Marinatos, *Minoan Religion*, 153-5, and Minoan Kingship in Minoan Crete in *Aegeum*, forthcoming.

45. For a general summing up of the specifications of Minoan art, see S Hood, *The Arts of Prehistoric Greece*, Harmondsworth, 1978, 235ff. and *BCH*, Supplement, XI, Paris, 1985, 21-6.

46. E Davis, *AJA* 90 (1986), 399-406.

47. The chronological correlation is established by Late Cypriot White Slip I-Ware found in the old excavations at Thera; see W D Niemeier, *Jahrbuch des Deutschen Archäologischen Instituts* 95 (1980), 72-4, fig. 44. White Slip I-Ware appears

together with Proto White Slip-Ware, White Painted V-Ware, White Painted VI-Ware, Bichrome Ware and other Late Cypriot wares at Tell el-Dab'a only in the later phase of str. D/2 (the final Hyksos period), i.e. the same period to which the Minoan paintings of H/I date. See L C Maguire, *The Middle Cypriot Pottery from Tell el-Dab'a, Egypt*, MA dissertation, University of Edinburgh, 1986, 27-35 (see especially 32, fig. 16); *Ägypten und Levante* 3 (1992), 115-20, figs. 2-4; *The Circulation of Cypriot Pottery in the Middle Bronze Age*, Ph.D. University of Edinburgh; and M Bietak, *Tell el-Dab'a*, V, Part 1, Vienna, 1992, 312ff., fig. 288,4.

48. See W D Niemeier in *Thera and the Aegean World*, III, London, 1990, 267-84.

49. W D Niemeier, *Aegeum* (1991), 188-201.

50. See S Hood, *The Arts of Prehistoric Greece*, 48-77; N Marinatos, *Art and Religion in Thera*, Athens, 1984.

51. I presented this idea in a public lecture at the Archaeological Society in Athens, June 1992, and in *The Raymond and Beverly Sackler Foundation Distinguished Lecture in Egyptology* at the British Museum in July 1992; see also my article in *Egyptian Archaeology* 2 (1992), 28.

52. *Minerva* 4, no. 3 (1993), 13-14.

53. There is additional evidence of Aegean contacts on the part of the rulers of the 17th/18th Dynasties. A tomb context, attributed to a queen Ahhotep of the 17th Dynasty, has yielded a Minoan-style dagger. There is also an Aegean-style griffin on the axe of Ahmose. Finally there is the epithet of one of the two queens Ahhotep: *ḥnwt idbw Ḥ3w-nbwt*, 'Mistress of the shores of Hau-nebu'. This has a disputed meaning but Hau-nebu can probably be regarded as referring to Asia or the Aegean islands. For a recent discussion of this problem, see P Jánosi, *Journal of the Ancient Chronology Forum* 5 (1991/92), 99-101, and V Hankey, op. cit.

54. Pointed out by L Morgan at the British Museum colloquium.

55. We need to be cautious, however, because some of the frescoes from Tell el-Dab'a (found in an 18th Dynasty context) show connections with the few preserved paintings from the palace of Phaistos, which is closer to Egypt. We know practically nothing about the Phaistos paintings and it is highly unlikely that the palace did not have substantial amounts of wall-painting.

56. The monkey motif appears already in jewellery of the 18th century and in seals of the pre-palatial Minoan period. Some of the motifs may have penetrated through Syrian glyptic art. See R Higgins, *The Aegina Treasure*, London, 1979, 22-9.

MINOAN PAINTING AND EGYPT
THE CASE OF TELL EL-DAB'A[1]

Lyvia Morgan

Aegean Painting and Egypt

In discussing artistic connections between Egypt and the Aegean, Fritz Schachermeyer in 1967 suggested that paintings by Egyptian artists in Avaris may have been seen by Minoan envoys.[2] The truth is altogether more startling.

Excavations conducted by the Austrian Institute under the direction of Professor Manfred Bietak at Tell el-Dab'a, identified with ancient Avaris, have now revealed thousands of fragments of wall-painting apparently stripped from the walls of the late Hyksos palace when it was overthrown by the Thebans who founded the 18th Dynasty and the beginning of the New Kingdom.[3] There on Egyptian soil were wall-paintings which are unmistakably Minoan in character. What were they doing there? Who painted them, and why?

This paper is concerned with the figurative paintings of the late Hyksos palace (c. 1590-1540 BC), which corresponds to transitional Middle Minoan IIIB - Late Minoan IA and the first half of Late Minoan IA (Late Cycladic I/Late Helladic I) in the Aegean.[4] Correlations between the dating of the Tell el-Dab'a paintings and those from the Cycladic island of Thera (LC I) arise from finds of Late Cypriot White Slip I ware at both sites.[5] Other paintings, non-figurative but with plant designs and still thought by their technique to be Minoan, have been found at Tell el-Dab'a in contexts indicating an early 18th Dynasty date. These are not considered here. The question of why Minoan or Minoan-style paintings, albeit non-figurative and hence without obvious iconographic significance, should have decorated the walls of the palace after the Hyksos were expelled is as puzzling as the question of why Minoan figurative images decorated a Hyksos palace in the first place. Were the Minoan artists working for the Hyksos (who, after all, became thoroughly Egyptianized in terms of their material culture)[6] or for the Egyptians or for both? Why the particular association with Avaris? These are questions which must hang in abeyance until excavation, conservation and study are complete. It is early days, and this paper offers no more than first impressions in placing the first figurative fragments to be published within the context of Minoan art.

It is important, first, to remind ourselves of the difficulties in comparing Aegean and Egyptian wall-painting owing to the fundamental differences of context and function. The vast majority of paintings in Egypt come from tombs. They are well preserved and a study of iconographic programmes is feasible. Aegean paintings come from palaces, town houses and country villas. In the course of time they have fallen from the mud-brick upper storeys that they decorated and are found in small pieces. Large quantities of the compositions have disappeared forever. While comments can be made on differences in technique and idiom, it is, therefore, only with caution that we make comments on the fundamental differences (which are real enough) in the iconography of the two cultures. The paintings have a different context - funerary versus non-funerary - and hence a different function. The dangers inherent in comparing are evident when we look to the rare instances of palace art in Egypt and tomb art in the Aegean. The Ayia Triada sarcophagus and related contemporary paintings from a tomb at Ayia Triada (LM IIIA) show evident funerary themes which, while by no means the same, have something in common with funerary themes of Egyptian tombs - sacrifice, offering bearers and, on the sarcophagus, the depiction of the deceased before his tomb.[7] Conversely, in the wall-paintings of the palace of Amenophis III at Malkata in Thebes and of his son Akhenaten at Amarna the themes are radically different from those of Egyptian tombs.[8] The question here, of course, is whether that difference has to do solely with the Amarna revolution in religion or whether it reflects a palace/tomb dichotomy. The fact that the themes of plants and animals appear in the pre-Amarna Malkata palace as well as at Amarna and are less evident in the Amarna tombs suggests that palace art may always have differed from tomb art, something that we might in any case have suspected. Much comment has been made on the Minoan character of the nature scenes at Amarna, which, along with the large quantities of Mycenaean pottery found at the site, has suggested to some an Aegean influence in the art.[9] However, nature scenes are typical not of Mycenaean art but of Minoan art and Minoan painting was a thing of the past by the time of Amarna. This is not to say that there is no flavour of Minoan art in the paintings, only to point out that such a flavour is unlikely to have emanated directly from the contemporary Aegean. What might, however, have happened, is that earlier New Kingdom palaces picked up on Minoan themes and idioms (such as the flying gallop discussed below) and that Malkata and Amarna built their palace iconography as much from earlier, lost, palace art in Egypt as from a pantheistic approach to nature. The Aegean paintings of Tell el-

Dab'a may well provide the first, and crucial, example of the missing links.

But what paintings did the Minoans who travelled to Tell el-Dab'a bring in their minds? What had they seen and executed at home? The answer is unclear since the dating of Minoan wall-paintings, and hence their correlations with Egyptian chronology, is a hazardous affair. But looking at those paintings which are generally accepted as the earliest pictorial murals of Crete, we find themes which are, on the whole, analogous with those from Tell el-Dab'a. A few themes, however, appear to predate known Cretan examples.

The earliest pictorial wall-paintings on Crete date to the beginning of the Second Palace period at Knossos (MM IIIa, c.1700 BC), with the possible exception of a few plant fragments said to be of MM II date from the palace of Phaistos. Prior to that, houses had been painted red (since Early Minoan times), and geometric designs had been painted in the first palaces of Knossos and Phaistos.[10]

A gradual internal development of pictorial art is evident in pottery and sealstones but the sudden appearance of fully developed mural painting in the New Palace period has suggested to some scholars the importance of outside influence. It was in this context that Schachermeyer thought of Minoans at Avaris. Maria Shaw and Sarah Immerwahr have both drawn attention to the probable influence of Egyptian painting on the earliest Minoan wall-painting.[11] Quantities of Minoan and Minoanizing pottery were found in rubbish deposits at the Middle Kingdom workmen's villages at Kahun and Haraga in the Faiyum.[12] Might Aegean craftsmen, it has been asked, have seen paintings and reliefs in Egyptian tomb chapels? The actual mechanism for the arrival of Minoan pottery in Egypt has been a matter of discussion. Was Aegean pottery traded down to Egypt through the Levantine coast, or did Aegean people actually visit and even live in Egypt prior to the 18th Dynasty when evidence of direct trading appears in tomb representations of the Keftiu?[13]

The discovery of Minoan-style wall-paintings at Tell el-Dab'a provides startling and unexpected new evidence for the presence of Minoans in Egypt at the time of some of the earliest figural paintings in the Aegean. Clearly Minoan artists could have had the opportunity to see Egyptian painting. Equally important, Egyptians would have seen Minoan painting.

The subjects of Aegean painting are restricted to certain themes. In Minoan villas the dominant theme was the nature goddess and her world of plants and animals. At the palace of Knossos we see public festivals in miniature style (also evident at the villa of Tylissos), human figures involved in ritual action, processions, and bull sports. On the Cycladic islands of Thera, Kea and Melos, we encounter miniature scenes of festivals, nature scenes and scenes connected with the cult of the goddess of nature. Because of their exceptional state of preservation in volcanic ash, the wall-paintings of Thera are particularly important. Little is known of the earliest Mycenaean painting owing to the lack of architectural remains for the 16th-15th centuries on the mainland. Mycenaean palatial wall-painting (14th-13th centuries, and therefore outside the period we are considering) concentrates on the human figure, and processions and scenes of hunting and warfare were especially popular.

The basic conventions of colour and form are in keeping with Egyptian art: dark-skinned male (red ochre) and pale-skinned female (white in the Aegean, yellow in Egypt); frontal shoulders, profile legs, profile head with frontal eye. Some basic techniques are also comparable: the use of guide lines, the composition of pigments. Other conventions and techniques differ significantly, notably the lack of canonical grid-lines in the Aegean and the use of lime plaster and some buon fresco technique in the Aegean as opposed to gypsum or mud plaster and entire tempera technique in Egypt.[14] Although flat painting is the norm in the Aegean, relief work was popular, particularly at Knossos, in the earlier, MM IIIB, period. The technique, however, differs from relief painting in Egypt, in that the material is plaster, built up in layers, rather than stone chiselled into relief.

The idioms of the Tell el-Dab'a paintings are, as we shall see, distinctly Aegean. Even more significant in terms of determining the origins of the painters is the fact that the techniques are Aegean. They are executed on lime plaster, and there is a mixed technique of buon fresco for ground colour and secco for the majority of the design and its details.

Until recently, the idea that Aegean artists were travelling such distances to paint in foreign lands was unheard of. But the situation at Tell el-Dab'a has a parallel on a somewhat smaller scale at Tel Kabri (in northern Israel). Recent excavations by Aaron Kempinski and Wolf Dietrich Niemeier have revealed fragments of wall- and floor-paintings of Minoan rather than Near Eastern style and technique.[15] A pattern of grid-lines with traces of plants between decorated the threshold of the palace. The most recent excavations have revealed numerous fragments of miniature scenes with close parallels to the subjects of the Theran miniatures: 'a rocky shore; boats on the sea; a town of houses with ashlar buildings with rounded, "beam heads"; a swallow in flight and a winged griffin'.[16] Some of the colours are applied in true fresco, string lines are used as guides, and imitation marbling is painted within the squares. These are all Aegean features. Imitation marbling, known primarily from dados at Knossos and at Thera, was also used at Yarim-Lin's palace at Alalakh. There too, it has been said, the technique includes true fresco, while plants and bull's horns and a bucranium with a disc recall Aegean themes. With new dating correlations (which are not without problems) Niemeier proposes the reverse of Wooley's suggestion of influence on the Aegean, by postulating travelling artisans from Crete working at Alalakh and Tel Kabri.[17] According to Niemeier's proposal, the rulers of the palaces at Tel Kabri, Alalakh and possibly Qatna in Syria (where there is also painted imitation marbling) asked the Cretan rulers to send their artisans to decorate their palaces with wall-paintings. He cites Ugaritic mythological poetry in which the god of handicrafts, Kothar Wa-Khasis, was brought from his throne in *Kptr* (= Caphtor = Crete) to build a palace for the god Baal and to furnish it with works of art.

What is now emerging is a situation in which Minoan artists travelled to selected palaces in the Near East and at least one palace in Egypt (one ruled by Egyptianized Near Easterners of uncertain origin), apparently commissioned to paint by the local rulers. It puts an entirely new perspective on relations between the Aegean and Egypt and the Near East at this time.

Tell el-Dab'a has yielded literally thousands of fragments of wall-paintings and the iconography needs to be closely analysed in order to ascertain which elements are exclusively Aegean and which might have been at home in Egypt. At present, there do not appear to be any elements which are exclusively Egyptian.

A first step in such an analysis would be to determine the forms of iconographic transfer which are known to have occured between Egypt and the Aegean and to examine the mechanism for such transfer.[18] I would propose three main forms of iconographic transfer (without precluding others):

1. *Motif distilled.* An example is provided by the theme of cat chasing bird. The theme, which first occurs on two relief cups and a relief jug from Quartier Mu at Mallia of Middle Minoan II,[19] became popular at the beginning of the Late Bronze Age, with examples from Ayia Triada, Knossos, Thera, and the Mycenae Shaft Graves.[20] On the Mallia cups and jug, the bird is not actually present but the pose of the cat in relation to the relief trees is immediately suggestive of the cat poised to pounce on birds in a papyrus thicket from the tomb of Khnumhotep (Tomb 3) at Middle Kingdom Beni Hasan.[21] In Egyptian paintings the scene is part of a wider theme of hunting and fishing in the marshes. The cat chasing birds is an adjunct to the tomb owner's own hunt as he stands with his family on a papyrus skiff.[22] In the Aegean, the theme is distilled into one belonging entirely to the natural world without the inclusion of man. Only those elements which would make sense within an Aegean context - cat, bird (waterfowl), river and riverine plants (or in the case of Ayia Triada, Cretan plants) - are included. Those elements which cannot be transported - the nobleman and family, the papyrus skiff, the variety of Egyptian birds - are excluded. The motif is distilled.

2. *Motif developed.* Our example here again has its Egyptian prototype at Beni Hasan. It is the monkey. In the tomb of Khnumhotep (Tomb 3) baboons reach out

for figs.[23] The natural imagery of monkeys as fruit gatherers is juxtaposed with human activity. In the Aegean, monkeys occur most notably in the iconography of MM III - LM I. As they are not indigenous to the region, they or their imagery must have been imported.[24] A primary iconographic role is again that of collecting. In two important instances the item to be collected is a plant - this time the crocus with its valuable commodity of saffron. At Knossos the animal collects it in baskets while wearing a halter showing that it is in the service of humans (Knossos Saffron Gatherer). At Thera the saffron is collected by women and delivered by a monkey to a seated goddess protected by a griffin (Xeste 3).[25] Here, in the iconographic transfer, the motif has been developed, the meaning of the animal symbol elaborated to fit the local flora as well as the local religion.

3. *Iconographic parallelism.* In these instances, the meaning of the motif remains the same or is parallel in its communicative power. The prime example in the ancient world is the lion. As a beast of ultimate power and ferocity, it is appropriated in visual and poetic imagery as a metaphor for male heroism and conquest. Though the idioms differ, the messages of such items as the Mycenae Shaft Grave lion-hunt dagger and the lion cosmetic jar from the tomb of Tutankhamun are parallel.[26] The former shows heroic men attacking lions on one side of the dagger and fearsome lions attacking deer on the other, affording a comparison between man and beast. The latter shows a large recumbent lion on the lid of the jar with the cartouche of Tutankhamun on his back by way of identification. Beneath, on the jar, a lion attacks its prey, while at the bottom, squashed as it were by the weight of the jar, are the heads of the enemies of the Pharaoh from the four corners of the earth. These examples of lion-man imagery are two of many from the repetoire of ancient art. Where the example differs radically from those previously discussed is in the fact that the two groups of images do not physically resemble one another. No-one could say that one object influenced the other. On the other hand, the iconographic message (which derives from the natural symbolism of the behaviour of the animal) is unequivocally parallel.

It is in the context of an understanding of these forms of iconographic transfer, as well as through an awareness of what is specifically Egyptian and what specifically Aegean in the repetoire of imagery of the time, that an analysis of the iconography of the Tell el-Dab'a paintings can begin.

The Paintings of Tell el-Dab'a
There appear to be two scales of painting - small friezes (akin to the House of the Frescoes and the Taureador frescoes at Knossos but not as small as the miniature friezes of Knossos, Tylissos, Thera and Kea), and large, almost life-size compositions (which correspond to the

Fig. 2.   Detail from an inlaid dagger from
Shaft Grave V, Mycenae.
(Smith, *Interconnections*, fig. 36).

Fig. 1.   MM II sealstone from Crete. (*CMS* VII, 35).

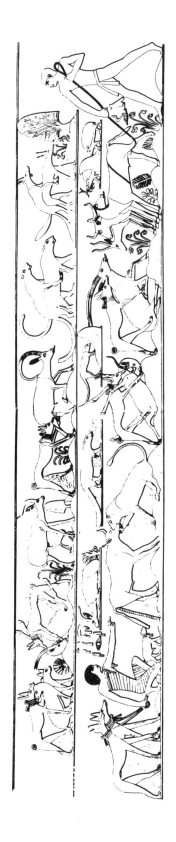

Fig. 3.   Detail from a hunt in the desert, Tomb of Ptahhotep, Saqqara,
East Wall, 5th dynasty. (Davies 1900, pl. XXII).

scale of the larger figurative paintings of Thera).

Backgrounds of the small-scale paintings are either light yellow ochre or red. While white is the most common background colour of Minoan and Cycladic painting, the use of red background corresponds with the earliest figurative painting in Crete, as in the Saffron Gatherer from Knossos.[27] Conversely, yellow ochre backgrounds are characteristic of later Minoan and Mycenaean wall-painting. However, there is a notable exception in the miniature paintings from the North East Bastion at Ayia Irini on Kea, which is datable to LC I.[28] Here the composition of plaster and the colour of the background correspond strikingly with the Tell el-Dab'a small-scale fragments with yellow ground. In the LM IA Birds and Monkeys frieze from the House of the Frescoes the background changes from red to white in undulating areas.[29] The question is whether we are looking at similar shifts of background colour or separate compositions from different rooms.[30]

The plaster is lime, as was always used in the Aegean, and not gypsum as was used in Egypt for the fine, painted layer. The majority of the fragments are executed in flat painting. The technique, as mentioned above, is mainly a mixture of buon fresco for the ground and secco for subsequent colours. There are also examples of stucco relief. This technique, in which the plaster is built up in layers, is quite different from the majority of Egyptian relief, which is carved from stone (plaster being used only occasionally in a subsidiary capacity). Colours correspond exactly to those used in the Aegean - yellow ochre, red ochre (both with various shades), blue, black and white. In accordance with Aegean painting and unlike Egyptian painting, there is very little green (used only occasionally as an admix of blue and yellow) and plants are painted a substitute blue.

Landscape

It is significant that of the plants depicted in Minoan painting, those which are found at Tell el-Dab'a agree with the vegetative surroundings of the Nile Delta. Water courses (rivers or streams), reeds, papyrus, *waz*-lilies and palms are all plants at home in Egypt. Indeed, the latter three are more at home in Egypt than in the Aegean and have arguably been imported (either as live plants or as artistic motifs) when found in Aegean art.[31] This is the principle discussed above under iconographic transference (1) now in reverse - Aegean to Egypt. It means that the painted plants make sense within their real context. The most significant of the missing plants - crocuses - are missing perhaps because of their quintessentially Aegean context. They are not indigenous to Egypt. Lilies, which are also not indigenous, do apparently appear in the paintings (as yet unpublished). But lilies, it seems, were imported to Egypt.[32] At the same time, there do not appear to be any plants in the paintings which, though common in Egypt, are not applicable to the Aegean flora and are

not found in Aegean painting.

Amongst the fragments is a large piece depicting mountains or hills in red ochre on a yellowish-white ground (or white hills on a red ground depending on one's perception).[33] The hills are barren, no plants growing. Parallels for this format are known from Cycladic paintings from Kea and Thera, both Late Cycladic I (LM Ia). Amongst the Kea miniature fragments are many pieces of multi-coloured rockwork (blue-grey, red ochre, yellow ochre, white), with occasional plants rising from them.[34] From Thera, multi-coloured rockwork provides a dominant landscape setting in the Xeste 3 adyton paintings of the Crocus Gatherers, and, along with flying swallows, the sole subject matter of the paintings from Delta 2 (the Spring Fresco). Closer to the Tell el-Dab'a fragment is the painting from the main stairway in Xeste 3, leading from the entrance up to the shrine or adyton area above. These are monochrome rather than multi-coloured. Small bushes rise from their heights.[35] All these Cycladic instances share the same sinuous shape as the Tell el-Dab'a fragment. There are no further colours on the red in the fragment, but faint traces of blue and pink on the white suggest vertical streaks. These may well represent descending rockwork, such as is found in the Kea miniature fragments mentioned above.

Other fragments depict the ground in terms of pebbles or gravel, a characteristic of Minoan art though it is not unknown in Egyptian painting, and the so-called 'easter egg' pebbles which are very much a Minoan iconographic form.[36]

A frequently repeated plant amongst the Tell el-Dab'a fragments consists of lanceolate leaves on narrow stems. A large-scale version of this plant is published in Bietak 1994, pl. 14 A. It has blue leaves and stalks and black stem. The blue is mixed with white and is applied in impasto. Numerous fragments of a smaller version of the plant also have a red ground, with leaves either in blue or yellow ochre. A similar, though not identical, plant appears against a yellow background with red stem and blue leaves (Bietak 1994, pl. 19 B), and the same leaf-shape again appears in connection with the large-scale griffin fragment (mentioned below), here in white and pale blue leaves with red stems (Bietak 1994, pl. 21 A).

Bietak calls the large-scale plant 'olive' (1994, 46). Olive trees, at least those clearly recognizable as such, have a somewhat different appearance in Aegean art, however, with a dense proliferation of leaves.[37] The earliest finds of olive in Egypt date from the 14th century (18th Dynasty) and it may not have been planted there until yet later.[38] If this were olive it would be the only case of a plant not equally at home in Egypt and the Aegean being represented in the paintings (though of course the material is neither fully digested nor fully excavated and further surprises may be in store).

It is hard to say what the plant actually is. However, there are a number of close parallels for the plant in

Aegean painting, where it is usually called myrtle *(Myrtus communis)*. In no case is the plant clearly identifiable, but the shape is characteristic of the myrtle shrub. A large painting from the Royal Road at Knossos shows myrtle plants with relief rockwork, datable between MM IIIA - LM IB (destruction). If the former, as Mark Cameron thought, it is the earliest example.[39] The same plant occurs amongst the paintings of the House of the Frescoes at Knossos (MM IIIB - LM IA).[40] While the plant of all these paintings has the characteristic leaves of myrtle, they have no flowers or berries to confirm the identification. In contrast, a flowering plant in the Cat and Bird frieze of the wall-paintings from Room 14 at Ayia Triada has the accurately depicted blossoms of myrtle but with inaccurately long leaves.[41] In the Cyclades, fragments of yellow ochre myrtle leaves were found in Building Gamma at Thera, and a large panel of myrtle and bramble (blackberry) decorated the wall of a room adjacent to the room with the miniatures at Kea.[42] The stalks of the Kea plants are red ochre and the leaves are mainly yellow ochre though some are blue. The scale corresponds to that of the larger scale 'myrtle' at Tell el-Dab'a (Bietak 1994, pl. 14 A). Another plant, of the same scale and also on a red background, may belong to the same composition as this piece (not yet published). It has a wavy-edged blue leaf and as such is a perfect corollary for the Kea bramble which occurs in the same panel as the myrtle. This piece also has a white border on two sides, as has the Kea panel.

Myrtle, if that is indeed what the plant is, is a Mediterranean shrub which, while not generally included among the garden plants of Egyptian wall-paintings, is thought to have been used by the Egyptians for its medicinal, aromatic and other properties.[43]

Animals
All the animals in the Tell el-Dab'a paintings are found in Egyptian as well as in Aegean art, though not always in the same iconographic context.

Bietak, this volume, **Plate 4,1**, shows a greyish-white ungulate in a landscape of blue rocks with a dark greenish small-leaved plant. A white dog with a red collar nips at the belly of the animal. Bietak identifies the animal as antelope (the creature lacks head and tail for certain identification but the hooves and thin legs are characterisic of ungulates in general, while the colouration might suggest caprid). Only one clear example of antelope exists in Aegean painting, in the Boxers and Antelopes from B6 at Thera.[44] These are white (the ground plaster) with black outlines like here.

Antelope is one of the creatures which inhabited the desert and mountain areas of ancient Egypt, as did gazelle, ibex and other ungulates (any of whom would be candidates for the animal in **Plate 4,1**). As such it is hunted by sportsmen accompanied by packs of trained dogs. This is a frequent subject in Egyptian art, from the Old Kingdom on.[45] The dogs, which from the earliest representations wear collars indicating their relationship with man, mainly attack ungulates.

The theme of dogs hunting ungulates is certainly Egyptian long before it is Aegean, though the treatment of the subject here is totally in keeping with Minoan art. In the Aegean, dogs were occasionally depicted in glyptic art of the Early and Middle Minoan periods and a magnificent sculptural version adorns the lid of an Early Minoan II stone lid from Mochlos.[46] Four almost identical pieces of Middle Minoan jewellery from the Aegina Treasure show antithetic dogs,[47] while a gold pendant with the same motif was found at Tell el-Dab'a in a 13th Dynasty stratum (Bietak, this volume **Plate 14,1**).[48] The iconography of the dog hunting an ungulate first occurs in glyptic art of MM II (**Fig. 1**),[49] and though not common continues into Late Minoan/Late Helladic. But until recently the dog was unknown in wall-painting prior to the Mycenaean palace period. There are no dogs in the surviving Cretan wall-paintings and none at Thera. The earliest known painting with hunting dogs is from Kea (LC I), amongst the fragments of the miniatures from the North East Bastion (note 28). Thin white dogs of greyhound type bound after fallow deer, the favourite prey of predators and man alike in Aegean art. One nips at the belly of its prey. There is no evidence for collars in the extant Kea fragments, though in the later Mycenaean paintings hunting dogs do wear them, as do some dogs in Minoan glyptic art.[50] In the Tell el-Dab'a fragment the animals enact their drama in a landscape of blue rocks and delicate leaved plants. Numerous other parts of the Kea miniatures show white hooved animals amidst landscape elements, but the deer and dogs are isolated from environmental context, existing in their own empty space of the plaster wall. This is characteristic of certain Kean animal scenes (cf. the Bluebirds frieze and the Dolphins frieze). Egyptian hunt scenes are usually set within landscape elements of small desert plants, occasional trees and an undulating ground line (**Fig. 3**). The fact that the dog wears a collar is also a feature in keeping with Egyptian scenes. It could well be argued that this iconography is derived from Egypt. Yet, though the iconographic features - dog hunting ungulate, collar, undulating rocks and small plants - are all at home in Egyptian painting, their execution (in particular that of the plants) is Minoan, and those features which do not occur in extant contemporary wall-paintings do nonetheless have predecessors in Minoan glyptic art.

Lions and leopards appear in the Tell el-Dab'a paintings, the former in association with reeds, the latter on a red background with blue leaves (Bietak, this volume, **Plate 4,2**). It is not yet clear if the two appeared together or in separate paintings, though the different backgrounds suggest the latter. All these hunting scenes are currently being studied by Nanno Marinatos.[51]

Hunting lions, as my example (3) in the introductory comments on iconographic transfer shows, are charac-

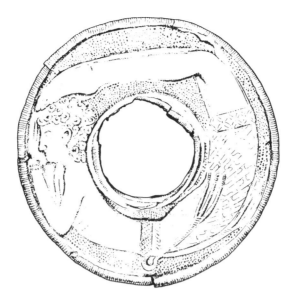

Fig. 4. Acrobat on a gold sword pommel roundel from Mallia, LM 1a. (Hood 1978, fig. 171).

Fig. 5. Acrobats on a sealstone from Knossos. (*PM* IV, 502, fig. 443).

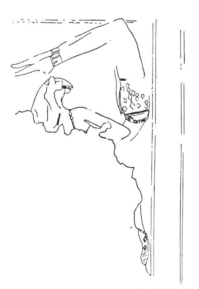

Fig. 6. Acrobatic dance from the Tomb of Ouahka II at Antaeopolis, Middle Kingdom. (Vandier Vol. IV, fig. 232).

teristic of Aegean art, especially, though not exclusively, Mycenaean art of the Shaft Graves. On Crete, hunting lions are found on a few sealings from Knossos, Ayia Triada and Zakro but, with one possible exception, not in wall-paintings. The exception is a fragment of stucco relief of a lion's mane (or bull?) from under the southeast staircase of the palace of Knossos.[52] Evans dated it to MM III. Otherwise, the earliest wall-painting with lions is the miniature Ship Procession from the West House at Thera. Here, lions in flying gallop chase fallow deer bucks on hilltops, while painted lions in the same posture glide along the side of the hull of the flagship and lion skins (?) adorn the sterns of some of the ships.[53]

The animal in **Plate 4,2,** has been identified by Bietak as a leopard. It has a yellow ochre coat with black spots on the leg, white spots on the back, and a white far leg (i.e. the underleg), with a long tail which may be striped rather than spotted. The animal is in a flying gallop and bounds past blue plants on a red background. Its feet are pointing downwards and the claws are white.

The white spots on the back have black around them, making the identification with leopard secure. The leopard is the only feline with rosette-like spots. It is notable that the East African leopard has solid black spots on the legs and rosette spots (white surrounded by black) on the body, exactly the combination in the painting.[54] The other details - spots turning into stripes towards the end of the tail and a lighter inside (far) leg - are equally characteristic and it appears that the artist had either seen the animal first-hand or had examined detailed Egyptian representations of the creature. Clearly the animal was not seen in Greece.

Perhaps the earliest representation of a leopard, or large spotted feline, in Aegean art is the stone macehead in the form of a leopard (one end) and battle-axe (the other end) from the Old Palace of Mallia (MM III, c.1650-1600 BC). The creature has large spots on the head.[55]

A fragment of wall-painting from Knossos shows the head of a feline with large spots, which strongly resembles a leopard.[56] In the miniature Landscape frieze from Thera, a blue feline with spotted coat and ringed tail bounds after waterfowl along a river course flanked by Nilotic plants of palms, papyrus and reeds. The identification of the feline here is difficult. If it is a leopard its environmental context is incorrect (leopards prey on mammals). With its long neck it most resembles a serval.[57] The combination of spotted coat with ringed tail is also known from Mycenae, on a dagger blade from Shaft Grave V (**Fig. 2**), where the creature again hunts fowl, and on a dagger blade from Rutsi near Pylos.[58] The artists could be thinking of feral cats, but with the discovery of the Tell el-Dab'a paintings an iconographic reference derived from Minoan artists working in Egypt seems plausible. The majority of representations of cats in the Aegean belong to scenes in which the animals hunt birds.[59] But sometimes the cats appear only with plants and in gold cut-outs from Shaft Grave III at Mycenae cats are associated with palms. In gold inlays from Shaft Grave III, a spotted feline with a ringed tail hunts alongside lions in a setting of palm trees.[60] On a pommel from Shaft Grave IV at Mycenae a lion attacks a leopard, biting into its neck.[61] These are the only two instances in Aegean art of which I am aware where lion and leopard appear together.

In Egyptian hunting scenes in the desert, dogs are not the only predators. In some Old and Middle Kingdom tombs, on the same wall lions attack bulls, and sometimes a leopard also appears in the same scene.[62]

The likelihood is that the fragment in **Plate 4,2,** was part of a chase or a hunt. The flying gallop would certainly suggest this. Other fragments with a red background (and on the same relative scale) include men wearing boots or greaves who could therefore be hunters or warriors (see below).

The so-called flying gallop, in which the four limbs are all extended, is a typical movement expressing animal speed in Aegean art. It is applied (particularly by the Mycenaeans) indiscriminately to various animals, not only to cats and dogs, who have considerable flexibility in their extended movements, but even to deer, horses and wild boar, none of whom could have achieved such a pose without splitting their limbs. However, it is quite likely that the origin of the flying gallop is the observation of the feline gallop. Modern stop-motion photography has shown that cats (unlike other animals) do indeed extend all four legs simultaneously in a spring-like moment of their gallop,[63] and an impression of this is quite possible to catch in the retinal image. The Minoan, gentler version when applied to cats is quite life-like.

The flying gallop first appears in Minoan art in Middle Minoan II (equivalent to the 13th Dynasty).[64] Inexplicably, an isolated example of a dog chasing a hare, both in an extended or flying gallop, occurs in a painting from a 1st Intermediate Period tomb at Moalla,[65] hence pre-dating the earliest Aegean examples. It does not, however, recur in Egyptian art until the period of the Dab'a paintings and its immediate aftermath, so remains an anomaly. Otherwise, prior to the discovery of this painting, the earliest known examples in Egypt were said to be on a dagger hilt of the Hyksos king Apophis (c.1585-1542 BC) (which is, however, not a full flying gallop)[66] and that on a dagger and gold collar of Ahhotep, mother of Ahmose, founder of the 18th Dynasty (which is).[67] The first example in tomb painting is not until the tomb of Puyemre in the time of Hatshepsut and Tuthmosis III.[68] This is surely significant, since it provides a rare chance to observe the process of iconographic transference from one region to another. The Aegean artist in Egypt painted a movement previously uncharacteristic of Egyptian art but applying it to an animal more at home in Egypt than in the Aegean. The movement is immediately adopted first

Fig. 7.   Bull capture and bull fighting. Detail from the Tomb of Baqt I, no. 29,
at Beni Hasan, South Wall. (Newberry and Griffith Vol II, pl. XXXI).

Fig. 8.   Sealing from the Temple
Repositories at Knossos,
MM IIIB-LM 1A.
(*PM* I, 694, fig. 514).

Fig. 9.   Sealstone from Gournes.
(*CMS* II, 4, 157).

Fig. 10.   Fragment of painted plaster
from the first palace of
Phaistos, MM II.
(Immerwahr 1990, fig. 6d).

Fig. 11.   Fragment of painted plaster
from the Domestic Quarter
of the palace of Knossos,
MM IIIa. (*PM* I, fig. 256).

by Hyksos/Egyptian artists and then Egyptian in the period immediately following its inception in Egypt, on portable objects. Its appearance in Egyptian wall-paintings follows some time later. The technique of the Ahhotep dagger is niello, a technique which was used in Byblos during the equivalant of the 12th Dynasty and which at the time of the dagger had its now famous examples at Mycenae, in the dagger blades of the Shaft Graves. They too use an exagerrated version of the flying gallop (which may well have arisen from the physical constraints of the narrow blade) for lions and griffins as well as for the cats (leopards?) in a Nilotic landscape.

Bietak has identified the wings of a large griffin against a background of aquatic plants (this volume, 24). The running spiral is in black, with traces of blue at the bottom of the fragment suggesting continuation of the motif in different format. The blue horizontal strip is irregular and painted freehand with traces of black over parts. Two of the leaves emerge from the blue, half hidden by it. This device indicates that the blue was painted afterwards and accords well with the interpretation of a griffin in a landscape as opposed to a plant scene with abstract dado. The wings of a small-scale griffin are represented in a fragment illustrated in Bietak 1994, pl. 21 B and this volume, 24, **Plate 4,3.**

Griffins are a familiar part of the iconography of both regions - the Aegean and Egypt - as well as of the Levant. Indeed, Frankfort first suggested that the Aegean griffin had its origin in textiles from Syria.[69] What is different about the Aegean griffin is its crest and its notched wing pattern (marking the flight feathers) with running spirals at the neck.

Not all Aegean griffins have wings. Those from the Throne Rooms at Knossos and Pylos have none. Again, the closest parallels to the fragments from Dab'a are from Thera, both in the Xeste 3 griffin guarding the goddess (**Plate 4,4**) and in the griffin in flying gallop in the Landscape from the West House. Fragments of griffin wings have also come to light in House A at Kea.[70]

As significant as the sudden appearance of the flying gallop in Egypt is the first Minoan-style griffin in Egyptan art, which appears at the same time - on an axe of Ahmose.[71] One weapon of a late Hyksos king and two weapons of Ahmose, the king responsible for the overthrow of the Hyksos, were thus decorated with two Aegean motifs whose first appearance in Egypt is in paintings decorating a building in the Hyksos capital, itself sacked by the warriors of Ahmose.

Large-scale human figures
Numerous fragments of patterns suggest dresses of large-scale female figures. One has a divided pattern indicative of flouncing and in particular brings to mind the dresses of the women in the House of the Ladies paintings from Thera.[72] However, unless other parts of female figures are found, it will be necessary to keep an open mind with regards to the interpretation of these patterns.

The fragment of a large-scale male head (Bietak, this volume, **Plate 3,2**) is unusual. Having said that, it should be remembered that large-scale male figures are not typical of Minoan painting from Crete and indeed occur only in the Knossos Procession Fresco from the Corridor running between the West Entrance and the Propylaeum, the best preserved figure being the Cup-Bearer. This procession is probably datable to LM II but an earlier prototype has been postulated by Mark Cameron for the Grand East Staircase.[73]

Processional male figures are also known from Thera. One led the way up the stairway in Xeste 3, while others were situated on the west wall and corridor of the ground floor of the adyton. Others (not yet fully excavated or fully published) have been found in the adjacent building, Xeste 4. Two large-scale naked fishermen from the West House also have a processional quality as they display their catch of fish.[74]

Two fragments from House B at Ayia Irini on Kea indicate that large-scale male figures were here too (most of this building has fallen into the sea). One fragment shows a large eye, the other has an arm holding a rhyton.[75]

The inspiration for large-scale processional male figures is surely Egyptian painting and relief, where the theme has a history stretching back into the Old Kingdom. But its popularity in Egypt was never matched in the Aegean, even when processions became standard in Mycenaean palaces, for there (Pylos excepted) the majority of figures were female.

The unusual features of the Tell el-Dab'a fragment in **Plate 3,2**, are the painting of a beard in parallel lines and the outlining of the mouth apparently in black (most of the black on this fragment has come off, revealing a pale blue-grey underneath). The ear is provided with internal markings in sinuous lines, a feature which is paralleled on both male and female large-scale figures from Thera,[76] while the best-preserved Fisherman from Thera also has lips defined by pink and black. The shape of the eye is of a more rounded type than in Egyptian art and comparable to those of the large-scale figures from Thera, as is the use of red ochre with black dot for iris and pupil. Beards, though not commonly worn by men in the Aegean, are depicted in a number of representations on sealstones. Nanno Marinatos identifies their wearers as priests.[77] A beard is also worn by at least one of the mariners (further distinguished by a hair-lock) in the miniature Ship Procession from Thera.[78]

Two other fragments of an arm and part of a torso have the characteristic curve of both the Knossos and Thera examples, which differs from Egyptian anatomical detail.[79] However, the red ochre skin is (rather carelessly) outlined in black, which is not a feature of Minoan or Cycladic painting.

Human figures against a red ground

Two fragments show a human leg wearing footgear. Both are against a red ground. One wears a black boot on the foot with an extension in white up the leg or, more likely, a white greave (Bietak 1994, pl. 20 A). The boot is held on by a blue strap, which is attached to the blue sole. The other figure wears a white boot with indications of black on the foot (Bietak 1994, pl. 20 B). Bietak is of the opinion that the white (painted over the red ground) is a sign of female skin and that these are women. The second fragment, he suggests, may be an arm rather than a leg. However, traces of black lines are surely indicative of a boot, like those worn by the bull-leaper in **Plate 2,1**, and the acrobat in **Plate 3,1**. There is no problem in turning the angle of the blue plants next to the limb in accordance with the orientation of the leg; Minoan plants frequently veer at an angle from the ground. On both, white colouration extends beyond the short white boot (whose top is outlined) up the calf. It is hard to be sure of the gender of these limbs. The white on the first fragment could perhaps be a greave, while the white on the second fragment is no more than a thin wash.

The boots worn by white-skinned bull-leapers in the Knossos paintings (**Plate 18,2**, discussed below) are also black and white, either with black foot and white ankle parts, or vice versa. White boots are also worn by miniature male figures in paintings from Tylissos and Melos.[80] Greaves are worn by Mycenaean warriors and hunters.[81] That white boots with straps and patterns were characteristic of Aegean people (or at least men) is shown by the fact that the Keftiu in Egyptian tombs are depicted wearing them.[82]

As these are isolated fragments, their iconographic context is hard to determine. Two possibilities present themselves. The first is that these are bull-leapers and that the bull-sports (like the later ones from Knossos which have both blue and yellow backgrounds) were painted in sections with different coloured backgrounds (cf. House of the Frescoes where the action of the animals takes place against red and white areas). The second possibility is that these are actually hunters and that they should be associated with the leopard fragments, which also have red backgrounds. It will be remembered that **Plate 4,2**, has blue plants on the red ground around the leopard. In Bietak 1994, pl. 20 B, indications of an environmental setting are provided by blue plants only slightly different in size and shape (here more ivy shaped). We may be looking at a frieze with human and animal action.

The acrobat

There are three fragments of acrobats from Tell el-Dab'a, apparently performing in a grove of palm trees.[83] Bietak, this volume, **Plate 3,1**, shows a male figure midway through an elegant somersault. To his left are the blue leaves of a palm tree. The man wears a white loincloth, shaped like that of the bull-sports man in **Plate 2,1**, though cut lower. It defies gravity as the man turns upside-down. On his feet are white boots with black markings, again like those of the man vaulting the bull. The only fundamental difference in him and the other figure is the head-gear, which is visible at the lower edge of the fragment. It consists of a lily-shape and papyrus (a variation of the *waz*-lily), from which arise two short streamers. It is reminiscent of the hat once attributed to, now associated with, the so-called Priest King from Knossos, on a smaller scale.[84] Similar head-gear is worn by Aegean sphinxes, by a goddess or priestess in the wall-painting from the Citadel House at Mycenae, and by a goddess in a griffin-drawn chariot on one of the ends of the Ayia Triada sarcophagus,[85] all of which are later in date than the Tell el-Dab'a painting. This head-gear clearly marks the figure's activity as of special significance. Here is no simple 'joi de vivre' but a movement probably with cultic meaning.

The palm tree provides an important contextual clue. First it should be mentioned that although palm trees are clearly Nilotic in inspiration and in reality, this palm tree is wholly Aegean in conception. It is painted blue, not green, a colour which Aegean artists used for vegetation but which Egyptian artists would not have used for a palm. Palm trees are only rarely represented in Aegean painting and the best examples come from Thera, in the Landscape painting (where they dominate the environment) and in a fragment from A1.[86] This fragment is particularly significant as next to the tree (also to the right of it) is a man. He too wears something on his head, though as the fragment ends at this point we cannot tell whether they are simply streamers or feathers or if they ended in a motif. The angle of the man to the tree indicates either that the tree is bent or that the man is bent, or both, and the angle of the man's head to his neck shows the same. That he too is an acrobat has been suggested by Nanno Marinatos, who has recently prepared a paper on the subject of acrobats in Minoan art.[87]

The acrobatic movement of the somersault, which is that represented here and in other examples of Minoan acrobats, appears not infrequently in Egyptian tombs, where it is one of many forms of athletic dance. Although there are antecedents in Middle Kingdom tombs, such as that in **Fig. 6**, where an acrobatic dance is performed in honour of Hathor, the somersault is essentially part of New Kingdom dance sequences, when it appears in both tombs and temples, always as part of a cultic performance.[88]

Acrobats occur in other instances of Minoan art, though they are not common. One stretches head to toe around the pommel of a Middle Minoan III sword from Mallia (**Fig. 4**).[89] Two others on a sealstone from Knossos (**Fig. 5**) have the same ribbon-like head-pieces seen on the man with palm from Thera and on top of the flower motif on the man in the Dab'a fragment.[90] Here, as on a comparable seal from Mycenae (Bietak, this volume, **Fig. 4**), the acrobats are in a setting of papyrus (?), showing that, there too, the activity took place out of doors.[91]

Palm trees had a special significance in Aegean iconography.[92] They are frequently associated with killer-lions and griffins, and sometimes with wild bulls (the Vapheio cups). At other times they appear to mark the sanctity of the place of sacrificial ritual. On a seal from Mycenae (?) a palm tree is bent over a sacrificial bull lying trussed up on an altar.[93] On another seal, from Aplomata on Naxos (later in date, probably LH III), a man holding a spear guards or salutes a palm tree, the accoutrements of sacrifice and (presumably blood) libation in front of him on an altar.[94] Interestingly, he wears a loin-cloth (not a Mycenaean kilt, in spite of the period) and some form of head-gear which terminates in a ribbon-like extension at the top.

This association of palm trees with death, sanctity and sacrifice may be relevant in terms of the associated bull-sports of these paintings. Most notably, the acrobat, who wears the same clothes as the vaulters with only the addition of the head-piece, performs a movement which is an echo of that of vaulting over the bull.

Bull-sports and the Labyrinth

The images which have created the most interest amongst the paintings from Tell el-Dab'a are those of the bull-sports. Of all animals, the bull is the most closely identified with Minoan cult and Minoan culture, from the sacrificial creature to the head of the bull, exemplified by the rhyta from Knossos (LM I, serpentine) and Mycenae (Shaft Grave IV, silver, with a rosette between its horns).[95] Bull's head rhyta are, of course, amongst the goods brought by Keftiu in Egyptian New Kingdom tombs of the 15th century, as are models of bulls and frontal-faced bulls painted on pottery including, in the tomb of Senenmut, examples with rosettes between the horns.[96]

Bull-sports are quintessentially Minoan in subject.[97] This was a ritual sport closely associated with the palace of Knossos, which had a number of examples both in flat painting (**Plate 18,2**) and relief. The sport expresses physical challenge and human dominance. The participants are youthful and full of vigour. The earliest instances of the sport are in the form of bull-vessels with small acrobats attached to their horns, dating to EM III - MM Ia (c. 2000 BC, equivalent to the early part of the Middle Kingdom) and found in tombs in the Cretan Mesara at Koumasa and Porti.[98] The earliest two-dimensional representations of the sport occur in MM IIIB-LM I, on sealings from Ayia Triada and the Knossos Temple Repositories (**Fig. 8**),[99] and on the Ayia Triada stone Sports Rhyton.[100] It continues as a fairly popular theme in glyptic art throughout the LM period, with examples from the mainland as well as from Crete. But the greatest concentration of bull-sports occurs in paintings and reliefs at Knossos.

It is largely a Minoan theme. Two bulls (one pink, one blue) came from the north wall of the West House

miniatures at Thera.[101] A human arm at the edge of the fragment might suggest a bull-grappling scene. Otherwise this is not a Cycladic theme. On mainland Greece there are examples of bull-leaping in wall-paintings from the Ramp House at Mycenae (LM II/IIIA), Pylos (LH IIIA) and Tiryns (LH IIIB),[102] but these later examples are isolated instances and give an unconvincing impression of the sport, suggesting to some commentators an iconographic hangover with little or no remaining relevance.

In Egyptian art, an isolated example of bull-leaping occurs on an ointment box from Kahun of the time of Tutankhamun.[103] Not only is it late in relation to the majority of Aegean examples, but it shows in the postures of the men little visible familiarity with the actual sport. The theme, otherwise, does not appear to have been appropriated by Egyptian artists. Bull-fighting - bull with bull, men watching - occurs as a theme in Old and Middle Kingdom tombs (**Fig. 7, lower**).[104] Occasional related capture scenes include strenuous acrobatic manoeuvres involving clinging to the bull's horns.[105] **In Fig. 7, upper,** from the tomb of Baqt, no. 29, at Beni Hasan a man actually springs over the horns of a bull.[106]

The funerary context of the Egyptian bull-fighting scenes differs fundamentally from the palatial scenes of Knossos, but it should be remembered that the first instances of the Aegean bull-sports - on the bull-vessels from the Mesara - were found in tombs, and of very much later date there is an isolated instance of bull-sports on a larnax from Tanagra on the mainland.[107]

Although it has always been contended that bull-sports originated in Crete, a recent study by Dominique Collon suggests that the immediate antecedants to the Minoan examples may be found in Syria, where some seals of the 17th century depict bull-sports.[108] **Plate 18,1**, is an example. It is interesting to note that the posture of the bull-leapers echoes that of the Tell el-Dab'a acrobat in **Plate 3,1**. Bietak nonetheless maintains that Minoan influence must be assumed.[109]

Where the origins of this sport were or whether there were pockets of independant origin remain open questions. A series of rock paintings in northern India of the 3rd millennium show scenes of bull-leaping, including three figures in positions uncannily like those in the Knossos paintings - in front of the bull, vaulting, and behind the bull - either as three participants or as three moments in the jump.[110] Surely an uncanny coincidence.

No doubt the Tell el-Dab'a examples have Knossian associations. However, the dating is significant. The earliest Cretan wall-paintings (as opposed to other media) which unequivocally show bull-leaping date, in all liklihood, to LM II. This is not, however, as problematic as it at first seems. As was the case with processions, there must have been earlier examples than those left on the walls at the time of the destruction of the palace of Knossos in LM IIIa.

At Tell el-Dab'a, besides the bull-sports, which are discussed in detail below, there is part of a bull's hoof in relief. The use of relief stucco is particularly significant in terms of Knossian parallels.

Relief bulls in action - a theme which seems to be an abbreviation for the sports or perhaps for the ritual context in which the sports were played - were an important element in the decoration of entrances to the palace at Knossos. At the North Entrance, fragments of at least two bulls in relief were associated with a woman's leg (a leaper?) and a landscape of olive and myrtle.[111] These were burnt at the final destruction and Evans suggested that they stood in situ until the Greek period when the legend of the Minotaur was established. The date of the reliefs is thought to be LM IB/LM II but as relief work was popular during MM III it is usually thought that it relates back to an earlier prototype. At the South-West Entrance a dado with a fragment of a bull was found in situ on the east wall of the west porch, before the Procession Fresco.[112] Two earlier paintings showing parts of bulls were preserved on the wall underneath. These are thought to be a late renewal (LM IIIa) of an earlier painting (MM IIIb-LM Ia). At both entrances the bulls face outwards, greeting or fending off the approaching visitor, like the heraldic emblem of the palace. A life-size bull, of which the foot was found in situ, in the Antechamber to the Throne Room (LM II-IIIA) no doubt had the same function.[113]

The theme of bulls continued outside the palace, with pieces of relief bulls having come from the Royal Road and the House of the Sacrificed Oxen (the latter, Evans suggested, may have fallen from the palace).[114] Flat painted fragments of a tree, part of a bull and the locks of a taureador came from the North-West Treasury.[115] Several other bull fragments came from the Domestic Quarter of the palace, some associated with plants and dress fragments which include the motif of the sacrificial double axe and one from a miniature scene of bull-sports.[116]

However, in the palace the main iconographic context of bulls is that of bull-leaping or associated sports. In the East Magazines and the Lapidary's Workshop bull reliefs were associated with boxers or wrestlers, fragments of female figures, and griffins (High Reliefs Deposit).[117] These are datable to MM IIIb-LM Ia, in other words contemporary with the Tell el-Dab'a paintings.

Although the main series of bull-sports wall-paintings at Knossos, the so-called Taureador Frescoes of the Court of the Stone Spout in the North East Quarters (the best-known example of which is shown in **Plate 18,2**), came from a level above LM II pottery and so must date to LM II/IIIA, other fragments from the cists of the 13th Magazine on the west side of the palace seem to show the same theme but in a style which might suggest an earlier date.[118] These had apparently fallen from a hall above. They show a bull's head with locks

of hair flowing out in the manner of bull-leapers. They were associated with fragments of miniature shrines, one with double axes, and miniature spectators, presumably of the bull-sports. Evans dated these to MM IIIb, though more recently on contextual grounds an LM II date has been preferred.[119] It should be noted that they are in a freer style than either the Taureador Frescoes of LM II or the Miniature Frescoes of LM Ia, which is what led Evans to postulate the earlier date.

The dating of Minoan wall-paintings is fraught with difficulties. But the absence of a clear example of a bull-leaping scene firmly datable to the earliest period of Minoan figurative painting (MM IIIb-LM Ia) should not necessarily lead to the conclusion that such did not exist. The evidence overwhelmingly shows that bull-sports were important at this time (as seen on other media) and had been known on Crete for hundreds of years. The emphasis on bull iconography at Knossos underlines this point.

Perhaps the most characteristically Minoan of all the Dab'a fragments is Bietak, this volume, **Plate 2,1**. It shows a large bull with a piebald hide, an indication of domestication of the species. As with the Knossos bulls, we are likely to be seeing a feral speciman descended from *Bos primigenius*.[120] The neck rises on the right side of the fragment, the tail extends upwards to the left. The man has vaulted over the bull's head and is in the process of beginning his land. It looks like the moment after that shown in the Knossos painting in **Plate 18,2**. However, the leaper's front faces the back of the bull, whereas in the Knossos painting the leaper faces the front, in the middle of an elegant somersault, lifting his head between his shoulders. It is an altogether more controlled position than in the Tell el-Dab'a painting.

The similarities with the Taureador Frescoes from Knossos are obvious, though, as we are seeing an earlier version here, both man and bull are more naturalistically rendered. This said, several idiomatic details are uncannily similar. The method of depicting hands - fingers together and thumb out, like a child stretching its hands in mittens - is identical.[121]

The picture in **Plate 18,2**, is one of perhaps seven panels, each of which is divided by a horizontal strip of stylized variagated stone, a pattern which also frames top and bottom so that the panels form a frieze. The panels mainly show bull-leaping though one, unusually, depicts an accident in which the sportsman has fallen.[122]

In the Tell el-Dab'a fragment, the young man has long black locks which flow back with his head in a more naturalistic manner than the free-standing locks of his later Knossian counterpart. Like the Knossos painting, however, the locks are divided into those at the forehead and those at the nape of the neck. This long flowing hair was characteristically worn by men taking part in ritual sports.[123] It is one indication of the special nature of the activity. Another is the jewellery worn by the figures. Here blue bands - perhaps indicative of silver - are worn on the upper arms. Such arm bands are worn in the Knossos paintings by several of the bull-leapers as well as by the Cup-Bearer in the Procession Fresco. The loin-cloth is cut up at the side like the Knossos versions, but here it is a softer, unpadded version with no indication of a cod-piece. Boots, such as the man wears here, are worn by the white-skinned figures rather than the red in the Knossos bull-sports, though, as mentioned above, a miniature fragment from Phylakopi on Melos shows a male (red) leg with a white boot as here. As this was found out of context and is a solitary find the activity of the man is unknown. The Tylissos miniatures, which have the same feature, depict a probable festival (as, in my opinion, do all the miniature wall-paintings in Crete and the Cyclades). In the earliest of the Mycenaean bull-sports from the Ramp House at Mycenae, white boots or greaves are worn by the men, with a white strap over the foot.[124] The question of whether the white-skinned bull-leapers from Knossos are intended to be women is an open one, which is discussed below in relation to the fragment from Tell el-Dab'a in **Plate 1,1** (at Tiryns, too, the acrobat is white-skinned).

The joined fragments in Bietak, this volume, **Plate 2,2**, depict a man standing in an awkward and unusual posture in front of a large bull's head with the head of a second man to the left, both facing towards the standing man. The man's arms are bent but face the spectator and the hands are clenched. The garment - whether intended as a loin cloth or a kilt - is also shown frontally. It is an experimental pose and must have an iconographic function. It almost looks as though he was holding a rope in his hands and pulling the bull with it. But no rope is visible. The bull has his mouth open and his tongue extended. His head must be sloping upwards. The second man, to the left, has a bemused expression (perhaps accidentally) as he looks towards his partner. The angle of his head to his neck indicates that he is stretching forward and his body must be bent. On the right of the fragment (behind the man) is a white area with blue 'flowers', which Bietak suggests may be a kiosk or altar.[125] If the latter, this would imply a sacrificial intention, but too little survives of this part for clear identification.

Either this is another bull-leaping scene, in which we are seeing both the leaper and the catcher, or it is a related bull-grappling scene. The two types of scene - vaulting and hunting - are shown together on an LM I ivory circular box from Katsamba. Men catching bulls are also depicted on the gold cups from Vapheio.[126] The angle of the bull's head and his open mouth with extended tongue suggest to me that the bull is in pain and therefore probably being captured. Such events must have taken place prior to the bull-leaping, though perhaps symbolically as part of the spectacle.

The most astonishing of all the Tell el-Dab'a pieces is Bietak, this volume, **Plate 1,1**. A leaper with light-coloured skin vaults over the back of a bull who turns his massive head to stare impassively at the spectator. Behind him is a maze-like pattern in red and black suggestive of a labyrinth. The related piece in **Plate 1,2**, shows that the maze-like pattern continued, punctuated by or ending in an area of blue.

The pale-yellowish skin raises the question of the flexibility of colour conventions in ancient art. The white-skinned bull-leapers from Knossos were always assumed to be female, as white is the Aegean convention for female skin. However, recently some scholars have questioned the rigidity of the convention on the grounds that these figures have all the musculature of men and none of the curves of women[127] (this does not apply to stucco reliefs of figures from the High Reliefs Deposit thought to be bull-leapers, who have female breasts).[128] The confusion is not restricted to bull-leapers. The so-called 'Priest-King' has white skin with male musculature and clothing, while figures in the Camp Stool fresco have red skins with female dresses (unless this is a priestly garment).[129] In fact, colour conventions may have been less strictly codified throughout the ancient world than is usually assumed. In the wall-paintings of Mari, both male and female skin is depicted red-ochre, but several male faces (with moustache and beard) are white, pink or white with pink cheeks.[130] In Egypt, male deities and by extension deified kings are sometimes depicted yellow-skinned, sometimes red, while in the Amarna period women were sometimes painted red-ochre. Foreign men from east and west - Libyans, Bedouin, Syrians, Hittites (but not northerners from the Aegean, who in 18th Dynasty tomb representations are, like Egyptian men, red-ochre) - were represented with light-yellow skin, like Egyptian women; so, occasionally, were elderly Egyptian men.[131]

Whatever the white/red distinction in the Knossos Taureador paintings signifies, the important factor is that a distinction has been made between two types of people - those with pale skin and those with dark skin - and that this distinction is made at Tell el-Dab'a, just as it is at Knossos, within the same iconographic context.

One possible interpretation for the yellow skin in **Plate 1,1**, is that the distinctions at Knossos are indeed about male and female and that this is picked up here but using the Egyptian convention for female skin - light yellow - rather than the Aegean - white. Another possibility is that we are seeing either a distinction of cultural or racial differentiation (as Egyptian artists used, but this is unlikely as the hair is clearly Aegean) or that the figure was overlapping with another and a lighter skin was used to differentiate the bodies (again as Egyptian artists did, including in sport activities).[132] However, an interesting Aegean parallel presents itself in the wall-paintings from Xeste 3, Thera. Here, uniquely in the Aegean, yellow skin is used to differentiate a young boy from the red-ochre men.[133] Given the direct parallel with the Theran paintings presented by the blue shaved head with hair locks (see below), this seems the most plausible explanation for the colour change - a distinction in age.

The person in the Dab'a fragment again has long black locks of hair but underneath them the head, following the hair-line, is blue. Again, only one parallel presents itself from the Aegean: Thera. There are no examples of blue heads in the paintings at Knossos or anywhere else. On Thera, the idiom is used for young men and women - the Fishermen and Priestess from the West House, the Boxing Boys, the Xeste 3 boys and girls.[134] It appears to denote a shaved head from which locks are allowed to grow. Parallels for such a practice exist from throughout the ancient world.[135] In Egypt, the hair lock was a sign of youth.[136] But to my knowledge, there are no painted depictions from Egypt of this period or anywhere else in the ancient world which show the shaved head as blue in conjunction with hair locks for non-divine figures,[137] other than at Thera and Tell el-Dab'a. That the practice of wearing hair locks was known on Crete is suggested by sculptures with holes in the head for locks, notably on ivory acrobats from the Ivory Deposit at Knossos, who were most likely bull-leapers.[138] That we have no examples of blue heads in wall-paintings from Crete may well be due to the accident of survival, but it should also be remembered that Thera provides the only known example of the convention of yellow skin for a young boy.

The figure wears a blue arm-band, as the other leaper, and a bracelet with a form which (judging by the drawing) can only be intended as a cushion-shaped sealstone on his wrist. The wearing of sealstones (which are indeed pierced to take a string) on the wrist is evidenced by the Cup-Bearer from the Knossos Procession Fresco. The leaper's hand grasps the bull, which is most unusual. The line of his torso is such that the only possible reconstruction involves a backwards flip. He is at the beginning of his vault over the bull.

The bull is again piebald, with hairs individually delineated on the patches, like the bulls from Knossos. There the colours are yellow ochre and white, black and white, or blue. Here two shades of ochre are used and on the patches reddish streaks on yellow define the hairs. The technique is directly paralleled at Knossos.[139] The blue horns are unique. The only surviving horns (shown in two compositions) at Knossos are yellow. But the blue bull from the Theran miniatures has black horns.

The frontal face of the bull is unique in Aegean wall-painting but it is not unique in other media in Aegean art. It occurs on a number of sealstones, including, in some instances, in bull-leaping scenes (Fig. 9).[140] The most usual context for frontal face in Aegean art is, however, in association with death and sacrifice.[141] Killer-lions are frequently depicted in frontal face in the act of slaughter. The sacrificed bull on the Ayia Triada sarcophagus, already cut, blood dripping from the slash, turns with eyes open to face us.[142] On a sealstone from Argos a sacrificial double axe sits above a disembodied frontal bull's head, flanked by two cult robes, a reference to the ritual robing of the priestess or goddess impersonator.[143]

The implication is that it is the sacrificial bull that has the frontal face and that sacrifice is associated with the goddess for whom the robing ceremony is performed and in whose honour the bull-sports were, in all probability, performed.

In this context, it is as well to remember the associations of palm trees with sacrifice and the juxtaposition of a palm tree with an acrobat - whose movement echoes that of the bull-vaulters - in a related fragment, as well as the palm tree fragments associated by Bietak with the labyrinth (this volume, 24).

A dado associated with this painting shows a triglyph and rosette frieze, which, as Bietak points out, is an important element in the decoration of the palace of Knossos.[144]

But what is the significance of the maze-like pattern which provides the environmental context for the bull and his vaulter?

In Greek mythology the Cretan palace of Knossos was known for its maze-like qualities as a labyrinth, inside of which lived a minotaur - half man, half bull. The word labyrinth is derived from 'labrys', meaning 'double axe', one of the most common Minoan religious motifs and indicative of sacrificial slaughter.[145] In the Linear B tablets from Knossos we learn of a 'Lady of the Labyrinth', Da-po-ri-te-re, a goddess of a place which could be meant for the palace.[146]

In Classical Greek art the minotaur is depicted pulled by the hero Theseus from a maze-like pattern - the labyrinth, symbolic of the palace.[147] To find, in the Bronze Age, a painting showing bull-sports associated with a maze-like pattern is, at the very least, evocative of the myths which later arose from the period - not least because a bull-man already existed in the iconography of the time. Futhermore, the Minoan bull-man, who is found exclusively on sealstones, clearly derives his form from the joint postures of man and bull during the vaulting of the bull-sports.[148]

The maze-pattern, or labyrinth, itself is known from two wall-paintings on Crete, both early in date (Figs. 10-11). Neither is identical with the pattern in the Tell el-Dab'a painting, but the one from Knossos in particular is closely related. The fragment in Fig. 10, from the first palace of Phaistos (Phase III, MM II), shows a brown on white maze-pattern, belonging either to a floor or wall.[149] The fragment in Fig. 11 (= Bietak, this volume, Fig. 3) from the Domestic Quarter of the palace at Knossos (Lower East-West Corridor, just east of the Hall of Double Axes), datable to the close of MM IIIa, shows a maze-pattern executed in incavo technique with dark reddish-brown on a yellowish ground, and associated with a marbled dado.[150] Evans saw in this fragment a more elaborate development of the key and meander patterns on ivory and other seals of EM III. He pointed to similar motifs on Egyptian seals and plaques of the 6th Dynasty on. The 12th Dynasty tomb of Hepzefa has two ceilings with such patterns.[151] Such meander patterns are assumed to be derived from textiles or perhaps basket work. Particularly significant is the relationship which Evans saw between this pattern and those Egyptian hieroglyphs in the form of a 'key pattern' which represent a building, walls or enclosures and are in certain cases associated with 'palace'.[152] Evans argued that the Cretan meander was derived from this pattern. If so, might it have taken meaning with motif in being applied to the maze-like structure of the palace with its central court? On Egyptian seals human figures sometimes appear beside or in the middle of the maze patterns. In the Aegean the pattern stands alone, but significantly in wall-paintings it occurs only at palatial sites.

This significant fragment from Tell el-Dab'a provides, I suggest, a cognitive link between the Egyptian picture-word-signs, the Minoan maze and bull-sports, and the later Greek myth of the labyrinth and the minotaur.

Did bull-sports take place in the vicinity of Tell el-Dab'a? Or was the iconographic theme brought there by travelling Minoans? The latter is, in my opinion, more plausible. The bull-sports were painted on the walls of what was, in all likelihood, a Minoan shrine abroad. Such bull-sports would, in reality, have taken place at Knossos but are here offered to the goddess as a painting rather than as an actual rite. The acrobat next to the palm may be representative of another stage in the proceedings, another rite in honour of the goddess prior to the sacrifice of the bull. The palace of Knossos is represented by the labyrinth pattern - a necessary adjunct in absentia - and the promise of sacrificial ritual after the games is implied by the frontal face of the bull.

Concluding Thoughts
Until the momentous discovery of the paintings from Tell el-Dab'a, the Keftiu and the Peoples from the Isles in the Midst of the Sea were known through Egyptian eyes in 18th Dynasty tomb tribute scenes and from literary texts from the Middle and New Kingdoms. Now we see, for the first time, the presence of the people presumed to be from these lands painted by Aegean artists in what was probably a shrine at the late Hyksos capital on Egyptian soil. Whether we are seeing Knossians (as is suggested by the sport) or Therans (as suggested by the blue hair) or indeed both, Keftiu and the Peoples from the Isles in the Midst of the Sea not only came to Egypt but brought with them images of their religious practices, which they painted on walls while in Egypt. With absolutely no Minoan pottery associated with the paintings, the mystery of what they were doing there and why the paintings were commissioned remains unsolved.

The discovery of the wall-paintings at Tell el-Dab'a, unique though they are, should be seen in relation to those recently unearthed at Tell Kabri. Together, they

have thrown into relief the cultural interrelationships between Hyksos Egypt, the Levant and the Aegean. The question of whether the paintings were in fact executed by Hyksos artists will inevitably be raised. It is true that our knowledge of Hyksos painting is nil, while those few examples from the Levant of this period all seem to have Aegean characteristics. But is it really conceivable that Hyksos painting (in Egypt and in its homeland) was identical in technique and comparable in its iconographic approach to Aegean painting[153] but not actually painted by Aegean artists? I hardly think so. Yet the discoveries at Tell el-Dab'a clearly imply a special relationship between Hyksos and Aegeans. If the Hyksos took over the cultural and artistic traits of the Egyptians whilst living in their land, as they seem to have done, why did they not use Egyptian painters and painting techniques as well? Nor do the paintings suggest copies of Aegean models by local artists: they exhibit no provincial characteristics; on the whole these are top quality wall-paintings by highly experienced artists. The idea of travelling Aegean artists, as proposed by Niemeier for the Levant, seems much more likely. But why did they travel to Egypt to paint, where there was a long and rich tradition of mural decoration from which the Hyksos artists could have drawn?

The idea that we are dealing with a dynastic marriage has the advantage of being the only plausible suggestion to date,[154] but if this is the case we have to imagine that the in-coming Minoan brought no domestic accoutrements or servants but nonetheless insisted on Minoan artists providing a painted shrine for personal worship. It is a curious scenario. It also leaves unanswered the question of why Aegean painters continued to work at Tell el-Dab'a after the overthrow of the Hyksos by Ahmose at the beginning of the New Kingdom.

Further excavation may throw unexpected light on the situation. In the meantime all we can say with certainty is that we have at Tell el-Dab'a an unprecedented instance of Minoan artists apparently commissioned to paint images from their culture and religion on the walls of a palace in Egypt.

Notes
1. I would like to thank Professor Manfred Bietak for generously inviting me to see the fragments at Tell el-Dab'a and for providing me with a number of slides from which to work. I would also like to thank Vivian Davies for inviting me to speak at the British Museum Colloquium on Tell el-Dab'a on the subject of Minoan wall-painting and Egypt. This paper is based on my talk at the British Museum, subsequently updated and corrected. The comments on the Tell el-Dab'a paintings refer to fragments published by Manfred Bietak in this volume and in the references given below in note 3, or shown at the Colloquium.

2. Schachermeyer 1967, 43-9.

3. For references to the Tell el-Dab'a excavations see M Bietak's paper in this volume. On the wall-paintings see also Bietak 1992 and for a preliminary report on the paintings and their context, Bietak 1994 and Jánosi 1994.

4. On Aegean chronology of this period see: Warren and Hankey 1989, 135-41, 164, with references to alternative views; cf. Warren 1990. LM IA is placed c.1600/1580, i.e. late Hyksos, early reign of Kamose, before the beginning of the 18th Dynasty. LM IA spans the 16th century (c.1600/1580-1504/1480) according to this chronology. According to the preliminary report by Jánosi (1994, 27-38), the late Hyksos stratum at Tell el-Dab'a (Stratum V) covers the period c.1590-1530. Stratum IV covers c.1540-1390, early New Kingdom. The paintings were found in Stratum V-IV, a destruction horizon in which the finds were not in situ. This period covers the end of the Hyksos and the beginning of the New Kingdom in the reigns of Kamose and Ahmose (Jánosi 1994, 31-2). It may be assumed, then, that the destruction which resulted in the paintings being torn from the palace walls occurred c. 1540, midway through LM IA, while their execution was in early LM IA/late Hyksos, c.1580-1540.

5. Bietak 1994, 54, 58.

6. Hayes 1990, Vol II, 11-14, comments on the relative scarcity of firmly datable Hyksos material but assumes that Egyptian artists trained in the Middle Kingdom traditions were patronized by the Hyksos rulers.

7. Long 1974.

8. Malkata: Smith 1981, 286-95. Amarna: Frankfort 1929. The only earlier evidence of palatial wall-painting in Egypt comes from two fragments from the early New Kingdom palace at Deir el Ballas, showing a man's head and two axes, thought to represent the palace guard (Smith 1981, 281, fig. 277, A-B).

9. Aegean features of Amarna art were first pointed out by Frankfort (1929) and Evans (PM II, 474). Frankfort suggested that Egyptians at the time of Akhenaten had seen older paintings while trading in the Argolid. Kantor (1947, 83-4) and Smith (Interconnections 1965, 154-68, cf. 161-2) contend that such influences derive from earlier New Kingdom contacts with the Aegean rather than contemporary contacts. On the Mycenaean pottery found at Amarna see: Hankey 1981 and this volume; also Cline 1987 (esp. 13-14).

10. See Immerwahr 1990, Ch. 3.

11. Shaw 1967, 1970, 25-30; Immerwahr 1990, 35-7, 50-3, 90, 159-61. (I have not had an opportunity to see Shaw 1967, which is cited by Immerwahr.)

12. Kemp and Merrillees 1980, 6-102.

13. On the Keftiu see: Kantor 1947, 41-9; Furumark 1950, 223-46; Vercoutter 1956; Merrillees 1972; Strange 1980; E Sakellarakis and Y Sakellarakis 1984, 197-203; Wachsmann 1987. The question of trading routes is discussed by Kemp and Merrillees 1980, 268-86; contrast Watrous 1992, 172-3, 175-8.

14. Lucas and Harris 1962, 353-4.

15. Niemeier 1991, 189-200; Kempinski and Niemeier 1988, 1991, 1993.

16. Kempinski and Niemeier 1993, 258.

17. Niemeier 1990, 120-6, presents evidence from radiocarbon dates from Akrotiri, Thera, for a 17th rather than 16th century date for LM IA, and seeks to correlate the new chronology of Alalakh VII in the 17th century. However, the argument for a high date for LM IA/LC I (which is controversial) may be unnecessary, given that earlier (MM II) Knossian prototypes for marbled dadoes almost certainly existed (as pointed out by Niemeier, 1991, 193, n. 33). The high chronology is also proposed by P Betancourt, Archaeometry 29 (1987) 47-9, and in C Doumas (ed.) 1990, Vol. 3, 19-23; H N Michael and P Betancourt, Archaeometry 30 (1988), 169-75; S Manning, Journal of Mediterranean Archaeology (1988), 17-82. Cf. against: P Warren, Archaeometry 29 (1987), 205-11; 30 (1988) 176-9, 181-2; Warren and Hankey 1989, 140f.

18. Cf. Peter Warren in this volume.

19. Poursat 1980, 116-32, figs. 170-1, 174; Immerwahr 1985, 41-50; Immerwahr 1990, 35, pl. 5.

20. See Morgan 1988, 146-50.

21. Newberry and Griffith 1900, Vol. IV, pl. V; Immerwahr 1990, pl. 6.

22. Cf. Morgan 1988, 146-7 and pl. 187 (Tomb of Nebamun, 18th Dynasty, British Museum). On fowling in the marshes see Vandier 1964, Vol. IV, ch. IX. The cat is less frequently depicted amongst papyrus then the genet.

23. Newberry and Griffith 1893, Vol. I, pl. XXIX; Nina de Garis Davies 1936, Vol. I, pl. VII.

24. The tomb of Rekhmire in Thebes provides a later glimpse of how such animals might have reached the Aegean. In a register beneath the Keftiu in the well-known 'tribute' scene are Nubians and Sudanese who bring with them numerous southern animals including a monkey who climbs up the neck of a giraffe. Presumably such small creatures, like the ostrich-eggs and antelope which appear here, made good trading items. N de Garis Davies 1935, pls. VI-VII, XXII; 1973 (1943), pls. XIX-XX; Morgan 1988, pl. 197.

25. Saffron Gatherer: Immerwahr 1990, pl. 11; Xeste 3: Doumas 1992, pl. 122; Marinatos 1987, 123-32.

26. The parallel is discussed in Morgan forthcoming (Klados).

27. Colour reconstruction: N Platon, KrChron 1947, 505-24, pl.

28. The miniature wall-paintings from Ayia Irini, Kea, will be published by the present author in Keos: The Wall Paintings, E Davies and L Morgan (Philip von Zabern, Mainz). Preliminary publications: Abramovitz 1980; and Morgan 1990, 253-8.

29. *PM* II, pls. X-XI; *PM* III, pl. XXII; Cameron 1967, 45-74, pls. II-IV; 1968, 1-31; 1975, col. slide 56.

30. Since I wrote this paper, Manfred Bietak and Nanno Marinatos have shown new reconstructions drawn by Lyla Brock under their supervision of the the bull-leaping and hunting scenes respectively. In both cases the ground colour appears to change with undulating horizontal divisions. (Oxford Conference in honour of M S F Hood, *Crete and the Aegean World in the Bronze Age. Invasions, Migrations and Influences,* 15-17 April 1994.)

31. Morgan 1988, 23, 28.

32. Lily bulbs were apparently imported to Egypt from the Mediterranean and the flowers used to scent oil (Hepper 1990, 20-1, 25; cf. Manniche 1989, 50-1). They were not, however, depicted in the art (Manniche 1989, 13).

33. Not yet published but shown in a slide at the British Museum Colloquium. The red is painted over the yellow-white ground, though this does not conclusively solve the gestalt problem of which way round to read it.

34. See note 28. Preliminary photograph of the rockwork: Abramovitz 1980, pl. 12b (243).

35. Doumas 1992, pls. 66-9 (Spring Fresco); pls. 100, 116, 129 (Xeste 3 adyton); S Marinatos, *Thera* VI, pl. 23 (Xeste 3 stairway).

36. See Morgan 1988, 34, for Aegean examples of both types. Gravel or small pebbles in Egyptian painting: Tomb of Kenamun (TT 93), N de Garis Davies 1930, I, pls. xlviii-l, p.37; II, pl. xlviii A; Nina de Garis Davies 1936, I, pls. xxx, xxxi, discussed by Evans, *PM* II, 448-50, Kantor 1947, 72 (who cites other instances) and Smith, *Interconnections,* 156-8.

37. As in the 'Sacred Grove and Dance' miniature fresco from Knossos (*PM* III, pl. XVIII), fragments of relief stucco from the North West Entrance (*PM* III, 167-70, figs. 109B - 113; *PM* IV, 17, fig. 8; and one of the Vapheio cups, Marinatos and Hirmer, pls. 179, 181, 182-4.)

38. Manniche 1989, 128-9.

39. Cameron 1975, p.728, col. slide 34 (reconstruction).

40. Evans, *PM* II, 458, fig. 270; Cameron 1967, 45-74, p. 64, fig. 6; 1975, colour slide 35 (reconstruction).

41. Col. pl: Sakellarakis 1978, 121.

42. Thera: Doumas 1992, 19. Kea: to be published by the author (see note 28); preliminary publication, Abramovitz 1980, pls. 8-9c.

43. Manniche 1989, 124-5. Cf. Vedel 1978, 68. The ancient Egyptian word for the plant is not certainly known, though it has been identified by some scholars as *ḫt-ds*. The Theban tomb of Ineni (TT 81, period of Tuthmosis I) includes an inventory of trees in his garden in which *ḫt-ds* appears (Manniche 1989, 10). On the tomb of Ineni see Dziobek 1992;

the list of trees is discussed by Baum 1988 (I am grateful to Vivian Davies for these references).

44. Doumas 1992, pls. 82-4.

45. On the hunt in the desert see: Vandier 1964, Vol. IV, 787-833. On dogs, see also: H Fischer *Lexikon* III, 78-9; Janssen 1989, 9-13.

46. Marinatos and Hirmer 1960, pl. 6. Glyptic art: Yule 1980, 129-30. The earliest example referred to here is attributed to EM III-MM IA (*CMS* XII, 74a).

47. Higgins 1979, pls. 17, 64, 65, and pp. 26, 63 (2).

48. Walberg 1991.

49. *CMS* II.5, 258, 259, 284, Phaestos sealings, MM IB - MM IIA; *CMS* VII, 35, Crete, flattened cylinder, MM IIB.

50. Mycenaean paintings: Pylos: Lang 1969, 21 H 48, pls. 15, 116, 122. Tiryns: Rodenwaldt 1912, Abb. 47 = Tafel XIV (6); Abb. 55 = Tafel XIII (boar hunt). Minoan glyptic: *CMS* II.5, 276, 277 (Phaistos sealings, MM IB-IIA, animal in flying gallop); *CMS* XI, 171 (animal hunt); *CMS* XIII, 71; I, 363 (Pylos sealing, animal hunt); *CMS* I, 81 (Mycenae, antithetic/animal hunt); *CMS* II.3, 52 (Isopata, accompanied by men); *CMS* VIII, 115 (head).

51. A paper on the hunting scenes was given by Marinatos at the Oxford Conference in honour of M S F Hood, *Crete and the Aegean World in the Bronze Age. Invasions, Migrations and Influences*, 15-17 April 1994.

52. Stucco relief: *PM* II, 332-4, fig. 188; Kaiser 1976, 284, fig. 461 a-b. For Mycenaean and Cretan examples see Pini 1982, 1985; Morgan 1988, 46, with references; Bloedow 1992.

53. Morgan 1988, 44-9.

54. Haltennorth and Diller 1980, pl. 40 (2), 222-3.

55. Marinatos and Hirmer 1960, pl. 68.

56. *PM* I, 540, fig. 392; Cameron and Hood 1967, pl. D, fig. 6. Evans associates the piece with a fragment of a bird, but Cameron dissociates it on grounds of style.

57. Today the serval's habitat is mainly central and southern Africa (Haltennorth and Diller 1980, 226-7), but the question of whether it was previously indigenous to North Africa remains open. See Morgan 1988, 41 and note 5.

58. Marinatos and Hirmer col. pls. XXXV, XXXVII (above), Shaft Grave V; pl. XXXVIII (centre) and 171, Rutsi, near Pylos.

59. See Morgan 1988, 41-4.

60. Morgan 1988, pl. 58.

61. Hood 1978, fig. 174, 177.

62. See Vandier 1964, Vol. IV, 830-1. According to Vandier's list of 49 private tombs with the scene of hunting in the desert, dogs appear in 34, evenly distributed in time, lions appear in 15 and leopards in 9 (leopard/panther), all in the Old and Middle Kingdoms, with only one instance (a leopard) in a New Kingdom tomb.

63. Muybridge 1957, pl. 127, phases 8-10.

64. *CMS* II.5, 276, 277, sealings from Phaistos. In these first extant examples (others may be lost) the movement is applied to dogs rather than felines. Edgerton (1936) argued in relation to the proposed Aegean origin of the flying gallop in Egypt that this extended motion occurs naturally in dogs. Canines cannot, however, extend their legs as fully as felines, nor do they characteristically spring.

65. Smith, *Interconnections* 1965, fig. 190b. Smith also cites an ivory inlay of a gazelle from Kerma (155, fig. 190a).

66. Daressy 1906, 115-20, pl VII, fig. 2; *PM* I, 718-9, fig. 540; II, 619 and n. 4; Kantor 1947, 64, n. 39; Smith, *Interconnections* 1965, 155. This is not a full flying gallop because only the back legs of the gazelle are up, while the front stay firmly on the ground. The posture balances that of the lion underneath, who faces the other way, back legs on ground, forelegs up. According to Frankfort this dagger is of Syrian workmanship (1970, 245-6, fig. 282).

67. Dagger: von Bissing 1900, pl. II; *PM* I, 714-5, fig. 537; Kantor 1947, 63-4, pl. XIIIA; Smith *Interconnections* 1965, 155, fig. 37. Collar: Ibid 64; Bissing 1900, pls. VIII, 3, 7, 11, 12; VIII A, 1, 6, 8, 10; Kantor 1947, 64; Hankey 1993, 13-4, pl. on p.14.

68. N de Garis Davies 1922, vol I, pl. VII-VIII; Kantor 1947, 66-9, pl. XIII B.

69. Frankfort 1936, 106-22.

70. To be published by E Davies, in the Kea volume (see note 28).

71. Smith 1965, pl. 86 / 1981, revised ed., fig. 216. For illustrations of both sides of the axe: von Bissing 1900, pl. I (col.); Kühnert-Eggebrecht 1969, pl. XXXI; Hankey 1993, 14. The Aegean characteristics of the griffin have been discussed by a number of authors (Evans *PM* I, 550, fig. 402; IV, 191; Frankfort 1936, 112-4; Furumark 1950, 220; Smith 1981, 221-2; Kühnert-Eggebrecht 1969, 93; Flagge 1975, 18; Helck 1979, 57-8; Morgan 1988, 53, pl. 63.) Helck (55-60) argues that the dagger of Apophis and the dagger and axe of Ahmose are evidence for real and copied Aegean weapons in Egypt in the late Hyksos/early New Kingdom. None, however, is entirely Aegean in character.

72. Doumas 1992, pls. 6-7, 11-12.

73. Cameron 1978, 579-92, pl. 4. West Entrance and Propylaeum Procession: Immerwahr 1990, 88-90, 174-5, pls. 38-40.

74. Doumas 1992, pls. 109-15 (Xeste 3); pls. 138-41 (Xeste 4); pls. 18-23 (West House Fishermen).

75. See note 28. Preliminary photograph: Abramovitz 1980, pl. 7d (eye).

76. See in particular Doumas 1992, pl. 23 (Fisherman), pl. 106 (Xeste 3 woman).

77. Marinatos 1993, 128-9, figs. 88-93, 97-8.

78. Morgan 1988, pl. 126.

79. Shown as a slide in the British Museum Colloquium. Bietak is of the opinion that these pieces are by a different artist.

80. Tylissos: Shaw 1972, 171-88, figs. 3, 13. Melos: Morgan 1990, fig. 6. The Melos fragment is the only surviving piece from a miniature frieze thrown out during Mycenaean occupation of the town but dating to LC I.

81. Pylos: Lang 1969, 21 H 48, pls. 15, 116, 122; 16 H 43, pls. 12, 121, B; 22 H 64, pls. 16, 117, A, M. Tiryns: Rodenwaldt 1912, Tafel XI (4), Abb. 47; Tafel XIV (10-11). Orchomenos: Bulle 1907, pl. XXVIII, Smith, *Interconnections,* fig. 96. Mycenae Megaron: Smith, *Interconnections,* fig. 118.

82. Vercoutter 1956, 289-95, pls. XXX-XXXIV.

83. Bietak this volume.

84. *PM* II, Part II, Frontispiece, pl. XIV; Niemeier 1988, 235-44; 1987, 65-98.

85. Sphinxes: e.g. Hood 1978, pls. 122 A, D. Mycenae: Hood 1978, pl. 65. Ayia Triada sarcophagus: Marinatos and Hirmer 1960, col. pl. XXX.

86. Doumas 1992, pl. 148.

87. Forthcoming. I am grateful to Nanno Marinatos for providing me with a copy of her article in advance of its publication.

88. Vandier 1964, Part IV, ch. VI, II, 'La Danse', 435-7, figs. 231, 232 (MK) 446-54, figs. 239-44 (NK); Decker, 1992, Ch. 7, 'Acrobatics', 136-46. MK predecessors to the NK 'bridge' are seen at Beni Hasan in the tombs of Baqt, no. 15, and Khety, no. 17 (Newberry and Griffith Vol. II, pl. IV and pl. XIII).

89. Marinatos and Hirmer pl. 69; Pelon 1985, 35-40.

90. Kenna 1960, pl. 23, No. 204 = *PM* IV, 502, fig. 443. Both this and the Mycenae seal referred to below are illustrated by Bietak 1994, 50, fig. 17 (also this volume, fig. 4) and by Hood 1978, 228, pls. 231-2.

91. *CMS* I, 131 = *PM* IV, 502, fig. 444. Cf. *CMS* Suppl. I, 169, 3-sided prism with an acrobat with (papyrus-type) plant on one face, bird and bull's heads on the others.

92. Marinatos 1984; Morgan 1988, 24-8.

93. *CMS* XI, 52 = Marinatos 1986, 13, fig. 1.

94. *CMS* V, 608 = Marinatos 1986, 23, fig. 12.

95. Marinatos and Hirmer pls. 98 and 175.

96. Kantor 1947, 46-7; Vercoutter 1956, 317-21, 357-9, pls. XI-XLII, Pl. LXI; Wachsmann 1987, pls. XIII, XXVII (B), XXIX, XXXIV-XXVI, XLI, LIV-LVI, LVIII, pp. 56-7, 60-1, 73.

97. On Aegean bull-sports see: Reichel 1909, 85-99; A J Evans 1921, 247-59; *PM* III, 203f; Sakellariou 1958, 85-9; J D Evans 1963, 138-43; Ward 1968, 117-22; Younger 1976, 125-37; Marinatos 1989, 1994.

98. Koumasa: Branigan 1970, pl. 11a. Porti: Marinatos and Hirmer pl. 14 (below).

99. Ayia Triada: Levi 1925-26, 120-1, figs. 124-6, nos. 108-10. Knossos Temple Repositories: *PM* I, 694, fig. 514; III, 218, fig. 149; IV, 506, fig. 451.

100. Marinatos and Hirmer pls. 106-7.

101. C Doumas (ed.) 1978, frontispiece, colour plates, pl. K (lower photograph, upper right of centre); Morgan 1988, 56; Televantou 1990, 309-24 (318-9), fig. 10 (sketch).

102. Mycenae: Rodenwaldt 1911, 221-50, pl. 9,1; Lamb 1919-20, pl. VII. 4-6. Pylos: Lang 1969, 36 H 105, pls. 24, 116, 124, C. Tiryns: Rodenwaldt 1912, pl. XVIII. Also possibly Orchomenos: Bulle 1907, pl. XXVIII, 8, but fragment now thought to be swimmers rather than bull-leapers.

103. Kantor 1947, 84, pl. XX, 2D.

104. Vandier 1969, Vol. V, 58-62, 219-20.

105. Vandier, 1969, Vol. V, figs. 43, 52, 79, 88, 98.

106. Newberry and Griffith, Vol. II, pl. XXXI.

107. Demakopoulou and Konsola 1981, 42.

108. Collon 1994, 81-8.

109. Bietak 1994, 56.

110. Brooks and Wakankar 1976, 70.

111. *PM* III, 167-77, figs. 109B, 113, 115-20; *PM* IV, 13-7, fig. 8; Kaiser 1976, 271f, figs. 418-24, pl. 35; Marinatos and Hirmer col. pl. XIV; Immerwahr 1990, 85-8, 174, pls. 36-7.

112. *PM* II, 674-8, figs. 428-9; IV, 893-5, fig. 873.

113. *PM* IV, 893, fig. 872.

114. Royal Road: Cameron 1975, 728, pl. 78B (LM IB deposit). House of the Sacrificed Oxen: *PM* II, 310 (MM IIIB).

115. *PM* II, 620, fig. 389; Cameron and Hood 1967, pl. VIII, fig. 2 (LM II/III).

116. *PM* I, 337, n.1; *PM* III, 294, 339, fig. 225, 343, n.1; *PM* IV, 892 (Hall of the Double Axes: bull's foot and plants); *PM* III, 207-9, figs. 141-3, and p. 403 (Ivory Deposit: miniature bull's head, double axe. Area of Queen's Megaron: miniature bull-leapers).

117. *PM* III, 495-518; Kaiser 1976, 278-82. Bull fragments: Kaiser figs. 430-5, 437.

118. *PM* I, 529, fig. 385; Cameron and Hood 1967, pl. VII, fig. 1; Immerwahr 1990, 64, 173-4.

119. Evans, *PM* I, 527-8; P Warren, *BSA* 62 (1967) 197-8; Hallager 1977, 25-6; Cameron 1975, 428-9, 686-7.

120. See Morgan 1988, 56, with notes 138-9.

121. A bull-leaper from Knossos, now housed in the Ashmolean Museum, has straps on the hands - evidently to protect them - providing a reason for this conventional gesture even where the straps are not depicted (*PM* III, 216-7, fig. 148). I am grateful to Nanno Marinatos for drawing my attention to this.

122. Cameron 1975, slide 52. Slides 46-52 show reconstructions of the panels, notes to the panels indicating that there were probably seven in all.

123. Cf. the Ayia Triada Sports Rhyton (Marinatos and Hirmer pls. 106-7) and the Thera Boxing Boys (Doumas 1992, pls. 79, 81).

124. Immerwahr 1990, col. pl. XVI.

125. Bietak 1994, 46.

126. Katsamba ivory box: Hood 1978, 122, pl. 111. Vapheio cups: Marinatos and Hirmer pls. 178, 180.

127. In particular: Damiani-Indelicato 1988, who suggests that only one of the three figures in the Knossos scenes is an actual acrobat, the others being symbolic of the notion of time (the three stages in the jump) with white used "to convey a mental picture" (p.43); and Marinatos 1989, 28-32; 1994.

128. *PM* I, 531, fig. 387; III, 508-9, figs. 354, A, B.

129. On the colour of the 'Priest-King' see Cameron 1970 (female?). Camp Stool Fresco: *PM* IV, pl. XXXI; N Platon, *KrChron* 1959, 319-45, col. pl. (opp. p. 336); M A S Cameron, *KrChron* 1964, 38-53.

130. Parrot 1958. Fragments from debris of Court 106: fig. 31 (pp. 38-9), nos. 36, 37/39, 38, 39, 40, 42); fig. 37 (pp. 44-6), nos. 57, 58, 60, 63. The fragments lack context so it is not possible to determine any significance in the differentiation. But compare fig. 36, no. 36, with fig. 24, no. 11, where the profile is almost identical and both have moustache and beard, but one is white and the other red-skinned. Possible example from Audience Hall 132: small-scale fisherman, pp. 81-2, pl. XVII (lower left), XIX and col. pl. E, but cf. p. 82, no. 2.

131. Wilkinson 1994, 114-5 and 125, 121-3. A full study of the question of skin colour in Egyptian tomb paintings would,

I suspect, reveal more instances. A number of early publications of Middle Kingdom tombs with black and white drawings distinguish dark and light coloured men (who are not overlapping) without textual comment.

132. E.g. Beni Hasan: Newberry and Griffith Vol. II, pls. V and VIII (tomb 15), pl. XV (tomb 17). pl. XXXII (tomb 29); Vol. I, pls. XIV-XVI (tomb 2). Cf. the Boxers wall-painting from Thera, where the face (though not the body) of the boy on the left is slightly paler (Doumas 1992, pl. 81).

133. Doumas 1992, pl. 112. Pointed out by Bietak, this volume, 23.

134. See Davies 1986; Doumas 1992, 23-5 (West House), 80 (Boxing Boys), 109, 112-3, 115, 1221 (Xeste 3).

135. Exs: Pritchard 1969, pls. 5, 7, 8 (Libyan men); pls. 33, 51 (Hittite men); 45-7, 49 (Syrian children); 326 (Shasu-Bedouin men).

136. Janssen 1990, 37-41; *Lexikon,* Vol. 3, 274, 'Jugendlocke'. Egyptian statuettes of children were sometimes provided with a hole in the crown or side of the head for the insertion of real or imitation hair (Hayes 1990, 220-1; Lloyd 1965, pl. 124).

137. Blue may occasionally be used for the (shaved?) heads of southerners (e.g. tomb of Rekhmire, Davies 1935, pl. VI, left, pl. VII, right, pl. XVII, left). Blue was also used for the beards and hair of divinities (Wilkinson 1994, 111).

138. *PM* III, 428ff., figs. 296-300; Marinatos and Hirmer pls. 96-7 and p. 146. (Locks of twisted gold-plated bronze wire were inserted into the holes, see *PM* III, 432). Similarly, large bronze locks of hair found near the conjectured East Hall at Knossos were thought by Evans to have belonged to a massive wooden statue, see *PM* III, 522-3, figs. 365-6). Cf. clay figurine from Juktas, *Praktika* 1974, pl. 177.

139. Cameron 1975, col. pls. 49, 52.

140. *CMS* II.4, 157 (Gournes); *CMS* VII, 108; *CMS* X, 141; Kenna 1960, No. 341, pl. 13.

141. Morgan forthcoming (*CMS* Beiheft).

142. Col. pl: Marinatos and Hirmer pl. XXVIII.

143. *CMS* XI, 259. Cf. Knossos, *CMS* II.3, 8, priestess carries robe (skirt) and holds double axe; Sitea, *CMS* II.3, 310, two mirror image bulls in frontal face, a double axe between them; *CMS* XI, 330, unknown provenance, frontal lion's mask on female figure associated with sacrificed animal and two figure of eight shields.

144. Bietak 1994, 51 and pl. 18B.

145. Evans, *PM* III, 283.

146. Ventris and Chadwick 1973, 310 (205 = Gg 702), 538. I am grateful to Peter Warren for reminding me of this.

147. Charbonneaux et. al. 1972, fig. 308.

148. Morgan 1989, 151-2, figs. 8-11.

149. Levi 1976, pl. LXXXVb; Immerwahr 1990, 22 and fig. 6d.

150. Evans, *PM* I, 356f, fig. 256. No associated pottery is described and an MM III attribution is on stylistic grounds (Cameron, 1975, 709, who agrees with the attribution).

151. Shaw 1970, 25-30.

152. Evans, *PM* I, 358-9, fig. 257. Cf. Gardiner 1957, 492-4, sign list O, nos. 4, 5, 11, 13, 15.

153. The iconography would not be identical as no two paintings in Aegean art are ever exactly the same. But all features of these paintings would be at home in the Aegean.

154. Bietak 1992, 28; 1994, 58; this volume, 26; Hankey 1993, 13-4.

Abbreviations

CMS - Corpus der minoischen und mykenischen Siegel. General eds. F Matz, H Biesantz and I Pini. Berlin, Gebr. Mann Verlag, 1964- .

Lexikon - Lexikon der Ägyptologie. General eds. W Helck and E Otto. Wiesbaden, Otto Harrassowitz, 1972-1990.

PM - Evans, A J 1921, 1928, 1930, 1935. *The Palace of Minos at Knossos* I-IV. London, Macmillan.

References

Abramovitz, K 1980. Frescoes from Ayia Irini, Keos, Parts II-IV. *Hesperia* 49, 57-85.
Baum, N 1988. *Arbres et Arbustes de l'Egypte Ancienne, La liste de la tombe thébaine d'Ineni (no. 81).* Leuven, Peeters.
Bietak, M 1992. Minoan Wall-Paintings Unearthed at Ancient Avaris. *Egyptian Archaeology* 2, 26-8.
Bietak, M 1994. Die Wandmalereien aus Tell el-Dab'a/ 'Ezbet Helmi, Erste Eindrucke. *Ägypten und Levante* 4, 44-81.
Bissing, F W von 1900. *Ein thebanischer Grabfund aus dem Anfang des neuen Reiches.* Berlin.
Bloedow, E 1992. On lions in Mycenaean and Minoan Culture. In R Laffineur and J L Crowley (eds.), *Aegean Bronze Age Iconography: Shaping a Methodology.* Proceedings of the 4th International Aegean Conference, University of Tasmania, Hobart, Australia, 6-9 April 1992. Liège, University of Liège.
Branigan, K 1970. *The Foundations of Palatial Crete, A Study of Crete in the Early Bronze Age.* London, Routledge and Kegan Paul.
Brooks, R R and Wakankar, V S 1976. *Stone Age Paint-*

ing in India. New Haven and London, Yale University Press.

Bulle, H 1907. *Orchomenos* I. Munich, Verlag der KB Akad. der Wissenschaft.

Cameron, M A S 1967. Notes on Some New Joins and Additions to Well-Known Frescoes from Knossos. In W Brice (ed.), *Europa, Studien zur Geschichte und Epigraphik der frühen Aegaeis. Festschrift für Ernst Grumach.* Berlin, 45-74.

Cameron, M A S 1968. Unpublished Paintings from the 'House of the Frescoes' at Knossos. *BSA* 63, 1-31.

Cameron, M A S 1968. A Graffito Related to a Myrtle Composition on a Minoan Fresco from Knossos. *Kadmos* VII, 97-9.

Cameron, M A S 1970. New Restorations of Minoan Frescoes from Knossos. *Bulletin of the Institute of Classical Studies* 17, 163-6.

Cameron, M A S 1978. Theran, Cretan and Mainland Frescoes. In C Doumas (ed.), *Thera and the Aegean World* I. London, The Thera Foundation, 579-92.

Cameron, M A S 1975. *A General Study of Minoan Frescoes with particular reference to wall paintings from Knossos*, 4 vols. Doctoral thesis housed at the British School at Athens, to be published by BSA edited by L Morgan.

Cameron, M A S and Hood, S 1967. *Catalogue of Plates in Sir Arthur Evans' Knossos Fresco Atlas.* London, Gregg Press.

Charbonneaux, J, Martin, R, Villard, F 1972. *Classical Greek Art.* London, Thames and Hudson.

Cline, E 1987. Amenhotep III and the Aegean: A Reassessment of Egypto-Aegean Relations in the 14th Century B.C. *Orientalia* 56, 1-36.

Collon, D 1994. Bull-Leaping in Syria. *Ägypten und Levante* 4, 81-8.

Damiani-Indelicato, S 1988. Were Cretan girls playing at bull-leaping? *Cretan Studies* 1, 39-47.

Darcque, P and Poursat, J-C (eds.) 1985. *L'iconographie minoenne.* Actes de la table ronde d'Athènes, (21-22 avril 1983). Paris, École Française d'Athènes.

Daressy, G 1906. Un Poignard du Temps des Rois Pasteurs. *Annales du service des antiquitées de l'Égypte* vii, 115-20.

Davies, E 1986. Youth and Age in the Thera Frescoes. *AJA* 90, 399-406.

Davies, Nina de Garis 1936. *Ancient Egyptian Paintings.* Chicago, University of Chicago Press.

Davies, N de Garis 1900. *The Mastaba of Ptahhetep and Akhethetep at Saqqareh*, Part I. London, Egypt Exploration Fund.

Davies, N de Garis 1922-3. *The Tomb of Puyemrê at Thebes,* Vol. I. New York, Metropolitan Museum of Art Egypt Expedition, Rob de Peyster Tytus Memorial Series, Vols. II-III.

Davies, N de Garis, 1930. *The Tomb of Ken-Amun at Thebes.* New York, Metropolitan Museum of Art Egyptian Expedition, Vol. V.

Davies, N de Garis 1935. *Paintings from the Tomb of Rekh-mi-re at Thebes.* New York, Metropolitan Museum of Art Egyptian Expedition, Vol. X.

Davies, N de Garis 1943. *The Tomb of Rekh-mi-re at Thebes*, Vol. I. New York, Metropolitan Museum of Art Egyptian Expedition, Vol. XI, reprint 1973.

Decker, W 1992. *Sports and Games of Ancient Egypt.* New Haven and London, Yale University Press.

Demakopoulou, K and Konsola, D 1981. *Archaeological Museum of Thebes.* Athens, General Direction of Antiquities and Restoration.

Doumas, C (ed.) 1978. *Thera and the Aegean World* I. Papers Presented at the Second International Scientific Congress, Santorini, Greece, August 1978. London, The Thera Foundation.

Doumas, C 1992. *The Wall Paintings of Thera.* Athens, The Thera Foundation.

Dziobek, E 1992. *Das Grab des Ineni Theben Nr. 81.* Mainz am Rhein, Philipp von Zabern.

Edgerton, W F 1936. Two Notes on the Flying Gallop. *Journal of the American Oriental Society* 56, 176-88.

Evans, A J 1921. On a Minoan bronze group of a galloping bull and acrobatic figure from Crete. *JHS* 41, 247-59

Evans, J D 1963. Cretan cattle-cults and sports. In A E Mourant and F E Zeuner (eds.), *Man and Cattle, Proceedings of a Symposium on Domestication.* London, Royal Anthropological Institute, Occasional Paper no. 18, 138-43.

Flagge, I 1975. *Untersuchungen zur Bedeutung des Greifen.* Sankt Augustin, Verlag Hans Richarz.

Frankfort, H 1929. *The Mural Painting of El-'Amarneh.* F. G. Newton Memorial Volume. London, Egypt Exploration Society.

Frankfort, H 1936. Notes on the Cretan griffin. *BSA* 37, 106-22.

Frankfort, H 1970. *The Art and Architecture of the Ancient Orient.* Harmondsworth, Penguin Books, 4th ed.

Furumark, A (ed.) 1950. The settlement at Ialysos and Aegean history c. 1550-1400 B.C. *Opuscula Archaeologica* VI, 150-271.

Gardiner, A H 1957. *Egyptian Grammar* (3rd ed.). Oxford, Griffith Institute.

Hallager, E 1977. *The Mycenaean Palace at Knossos: Evidence for Final Destruction in the IIIB Period.* Stockholm, Medelhavsmuseet Memoir I.

Haltennorth, T and Diller, H 1980. *Mammals of Africa including Madagascar.* London, William Collins Sons & Co. Ltd.

Hankey, V 1981. The Aegean Interest in El-Amarna. *Journal of Mediterranean Anthropology and Archaeology* I, 38-49.

Hankey, V 1993. A Theban 'Battle Axe'. Queen Aahotpe and the Minoans. *Minerva* 4:3, May/June, 13-14.

Hardy, D A (ed.) 1990. *Thera and the Aegean World*

III. Proceedings of the Third International Congress, Santorini, Greece, 3-9 September 1989. Vols. 1-3. London, The Thera Foundation.

Hayes, W C 1990. *The Scepter of Egypt* I and II. New York, The Metropolitan Museum of Art/Harry N. Abrams Inc. (revised ed.).

Helck, W 1979. *Die Beziehungen Ägyptens und Vorderasiens zur Ägäis bis ins 7 Jahrhundert v. Chr.* Darmstadt, Wissenschaftliche Buchgesellschaft.

Hepper, N F 1990. *Pharaoh's Flowers.* London, Royal Botanic Gardens, Kew, HMSO.

Higgins, R A 1979. *The Aegina Treasure.* London, British Museum Publications.

Hood, S 1978. *The Arts in Prehistoric Greece.* Harmondsworth, Penguin Books.

Immerwahr, S A 1985. A Possible Influence of Egyptian Art in the Creation of Minoan Wall Painting. In P Darque and J-C Poursat (eds.), *L'iconographie minoenne.* Actes de la table ronde d'Athènes (21-22 avril 1983). Paris, École Française d'Athènes, 41-50.

Immerwahr, S A 1990. *Aegean Painting in the Bronze Age.* Pennsylvania and London, Pennsylvania State University Press.

Janssen, R M and J J 1989. *Egyptian Household Animals.* Aylesbury, Shire Egyptology.

Janssen, R M and J J 1990. *Growing up in Ancient Egypt.* London, The Rubicon Press.

Jánosi, P 1994. The Queens Ahhotep I & II and Egypt's Foreign Relations. *Journal of the Ancient Chronology Forum* 5, 99-105.

Jánosi, P 1994. Tell el-Dab'a - 'Ezbet Helmi. Vorbericht über den Grabungsplatz H/I (1989-1992). *Ägypten und Levante* 4, 20-38.

Kaiser, B 1976. *Untersuchungen zum minoischen Relief.* Bonn, Rudolf Habelt Verlag GMBH.

Kantor, H 1947. The Aegean and the Orient in the Second Millennium B.C. *AJA* 51, 1-108.

Kemp, B J and Merrillees, R S 1980. *Minoan Pottery in Second Millennium Egypt.* Mainz am Rhein, Philipp von Zabern.

Kempinski, A and Niemeier, W-D 1988. *Excavations at Kabri. Preliminary Report of 1987 Season* 4. Tel Aviv, Tel Aviv University.

Kempinski, A and Niemeier, W-D 1991. *Excavations at Kabri. Preliminary Report of 1990 Season* 5. Tel Aviv, Tel Aviv University.

Kempinski, A and Niemeier, W-D 1993. Kabri, 1993. *Israel Exploration Journal* 43, No. 4, 256-9.

Kenna, V E 1960. *Cretan Seals with a Catalogue of the Minoan Gems in the Ashmolean Museum.* Oxford, Clarendon Press.

Kühnert-Eggebrecht, E 1969. *Die Axt als Waffe und Werkzeug im alten Ägypten.* Berlin, Verlag Bruno Hessling.

Lamb, W 1919-20. Frescoes from the Ramp House. *BSA* 24, 189-99.

Lang, M L 1969. *The Palace of Nestor at Pylos in West-ern Messenia* II: *The Frescoes.* Princeton, University of Cincinnati/Princeton University Press.

Levi, D 1925-26. Le cretule di Haghia Triada e di Zakro. *Annuario* 8-9, 71-201.

Levi, D 1976. *Festos e la civilta minoica* I. Rome, Ediz. dell Atene Inamabula Graeca, Vol. LXXVII.

Lloyd, S 1965. *The Art of the Ancient Near East.* London, Thames and Hudson.

Long, C R 1974. *The Ayia Triada Sarcophagus. A Study of Late Minoan and Mycenaean Funerary Practices and Beliefs.* Studies in Mediterranean Archaeology XLI. Göteborg, Paul Åströms Förlag.

Lucas, A and Harris, J R 1962. *Ancient Egyptian Materials and Industries*, 4th ed. London, Edward Arnold.

Manniche, L 1989. *An Ancient Egyptian Herbal.* London, British Museum Press.

Marinatos, N 1984. The date-palm in Minoan iconography and religion. *Opuscula Atheniensia* 15, 115-22.

Marinatos, N 1986. *Minoan Sacrificial Ritual.* Stockholm, Paul Åströms Förlag.

Marinatos, N 1987. An Offering of Saffron to the Minoan Goddess of Nature: The Role of the Monkey and the Importance of Saffron. In T Linders and G Nordquist (eds.), *Gifts to the Gods.* Proceedings of Uppsala Symposium 1985 (Boreas 15). Uppsala, 123-32.

Marinatos, N 1989. The Bull as an Adversary: Some Observations on Bull-Hunting and Bull-Leaping. In *Aphieroma sto Styliano Alexiou. Ariadne* 5, 23-32.

Marinatos, N 1993. *Minoan Religion. Ritual, Image and Symbol.* South Carolina, University of South Carolina Press.

Marinatos, N 1994. The 'Export' Significance of Minoan Bull-Hunting and Bull-Leaping Scenes. *Ägypten und Levante* 4, 89-93.

Marinatos, N forthcoming. Acrobats in Minoan Art. *Ägypten und Levante* 5.

Marinatos, S 1968-76. *Excavations at Thera* I-VII. Athens, Bibliothiki tis en Athinais, Athens, Archaeologike Etaireias.

Marinatos, S and Hirmer, M 1960. *Crete and Mycenae.* London, Thames and Hudson.

Merrillees, R S 1972. Aegean Bronze Age Relations with Egypt. *AJA* 76, 281-94.

Morgan, L 1988. *The Miniature Wall Paintings from Thera. A Study in Aegean Culture and Iconography.* Cambridge, Cambridge University Press.

Morgan, L 1989. Ambiguity and Interpretation. In *Fragen und Probleme der Bronzezeitlichen Ägaischen Glyptik. CMS* Beiheft 3. Berlin, Gebr. Mann Verlag, 145-61.

Morgan, L 1990. Island Iconography: Thera, Kea, Milos. In D A Hardy (ed.), *Thera and the Aegean World* III. London, The Thera Foundation, 252-66.

Morgan, L forthcoming. Of Animals and Men: The Symbolic Parallel. In C Morris, (ed.), *Klados. Es-*

says in Honour of Professor J. N. Coldstream. London, Institute of Classical Studies Bulletin, Supplement 63.

Morgan, L forthcoming. Frontal Face and the Symbolism of Death in Aegean Glyptic. In *CMS* Beiheft 4.

Muybridge, E 1957. *Animals in Motion.* L S Brown (ed.). New York, Dover (originally *Animal Locomotion*, 1887).

Newberry, P E and Griffith, F L 1893-1900. *Beni Hasan* I-IV. London, Egypt Exploration Fund.

Niemeier, W-D 1987. Das Stuckrelief des 'Prinzen mit der Federkrone' aus Knossos und minoische Götter Darstellungen. *AM* 102, 65-98.

Niemeier, W-D 1988. 'The Priest King' Fresco from Knossos, A New Reconstruction and Interpretation. In E B French and K Wardle (eds.), *Problems in Greek Prehistory.* Bristol, Bristol Classical Press, 135-244.

Niemeier, W-D 1990. New Archaeological Evidence for a 17th Century Date of the 'Minoan Eruption' from Israel (Tel Kabri, Western Galilee). In D Hardy (ed.), *Thera and the Aegean World* III, Vol. 3. London, The Thera Foundation, 120-6.

Niemeier, W-D 1991. Minoan Artisans Travelling Overseas: The Alalakh Frescoes and the Painted Plaster Floor at Tel Kabri (Western Galilee). In R Laffineur and L Basch (eds.), *Thalassa. L'Égée Préhistorique et la Mer, Aegaeum* 7. Liège, 189-200.

Parrot, A 1958. *Mission Archéologique de Mari II. Le Palais. Peinture murales.* Bibliothèque archéologique et historique, Tome LXIX. Paris, Libraire Orientaliste Paul Geuthner, Institut Français d'Archéologie de Beyrouth.

Pelon, O 1985. L'acrobate de Malia et l'art de l'époque protopalatiale en Crète. In P Darcque and J-C Poursat (eds.), *L'iconographie minoenne.* Actes de la table ronde d'Athènes (21-22 avril 1983). Paris, École Française d'Athènes, 15-40.

Pini, I 1982. Ein Löwenjagd-Motiv. *AA*, 604-6.

Pini, I 1985. Das Motiv des Löwenüberfalls in der spätminoischen und mykenischen Glyptik. In P Darque and J-C Poursat (cds.), *L'iconographie minoenne.* Actes de la table ronde d'Athenes (21-22 Avril 1983). Paris, École Française d'Athènes, 153-66.

Poursat, J-C 1980. *Fouilles Exécutées à Mallia: Le Quartier Mu II. Études Cretoises* XXVI. Paris, École Française d'Athènes.

Pritchard, J B 1969. *The Ancient Near East in Pictures Relating to the Old Testament.* Princeton, Princeton University Press.

Reichel, A 1909. Stierspiele in der kretisch-mykenischen Kultur. *AM* 34, 85-99.

Rodenwaldt, G 1911. Fragmente mykenischer Wandgemälde. *Ath Mitt* 36, 221-50.

Rodenwaldt, G 1912. *Tiryns* II: *Die Fresken des Palastes.* Athens, Deutsches Archäologisches Institut, Eleutheroudakis and Barth. (Reprinted:

Mainz am Rhein, Philipp von Zabern, 1976.)

Sakellarakis, J A 1978. *Herakleion Museum.* Athens, Ekdotike Athenon, S. A.

Sakellarakis, E and Sakellarakis, Y 1984. The Keftiu and the Minoan Thalassocracy. In R Hägg and N Marinatos (eds.), *The Minoan Thalassocracy. Myth and Reality.* Stockholm, Proceedings of the Third International Symposium at the Swedish Institute in Athens, 31 May - 5 June 1982, 197-203.

Schachermeyer, F 1967. *Ägäis und Orient.* Vienna, Österreichische Akademie der Wissenschaften.

Shaw, M 1967. *An Evaluation of Possible Affinities between Egyptian and Minoan Wall Paintings before the New Kingdom.* Doctoral dissertation, Bryn Mawr.

Shaw, M 1970. Ceiling Patterns from the Tomb of Hepsefa. *AJA* 74, 25-30.

Shaw, M 1972. The Miniature Frescoes of Tylissos Reconsidered. *AA* 87, 171-88.

Stevenson Smith, W 1965. *Interconnections in the Ancient Near East.* New Haven and London, Yale University Press.

Stevenson Smith, W 1965. *The Art and Architecture of Ancient Egypt.* Harmondsworth-Baltimore-Victoria/ 2nd ed. (revised W K Simpson). London, Penguin Books, 1981.

Strange, J 1980. *Caphtor/Keftiu: A New Investigation.* Leiden, E J Brill.

Televandou, C 1990. New Light on the West House Wall-Paintings. In D Hardy (ed.), *Thera and the Aegean World* III, Vol. I. London, The Thera Foundation, 309-24.

Vandier, J 1964/69. *Manuel d'Archéologie Égyptienne,* Vols. IV and V, *Bas reliefs et peintures, scènes de la vie quotidienne.* Paris, Éditions A et J Picard.

Vedel, H 1978. *Trees and Shrubs of the Mediterranean.* Harmondsworth, Penguin Books.

Ventris, M and Chadwick, J 1973. *Documents in Mycenaean Greek.* Cambridge, Cambridge University Press (2nd ed.).

Vercoutter, J 1956. *L'Égypte et le monde égéen préhellénique.* Bibliothèque d'Étude, XXII. Cairo, Inst. Fran. d'Archéol. Orientale.

Wachsmann, S 1987. *Aegeans in the Theban Tombs.* Leuven, Peeters.

Walberg, G 1991. A Gold Pendant from Tell el-Dab'a. *Ägypten und Levante* 2, 111-4.

Ward, A 1968. The Cretan bull sports. *Antiquity* 42, 117-22.

Warren, P 1990. Summary of the Evidence for the Absolute Chronology of the Early Part of the Aegean Late Bronze Age. In D Hardy (ed.), *Thera and the Aegean World* III, Vol. 3. London, The Thera Foundation, 24-6.

Warren, P and Hankey, V 1989. *Aegean Bronze Age Chronology.* Bristol, Bristol Classical Press.

Watrous, L V 1992. *Kommos* III. *The Late Bronze Age Pottery.* Princeton, Princeton University Press.

Wilkinson, R W 1994. *Symbol and Magic in Egyptian Art*. London, Thames and Hudson.

Xenaki-Sakellariou, A 1958. *Les cachets minoens de la collection Giamalakis* (*Études Cretoise* 10). Paris, École Française d'Athènes.

Younger, J G 1976. Bronze Age Representations of Aegean Bull-Leaping. *AJA* 80, 125-37.

Yule, P 1980. *Early Cretan Seals: A Study of Chronology*. Marburger Studien zur Vor- und Frühgeschichte Band 4. Mainz am Rhein, Philipp von Zabern.

TELL EL-DAB'A
THE CYPRIOT CONNECTION[1]

Louise C Maguire

The excavations at Tell el-Dab'a (Bietak 1979; 1989; 1991; this volume, 19-28) have produced an exceptional amount of Cypriot pottery, in the range of 500 pieces (Maguire 1990; 1992). Prior to these excavations, very few pieces of Cypriot Middle Bronze Age pottery had been found in Egypt (Merrillees 1968, 145-6). Indeed, Tell el-Dab'a has produced the largest corpus of Cypriot Middle Bronze Age pottery found abroad. Ras Shamra and Akko have each produced in the region of 200 pieces (Maguire 1990).

The Cypriot pottery from Tell el-Dab'a is primarily of Middle Bronze (MB) II character from the main Tell areas AII (Bietak 1991, Abb. 2) to AV (Hein and Jánosi forthcoming) and the palace area FI (Bietak 1984; 1989; 1991). It comprises the popular Middle Cypriot styles: White Painted Pendent Line Style (WP PLS) (**Plate 5,1 and Fig. 1**), White Painted Cross Line Style (WP CLS) (**Plate 5,2**), White Painted V (WP V) (**Plate 5,3**), as well as White Painted Alternating Broad Band and Wavy Line Style (WP ABBWLS) and White Painted Composite Style (WP Comp), Red on Black (RoB) and Plain Ware (Plain) (**Plate 5,4**). Cypriot Bichrome Ware (BICH (Cyp) or (C)) is also present (**Figs. 2-3**), as well as imitations (IMIT) of WP PLS (**Figs. 9-10**).[2]

In addition to presenting some of this Dab'a material, it will also be possible to discuss some of the recently excavated Cypriot material of Late Bronze Age (LB) character from the site of 'Ezbet Helmi (Bietak this volume, 20; Jánosi 1994; Hein 1994). The Cypriot wares from 'Ezbet Helmi comprise Base Ring (BR) (**Plate 5,5**), White Slip (WS), White Painted VI, Red Lustrous Wheelmade Ware (RLWM) (**Plate 5,6**) and Red Slip Wheelmade Ware (RS), as well as Cypriot Bichrome and imitations of Cypriot wares (**Fig. 4**).

In introducing these two assemblages we touch upon the changes which take place in the Middle Bronze to Late Bronze transitional period. While this period presents difficulties in understanding the details of the political manoeuvres of the Hyksos, certain patterns in the production and circulation of jugs and juglets throughout the Levant may emphasise the intensity of the political and economic cohesion created by the Hyksos - who may eventually be shown to have been élite groups of people operating in Syria, Palestine and Egypt in the Middle Bronze Age period.[3] Likewise, in the aftermath of the 'expulsion' of the Hyksos or the breakdown of that political and economic cohesion, the Late Bronze Age pattern of exchange in jugs and juglets throughout the Levant, which is quite different from the Middle Bronze distributions, may provide some interesting information.

Cyprus itself at the end of the MBA (MCIII-LCI) is witness to possible social change attested in the archaeological record, particularly in the south-east of the island - new pottery types as well as imports, for example Bichrome Ware (and most probably at this time the introduction of the pottery wheel), weaponry, metal belts, 'fortifications', 'mass' burials and equid burials.[4] As yet it has not been possible to identify the impetus for social change which culminates in an intensity in international contact in the Late Bronze Age. In fact, in economic terms, the repercussions associated with the end of the Hyksos may be widespread and disruptive. In looking at the intensity of external contact prior to the demise of the Hyksos and immediately after it, the patterns emerging indicate radical change. This can be illustrated initially in the circulation of generically similar jugs and juglets produced in Cyprus, as well as in Syria, Palestine and Egypt.

For the purposes of this article, attention has been drawn to the Cypriot jugs and juglets from Tell el-Dab'a and 'Ezbet Helmi; the full repertoire of Cypriot pottery abroad is dealt with elsewhere (Maguire 1990).

Essentially, we will be looking at a diversified exchange network in small precious commodity containers in the Middle Bronze Age, comprising several facets, which undergoes radical transformation in the Late Bronze Age and is reduced to one facet, probably as a result of the demise of Middle Bronze Age production centres but certainly of a fall in demand.

Figures 5-8 indicate the proportional occurrence of the different types of Cypriot pottery found at Tell el-Dab'a. The distributions of these wares within Cyprus are primarily southern, where linear styles predominate as opposed to geometric in the north (Frankel 1974; Maguire 1992). The WP PLS and the WP CLS comprise only bottles, jugs and juglets in Cyprus and abroad, and carry, one would assume, a commodity which may or may not originate in Cyprus. Jugs and juglets comprise the largest groups of exported forms; bowls and jars are known in WP V, and jars in Plain Ware. Cypriot Bichrome (Åström 1972; Artzy and Asaro 1979; and Artzy, Asaro and Perlman 1973) occurs at Dab'a but alongside that are examples of Palestinian Bichrome (Amiran 1969) and even Egyptian Bichrome (Merrillees 1970; Maguire 1990), and these origins have been confirmed in a preliminary study using neutron-activation analysis (Maguire 1990). Most of the Cypriot material at both Tell el-Dab'a and 'Ezbet Helmi is sherdage.

Also at Tell el-Dab'a in MB contexts are imitations of WP PLS pots in Tell el-Yahudiyeh shape and fabric (**Figs. 9-10**). Parallels for these examples can be found at Tell el-Yahudiyeh and Tarkhan (Bagh 1988). **Figures 9 and 10** are very distinctive pieces but in both cases the potter is selective with regard to either the decoration or the shape and decoration. Imitations may have been produced in response to demand or the style may have been aesthetically pleasing - but the very fact that such imitation exists demonstrates the significance of the PLS style and the globular shape.

Early examples of a possible Cypriot influence are already observed in Stratum G, where the technique is used of inserting the handle through the vessel wall to leave a protrusion on the interior which could not be smoothed off, since the body of the vessel was already shaped (**Fig. 11**). This technique is popular throughout the Bronze Age of Cyprus, but it is also known outside Cyprus on Crete (Betancourt 1985, Fig. 26D).

The stratigraphic occurrence of WP PLS and WP CLS at Tell el-Dab'a shows a floruit in the E/1 levels (Maguire 1992, Fig. 2), and in some sense we are seeing a chronological distinction between Cypriot MBA wares, such as the classic PLS and CLS styles, and what would appear to be the later so-called WP V wares (Maguire 1992, 116-18). The late Hyksos settlement revealed in Area AV (Hein and Jánosi forthcoming) illustrates this succession (**Fig. 7**), but overall we are dealing with sherdage within a Tell site and sherds reflect a date of deposition or even redeposition and not an accurate date of period of use or period of manufacture within either the country of origin or export.

The 'Ezbet Helmi examples are in complete contrast to the MBA repertoire found on the main Tell area (**Fig. 4**). Jugs and juglets predominate but the wares themselves are very different. From the earliest levels of the 18th Dynasty occupation we have BR (**Plate 5,5**) and WS, which continue through to the reign of Tuthmosis III. All the material is sherdage and the processes of deposition and redeposition are difficult to reconstruct; in consequence, using BR found at 'Ezbet Helmi to date sequences in Cyprus should not be attempted. BR is now documented to have six regionally specific Cypriot groups (Vaughan 1991, 123). The numerical divisions (i.e. BR I, BR II) have been avoided for the moment, since, as with the WP sequence, the divisions place too much emphasis on chronological succession and the criteria originally used to define I and II are inadequate to establish a clear succession (Vaughan 1991, 119). RLWM is possibly a Cypro-Syrian product deriving from a close interaction between Cypriot and Syrian potters - probably already established in the Bronze Age. Eriksson (1991) has argued for a Cypriot origin for the ware but this has yet

to be conclusively proven. WP VI jugs are also present.

We can begin to understand the transition and the distribution of Cypriot pottery, if we look firstly at the Tell el-Dab'a material in the context of the distribution of Cypriot pottery abroad, and secondly, and more importantly, if we look at other small narrow-necked juglets which were in circulation at this time.

The emerging pattern is a coastal distribution, especially in Syria and Palestine, with sites as far west as Kommos and Zakro on Crete and as far east as Kültepe in Anatolia (Maguire 1990, Figs. 25-30). The characteristic wares - WP PLS, WP CLS, WP V, RoB - are present at over forty sites in Syria and Palestine, deposited in classic MB/Hyksos assemblages - alongside togglepins, knives, daggers, jugs, jars, pithoi and scarabs - a standardized tomb package (Maguire 1990, Appendix IV, Fig. 1). We know that primarily, though of course not exclusively, the Cypriot forms exported comprise jugs and juglets; the jugs are aesthetically pleasing - handmade and vibrantly decorated in contrast to the mainly wheelmade, burnished and polished monochrome repertoire of equivalent juglets in Syria, Palestine and the Delta.

A consistent element in the tomb assemblages especially are juglets, such as piriform juglets in the Palestinian and Dab'a record[5] and burnished juglets in the Syrian record,[6] as well as punctured and painted Tell el-Yahudiyeh ware of Egyptian and Palestinian origin (Bietak 1985; 1989; 1991).

They are *all* small, narrow-necked containers for holding a commodity which was precious, in that only a small amount of it was meant to be used at any one time - one might imagine an oil or perfume. Their position in many burials near the head or body of the deceased may indicate that they were important to the individual.[7] It is possible to summarize the circulation of all these jugs and juglets of Syrian, Palestinian and Egyptian origin in the following way.

In the Cypriot group (**Fig. 12, 1-6**) in the Middle Bronze Age, we see the export of Cypriot Middle Bronze Age forms, of distinctive styles. Within that group of styles there are remarkable interchanges between the Cypriot and Syrian group to produce what is effectively a hybrid (**Fig. 12, 6**). WP V 'Eyelet style' is produced in Cyprus, handmade as opposed to wheelmade, combining imitation of a wheelmade Syrian shape (**Fig. 12, 18**), using Syrian motifs, common on eyelet juglets from Alalakh, for example, and Cypriot motifs of the WP V south-eastern Broad Band styles. Even more unusual is the combination of the most distinctive Cypriot WP PLS and WP CLS style on ring vases (**Fig. 12, 3**). The Cypriot examples may be imitating the ring vases of monochrome finish, which have been found at Ugarit and Tell el-Dab'a (e.g. **Fig. 12, 14**). Within the Syrian, Palestinian and Egyptian groups, we see a generic form of jug and juglet (**Fig. 12, 14-20**) - small, narrow-necked - manufactured in different locales, whose distribution can remain ex-

Fig. 1.   White Painted Pendent Line Style (Scale 1:2).

Fig. 2.   Bichrome Ware (Cypriot) from Tell el-Dab'a (Scale 1:1).

Fig. 3.   Bichrome Ware (Cypriot) from Tell el-Dab'a (Scale 1:1).

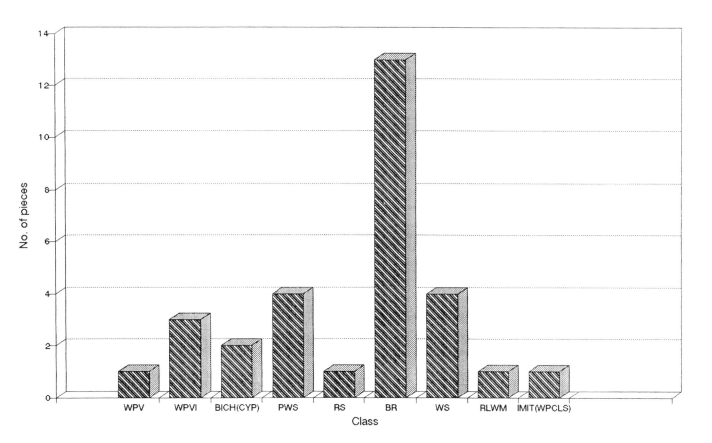

Fig. 4.   Proportional occurrence of Cypriot pottery.

Abbreviations   for   Figs   4-8

WP	White Painted Ware	Plain	Plain Ware
WP PLS	White Painted Pendent Line Style	PWS	Proto White Slip
		WS	White Slip
WP CLS	White Painted Cross Line Style	BR	Base Ring
WP ABBWLS	White Painted Alternating Broad Band and Wavy Line Style	IMIT	Imitation
		RLWM	Red Lustrous Wheelmade Ware
WP Comp	White Painted Composite		
BS	Black Slip	BICH (C) or (CYP)	Bichrome Ware (Cypriot)
RS	Red Slip	TYH	Tell el-Yahudiyeh Ware
RoB	Red on Black		

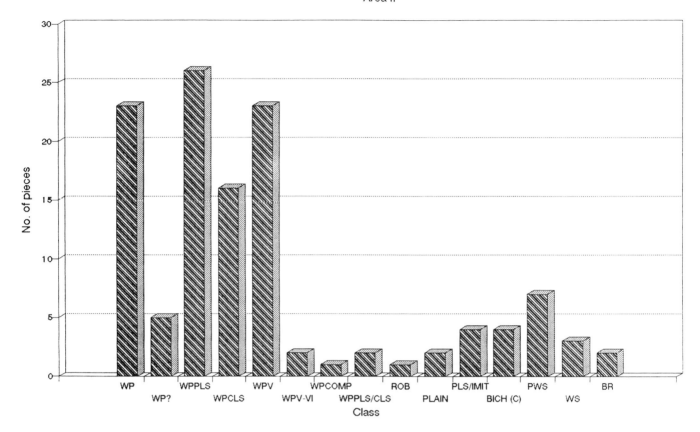

Fig. 5.   Proportional occurrence of Cypriot pottery.

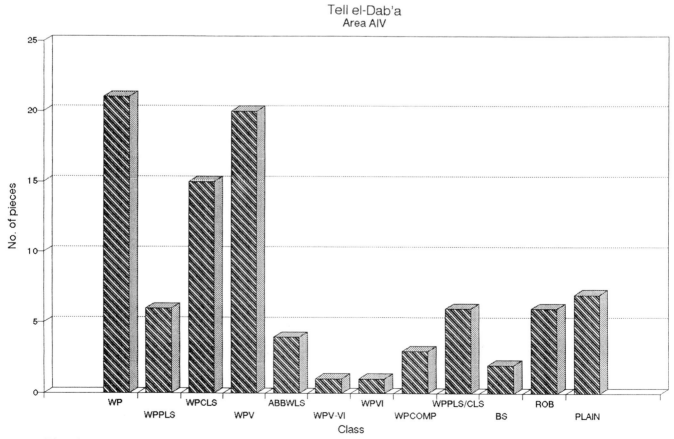

Fig. 6.   Proportional occurrence of Cypriot pottery.

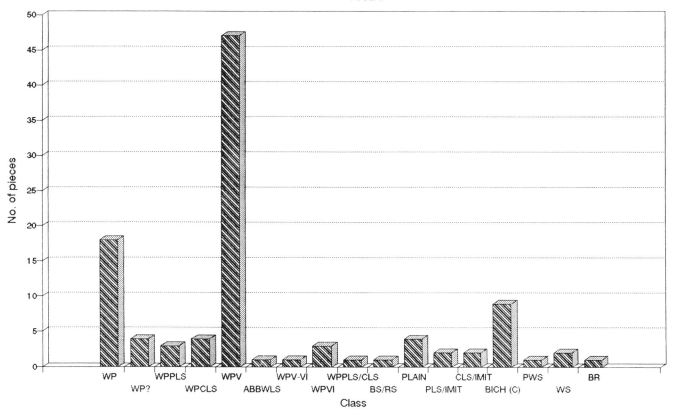

Fig. 7.   Proportional occurrence of Cypriot pottery.

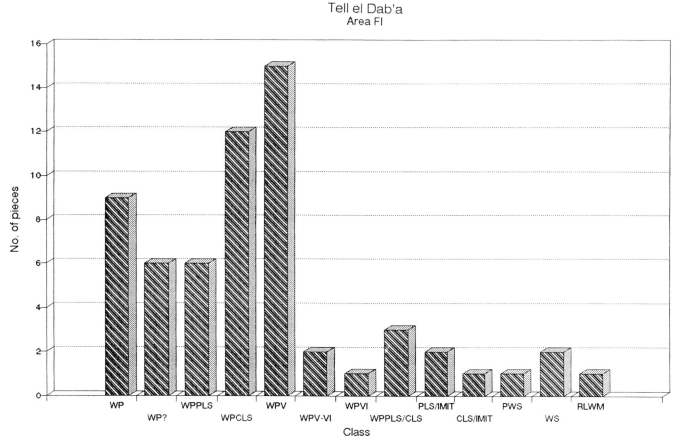

Fig. 8.   Proportional occurrence of Cypriot pottery.

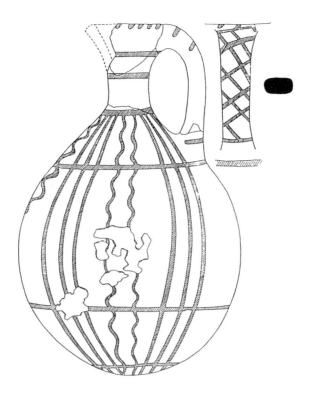

Fig. 9.   Imititation White Painted Pendent Line Style, Tell el-Dab'a (Scale 1:2).

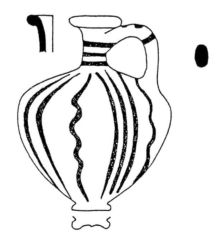

Fig. 10.   Imitation White Painted Pendent Line Style, Tell el-Dab'a (Scale 1:2).

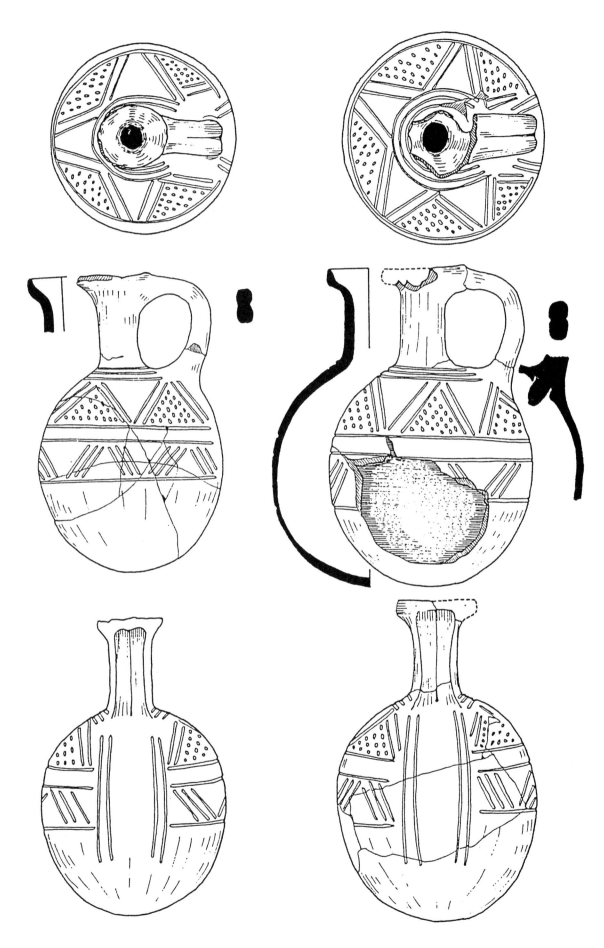

Fig. 11.   Globular handmade Tell el-Yahudiyeh Ware, Tell el-Dab'a (Scale 1:2).

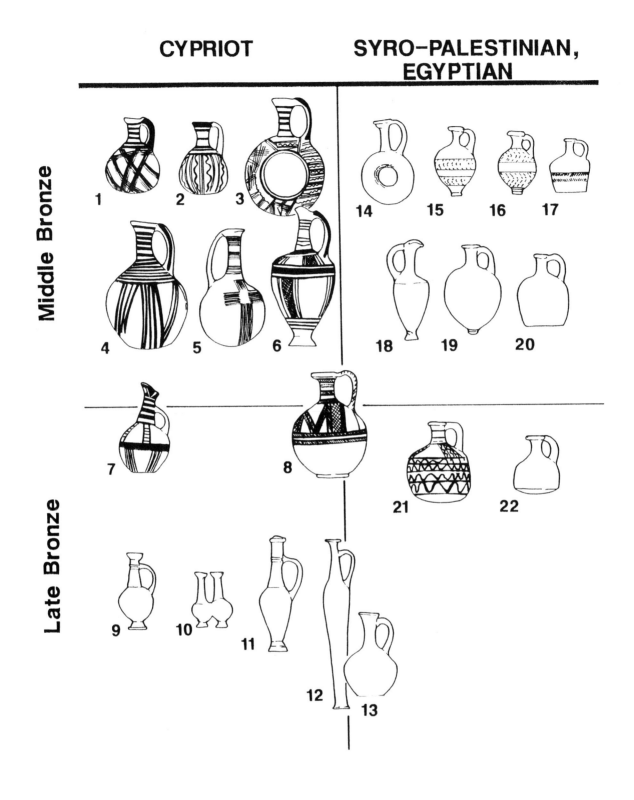

CYPRIOT

SYRO-PALESTINIAN, EGYPTIAN

Middle Bronze

Late Bronze

Fig. 12.   The relative occurrence of precious commodity containers of Cypriot,
Syrian and Egyptian origin in the Middle and Late Bronze Ages (Scale 1:2).

clusive to that locale or is exported beyond; for example, Red Burnished ware (**Fig. 12, 18**) is made in Syria and exported to Cyprus, but nowhere else. Tell el-Yahudiyeh ware (TYH) (**Fig. 12, 15-16**) is manufactured both in Palestine and Egypt - the Egyptian is exported to Cyprus and Syria but rarely to Palestine; the Palestinian TYH is peculiar to Palestine. The piriform (**Fig. 12, 19**) and cylindrical juglets (**Fig. 12, 20**) of Palestine are found all over Palestine and at Tell el-Dab'a.

Jugs and juglets are in circulation all over the Levant - juglets with overlapping as well as exclusive distribution. The Cypriot pottery cuts across all geographical and possible cultural barriers and is circulated throughout the Mediterranean.

The picture in the Late Bronze Age is drastically different. The narrow-necked juglets of the preceding Middle Bronze Age largely disappear - a few examples persist (**Fig. 12, 21-22**). Bichrome ware (**Fig. 12, 8**) of Cypriot, Palestinian and Egyptian origin appears at the transitional period and is a ware in which several pottery styles from different areas are brought together, manufactured and distributed throughout the Levant. The expanded Cypriot component, however, monopolizes the circulation with the introduction of BR jugs and juglets (**Fig. 12, 9-11**) and to a certain extent RLWM (**Fig. 12, 12-13**). The circulation of BR is far more extensive than the MBA Cypriot wares and emphasizes the exclusivity of Cypriot wares in contrast to the demise of the mainland production in other small narrow-necked juglets.

The questions yet to be answered include the reasons for the transformation within the production of Cypriot wares; within Cyprus, we have difficulty explaining the preference for monochrome wares. Had the demand changed in MBA Syria and Palestine and was Cyprus attempting to fill an empty market, if the production centres of the MBA especially Dab'a and Jericho had ceased to function? Had the disruptions in the Delta and Palestine affected the exchange network? Did Syria and Cyprus avoid or escape any disruption and adapt to fill the market demand? Was a particular commodity no longer in circulation? If the cargoes were circulated through a specific intermediary who could no longer operate, alternative routes of transport as well as new markets may have been found.

The Cypriot connection at Tell el-Dab'a is an impressive component of the complex circulation network of precious commodity containers in the Middle and Late Bronze Age. The patterns of distribution and circulation of Cypriot pottery in the context of the circulation of other small precious commodity containers illustrate that prior to the demise of the Hyksos phenomenon an impressive number of jugs and juglets were manufactured and distributed throughout the Levant. At the beginning of the Late Bronze Age the disappearance of the Palestirian and Tell el-Dab'a TYH and Red Polished repertoires, to be replaced in effect by a Cypriot

repertoire of BR, is an important observation, which highlights the ease of production and distribution of precious commodity containers in the Hyksos period, as well as the vulnerability of an exchange network, if a major component in that network is removed.

Acknowledgments

I would like to express my thanks to Vivian Davies for inviting me to speak at the colloquium; to Prof. Manfred Bietak for allowing me to study and publish the material from Tell el-Dab'a and 'Ezbet Helmi; to Prof. E Peltenburg for his continuing support and to Gordon Thomas for producing Figure 12.

Notes

1. This research is at present being funded by the Austrian Academy of Sciences, under the direction of Prof. Manfred Bietak, and is based at the Department of Archaeology, University of Edinburgh.

2. The properties of these wares, their geographical and chronological distribution both within and beyond Cyprus are discussed in detail in Åström 1972; Johnson 1982; Maguire 1990; 1992. A re-evaluation of the classification of these wares has been undertaken (Merrillees 1978; Frankel 1991; Maguire 1990; 1991): the numerical divisions of the White Painted sequence have been tailored in the case of unique styles to avoid chronological inferences being made from their succession.

3. An interesting point was brought up in discussion at the colloquium with Dr Stephen Quirke, who has provided the following references. In pre-New Kingdom Egyptian sources, the term *heqa-khasut* suggests in the majority of cases (the exception being the title of the man in the Beni Hasan scene of Asiatics, Newberry 1893, pls. xxxviii and xxx) that the Hyksos were referred to as either 'rulers of *foreign lands*' or a 'ruler of *foreign lands*'; at Beni Hasan we have 'ruler of a *foreign land*' (my italics). This is an observation which may be significant to our understanding of the Hyksos. Archaeologically, we are restricted to identifying the origin of the Hyksos through their material culture, which does not necessarily reflect the political or economic control obtained or exercised by them over a wider geographical or cultural area. Equally, the fact that 'rulers' is in the plural reminds us that we are not necessarily dealing with an individual person but rather a group of people, possibly élite, and potentially a 'warrior aristocracy' (Philip, this volume, 74, 77 and 81).

4. The nature of this material is discussed in Masson 1976, Knapp 1979, Baurain 1984, and more recently Philip 1991.

5. **Palestine**, e.g. Tufnell 1958, pl. 77, 727-9, 750, TYH; 732-49, RP piriform; 751-71, RP cylindrical. Kenyon 1965, Fig. 214, 6-10, TYH; Fig. 214, 1-5, 11, 12, RP piriform; Fig. 214, 13-16, RP cylindrical. **Egypt**, e.g. Bietak 1991b, Abb. 140, 3-12, TYH; Abb. 140, 13-20, BP (Black Polished)/RP (RP type 'piriform'); Abb. 145, 3-6, TYH; Abb. 145, 7, BP/RP.

6. **Syria**, e.g. *Syria* 17, Fig. 16, D-F, J-N, Red Burnished (RB) carinated; Fig. 18, D, TYH; L-O, RB carinated. *Syria*

19, Fig. 26,C, RB cylindrical; Fig. 26, K-M, RB carinated. *Ugaritica* VII, Fig. 1, 2, TYH; Fig. 1, 3-7, RB carinated; Fig. 1, 4 RB cylindrical.

7. E.g.: **Tell el-Dab'a**, Bietak 1991b, Abb. 139-45; **Tell el 'Ajjul**, Petrie 1931, pl. x, top left, Tb 406; **Tell Fara**, Petrie 1930, pl. xvii, e.g. 740[5] left chamber.

References

Amiran, R 1969. *Ancient Pottery of the Holy Land.* Israel, Massada Press.

Artzy, M and Asaro, F 1979. Origin of Tell el-Yahudiyeh Ware Found in Cyprus. *Report of the Department of Antiquities, Cyprus,* 135-50.

Artzy, M, Asaro, F and Perlman, I 1973. The Origin of the 'Palestinian' Bichrome Ware. *JAOS* 93, 446-61.

Åström, P 1972. The Middle Cypriote Bronze Age. *Swedish Cyprus Expedition,* IV, Part 1, B. Lund, Swedish Cyprus Expedition..

Bagh, T 1988. *Bemalet MBIIA keramik & Bemalet Tell el-Yahudiyeh ware fundet i Aeygpten.* Unpublished dissertation, Københavns Universitet.

Baurain, C 1984. *Chypre et la Méditerranée Orientale au Bronze Récent Synthèse Historique.* Études Chypriotes VI. Athens, École Française d'Athènes.

Betancourt, P P 1985. *The History of Minoan Pottery.* New Jersey, Princeton University Press.

Bietak, M 1979. Avaris and Piramesse, Archaeological Exploration in the Eastern Nile Delta. *Proceedings of the British Academy* 65, 225-90. London.

Bietak, M 1984. Eine Palastanlage aus der Zeit des späten Mittleren Reiches und andere Forschungsergebnisse aus dem östlichen Nildelta (Tell el-Dab'a 1979-1984). *Anzeiger der Philosophisch-historischen Klasse der Österreichischen Akademie der Wissenschaften* 121, 313-49.

Bietak, M 1985. Tell el-Jahudija-Keramik. *Lexikon der Ägyptologie,* VI, 335-47.

Bietak, M 1989. The Middle Bronze Age of the Levant - A New Approach to Relative and Absolute Chronology. In P Åström (ed.), *High, Middle or Low? Acts of an International Colloquium on Absolute Chronology held at the University of Gothenburg 20th-22nd August 1987,* Part 3. Gothenburg, Paul Åströms Förlag, 78-120.

Bietak, M 1991a. Der Friedhof in einem Palastgarten aus der Zeit des späten Mittleren Reiches und andere Forschungsergebnisse aus dem östlichen Nildelta (Tell el-Dab'a 1984-1987). *Ägypten und Levante* 2, 47-109.

Bietak, M 1991b. *Tell el-Dab'a, V: Ein Friedhofsbezirk der Mit-tleren Bronzezeitkultur mit Totentempel und Siedlungs-schichten,* Teil I. Österreichische Akademie der Wissenschaften, Denkschriften der Gesamtakademie, IX. Vienna, Österreichische Akademie der Wissenschaften.

Courtois, J-C 1978. Corpus céramique de Ras Shamra-Ugarit, II. *Ugaritica* VII, 191-370

Eriksson, K 1991. Red Lustrous Wheel-made Ware: a product of Late Bronze Age Cyprus. In J Barlow, D Bolger and B Kling (eds.), *Cypriot Ceramics: Reading the Prehistoric Record.* The University Museum, Monograph 74. Philadelphia, The University of Pennsylvania, 81-96.

Frankel, D 1991. Ceramic variability: measurement and meaning. In J Barlow, D Bolger and B Kling (eds.), *Cypriot Ceramics: Reading the Prehistoric Record.* The University Museum, Monograph 74. Philadelphia, The University of Pennsylvania, 241-51.

Hein, I and Jánosi, P forthcoming. *Tell el-Dab'a. Siedungsrelikte der späten Hyksoszeit (Area A/V).*

Hein, I 1994. Erste Beobachtungen zur Keramik aus 'Ezbet Helmi. *Ägypten und Levante* 4, 39-43.

Jánosi, P 1994. Tell el-Dab'a/'Ezbet Helmi. Vorbericht über den Grabungsplatz H/I (1989-1992). *Ägypten und Levante* 4, 20-38.

Johnson, P 1982. The Middle Cypriot pottery found in Palestine. *OpAth* XIV, 49-72.

Kenyon, K M 1965. *Excavations at Jericho,* II: *the tombs excavated in 1955-8.* London, British School of Archaeology in Jerusalem.

Knapp, A B 1979. *A Re-examination of the Interpretation of Cypriot Material in the MCIII-LCI Period in the Light of Textual Data.* Ph.D. thesis, University of California at Berkeley.

Maguire, L C 1990. *The Circulation of Cypriot Pottery in the Middle Bronze Age.* Ph.D. thesis, University of Edinburgh.

Maguire, L C 1991. The classification of Middle Bronze Age painted pottery: wares, styles... workshops? In J Barlow, D Bolger and B Kling (eds.), *Cypriot Ceramics: Reading the Prehistoric Record.* The University Museum, Monograph 74. Philadelphia, The University of Pennsylvania, 59-65.

Maguire, L C 1992. A Cautious Approach to the Middle Bronze Age Chronology of Cyprus. *Ägypten und Levante* 3, 115-20.

Masson, E 1976. À la recherche des vestiges Proche-Orientaux à Chypre, Fin du Bronze Moyen et Début du Bronze Récent. *Archäologischer Anzeiger,* 139-65

Merrillees, R S 1968. The Cypriote Bronze Age Pottery Found in Egypt. *Studies in Mediterranean Archaeology* XVIII. Lund, Paul Åströms Forlag.

Merrillees, R S 1970. Evidence for the Bichrome Wheel-made Ware in Egypt. *The Australian Journal of Biblical Archaeology* 1, No. 3.

Merrillees, R S 1978. Introduction to the Bronze Age Archaeology of Cyprus. *Studies in Mediterranean Archaeology Pocket-book* 9. Göteborg, Paul Åströms Förlag.

Newberry, P E 1893. *Beni Hasan,* Part I. London, Egypt Exploration Fund.

Petrie, W M F 1931. *Ancient Gaza,* I. London, British School of Archaeology in Egypt.

64

Petrie, W M F 1930. *Beth Pelet,* I (Tell Fara). London, British School of Archaeology in Egypt.

Philip, G 1991. Cypriot bronzework in the Levantine world: conservatism, innovation and social change. *J Medit. Arch.* 4/1, 59-107.

Schaeffer, C F-A 1938. Les fouilles de Ras Shamra-Ugarit. Neuvième Campagne (printemps 1937). *Syria* 19, 193-255.

Tufnell, O 1958. *Lachish,* IV. *The Bronze Age.* London, New York, Toronto, Oxford University Press.

Vaughan, S 1991. Material and technical characterization of Base Ring Ware: a new fabric typology. In J Barlow, D Bolger and B Kling (eds.), *Cypriot Ceramics: Reading the Prehistoric Record.* The University Museum, Monograph 74. Philadelphia, University of Pennsylvania, 119-30.

TELL EL-DAB'A METALWORK
PATTERNS AND PURPOSE

Graham Philip

Abstract

The following summarizes work to date on the metal-work from the Middle Kingdom - Second Intermediate Period site of Tell el-Dab'a in the eastern Nile Delta. The data reveals patterning in several dimensions: temporal, typological, contextual and metallurgical. After a summary description of the material, both the contextual evidence and archaeometallurgical data are described. The metallurgy of the Tell el-Dab'a assemblage is compared with that of similar metalwork from MBA Jericho. Finally, the evidence is discussed in the context of wider aspects of material culture in the Nile Delta and of socio-economic developments in the region generally.

Introduction

The site of Tell el-Dab'a provides a prime example of the hybrid of Egyptian and Syro-Palestinian traits present in the eastern Nile Delta during the Second Intermediate Period, which represents the material culture of the Hyksos. The present study aims to provide a synopsis of the metalwork found at Tell el-Dab'a and of its typological relationships with both the Egyptian and Syro-Palestinian metalworking traditions. An outline of the contexts in which different types of artefact appear is also given, and a comparison made of metallurgical practices at Tell el-Dab'a with those of MBA Jericho. This contemporary Palestinian settlement has produced material typologically akin to that from Tell el-Dab'a. Study of the metalwork from the site is continuing: remarks made here should be regarded as a preliminary, and will require modification as research proceeds.

A cautionary note is required concerning matters of context. As most of the well-preserved metalwork from Tell el-Dab'a comes from graves, we are not dealing with a random sample of the complete range of metalwork once used at Tell el-Dab'a. Rather, we have a selection of material deposited according to particular conceptual schemes. Hence the reference to 'purpose' in the title. The burials concerned cover the greater part of the duration of the site, that is from the later 19th century BC to the mid 16th century BC. Several summaries of work at Tell el-Dab'a are now available and the reader is referred to these for general information (Bietak 1979; 1984; 1991a; 1991b). The individual areas of excavation within the site have distinct stratigraphic sequences which are tied to overall site phases designated A-H (Bietak 1991a, Fig. 3). For the sake of clarity, I refer here only to the overall phasing, rather than those of the separate excavation areas. For age-sex data, I have drawn on new published material (Winkler and Wilfing 1991), and additional unpublished data kindly supplied by Dr. Eike Winkler.

A major concern of archaeology is the identification of material culture patterning. In pursuing this idea, Binford argued that in burial contexts it should be possible to establish a connection between 'formal classes' and the social persona of the deceased (Binford 1972a, 225-6). In practice, the transition from describing patterns visible in the archaeological record to understanding past human action is complex and fraught with problems. Binford's original suggestions have been revised in subsequent studies which have revealed burial as representing a transformation of that behaviour (see Hodder 1991, 2-3 and references therein). However, there is still considerable value in an investigation of observable patterns.

Elsewhere, Binford (1972b, 198-200) has stressed the importance of analysing separately the several dimensions of observed variation. This he contrasts with procedures which seek normative groupings which may mask important differences in the patterning of particular aspects of material culture. In the case of the Tell el-Dab'a metalwork four main dimensions of variation have been identified: temporal, typological, contextual and metallurgical. As these display various degrees of interrelationship, some are treated individually, while others must be considered together.

It is currently too early to undertake an overall analysis of funerary practices at Tell el-Dab'a. For the purpose of the present investigation, the data base consists of typological and chemical-analytical information relevant to the metal objects themselves, their positioning within individual graves, and age-sex data pertaining to those graves which have produced metal objects. I have therefore taken an artefact-centred approach in my analysis.

While Wobst (1977, 320) drew attention to the role of material culture in communication, Hodder (1987, 2) has made the point that the selection of artefacts to carry particular information is not arbitrary: it is done according to culturally developed, organizational schemes. As the Mari texts have made clear, metalworking in ancient western Asia was a specialist activity, with workshops and their supplies controlled by the dominant socio-economic groups (Rouault 1977; Limet 1986). These were among the largest consumers of metal goods, whether as personal items, as gifts for others including offerings to deities, or as military and agricultural equipment. Certain metal objects may have functioned as status items (Philip 1989, 156-9), so an analysis of changing types, their associations, and foreign parallels, should provide a potentially fruitful means of investigating aspects of the social and economic organization of the Nile Delta.

A complication of particular significance to the present case is the likelihood that the patterns detectable archaeologically are composites relating to several quite different processes or structures, resulting in complex patterns, within which it is hard to isolate the various strands of meaning. Were material culture to be 'read' like a text as some have suggested (Hodder 1991, 153), we may have to deal with the simultaneous transmission, within burial contexts, of messages referring to the deceased's wealth, sex, group-affiliations or ethnicity, each aimed at slightly different audiences. Furthermore, the possibility of the deliberate manipulation of such 'symbolic language' by those involved in the funerary rites, when allied to periodic fluctuations in the availability of particular items or materials, could result in very muddy waters indeed. (See Hodder 1991 and references there for a detailed exposition of these problems).

Attempts to find a single, constant 'meaning' for any one artefact will run up against the diachronic dimension of mortuary practices. The importance of this factor has been illustrated in a recent study of burial in Iron Age Greece. Here, Morris (1987) observed the changing amounts of metalwork deposited in graves over a period of several centuries, suggesting that this represented diachronic variation in the significance of particular artefacts or groups of material. The marked concentration of specific types and artefacts at particular chronological phases within the duration of the site suggests that a similar process may have been operating at Tell el-Dab'a. In circumstances of competitive display, there will be constant pressure to change the format of existing artefacts, to 'consume' new types of material, or even to move the focus of attention away from burial offerings to other arenas such as commemorative building operations. In the case of a major site such as Tell el-Dab'a, likely to have been a focus of intense social and political change, and where the occupation spans several centuries, we should be alert to the likelihood of such processes.

Yet more confusion is added because of the degree of disturbance, often deliberate robbing, of many graves. In numerous instances we have only partial artefact repertoires, and poor preservation of human skeletal material. In practice, patterns are most readily observed in well-preserved graves. Although these are relatively few, there are many partially disturbed burials which provide supporting evidence and confirm the once widespread existence of the patterns seen in the former group of tombs. On a more optimistic note, and in contrast to many Syro-Palestinian sites, large-scale multiple successive interments containing tens of individuals are not a feature of mortuary practices at Tell el-Dab'a. Here, one to three burials per chamber is the norm (Bietak 1979, 286), increasing our ability to relate artefacts to particular individuals, as well as facilitating analysis of human skeletal remains.

In the long run, a complete contextual analysis of the material culture of the site, or at least a comprehensive study of the mortuary remains, is required. While the present investigation is restricted to patterns observable in metalwork alone, I hope that it will give some indication of promising lines of approach for a more thorough examination in the future.

The observable patterns fall into four main areas:

1. Changing artefact-types.
2. Chronological and spatial patterning (traditional time-space distributions).
3. Patterns of association between artefacts, between artefacts and burial age-sex data, and the spatial positioning of objects within graves.
4. Patterns of alloy-use: by artefact-type, by chronological phase and contrasting modes of alloy usage at Jericho and Tell el-Dab'a.

For the purpose of discussion, it is convenient to treat the first three types of patterning together.

Typological Patterning and Patterns of Association and Co-occurrence: Age-sex Patterning of Metalwork from Mortuary Contexts

Weapons and Related Items

The term weapons is here applied to daggers, axes and spearheads. Other forms of weaponry such as archery equipment and sling-bolts are not found in funerary contexts at the site: these seem to have played little part in the signalling of status messages in the culture of the MBA Levant (Philip 1989, 146).

While individual examples are found, most daggers and axes from well-preserved graves occur as sets consisting of one dagger and one axe. All daggers, axes and spearheads from contexts where the skeletal evidence has been amenable to sex identification have come from adult male burials. Daggers were usually positioned across the abdomen of the deceased, axes at the head or shoulder with the handle pointing towards the feet. A similar layout was employed widely throughout Syria-Palestine in the MBA (Philip forthcoming [a]). Spearheads often occur in pairs, in several cases placed against the blocking bricks of the tomb-chamber.

Dominant types showing high stylistic similarity to contemporary Syro-Palestinian artefacts can be identified at various periods. These fall into a chronological

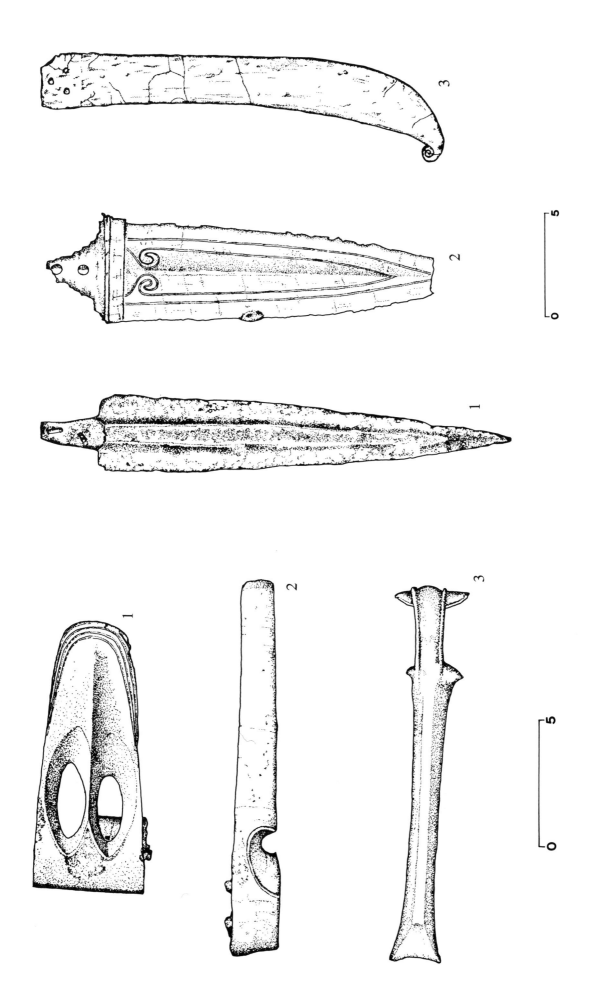

Fig. 2, 1-3.   Two daggers and curved knife,
reg. nos. 433, 7323 and 6143.

Fig. 1, 1-3.   Axes, reg. nos. 6139, 3082 and 4716.

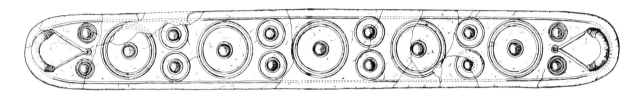

Fig. 4.
Metal belt,
reg. no. 6140,
restored,
estimated original
length c. 80 cm.

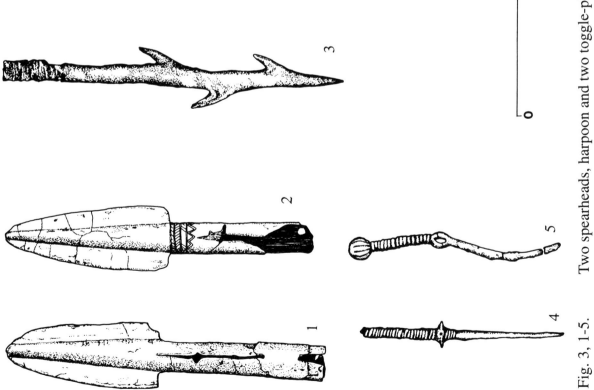

Fig. 3, 1-5.   Two spearheads, harpoon and two toggle-pins,
reg. nos. 6106, 6107, 2506, 375 and 4966.

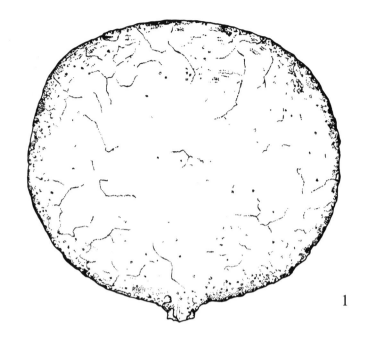

1

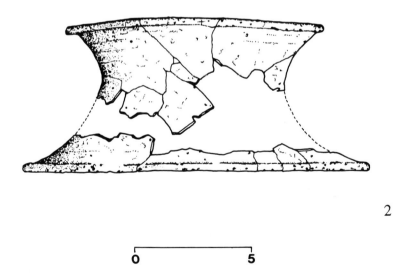

2

0   5

Fig. 5, 1-2.   Mirror and stand, reg. nos. 5425 and 3078.

succession, with shifts in the preferred types occuring broadly in line with corresponding changes in the southern Levant.

Axes

The earliest well-stratified axe from the site is a fenestrated example **(Fig. 1,1)**, of the narrow or 'duckbill' type (Philip 1989, Fenestrated axe Type 1). This piece comes from F/1-o/19 Grave 8, assigned to stratum H. No additional examples have yet been excavated at Tell el-Dab'a. Notched, narrow-bladed axes (Philip 1989, Narrow-bladed axe Type 1, **Fig. 1,2** here) are predominant in graves assigned to levels F and G, and types with flanges or a hook at the socket are found in graves of strata D/3 and E (Philip 1989, Narrow-bladed axe Types 2 and 3, **Fig. 1,3** here).

Moulds indicating production of axes of both Egyptian and foreign styles have been found at the site. Traditional Egyptian forms, Davies (1987, 43) 'lugged forms with incurved or splayed sides', could have been cast in limestone moulds (Bietak 1985, Abb. 10). Socketed axes of Levantine style could have been produced in a two-piece stone mould, a fragment of which was also found (Reg. No. 300, unpublished). However, only the socketed form occurs in grave contexts suggesting that flat axes, deemed perfectly adequate for graves elsewhere in Egypt, were not considered 'correct' for graves in the Nile Delta. Equally, in contrast to the prevalence of socketed axes in the Delta, examples have not yet been reported from secure contexts in other parts of Egypt (Davies 1987, 54). The implication is that the socketed axes were associated with Asiatic groups.

Daggers

The earliest dagger form appears in F/1-o/20 Grave 17, assigned to stratum H. The blade bears two pronounced ribs separated by a deep central groove (Philip 1989, Type 12), and is related to those from early MB IIA Levantine warrior graves such as Tomb 92 at Beth Shan (Oren 1971, 116, Fig. 2,1) and Tomb 21 at Tell Rehov (Yogev 1985, 93, Fig. 4,2), as well as numerous examples from the 'Dépôts des Offrandes' at Byblos (Dunand 1954, 302, Nos. 9652-9658, Pl. LXVIII). As is the case with the dagger from Tell el-Dab'a, a number of these bore crescent-shaped handles.

Slightly later, daggers with blades showing multiple cast-in ribs appear (Philip 1989, Type 13), in graves spanning strata G and F **(Fig. 2,2, and Bietak, this volume, Plate 14,2)**. The latest easily identifiable type are daggers with a broad flat mid-rib (Philip 1989, Type 17, **Fig. 2,1** here). These are the dominant dagger form in graves of phases E and D, and are common in south Levantine MB IIB/C contexts (Philip 1989, 120). As in the Levant, the earlier crescent-shaped pommels are replaced by limestone globular examples in the later daggers. A point of interest is that while the earlier two styles of both axe and dagger occur throughout the

Levant, the latest type of each is restricted to the southern Levant only (Philip 1989, 169-70).

Spearheads

With one exception (Reg. No. 4802), the spearheads from Tell el-Dab'a are small, relatively light, and most likely represent throwing weapons. Most examples come from the graves in the early phases of the site, strata H-F, often occurring in pairs **(Fig. 3,1 and 2)**. Yet again practices at Tell el-Dab'a reflect trends familiar from the contemporary Levant, where small spearheads are largely restricted to the MB IIA period (Philip 1989, 169). The rarity of large spearheads at Tell el-Dab'a indicates a pattern closer to that of the southern Levant than to Syria, where these occur in MB IIB/C contexts at Ras Shamra and Tell Mardikh (Philip 1989, 99). It is worth noting that the single combat scene described in the Tale of Sinuhe, which should illustrate Egyptian perceptions of south Levantine society in the early second millennium BC, describes the two warriors as shooting arrows and throwing javelins prior to final hand-to-hand combat which would have involved the use of daggers and axes (Pritchard 1955, 20).

Most weapons found in the graves from Tell el-Dab'a conform to a limited range of standard types. This contrasts with the picture in the southern Levant where alongside weapons of these forms many daggers of less highly stylized designs are also found (Philip 1989, 214). The metal artefacts from Tell el-Dab'a include highly decorated pieces, and examples using precious metals.

One axe (Reg. No. 2193) revealed fragments of a decorated, silver sleeve, which would originally have been wrapped around the weapon-haft. From an earlier grave came a dagger (Reg. No. 7323) which exhibits an unusual variant of the widely occurring ribbed decoration on the blade (**Fig. 2, 2**, and Bietak, this volume, **Plate 14,2**). In addition, the rivets which secured the haft of this piece showed traces of gold caps. This tomb also produced two silver spearheads (Reg. Nos. 7017 and 7018). In terms of shape, however, all these examples are clear variations on conventional designs.

There are good parallels for decorated weapons from the 'Dépôts des Offrandes' at Byblos (e.g. Dunand 1954, 695, Pl. CXX, No. 14439). There is also textual evidence revealing the significance of weapons as precious material. The Kamose Stela lists large quantities of copper axes among the precious goods carried away from Avaris, the Hyksos capital, following a successful attack on the town by the 17th Dynasty Pharaoh (Smith and Smith 1976, 60).

Northern (1981, 3-4) has developed the concept of the 'ornate implement', objects structurally similar to utilitarian items but which have undergone morphological modification and elaboration and which should be understood as functioning to express cultural values or beliefs. While this idea seems applicable to certain types of grave equipment at Tell el-Dab'a, I would suggest that no clear division exists between utilitarian and ornate implements. Rather, there is a continuum of variation, extending from simple undecorated examples to highly stylized versions, with all artefacts playing a variable role in the symbolic world depending on particular circumstances. In the case of daggers and axes, all are to some extent 'ornate', in that they show stylistic features unnecessary for mechanical function alone.

Metal Belts

Tell el-Dab'a has produced four good instances of metal belts, generally similar to Syro-Palestinian examples, and all from contexts producing weapons. Although they are all slightly different, they share many features in common: spring-clip fastenings, small perforations around the edge of the metal to permit the attachment of a leather backing, and a stamped, decorative motif of concentric circles (**Fig. 4**). Broadly similar belts have a wide distribution in the earlier second millennium BC.

A silver example is reported from a level Ib context at Kültepe (Emre 1971, Pl. XVI, a-c), and copper-alloy cases include those from Tell el-Far'ah (N) (de Vaux 1947, 432, Pl. XX,1) and Jericho (Kenyon 1960, 313, Fig. 117,3), both of MB IIB date. Small groups of decorated discs, which would produce a similar effect when sewn in a group on to leather belts, are known from the 'Dépôts des Offrandes' at Byblos (Dunand 1954, LXIX, Nos. 10093-10095), and from MB IIA tombs at Tell et-Tin near Homs, where they were interpreted as parts of shields by the excavator (Gautier 1895, 459). Both complete belts and groups of discs are known from graves in Cyprus spanning the later Middle and Late Cypriot Periods (Philip 1991, 84-5).

Curved Knives

The distinctive curved knife forms an important part of the MBA funerary equipment from Tell el-Dab'a, and from the Levant generally (Philip 1989, 141-2). They have thin blades, with a sharp cutting-edge which curves back towards the tip (**Fig. 2,3**). The back of the blade is straight and blunt. As these items were made of thin metal, they are frequently incomplete when found. The shape of these items implies that they were designed for cutting rather than stabbing. Most had a wooden handle secured by three or four rivets driven through the butt, which was usually of trapezoidal form: traces of wood may often be observed around the rivets. Several examples have a longer, rectangular tang, usually unriveted.

At Tell el-Dab'a many curved knives were found in secondary contexts. Most of those found within graves were no longer in their original position. Of those which appear to be in situ, one was found in the offering chamber of a grave, another on a plate at the head of the burial, yet another below the head of a slaughtered ram. Two others were positioned by the right side of the abdomen of the deceased, lying point downwards as if originally worn on a belt.

It may be instructive to compare the percentage of different kinds of artefact apparently in situ when found in grave contexts.

Percentage of Each Group of Artefacts Found In Situ

Toggle-pins	66%
Daggers	62%
Axes	46%
Curved Knives	22%

(The figures above include only those items found within tomb chambers.)

Daggers and toggle-pins were usually positioned by the abdomen or chest respectively, as if worn by the deceased, and seem frequently to have remained in situ, even in robbed graves. Those items located slightly further away from the body seem to have been more subject to movement. Hence axes, frequently placed above the skull, were more often found in secondary positions than were daggers or pins. That being so, the very low percentage of knives remaining in situ indicates that they were frequently (though not always) situated further from the deceased than daggers or axes, resulting in a greater likelihood of disturbance, an indication that they were not treated as weapons proper.

Additional support for this argument comes from the presence of several examples in association with adult female, as well as adult male burials, a point paralleled in southern Palestine at Dhahrat el-Humraiya Grave 44 (Ory 1948, 85). The fact that they were designed for cutting, suggests that curved knives may have had a symbolic association with the meat offerings which are a feature of a number of MBA graves, but which at Tell el-Dab'a are generally placed some distance from the deceased. It is planned to investigate this hypothesis more fully when additional data becomes available. Curved knives are frequently found at Palestinian MBA sites (Philip 1989, 141-2), and several, including examples with handles decorated in precious metals, are known from the Royal Tombs at Byblos (Montet 1928, 181, Pl. CII, Nos. 656-8). The existence of a similar 'ornamental' trend at Tell el-Dab'a is underlined by the presence there of an example, so far unique (**Fig. 2,3**), the point of which has been turned-up to form a small curl.

Other Metal Artefacts
Pins

In comparison to sites such as Tell el-'Ajjul or Jericho, Tell el-Dab'a shows a fairly limited repertoire of pin types. Most well-preserved examples from the site are in fact toggle-pins. These have a perforation through the shaft and were probably employed in fastening clothing (Henschel-Simon 1938). Although many fragmentary examples are referred to simply as 'pins', the bulk of these are likely to represent parts of toggle-pins. A single example (Reg. No. 4966) is known of a toggle-pin with a lobed-head (**Fig. 3,5**). In comparison with Jericho, Tell el-Dab'a shows rather fewer pins with flattened-heads: beaded and fluted-head varieties are also rare.

Most pins are made of copper-alloy, although several silver examples were found. The latter are all of one type, a toggle-pin with a pair of half-discs located in the vicinity of the perforation (**Fig. 3,4**). This particular form does not occur among the copper-alloy pins from the site, suggesting that it was reserved for silver artefacts. Exact parallels for these are rare. There are none published from Jericho or Megiddo, for example. A parallel found in a MB II B/C tomb at el-Jisr, some 14 km south of Jaffa (Ory 1946, 37, Pl. XIII,45), may indicate that the distribution of this type of pin was restricted to southern regions.

Pins are found in association with both male and female burials, generally, although not exclusively, with adults. When positions can be established they are usually found in the neck or shoulder region, in most cases on the left-hand side.

Rings

Rings from Tell el-Dab'a are usually made from silver. Several gold rings occur, but copper-alloy examples are rare. Rings occur in a wide range of sizes, probably indicative of different functions, in particular earrings and finger-rings. Most rings come from adult female burials, but several silver rings were found in association with infant or child graves. As these are usually interred without grave goods, the occasional occurrence of silver rings is of some interest. An impressionistic assessment suggests that both pins and rings are relatively more frequent in graves assigned to strata E and D than in those from the earlier phases of occupation. However, a full breakdown of the overall number of interments excavated from each stratum and an estimate of their degree of disturbance would be required in order to put this on a firm statistical basis.

Mirrors

Three flat, sub-circular mirrors have been excavated (**Fig. 5,1**). One was in a fragmentary condition, the other two had short, rectangular tangs cast as one piece with the disc of the mirror. Mirrors are a common feature of Egyptian burial customs, but are rare in MBA contexts in Syria-Palestine (Lilyquist 1979). The silver examples from the Royal Graves at Byblos (Montet 1928, 161, Pl. 98 [No. 615], Pls. 92, 93 [No. 616]) are probably of Egyptian workmanship rather than being local items.

In both instances where the associated skeletal remains could be identified, they were adult female interments, a trait in keeping with the pattern of Egypt proper, where mirrors generally show a closer association with females than with males (Lilyquist 1979, 97). One lay by the left hand of a burial, another by the head of the deceased. As at Tell el-Dab'a, mirrors from Egyptian burials are found in a variety of positions vis-à-vis the body of the deceased (Lilyquist 1979: 71-80). In the Aegean, mirrors do not occur until the LM II and III periods, and when they do, they are distinguished from Egyptian examples by having a tang attached to the disc by means of rivets (Catling 1964, 226). The use of mirrors at Tell el-Dab'a should be seen as the adoption of an Egyptian funerary practice.

Tweezers

Three pairs of tweezers have been reported from Tell el-Dab'a, all from graves attributed to Stratum F. Each item is made from a single folded piece of metal. Like the mirrors, tweezers are rare in secure MBA contexts in Syria-Palestine. An example is known from the MB IIB/C Tomb LV at Ras Shamra (Schaeffer 1938, 232-3, Fig. 27,H), a grave which produced several weapons resembling the well-known Cypriot 'knives' see Philip 1991, 76, Fig. 8). As tweezers are common in both the Aegean and Cyprus, these may be a genuine import. In the Aegean, they appear around Early Minoan II and cease in the Late Bronze Age (Catling 1964, 228; Branigan 1974, 32). In Cyprus, tweezers appear in Early Cypriot III contexts continuing until Late Cypriot I (Balthazar 1990, 384), a floruit which covers the whole Second Intermediate Period occupation of Tell el-Dab'a. The typological parallels between Aegean and Cypriot examples (Branigan 1974, 123) extend to those from Tell el-Dab'a. The adoption of tweezers could, of course, be of Egyptian inspiration, but more work is required before this can be fully assessed.

Stands

Five circular metal stands have been excavated. One grave produced two rim-sections, of different diameters, but these may well represent two parts of a single stand (**Fig. 5,2**). The stands are between 12.0 and 17.0 cm in diameter, with a concave profile. In some cases they were accompanied by a lid. Three stands have been found in graves, one in a redeposited group of funerary metalwork F/1-d/23 Gr. 1 (Bietak 1984, Abb. 12), while another stand was found in a general fill deposit. While quite rare in metal, ceramic stands occur far more frequently, and are an Egyptian rather than a Syro-Palestinian trait (Bietak 1991a, Fig. 10,22). On analysis, one of the metal examples revealed a sufficiently high gold content to suggest that it might have originally been gilded. The original surface was heavily coated by corrosion products and no gilding was noticed during preparation of the surface for sampling. (It is hoped to re-examine this piece in the future.) The exact function of these stands is uncertain, but they may have supported small pottery jars.

Harpoons

Four metal harpoons have been found at the site. There are slight variations in exact size and in the number and location of the barbs. However, all have barbs lying in the same plane, no doubt a result of their being mould-made rather than hand-wrought (**Fig. 3,3**). A limestone mould for casting such harpoons was found in a secondary context in Area F (Bietak 1984, Abb. 10, 3111, Seite B), showing that these were locally produced and should be considered as an Egyptian trait. Metal harpoons are not a feature of MBA Levantine traditions. The Nile Delta has a greater annual flow, and wider range of both fish and aquatic mammals, than the smaller rivers of coastal Syria-Palestine, so this is hardly surprising. Stranger, though, is the choice of metal for the fabrication of objects so likely to be lost or damaged in use, especially given the ready availability of alternative materials such as bone. Perhaps metal harpoons were reserved for specific roles? This possibility is supported by the fact that one example was found below a square mudbrick platform near the door of Temple II.

Summary of Age-Sex Data

Tell el-Dab'a can provide useful information which might bear on the analysis of grave material from sites in the Levant where tombs were frequently re-used, and where grave groups are mixed as a result. Male burials have a monopoly on weapons and metal belts, the manifestations of 'warrior' roles. This material tends to occur in specific combinations. The axe-dagger pairing is the basis, while in the earlier phases of the site, this may be accompanied by a pair of small spearheads. Such weapons do not represent the military equipment of armies, but that of an élite. They are symbols of the individual 'heroic' warrior. These patterns constitute strong evidence for structured human behaviour, and are related to similar practices occurring throughout western Asia in the early second millennium BC (Philip forthcoming [a]). Their origins lie outside Egypt, where these sets occur only in the Nile Delta.

Female burials on the other hand have produced pins, rings, mirrors, and fragments of sheet metal, in essence jewellery and toilet items. As with warrior gear, these items must be understood as idealised sex associations. Quite how these related to everyday life is not clear. It is well known that the social categories distinguished in mortuary contexts may not be equivalent to those recognised in the living world (Parker Pearson 1982, 101).

The picture from Egypt proper is rather different, with arms reported from Middle Kingdom graves of both sexes at Lisht (Williams 1977, 45). Additional examples include the tombs of the princesses Ita and Noub-Hotep at Dahshur, both of which produced weapons (de Morgan 1895, 50-2, Pl. VI; 108, Figs. 255, 267).

In both cases the daggers were found within the sarcophagus. In the latter instance the material included archery equipment, which is notable for its absence from graves in the Delta. The different ways in which weapons are employed in burial contexts in the Delta, and in Egypt proper, may be significant.

I would argue that in western Asia the role of warrior equipment and of certain other items of material culture in the expression of particular social messages was the common factor underlying the high degree of typological conformity seen in the metal types throughout the Levant (Philip forthcoming [a]). The messages conveyed by these items were understood over a wide area, hence the need to possess, or to be buried with, the appropriate, standard items. The majority of burials at Tell el-Dab'a contained no metal grave goods at all. Metal finds were concentrated in a fraction of the total grave corpus.

If the foregoing sex-associations seem rather predictable, a contrast is provided by the association of curved knives with adult burials of both sexes. For reasons which I will address more fully elsewhere (the full evidence will be presented in the final publication of the Tell el-Dab'a material, once the faunal evidence has been assessed), I believe these to be connected with the presence of meat offerings in graves, a trait which may be associated with age or seniority, and applicable to both sexes. Whatever the exact situation, it is clear that curved knives played a rather different role to that of 'true' weapons, which were interred with male burials only.

Patterns of Alloy Usage

Previous analyses of Egyptian copper-based metalwork have shown that during the Second Intermediate Period unalloyed copper, arsenical copper and tin-bronze were all being used for the manufacture of functional artefacts. Not until the New Kingdom did tin-bronze emerge as the clearly preferred material for artefact manufacture (Cowell 1987, 99). While the composition of the Tell el-Dab'a material agrees generally with these findings, there are two points worthy of note (see Philip forthcoming [b] for fuller information).

1.   A range of copper-base metal is found at Tell el-Dab'a. Unalloyed copper was in use, as were low arsenic alloys (1-2%), and tin-bronzes. As relatively few artefacts showed a significant level of both tin and arsenic, more than 4% or 2% respectively, a degree of selectivity seems to have been exercised by smiths.

2.   There is no clear pattern of association between type of object and preferred alloy. Some daggers and axes were manufactured from unalloyed copper, proving that complex socketed axes made in two-piece moulds could be cast from unalloyed copper if desired. However, such weapons could never provide such hard cutting edges as their arsenical-copper or tin-bronze equivalents (Tylecote 1986, 29). The apparent lack of

74

selectivity contrasts with the pattern detected by Cowell in his recent investigation of the composition of a large group of Egyptian axes (1987, 99), which revealed a degree of association between particular axe-types and alloys. However, on closer inspection, there seems to be a chronological factor at work here. Among both the axes and the daggers, those from graves assigned to strata H-F are far more likely to be composed of tin-bronze than those from the later strata E-D.

The Tell el-Dab'a Metal Industry in Context

A comparison of the alloys employed at Tell el-Dab'a and MBA Jericho reveals a number of important differences in alloy usage between the two sites. Jericho is selected for comparison because it has a range of metalwork directly comparable typologically to that from Tell el-Dab'a, and has the only other substantial body of analyses from a MBA site (Khalil 1980). The patterns of alloy usage at the two sites are rather different and suggest that we have two distinct centres producing material in very similar styles.

All of the metalwork from Jericho comes from tombs dated to MB IIB/C, a period of no more than 200 years. That from Tell el-Dab'a covers the later part of the MB IIA period and all of MB IIB/C, perhaps nearer 300 years in all. Given the size of the samples, and the mixing of material within the Jericho tombs, no attempt has been made to provide more refined chronological sub-divisions.

Discussion of Analytical Results

All objects discussed below were analysed by the same method: Atomic Absorption Spectrophotometry (AAS) on drilled samples. The analytical methods employed on the Tell el-Dab'a material are those described by Hughes et al. (1976). Included are 44 objects from Jericho analysed by Dr. Lufti Khalil (Khalil 1980) and 40 objects from Tell el-Dab'a analysed by Mr Mike Cowell of the British Museum Research Laboratory in preparation for the final publication of the metalwork from the latter site.

In the case of the Tell el-Dab'a samples, the precision of the AAS technique is typically about 1-2% relative for most major and minor components and 10-50% relative for trace components, this depending on how closely the measured concentration approaches the detection limit. A description of the procedures employed on the material from Jericho is provided elsewhere (Khalil 1980, 55-7).

The data-sets are compared by means of a series of simple plots, namely histograms for the display of single variables, and scatterplots where it is desired to explicate the relationship between two alloying elements.

Tin (Sn)

Histograms showing the percentage of tin indicate that the material from both sites includes a number of good tin-bronzes. However, while the material from Jericho (**Fig. 6**) shows a relatively wide spread of tin contents, with few objects containing less than 2% Sn, and a median value of around 6% Sn, that from Tell el-Dab'a (**Fig. 7**) shows a more marked division into tin-copper alloys and a second group containing very low quantities of tin. Here the median value is below 0.2% Sn. (Those items on the histogram showing tin present at 0.2% or 0.1% actually represent real values of 'less than' these figures.)

Arsenic (As)

When the content of arsenic is plotted in the same way, the objects from Jericho (**Fig. 8**) can be seen to contain generally higher levels of arsenic, median c.1.3% As, than do objects from Tell el-Dab'a (**Fig. 9**), median 0.5% As. Almost 50% of the objects from Jericho contain more than 1.5% As, while only 20% contain less than 0.5% As. The Tell el-Dab'a material reveals a different picture (**Fig. 9**), with just under 15% containing more than 1.5% arsenic and around 55% less than 0.5% arsenic. This difference should be significant.

Recent work on the comparative properties of copper-tin and copper-arsenic alloys (Northover 1989, 113) suggests that the presence of around 2-4% arsenic is required to improve *significantly* the toughness and hardness of a worked copper object, although arsenic retains its effectiveness as a de-oxidant when present at lower levels. In the case of the Tell el-Dab'a objects, only 5% lie within this range, although around one quarter of those from Jericho do so.

Arsenic is volatile and can easily be removed from molten metal by heating under oxidizing conditions, during recycling or hot working for example (McKerrel and Tylecote 1972). As many of the Jericho objects contain arsenic at concentrations of between 1 and 2%, it is likely that the presence of arsenic in many of the objects from Jericho is owed to its presence in the original copper ore, rather than the deliberate addition of arsenic to the alloy. This is not to say that its presence was not recognized, and appreciated, by the metalworkers.

At Tell el-Dab'a, on the other hand, a good number of the objects were made from copper which was probably derived from a low-arsenic ore. Alternatively, this metal had been recylced so often as to have reduced significantly the original arsenic content, although this seems less likely. Other artefacts, however, contain arsenic at higher levels, more akin to those found at Jericho, perhaps indicating that copper from two different ore sources was in use at Tell el-Dab'a, or that the metal employed for these had been subject to less extensive recyling.

A comparison of the pattern of co-occurrence of tin and arsenic in artefacts from the two sites is revealing. In the case of Tell el-Dab'a (**Fig. 11**), objects containing tin at above 4% nearly always contain arsenic at levels of 0.5% or less. Equally, those objects containing levels of arsenic over 1.5% generally contain less than 0.5% tin. Pieces containing marked quantities of both tin and arsenic are relatively few, suggesting that a real distinction was made at the site between alloys containing tin and those containing arsenic above a certain level. Finally, the Tell el-Dab'a plot shows a group of objects low in both tin and arsenic. These represent the objects made from the low-arsenic copper discussed above.

Such low-arsenic coppers are all but absent from the plot of the equivalent data from Jericho (**Fig. 10**), suggesting that much of the raw copper coming to Jericho may have originated from arsenical ores. Here too a general trend is detectable in that a good proportion of objects containing 6% or more tin show arsenic at less than 2.0%, while most of those containing more than 2.5% arsenic contain less than 3% tin. Again, high arsenic levels and high tin levels are not usually present in the same artefact, although the degree of co-occurrence is higher than at Tell el-Dab'a. However, while a good proportion of the objects from Tell el-Dab'a contain very low levels of tin (**Fig. 7**), such alloys are relatively rare at Jericho, where all but four objects contain at least 1.0% tin. The bulk of objects from Jericho, therefore, contain some tin, many between 2 and 6%. Most of these also reveal arsenic levels ranging between 1 and 2%. At Jericho then, there is rather more mixing of tin and arsenic in individual pieces than at Tell el-Dab'a.

The suggested use at Jericho of copper with a higher natural arsenic content than that employed in many of the artefacts from Tell el-Dab'a would explain the generally higher arsenic levels noted in objects from the former site. However, this does not account for the more frequent co-occurrence of tin and arsenic in copper alloys at Jericho. Perhaps the answer lies in the role of scrap at the two sites. Tin is far less volatile than arsenic. Because of this, scrap tin-bronze will pass much of its tin content directly into the new alloy (Cowell 1987, 98).

Perhaps the underlying pattern at Jericho is that of smiths employing copper derived from arsenical ores, with the addition of a certain amount of tin through the mixing of this material with recycled metal, including scrap tin-bronze. The metal used at Jericho seems to have undergone considerably more mixing than that employed at Tell el-Dab'a, where a rather different alloying pattern can be observed, and where a significant number of objects are low in both arsenic and tin. This suggests that copper from a low-arsenic ore was in use alongside copper with a rather higher arsenic content. We might also argue that the relatively low tin levels of most unalloyed and arsenical copper objects from Tell el-Dab'a indicate that scrap tin-bronze was re-used in a more systematic manner than at Jericho. Whatever the exact mechanism, the general distribution of alloy types at the two sites suggests that we have two distinct industries, producing artefacts to

highly standardized designs.

The integration of the typological and metallurgical data provides important evidence for the reconstruction of socio-economic developments in the Middle Bronze Age of the region. The different alloying patterns at the two sites confirm that (at least) two separate metal industries were producing stylistically similar objects. Moulds for certain types are already known from Tell el-Dab'a (Bietak 1984, Abb. 10, and additional unpublished examples). Jericho has not produced such moulds, leaving open the question of whether the metalwork from the Jericho tombs was made at the site, at some larger Palestinian regional centre, or a combination of both.

Smiths in Palestine and in the Delta were making items to the same designs. Weapon types were not being produced at a single source and traded from there, although some degree of trading and exchange is likely. It is fairly certain then that these artefacts, the weapons in particular, were made with special roles in mind. This in turn reinforces our suggestion of a degree of common symbolic expression understood throughout a wide area, embracing the eastern Nile Delta and Palestine, during the later MB IIA and MB IIB/C periods. Elucidation of the exact relationship between these artefact style zones and the political organization of the later Middle Bronze Age in this region is the next task.

Chronological and Spatial Patterning
As noted earlier, the main weapon types found at Tell el-Dab'a fall into a definite chronological succession, with one preferred style dominant in any one period. The sequence at Dab'a mirrors that in the Levant generally. As there, types change relatively quickly, with later forms showing little mechanical advantage over their predecessors. The changes are essentially stylistic, not functional, supporting the notion that appearance and display were of vital importance. However, we should note that while the styles common during MB IIA and the very beginning of MB IIB/C conform to patterns widespread throughout the coastal Levant, those found at Tell el-Dab'a in strata E through D/3 are in styles with a more restricted spatial distribution, essentially covering the Delta and Palestine (Philip 1989, 211).

No weapons are reported from the latest Second Intermediate Period stratum (D/2) at the site. This might be attributed to the extensive looting of the late graves. However, the distinctive weapon sets are also absent in tombs assigned to Jericho phases IV-V (Kenyon 1960, 1965). A similar absence is notable at sites such as Tell Fara (S) and Tell el-'Ajjul (but for one dagger-axe pair of unusual forms from Tomb 1750 [Petrie 1934, Pl. XXII, 239 and 240]). Nor do weapons of MBA form occur in reliable LBA contexts, suggesting that the deposition of these types ceased a little before, or at the end of, the MBA. This point may be connected to other changes.

Both daggers and axes exhibit a diachronic shift in the preferred alloy forms. While those from strata H-F are uniformly composed of tin-bronze (all five examples analysed revealed a tin content of more than 6%), the majority of those from the later strata E/3 through D/3 are composed of copper containing little or no tin. It is not clear whether the same chronological pattern applies to metalwork generally, as there are too few analyses from well stratified, domestic copper-alloy objects to permit their use as a check on the results from the weapons. Even so, this phenomenon requires explanation, as one would generally expect weapons to be produced in those alloys which give a hard cutting-edge when worked. There are several reasons why this should not simply be attributed to an interruption of the tin-supply during the later part of the MBA:

1.   Tell el-Dab'a was a rich, important site producing quantities of gold, silver and other valuable materials. It seems unlikely that a prolonged interruption of the tin supply would have been tolerated.
2.   The analyses of 20 Second Intermediate Period axes carried out by the British Museum recently (Cowell 1987, 99) show a ratio of 30:30:40 for copper: arsenical-copper: tin-bronze, indicating that tin was available, and in regular use, during this period.
3.   There is no indication of a tin-shortage at Jericho, a site which was smaller, poorer and less accessible to international trade than Tell el-Dab'a. Here daggers and axes stylistically comparable to those from Tell el-Dab'a continued to be produced in tin-bronze (Khalil 1980).

Alternative explanations include the possibility that weapons made from inferior materials were produced as status goods, or as special grave items rather than for real combat, supporting the argument advanced above for the communicative role of weapons. While reasonable, this argument would have applied equally well at Jericho and in the earlier phases of Tell el-Dab'a where tin-bronze was used for weapons.

Perhaps we should approach this technical change through its temporal patterning. As discussed above, early weapon types have good parallels throughout the Levant, while later examples are restricted to the Delta and Palestine. The absence of such weapons in graves assigned to the latest stratum (D/2) and in LBA contexts suggests a decline in the significance of weapons during the later MBA. Considered alongside the Egyptianizing tendencies of later Hyksos rulers (Gardiner 1961, 157-8: Quirke 1991, 126-7), the pattern makes more sense. I would tentatively suggest that as the upper strata of Delta society adopted new, more Egyptianizing customs, traditionally Levantine symbols, such as weapons, gradually decreased in importance. The apparent 'debasing' of the alloys from which they were made may attest to a decline in their significance. If the distribution of metal itself was un-

der the control of the administration, the appearance of weapons in lower value alloys might indicate that these symbols were being adopted by people of lesser status than had been the case in the earlier part of the period

When warrior burials first appear in the Levant they contain relatively few grave goods in addition to the weapons themselves, usually a few ceramic vessesls (Oren 1971). By the later MBA many weapons come from tombs containing a fairly rich range of additional grave goods. Weapons are simply one aspect of status, a few consumer items among many: scarabs, faience and alabaster vessels, juglets containing scented oils, amphorae, various ceramic items and so on. At Jericho the process of change may have been slower, and the adoption of Egyptian symbols by the élite, if it happened at all, may have been less apparent than in the Nile Delta.

Summary and Implications

As smiths throughout the region were producing material to virtually the same designs, it is fairly certain that these artefacts, the weapons in particular, were made with special roles in mind. This in turn implies a degree of common symbolic expression understood throughout a wide area embracing the eastern Nile Delta and the southern Levant. Such a system suggests the existence of a network of political and socio-economic ties connecting these two areas. The shared weapon-symbolism might simply represent the most visible manifestation of this structure, perhaps largely operating in the non-material world. However, the metalwork from Tell el-Dab'a is a mixture of Egyptian and Levantine types. Metal stands, mirrors and silver scarab-mounts are of Egyptian inspiration. These are found not only at Tell el-Dab'a, but were widely adopted within the Levant. The traffic in styles and fashions was not all one way.

The means of transmission should be sought in social, economic and political contacts between the fortified towns of the Levant and the Asiatic-dominated political units, however these functioned, in the Nile Delta. Perhaps we should envisage a situation in which the rulers of the Delta towns maintained regular relationships or defensive pacts with the towns of southern Palestine. In such circumstances we should be thinking in terms of the existence of common symbolic systems, the exchange of prestige goods, wives, horses, hostages, kinship relations, the education of sons at foreign courts and similar linkages, rather than an empire with a centralized administration.

Perhaps, in the warrior burials of Tell el-Dab'a, we see the archaeological expression of the warlike and 'predatory' nature of the Hyksos kingdoms as described in Manetho and other Egyptian sources (see Redford 1970). Perhaps it was the expression of élitism via military paraphernalia, and the imposition of a new and unfamiliar system of political control, as much as real violence, that coloured the Egyptian view of this epi-

Jericho MBA Metalwork

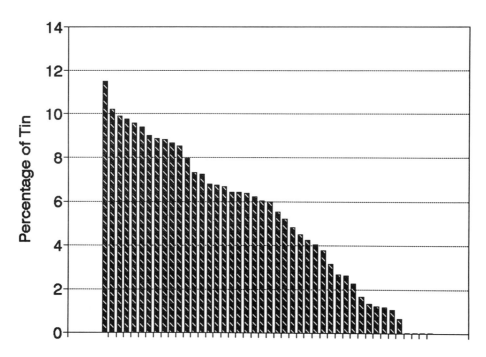

Fig. 6.

Tell el-Dab'a MBA Metalwork

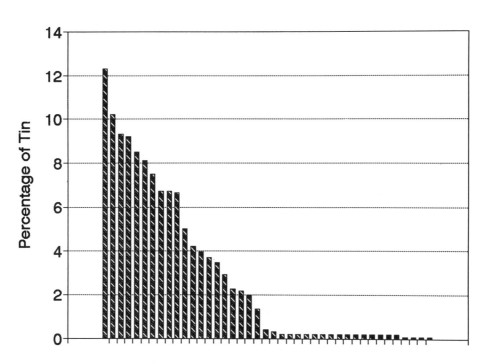

Fig. 7.

Jericho MBA Metalwork

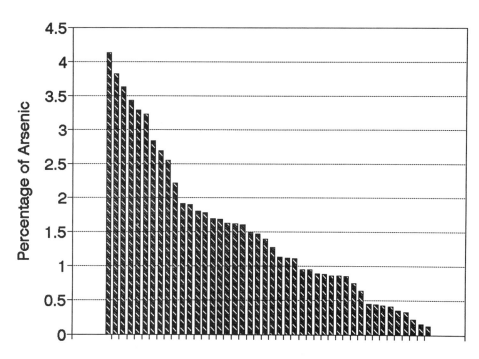

Fig. 8.

Tell el-Dab'a MBA Metalwork

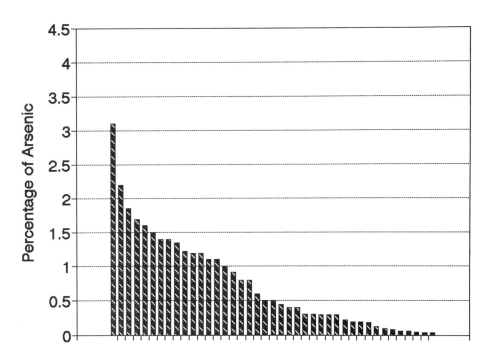

Fig. 9.

Tell el-Dab'a MBA Metalwork

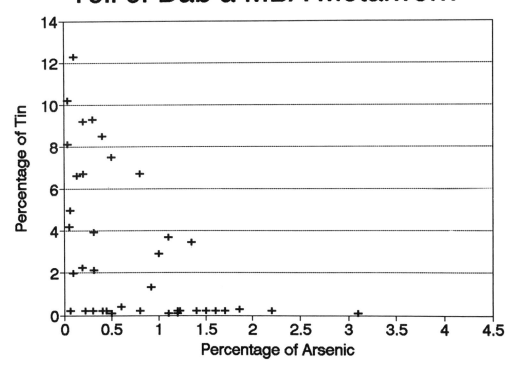

Fig. 10.

Jericho MBA Metalwork

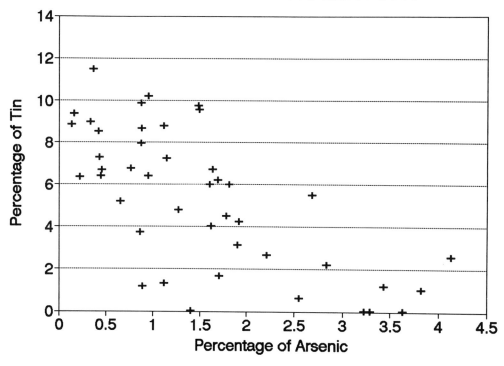

Fig. 11.

sode. Even quite small Palestinian towns were fortified in the Middle Bronze Age (Dever 1987, 153-4),
suggesting a need for substantial defences, even if these
were largely concerned with prestige (see Bunimovitz
1992). The intermittent local feuding which this implies was likely to have been far greater, both in scale
and in cost, were a similar situation prevalent in the
Delta. Here, raids and warfare could have been financed
from the products of the rich local agriculture and east
Mediterranean trade, an option not open to rulers of
small Palestinian sites. Perhaps we see in the tales of
Hyksos misrule not memories of one single event, but
endless, destructive, internecine warfare, and a system
of feudal or perhaps even tribal loyalties. Such a system would have been very different from the pattern of
rule prevalent during the Middle Kingdom, as recently
described by Quirke (1991).

The polemic of later times may not have been mere
18th Dynasty propaganda, intended to justify expan-
sionist policies in Asia. The expression of status through
arms may have been a concept strange to indigenous
Egyptian value systems, while the Hyksos, as their name
implies, were clearly categorised as 'foreign' by later
rulers. The long adherence of Tell el-Dab'a to particularly Asiatic status symbols such as warrior gear could
well be viewed in such a light.

As no Levantine weapons appear in Egypt proper at
this time, despite their presence in large numbers at
Dab'a, the implication is that they had no meaning
outwith the context of Levantine-Delta society and
were, therefore, not adopted in those regions of Egypt
controlled by more traditional ruling groups. The burial
of Egyptian dignitaries with their tomb paintings and
special grave goods involved an entirely different set
of values (Spencer 1982).

While a degree of acculturation can be detected in
certain aspects of Delta material culture (Bietak 1991a,
41-6), it was a long, slow process. Delta rulers, or individuals, may have maintained deliberate ties with kin
or allies in the lands to the north, sustaining their sense
of 'difference' from the indigenous population. Relationships of this kind could have formed the basis for
the occurrence of 'Egyptianizing', rather than genuine
Egyptian, goods in Palestine. A case in point is the
inlaid box from Pella. According to Potts (1987, 63-
9), the box, found in an early LBA context, may have
been produced a century or more prior to its deposition
and shows the use of Egyptian motifs, in a manner suggestive of Canaanite workmanship, perhaps in the Nile
Delta rather than Palestine itself. Egyptian ideas, then,
may not have been transmitted directly to Palestine,
but through the distorting lens of a partly acculturated,
partly Asiatic, Delta society.

It is probably no coincidence that the MB IIB/C period sees a high level of economic development in the
southern Levant. Covering around 250 Ha. during the
later Second Intermediate Period (Bietak 1991a, 29),
Tell el-Dab'a was larger than any Palestinian site, and

many times larger than most (see site areas quoted in
Broshi and Gophna 1986). When other, less well studied, MBA sites showing a similar 'Delta culture' are
taken into consideration, the economic differential between this region and Palestine becomes clearer. In
fact, the greater economic potential of the former region might suggest that the Delta sites acted as the 'lo-
comotive' for the economic developments throughout
the southern Levant, which led to the prosperity that
marks the Middle Bronze Age, a period which Dever
(1987) has described as 'the zenith of the urban
Canaanite era'.

We are still unsure as to whether dagger-axe sets disappear from the grave record at the end of the MBA or
are replaced by other material a little before this. Whatever the case, if we accept that southern Palestine and
the Nile Delta were linked by a network of social relationships, style zones and exchange networks, built
around the 'Hyksos Entity', then the destruction of this
entity by Ahmose and his predecessor may have severely damaged these networks, and hence affected the
deposition of the associated valuables, perhaps the final blow to a symbolic system which was already in
the process of change.

Acknowledgments
I have been able to examine the bulk of the material at
first hand through visits to the site in 1984 and 1990,
and to the Kunsthistorisches Museum in Vienna in 1985.
Chemical analysis of metal samples collected by the
author was kindly undertaken by Mr Mike Cowell of
the Department of Scientific Research of the British
Museum. The results will be published in a future final report on the metalwork from the site. Financial
assistance for this project has been provided by the following bodies: the Österreichisches Archäologisches
Institut Kairo; the British Institute at Amman for Archaeology and History; the Gerald Avery Wainwright
Fund, Oxford, and the Abercromby Fund, Edinburgh
University. The illustrations in Figures 1-5 were re-
drawn by my wife, Caroline Philip.

References
Åström, P 1972. *The Swedish Cyprus Expedition*, IV,
    Part 1,B, *The Middle Cypriote Bronze Age*. Lund,
    Berlingska Boktryckeriet.
Balthazar, J W 1990. *Copper and Bronze Working in
    Early through Middle Bronze Age Cyprus*.
    Jonsered, Paul Åströms Förlag.
Bietak, M 1979. Avaris and Piramesse: Archaeological
    Exploration in the Eastern Nile Delta. *Proceedings
    of the British Academy* 65, 225-90.
Bietak, M 1984. Eine Palastanlage aus der Zeit des
    späten Mittleren Reiches und andere
    Forschungsergebnisse aus dem östlichen Nildelta
    (Tell el-Dab'a 1979-1984). *Anzeiger der phil.-hist.
    Klasse der Österreichischen Akademie der
    Wissenschaften* 121, 313-49.

Bietak, M 1991a. Egypt and Canaan during the Middle Bronze Age. *Bulletin of the American Schools of Oriental Research* 281, 27-72.

Bietak, M 1991b. Der Friedhof in einem Palastgarten aus der Zeit des späten Mittleren Reiches und andere Forschungsergebnisse aus dem östlichen Nildelta (Tell el-Dab'a 1984-1987). *Ägypten und Levante* 2, 47-75.

Binford, L R 1972a. Mortuary Practices: Their Study and Their Potential. In L R Binford (ed.), *An Archaeological Perspective,* 208-43. New York. Reprinted from J A Brown (ed.), *Approaches to the Social Dimensions of Mortuary Practices.* Memoirs of the Society for American Archaeology, *American Antiquity* 36 (1971), 6-29.

Binford, L R 1972b. Archaeological Systematics and the Study of Culture Process. In L R Binford (ed.), *An Archaeological Perspective,* 195-207. New York. Reprinted from *American Antiquity* 31 (1965), 203-10.

Branigan, K 1974. *Aegean Metalwork of the Early and Middle Bronze Age.* Oxford, Clarendon Press.

Broshi, M and Gophna, R 1986. Middle Bronze Age II Palestine: Its Settlements and Population. *Bulletin of the American Schools of Oriental Research* 261, 73-90.

Bunimovitz, S 1992. Middle Bronze Age Fortifications in Palestine as a Social Phenomenon, *Tel Aviv* 19, 221-35.

Catling, H W 1964. *Cypriot Bronzework in the Mycenaean World.* Oxford, Clarendon Press.

Cowell, M R 1987. Scientific Appendix I: Chemical Analysis. In W V Davies *Catalogue of Egyptian Antiquities in the British Museum, VII, Tools and Weapons, I, Axes.* London, British Museum Publications, 96-118.

Cowell, M R pers. comm. Report on the analysis of some metalwork and associated items from Tell el-Dab'a and Tura, Egypt, March 1986.

Davies, W V 1987. *Catalogue of Egyptian Antiquities in the British Museum, VII, Tools and Weapons, I, Axes.* London, British Museum Publications.

Dever, W G 1987. The Middle Bronze Age: The Zenith of the Urban Canaanite Era. *Biblical Archaeologist* 50, 148-77.

Dunand, M 1954-58. *Fouilles de Byblos 1933-1938,* II. Paris, Paul Geuthner.

Emre, K 1971. *Anatolian Lead Figurines and Their Stone Moulds.* Türk Tarih Kurumu Vi Seri, Sa. 14. Ankara.

Gale, N H and Stos-Gale, Z A 1981. Ancient Egyptian Silver. *Journal of Egyptian Archaeology* 67, 103-15.

Gardiner, A H 1961. *Egypt of the Pharaohs.* Oxford, Oxford University Press.

Gautier, J E 1895. Notes sur les fouilles entrepris dans le haute Vallée de l'Oronte. *Comptes Rendue des Séances de l'Académie des Inscriptions et Belles-lettres* 23, 4th ser., 441-64.

Henschel-Simon, E 1938. The 'Toggle Pins' in the Palestine Archaeological Museum. *Quarterly of the Department of Antiquities of Palestine* 6, 169-209.

Hodder, I A 1987. The contextual analysis of symbolic meaning. In I A Hodder (ed.), *The Archaeology of Contextual Meaning.* Cambridge, Cambridge University Press, 1-10.

Hodder, I A, 1991. *Reading the Past. Current Approaches to Interpretation in Archaeology* (2nd edition). Cambridge, Cambridge University Press.

Hughes, M J, Cowell, M R and Craddock, P T 1976. Atomic Absorption Techniques in Archaeology. *Archaeometry* 18, 19-37.

Kenyon, K M 1960. *Excavations at Jericho,* I. London, British School of Archaeology in Jerusalem.

Kenyon, K M 1965. *Excavations at Jericho,* II. London, British School of Archaeology in Jerusalem.

Khalil, L 1980. *The Composition and Technology of Ancient Copper Alloy Artefacts from Jericho and Related Sites.* Unpublished Ph.D. Thesis, Institute of Archaeology, London.

Lilyquist, C 1979. *Ancient Egyptian Mirrors from the Earliest Times through the Middle Kingdom.* Münchner Ägyptologische Studien, Heft 27. München/Berlin, Deutscher Kunstverlag.

Limet, H 1986. *A.R.M. XXV, Textes administratifs relatifs aux métaux.* Paris, Éditions Recherche sur les Civilisations.

Mace, A C and Winlock, H E 1916. *The Tomb of Senebtisi at Lisht.* New York, Metropolitan Museum of Art.

McKerrel, H and Tylecote, R F 1972. The working of copper-arsenic alloys in the Early Bronze Age and the effect on the determination of provenance. *Proceedings of the Prehistoric Society* 38, 209-18.

Montet, P 1928. *Byblos et l'Égypte.* Paris, Paul Geuthner.

Morris, I 1987. *Burial and Ancient Society: The Rise of the Greek City-state.* Cambridge, Cambridge University Press.

de Morgan, J 1895. *Fouilles à Dahchour, Mars-Juin 1894.* Vienna, Holzhausen.

Northern, T 1981. *The Ornate Implement.* Dartmough College Museum and Galleries. Hanover, New Hampshire.

Northover, J P 1989. Properties and use of arsenic-copper alloys. In *Archäometallurgie der Alten Welt.* Heidelberg. *Der Anschnitt,* Beiheft 7, 113-8.

Oren, E D 1971. A Middle Bronze Age I Warrior Tomb at Beth Shan. *Zeitschrift der Deutschen Palästina-Vereins* 87, 109-39.

Ory, J 1946. A Middle Bronze Age Tomb et El-Jisr. *Quarterly of the Department of Antiquities of Palestine* 12, 21-42.

Ory, J 1948. A Bronze Age Cemetery at Dhahrat el-Humraiya. *Quarterly of the Department of Antiquities of Palestine* 13, 75-89.

Parker-Pearson, M 1982. Mortuary practices, society and ideology: an ethnoarchaeological study. In I A Hodder (ed.), *Symbolic and Structural Archaeology*. Cambridge, Cambridge University Press, 91-113.

Petrie, W M F 1934. *Ancient Gaza,* IV. London, British School of Archaeology in Egypt.

Philip, G 1989. *Metal Weapons of the Early and Middle Bronze Ages in Syria-Palestine*. BAR International Series 526 (i) and (ii), Oxford.

Philip, G 1991. Cypriot Bronzework in the Levantine World: conservatism, innovation and social change. *Journal of Mediterranean Archaeology* 4.1, 59-108.

Philip, G forthcoming [a]. Warrior Burials in the Ancient Near Eastern Bronze Age: the evidence from Mesopotamia, western Iran and Syria-Palestine. In A R Green and S Campbell (eds.), *The Archaeology of Death in the Ancient Near East*.

Philip, G forthcoming [b]. The Same but Different: a comparison of Middle Bronze Age metalwork from Jericho and Tell el-Dab'a. *Studies in the History and Archaeology of Jordan*, V. Amman, Department of Antiquities of the Hashemite Kingdom of Jordan.

Potts, T F 1987. A Bronze Age Ivory-Decorated Box from Pella (Pahel) and its Foreign Relations. In A Hadidi (ed.), *Studies in the History and Archaeology of Jordan*, III. London, 59-71.

Pritchard, J B 1955. *Ancient Near Eastern Texts Relating to the Old Testament* (2nd edition). Princeton, Princeton University Press.

Quirke, S 1991. Royal Power in the Thirteenth Dynasty. In S Quirke (ed.), *Middle Kingdom Studies*. New Malden SIA Publishing, 123-39.

Redford, D 1970. The Hyksos Invasion in History and Tradition. *Orientalia* 39, 1-51.

Rouault, O 1977. *A.R.M.* XVIII, *Mukannišum, l'administration et l'économie palatiales à Mari*. Paris, Paul Geuthner.

Schaeffer, C F A 1938. Les fouilles de Ras Shamra-Ugarit, neuvième campagne (Printemps 1937). *Syria* 19, 193-255.

Smith, H S and Smith, A 1976. A Reconsideration of the Kamose Texts. *Zeitschrift fur Ägyptische Spräche und Altertumskunde* 104, 46-78.

Spencer, A J 1982. *Death in Ancient Egypt*. Harmondsworth, Penguin Books.

Tylecote, R F 1986. *The Prehistory of Metallurgy in the British Isles*. London, The Institute of Metals.

Vaux de, R and Stève, A M 1947. La première campagne de fouilles à Tell el-Far'ah, près Naplouse. *Révue Biblique* 54, 394-433.

Williams, B 1977. The Date of Senebtisi at Lisht and the Chronology of Major Groups and Deposits of the Middle Kingdom. *Serapis* 3, 41-60.

Winkler, E-M and Wilfing, H 1991. *Tell el-Dab'a,* VI. *Anthropologische Untersuchungen an den Skelettresten der Kampagnen 1966-69, 1975-80, 1985*. Wien, Österreichische Akademie der Wissenschaftern, Denkschriften der Gesamtakademie, Bd 10.

Wobst, H M 1977. Stylistic behaviour and information exchange. In C E Cleland (ed.), *For the Director: Research Essays in Honor of James B Griffin*. University of Michigan, Museum of Anthropology, Anthropological Paper 61. Ann Arbor, 317-42.

Yogev, O 1985. A Middle Bronze Age Cemetery South of Tell Rehov. *Atiqot* 17, 90-114.

REFLECTIONS ON THE CHRONOLOGY
OF TELL EL-DAB'A

James M Weinstein

In 1966, John Van Seters published *The Hyksos: A New Investigation*. The book identified Manetho's 15th Dynasty as a line of foreign kings with close ties to the Amorite rulers and society of Middle Bronze Age Syria-Palestine, ending the notion that these Asiatics were Hurrian or other non-Semitic invaders from further north. It placed the Hyksos capital of Avaris in the area of Khata'na-Qantir rather than at Tanis, and it gave substantial attention to the Levantine background of the Hyksos, not, as many Egyptologists were wont to do, only to their activities in Egypt. The book quickly became a basic reference work on the topic.

Today, Van Seters's book receives only scattered mention in the burgeoning literature on the Hyksos, for much of its archaeological content is irrelevant or out of date. Since the mid 1960s, excavations in Syria-Palestine have provided a massive quantity of new data on the stratigraphic phasing, material culture, and relative chronology of the Middle Bronze Age. At the same time, detailed studies of already excavated finds, such as Tufnell's (1978) re-examination of the Asiatic burials excavated by Flinders Petrie at Tell el-Yahudiyeh, Gerstenblith's (1983) investigation of the MB IIA period in the Levant, Kaplan's (1980) study of Tell el-Yahudiyeh ware, and Philip's (1989) comprehensive investigation of Early and Middle Bronze Age weaponry have furnished a large body of new information on the typology, technology, and chronology of special categories of Middle Bronze Age materials, as well as on the commercial and other interconnections of the period. The most significant factor in the obsolescence of Van Seters's book, however, has been Manfred Bietak's excavations at Tell el-Dab'a, the site of ancient Avaris.

Until the mid 1960s, Tell el-Yahudiyeh was the only published site in the eastern Delta that had yielded evidence of Asiatic occupation during the Second Intermediate Period - and those finds pertain to the period of the 15th Dynasty rather than to the formative phase of Hyksos history. In 1966, the same year in which John Van Seters summed up the information then available on the Hyksos, Manfred Bietak began field investigations at Tell el-Dab'a. That project has opened up a whole new vista on Asiatic activity in Egypt during the late Middle Kingdom and Second Intermediate Period, on the Hyksos rise to power and their eventual demise, and on interconnections in the eastern Mediterranean world and north-eastern Africa during the Second In-

termediate Period. Even today, Tell el-Dab'a remains the only urban Middle Bronze Age settlement in Egypt, one of only two Delta sites (the other is Tell Farasha [Yacoub 1983]) to produce MB IIA materials, the only stratified Egyptian site with continuous Asiatic occupation from the late 12th Dynasty through the end of the Second Intermediate Period, and the source of more Syro-Palestinian finds in Second Intermediate Period contexts than all other sites in Egypt combined. While a few other MB II sites in Egypt have been excavated in the past couple of decades (e.g. Tell el-Maskhuta and Tell el-Habwe), none has the chronological range or breadth of archaeological materials of Tell el-Dab'a.

The Tell el-Dab'a project is conspicuous not only for the extraordinary discoveries it has made - the most recent of which are the spectacular Aegean-style frescoes and Theran tephra - but for the controversy it has generated. The principal points of debate relate to the precise dates that the excavator assigns to his strata and to his views on the comparative chronology of Egypt and Palestine during the early 2nd millennium BC (see, e.g., Dever 1985; 1991; 1992a; 1992b; Ward 1987; Weinstein 1992).

Tell el-Dab'a and Chronology
The low dates employed by the excavator are more than a minor inconvenience to many Syro-Palestinian archaeologists and Egyptologists. If correct, they force a substantial reduction in the terminal date for the MB IIA period and a compression of the succeeding MB IIB and IIC periods into a shorter span of time than the stratigraphic and ceramic remains in the southern Levant seem to permit. Even allowing for the possibility that the MB IIC period may have continued in Palestine for a generation or two past the campaigns of Ahmose in the third quarter of the 16th century BC, the dates still cause difficulties for Syro-Palestinian stratigraphy and chronology.

Levantine archaeologists agree that the chronology of Palestine during the Middle Bronze Age is largely dependent on connections with Egypt. Some of these linkages are direct - such as those established on the basis of Levantine materials found in Middle Kingdom and Second Intermediate Period deposits in Egypt, and Egyptian objects discovered in Middle Bronze Age contexts in Palestine. Others are indirect - most notably the Egyptian objects recovered from Syrian Middle Bronze Age contexts, which in turn are linked to materials found in the southern Levant.

The lack of agreement on Palestinian chronology during the first half of the 2nd millennium BC is evident from the current endorsement in the archaeological literature of no less than four dating schemes - the ultra-high, high, middle, and low - for the Middle Bronze Age (Weinstein 1992, 27, table 1). Since Tell el-Dab'a's Middle Bronze Age deposits are so extensive, it is essential that every effort be made to harmonize the dating of that Delta site with the chronology obtained from sites elsewhere in the south-eastern Mediterranean world.

The two excavation areas at Tell el-Dab'a that are of special importance for Middle Bronze Age chronology are Tell A in the eastern part of the site, and Area F/1 near the centre. Nine strata on Tell A (designated H through D/2) and six strata in Area F/1 (labelled d/2-b/1, and corresponding to Strata H-E/1 on Tell A) have yielded MB II materials. The end of the Second Intermediate Period sequence on Tell A, as well as at 'Ezbet Rushdi to the west of the main site, equates historically with Ahmose's capture of the city at the beginning of the 18th Dynasty. That event probably occurred in year 11 (or soon thereafter) of the king's reign,[1] i.e. about 1540 BC in terms of absolute dating.[2] The initial phase of Asiatic occupation at the site is represented by Stratum H = d/2 and belongs to the latter part of the 12th Dynasty, perhaps to the reign of Amenemhet III (1843-1798 BC). The time-span between the beginning and end of this sequence is, therefore, less than three centuries (the excavator uses 270 years in his publications).

Bietak (1989, 93) views each of the nine strata on Tell A as representing a single building 'generation'. He justifies his division of 270 (years) by nine (strata) by asserting that the resultant 30 years is an adequate lifetime for a single building 'generation'. Though he acknowledges that some buildings and strata lasted longer than others, the overall result of this 'scaled' approach is a series of precise dates of nearly equal duration for the nine levels. As set forth in Bietak's latest chronological discussion (1992, fig. 1), the absolute dates for the Tell A strata are as follows:

Stratum	Dates (BC)
H	1800-1770
G/4	1770-1750
G/1-3	1750-1710
F	1710-1680
E/3	1680-1650
E/2	1650-1620
E/1	1620-1590
D/3	1590-1560
D/2	1560-1540/30

I think the reaction of many archaeologists would be that there is no obvious reason why mudbrick structures in Egypt should collapse or require major rebuilding after so short a period of time. While one can easily cite settlements elsewhere in the ancient world where individual occupational phases lasted for only a brief period of time - Bietak (1989, 93 and n. 66) himself mentions the case of Hala Sultan Tekke during the LC IIIA period on Cyprus - the important question is why a major rebuilding effort should be required about every 30 years for nearly three centuries.

Bietak's comment (1989, 93) that 'in many other sites' - one assumes here that he is offering his interpretation of Syro-Palestinian archaeology - 'only overall destruction or abandonments were used to define strata' perhaps provides some room to manoeuvre. There are hints in the Tell el-Dab'a reports that some of the excavator's nine 'main strata' may be substrata, or 'phases', as used in the literature of Levantine archaeology. Stratum E/2 = b/1, for example, seems to represent only a gradual architectural and ceramic shift from Stratum E/3 = b/2 (see, e.g., Bietak 1991a, 40-1), not a major change either culturally or stratigraphically. If indeed some of the 'strata' at Tell el-Dab'a are equivalent to 'phase' as used in Syro-Palestinian archaeology, the excavator's identification of nine 'main strata' covering 270 years may not be such a major hurdle to overcome.

Middle Bronze IIA Strata

The MB IIA period is represented at Tell el-Dab'a in Strata H = d/2, G/4 = d/1, and G/1-3 = c, while the transitional MB IIA/B period is attested in Stratum F = b/3. Since no royal or private names, or datable inscriptions of any sort, appear on objects found in the lowest three levels, the excavator relies heavily on a seriation of the hemispherical drinking cups - linking those cups to ones found by Dieter and Dorothea Arnold in various deposits at Dahshur - to establish dates for those strata (Bietak 1984; 1985; 1991a, fig. 14). Lesser reliance is placed on parallels at Dahshur for several other types of Egyptian pottery, such as beer and water jars, and on the typological analysis of a few pieces of sculpture. Altogether, these three strata provide little evidence for exact dates, though they must fit mostly within the 18th century BC. More data need to be published, however, before we can eliminate the possibility that Stratum H = d/2 begins in the 19th century BC.[3] The dating of that stratum is an important matter for Syro-Palestinian archaeologists, since it is the linchpin for the entire early 2nd millennium BC stratigraphic sequence and contains the earliest MB IIA pottery on the site.

The Syro-Palestinian ceramic types in H = d/2 include Levantine Painted Ware, a single sherd from an Ovoid 1 Tell el-Yahudiyeh ware juglet, and possibly a few sherds of red-burnished juglets (Bietak 1989, 90; 1991a, 33).[4] The Levantine Painted Ware provides a correlation with the early MB IIA period at such Palestinian sites as Aphek and Tell el-Ifshar (Weinstein 1992, 28-9), while the Tell el-Yahudiyeh ware sherd and perhaps the few sherds of red-burnished pottery indicate a somewhat later date within the period, assuming they are not intrusive. The excavator assigns this stratum to his MB IIA2 period, thereby leaving room for an earlier phase of the Middle Bronze Age (MB IIA1), which is not attested at Tell el-Dab'a.

Since the earliest MB IIA materials at Tell el-Dab'a do not predate the late 12th Dynasty, we need to ask how much earlier the MB IIA period could have begun in the Levant. Until recently, Bietak seems to have preferred to start MB IIA in Syria-Palestine in about the second quarter of the 19th century BC (e.g. Bietak 1991a, fig. 3). In a new article, however, he has allowed for the possibility that MB IIA may go back to about 1900 BC (Bietak 1992, fig. 1), a time well before there is any sign of Asiatic occupation at Tell el-Dab'a.

The 'duckbill' axe found in a Stratum H = d/2 tomb (Bietak 1989, 94, fig. 8; 1991, 49, fig. 5) and a similar axe depicted on a cylinder seal from the pavement of the palace of Stratum G/4 = d/1 (Porada 1984) have generated considerable discussion. The duckbill axe is characteristic of MB IIA and perhaps transitional MB IIA/B in the Levant. The earliest representation of this weapon is on a wall scene in the tomb of Khnumhotep (Tomb 3) at Beni Hasan. There, in a group of visiting Asiatics, one man is shown holding a long wooden handle that has a distinctive curve at one end. Attached to the handle, away from the curved end, is an object that almost all Palestinian archaeologists interpret as a duckbill axe. Although questions have been raised about the identification of the object as this weapon type (e.g. Bietak 1989, 94; 1991a, 49 and n. 25; Williams 1975, 860), there is every reason to believe that it is indeed such an item.

Duckbill axes with long handles having the same pronounced curve as that represented in the Beni Hasan scene were found in several MB IIA tombs at Baghouz in Syria (du Mesnil du Buisson 1948, 53-4, pls. 45, 47-8, 54, 56). Bietak (1992, 33, fig. 7) has recently discussed an Egyptian model axe from Beni Hasan which also has a curving handle. The handle on the model axe is easily distinguishable from the Baghouz handles by its smaller curvature, however, and by the fact that the axe-blade is considerably wider, in relation to its length, than the axe shown in the Beni Hasan scene or found on true duckbill axes.

A question has also been raised about the Beni Hasan axe because the two 'eyes' typical of the duckbill axe blade are not shown in the original publications of the scene.[5] In my opinion, whether the 'eyes' were ever included in the wall scene is not a critical factor in the identification of the axe. What is important is that one has here an Asiatic holding a long stick with a distinctive curving handle. In each instance at Baghouz in which such a stick occurs with an axe, the axe-blade is

of the duckbill type. That a local artisan could be less than perfect in reproducing the features of the duckbill axe is clear from the specimen represented on the cylinder seal. On that item, which Porada (1984) thinks may be the work of a local craftsman and which Bietak (1989, 94, fig. 10; 1991a, 49) himself accepts as a duckbill axe, elongated lines appear in the axe in place of the 'eyes'. More interesting, however, is the fact that the object has a straight handle, a characteristic of Egyptian Middle Kingdom axes but unlike the curved handles associated with the Baghouz duckbill axes.

If the artisan who engraved the Tell el-Dab'a cylinder seal could cut an Egyptian-style handle for the duckbill axe, why should one be surprised if the Beni Hasan tomb painter neglected to show the 'eyes' inside the duckbill axe? Common sense tells us that in a scene composed of a group of Asiatics wearing foreign dress and carrying foreign goods, the axe being carried by an Asiatic man is intended to be a duckbill axe, not an Egyptian axe, whatever the precise details of the illustration. Since an inscription accompanying the scene dates the visit by the Asiatics to regnal year 6 of Senusert II (whose reign Kitchen places at 1868-1862 BC), that sets the beginning of MB IIA no later than the second quarter of the 19th century BC.

There is little evidence to support a date much earlier than about 1900 BC for the start of the MB IIA period in Palestine. Arguments have been put forward (e.g. by Rainey 1972) to put the Story of Sinuhe within an MB IIA cultural matrix and thereby to push early MB IIA back to the mid 20th century BC. The archaeological evidence for Egyptian-Palestinian relations in early MB IIA is so sparse, however, that it seems implausible that the mention in the Sinuhe account of Egyptians crisscrossing the land refers to Palestine in the mid 20th century BC (a Syrian context for that part of the Sinuhe narrative is more likely). In the southern Levant the MB IIA period probably began in the early 19th century BC, that is, 50-100 years earlier than it shows up at Tell el-Dab'a.

Although an overlapping of late MB IIA with the early 13th Dynasty is assured (Weinstein 1975; 1992), a debate exists over the length of that overlap. Stratum F = b/3, where the Levantine materials change from MB IIA to MB IIB, has been the subject of much controversy because the excavator dates the level quite late, i.e. to about 1710-1680 BC. While 13th Dynasty scarabs and pottery were found in this stratum, none of the material is precisely datable. As for the two fragmentary limestone blocks inscribed with the name of a Second Intermediate Period king, Aasehre Nehesy, and attributed to Temple III, which was started in this stratum, those blocks were found in pits of the much later Strata B and A/2 and may or may not relate to Temple III in Area A/III (Weinstein 1992, 30-1). The excavator may be correct in pushing the end of Stratum F = b/3 down into the early 17th century BC, but the finds published so far do not require such a low date.

Middle Bronze IIB Strata

Three strata at Tell el-Dab'a contain MB IIB remains: E/3 = b/2, E/2 = b/1, and E/1 = b/1-a/2. The Levantine pottery and metal finds in Stratum E/3 = b/2 belong in early MB IIB. A scarab from a tomb on Tell A which is inscribed with a corrupt form of the royal nomen Sobekhotep (Bietak 1970, pl. 19b, top row, 2nd from left; 1991a, fig. 17: 1840) may well belong in the second half of the 13th Dynasty, but that does not yield an explicit date for E/3 = b/2. Nothing published so far dates that stratum precisely or indicates how long it lasted.

The succeeding level, Stratum E/2 = b/1, could be attributed as easily to late Dynasty 13 as to early Dynasty 15. The meager chronological evidence for this stratum includes a scarab inscribed with the *rdi-R'* group of signs. Although this series of hieroglyphs was popular on scarabs in the 15th Dynasty, its initial appearance on those objects may have been as early as the late 13th Dynasty (Weinstein 1992, 40 n. 24). Other scarabs from this stratum are also of types that could be either late 13th Dynasty or 15th Dynasty and include none of the categories most typically associated with the Hyksos period.[6] I am, therefore, inclined to place Stratum E/2 = b/1 at the end of the 13th Dynasty and begin the Hyksos-period levels only with Stratum E/1 = b/1-a/2, where several scarab design-types considered characteristic of the Hyksos period appear (Bietak 1989, 96; 1991a, 52). That would push the date of E/2 = b/1 back about a quarter century from the excavator's 1650-1620 BC date. Admittedly, however, the evidence to support this slightly earlier dating is not strong.

Evidence from other sites for the precise dating of MB IIB is minimal. Several scarabs with Egyptian royal names are attested in MB IIB contexts in Palestine and Egypt. A recently excavated 'Middle Bronze Age II' tomb at Fassuṭa in northern Palestine yielded a scarab of Neferhotep I (1723-1712 BC) (Avi'am and Brandl 1989-90). Kempinski (1992, 71) assigns the context specifically to early MB IIB, though he does not state the basis on which he supplies that date. The brief preliminary report on the salvage excavation at Fassuṭa indicates that the royal-name scarab was the only scarab found in the tomb. That scarab may be close in date to its context and provide evidence for the beginning of MB IIB before the end of the 18th century BC, but it must be remembered that a single scarab has little more value than a solitary radio-carbon date. Additional scarabs or other data from the same context are necessary to determine whether the royal-name scarab is likely to be contemporary with the rest of the deposit or just an heirloom.

A tomb assigned to tomb group III at Jericho (= mid MB IIB) produced a scarab of Khahetepre Sobekhotep V (1705-1701 BC), while a late MB IIB tomb at Tell el-Maskhuta in the Wadi Tumilat had a scarab inscribed for Khaneferre Sobekhotep IV (1712-1705 BC)

(Holladay 1982, 45, figs. 75-6). The Maskhuta scarab is an heirloom, since the late MB IIB period overlaps the early 15th Dynasty. The Jericho scarab is also likely to be an heirloom, though the tenuous nature of the dating of the Jericho tombs requires us to be cautious in utilizing that material.

Bietak (1984, 483, ills. 4-5; 1989, 97; 1991a, 55-6) has interpreted two other scarabs from MB IIB tomb groups at Jericho as containing royal names. He reads one item (from tomb group III) as containing a corrupt writing of the name of the Hyksos king Maaibre Sheshi, and interprets another (from tomb group II) as having the name of Nubkheperre Intef V of the early 17th Dynasty. Ward (1987, 521-2) doubts that royal names should be read on either scarab, while Kempinski (1992, 71, n. 7) states that the 'Maaibre' scarab is 'certainly intrusive', while the second item may contain an amuletic combination of signs rather than a royal name. The labelling of the tomb group II scarab as a deliberate writing of the royal name Nubkheperre may be questioned, if for no other reason than it renders even Bietak's chronology too high. Tomb group II belongs typologically to early MB IIB. Making that phase contemporary with the late 17th century BC (the period of Intef V [Kitchen 1992, 329], unless that king's reign can be pushed back into the mid 17th century), effectively sets most or all of MB IIB *within* the 15th Dynasty, pulling the end of MB IIA down even lower than Bietak has proposed.

The other well-known Asiatic site in the eastern Delta with MB IIB materials is Tell el-Maskhuta, where a University of Toronto expedition under the direction of John S. Holladay, Jr., discovered a small, seasonally occupied settlement as well as tombs (Holladay 1982, 44-7; 1992; Weinstein 1992, 32-3). Many of the finds in the settlement and tombs are similar to those found at Tell el-Dab'a.

The scarabs from the early MB IIB contexts at Tell el-Maskhuta typologically belong to the second half of the 13th Dynasty and the early 15th Dynasty.[7] Their designs show little relationship to those found on the scarabs and seal impressions from the Middle Kingdom town of Kahun, whose occupation was confined mainly to the 19th and first three-quarters of the 18th centuries BC, and no contact at all with scarabs of the preceding 12th Dynasty. The designs on the scarabs from the late MB IIB tombs and one or two early MB IIC tombs at Tell el-Maskhuta are, again, late 13th and 15th Dynasty types (predominately the latter), and include such standard Hyksos-period motifs as the deeply cut mythical and animal figures. The best sphragistic parallels at Jericho for the early MB IIB materials at Tell el-Maskhuta come from tomb groups III and IV, and for the late MB IIB scarabs from tomb groups IV-V. As for Tell el-Dab'a, the best parallels at that site for the Tell el-Maskhuta scarabs come from Strata E/1 = b/1-a/2 and D/3 = a/2.[8] No scarabs at Tell el-Maskhuta need be dated to the late 15th Dynasty, which suggests that occupation at the site terminated prior to the end of the Second Intermediate Period.

The best published parallels at Tell el-Dab'a for the Tell el-Maskhuta pottery also come from Strata E/1 and D/3. They include the Piriform 2 Tell el-Yahudiyeh ware found in Strata E/1-D/2, the Tell el-Yahudiyeh ware jugs with horizontal combed decoration found in D/3-D/2, the cylindrical Tell el-Yahudiyeh ware jugs (late E/2-early D/3), and the flat-bottomed drinking cups (D/3-D/2). The ceramic parallels present something of a problem, since Bietak assigns Strata E/1 and D/3, respectively, to late MB IIB and to a transitional phase leading to a localized MB IIC, whereas much of the Palestinian pottery at Tell el-Maskhuta is classic MB IIB; in the earliest phases, there may even be some transitional MB IIA/B material (Holladay 1982, 45-6; 1992; and personal communication).

The drinking cups at Tell el-Maskhuta present a special concern. At Tell el-Dab'a, the flat-based cups appear only in Strata D/3 = a/2 and D/2 (e.g. Bietak 1989, 79-80, fig. 1; 1991a, 43, 46, fig. 13), which makes them contemporary with the excavator's late MB IIB and early MB IIC periods. Yet at Tell el-Maskhuta these cups occur throughout the MB IIB sequence (four examples being illustrated in Holladay 1982, pl. 1: 1-4). Only in the very earliest phases are there any round-bottomed cups such as typify the 18th and 17th century BC sequence at Tell el-Dab'a (John S. Holladay, Jr., personal communication).

It is difficult to reconcile the archaeological sequences at Tell el-Maskhuta and Tell el-Dab'a. At the same time, precise dates for the MB IIB remains at Tell el-Maskhuta remain elusive. These materials fit primarily within the 17th century BC, but they probably have a wider range than that proposed for the corresponding strata at Tell el-Dab'a.

Middle Bronze IIC Strata

Two strata at Tell el-Dab'a contain MB IIC materials: D/3 = a/2 and D/2 (the corresponding stratum in Area F/1 is missing). The scarabs in D/3 = a/2 and D/2 include a number of classic Hyksos types, with no scarabs attributable to the 18th Dynasty (Bietak 1989, 96; 1991a, 52-3). In addition, one scarab from D/3 = a/2 is inscribed with an otherwise unknown Hyksos royal name, Šnšk (Bietak 1989, 96; 1991a: 52, fig. 18: 6160), while a scarab from D/2 mentions the famous chancellor, Har (Bietak 1991a: 53, fig. 18: 6161). One of the latest scarabs at Tell el-Maskhuta also names a Hyksos ruler, Maaibre (Sheshi); that item comes from a disturbed tomb which may belong to the MB IIC period.[9] At Jericho, a scarab naming the same king comes from a tomb group V deposit (and possibly also III [but see above]).

It is during the MB IIC period that a dozen Asiatic burials found at Tell el-Yahudiyeh come into the picture (Tufnell 1978). Most of the Tell el-Yahudiyeh ware juglets in these graves have a piriform shape, while only three are of the later, cylindrical form. As at Tell el-Maskhuta, the piriform Tell el-Yahudiyeh juglets are much more common than the cylindrical juglets. There is also at least one example of Tell el-Yahudiyeh ware with horizontal combed decoration. The drinking cups in the Tell el-Yahudiyeh graves are uniformly of the flat-bottomed variety, a feature that occurs throughout most of the Tell el-Maskhuta sequence, but, as noted above, is apparently limited at Tell el-Dab'a to Strata D/3 = a/2 and D/2. The drinking cups and Tell el-Yahudiyeh ware vessels place the graves roughly contemporaneous with Strata E/1 = b/1-a/2 and D/3 = a/2 at Tell el-Dab'a, i.e. at about the same time as much of the Tell el-Maskhuta material.

The other finds at Tell el-Yahudiyeh include more than 150 scarabs. These are difficult to date because the excavators only published drawings of their bases and most are lacking an archaeological context. Of the 29 scarabs republished by Tufnell, the majority fit typologically in the latter part of the 13th Dynasty and at least the first half of the Hyksos period, i.e. to about the same period as the Tell el-Maskhuta scarabs. Three of the scarabs, for example, are of uninscribed amethyst and may be compared with those found at Tell el-Maskhuta as well as at Tell el-Dab'a starting in Stratum E/1 = b/1-a/2. The best parallels at Jericho for the designs on the Tell el-Yahudiyeh scarabs, like those at Tell el-Maskhuta, come from tomb group IV, though there is some overlapping with tomb groups III and V. Common designs include animals and heraldic beasts, human and mythical figures, concentric circles, and various combinations of signs and symbols. The average length of the Tell el-Yahudiyeh scarabs is close to that of Jericho tomb groups IV and V. As in the case of the Tell el-Maskhuta scarabs, there are no distinctively 12th Dynasty back types; instead, most of the scarabs have highly schematic heads and backs.[10]

Tufnell dated the graves to about 1700-1600 BC, which I take to be about a quarter century too high at both ends. Tell el-Yahudiyeh itself probably had a somewhat longer span of occupation, since objects found loose on the site contain royal names from the early 12th Dynasty (Amenemhet I and Senusert I) to Awoserre Apophis of the late 15th Dynasty. Unfortunately, the nature of the excavations and the materials published from the site make it impossible to discern anything about the chronology of the Asiatic activity at Tell el-Yahudiyeh prior to, or later than, the time of the burials.

Tell el-Maskhuta and Tell el-Yahudiyeh probably were abandoned early in the use-phase of the cylindrical juglets. The end came prior to the demise of Tell el-Dab'a and before the termination of Jericho tomb group V. As for the relative dating of Tell el-Yahudiyeh and Tell el-Maskhuta, it is likely that the former site lasted somewhat longer than the latter.

Conclusion

Archaeologists agree that the end of Stratum D/2 at Tell el-Dab'a should be linked to the capture of Avaris by Ahmose at the beginning of the 18th Dynasty. For the dating of many of the earlier levels at the site, however, there remains much controversy. There are no astronomical data, inscriptions or historical events to date precisely any of the earlier strata. It is, therefore, appropriate that some flexibility be allowed in assigning chronological limits to the individual strata and in determining the beginning of Stratum H = d/2. Exact dating of the Tell el-Dab'a strata remains a goal that (in my opinion) has not yet been achieved.[11]

The excavator's low dating of Stratum F = b/3 may be correct, or my own more moderate dates, about a quarter century higher, may prove closer to reality. Professor Bietak and I agree that the ultra-high and high chronologies proposed by a number of American and Israeli scholars for the MB IIA-B transition are too early: we do not agree on whether a middle or low dating is appropriate. Based on the *published* evidence, I believe that either dating scheme is possible, though I continue to support a middle chronology because of my concern regarding the compression of the succeeding MB IIB and IIC strata that is demanded by the low chronology.

We can relate the Tell el-Maskhuta and Tell el-Yahudiyeh materials in general terms to the finds at Tell el-Dab'a, but reconciliation of Bietak's dating of Tell el-Dab'a with that proposed for Tell el-Maskhuta is more problematic. Perhaps the individual strata at Tell el-Dab'a were of more uneven length than the excavator believes; possibly the pottery from domestic deposits at Tell el-Dab'a will prove to be somewhat different than those from the tombs. In the end, it may prove necessary to excavate another large Middle Bronze Age site in the eastern Delta to settle the chronological questions raised by Tell el-Dab'a.

The excavations at Tell el-Dab'a have given us a wealth of new and exciting material. If no consensus yet exists on the dating of the site's Middle Bronze Age remains, there is agreement that Tell el-Dab'a is critical to an understanding of the history and archaeology of the Middle Bronze Age in Palestine and the Second Intermediate Period in Egypt. In recent years, vigorous debate has arisen regarding the chronology of Tell el-Dab'a. A number of scholars, not all of whom are Syro-Palestinian archaeologists, feel that the published data are insufficient to support a low chronology. The current debate, however, does not overshadow the extraordinary contributions made by the Tell el-Dab'a project to the history of the eastern Mediterranean world in the 2nd millennium BC. All of us who work in this field are indebted to Manfred Bietak for his excavation and for the promptness with which he has made his spectacular discoveries known to the world.

Notes

1. The date of Ahmose's conquest of Avaris remains under discussion. The latest paper on the subject (el-Sabbahy 1993) returns to the possibility that the critical regnal year 11 on the verso of the Rhind Mathematical Papyrus refers to the reign of the Hyksos ruler Khamudy rather than to that of his Theban contemporary, Ahmose.

2. Absolute dates in this paper are from Kitchen 1992.

3. At the present time the excavator's date for the beginning of H = d/2 cannot be checked, since the pottery and other finds from that stratum are unpublished.

4. In 1989 (Bietak, 90), the excavator said that 'red-burnished juglets are not represented', while in 1991a (Bietak, 33) he stated that 'red-burnished vessels such as juglets are still extremely rare in this stratum'.

5. Newberry 1893, pls. 30-1. The photograph in Wreszinski 1935, pl. 6, is inadeqate to evaluate any interpretation.

6. My knowledge of the Tell el-Dab'a scarabs is due to the kindness of Professor Bietak. Several years ago, he put at my disposal copies of the drawings of the scarabs found through the 1988 season.

7. I thank Professor John S. Holladay, Jr., Professor Carol Redmount, and Ms Patricia Paice for facilitating my study of the scarabs, pottery, and other finds from Tell el-Maskhuta.

8. For example, uninscribed amethyst scarabs and a wide variety of designs, such as deeply-cut human, animal, and mythical figures, some with interior crosshatching and often shown between erect cobras facing each other; the Hathor or Bat symbol shown full face; and Red Crowns in a tête-bêche arrangement.

9. Field number M81-455, from Tomb 2054.

10. No Hyksos royal names occur on the scarabs from the graves, but scarabs found elsewhere on the site (mostly loose) had the names of Khyan, Sekhaenre, and Apophis (as well as the name of the Treasurer Har and the great Administrator of the City, Senaa).

11. Hence, efforts to assign dates to the Alalakh strata on the basis of Bietak's chronology for Tell el-Dab'a (Gates 1988, 78-9; Heinz 1992, 203-5) are premature.

References

Avi'am, M and Brandl, B 1989-90. Fassuṭa. *Excavations and Surveys in Israel 1989/1990* 9, 92.

Bietak, M 1970. Vorläufiger Bericht über die dritte Kampagne der österreichischen Ausgrabungen auf Tell ed Dab'a im Ostdelta Ägyptens (1968). *Mitteilungen des Deutschen Archäologischen Instituts Abteilung Kairo* 26, 15-42.

Bietak, M 1984. Problems of Middle Bronze Age Chronology: New Evidence from Egypt. *American Journal of Archaeology* 88, 471-85.

Bietak, M 1985. Stratigraphie und Seriation. Arbeiten zur Erschliessung der relativen Chronologie in Ägypten. In *Lebendige Altertumswissenschaft: Festgabe zur Vollendung des 70. Lebensjahres von Hermann Vetters.* Vienna, Adolf Holzhausens, 5-9.

Bietak, M 1989. The Middle Bronze Age of the Levant - A New Approach to Relative and Absolute Chronology. In P Åström (ed.), *High, Middle or Low? Acts of an International Colloquium on Absolute Chronology held at the University of Gothenburg 20th-22nd August* 1987, Part 3. Gothenburg, Paul Åströms Förlag, 78-120.

Bietak, M 1991a. Egypt and Canaan during the Middle Bronze Age. *Bulletin of the American Schools of Oriental Research* 281, 27-72.

Bietak, M 1991b. *Tell el-Dab'a V: Ein Friedhofsbezirk der Mittleren Bronzezeitkultur mit Totentempel und Siedlungsschichten,* Teil I. Österreichische Akademie der Wissenschaften, Denkschriften der Gesamtakademie, IX. Vienna, Österreichische Akademie der Wissenschaften.

Bietak, M 1992. Die Chronologie Ägyptens und der Beginn der Mittleren Bronzezeit-Kultur. *Ägypten und Levante* 3, 29-37.

Dever, W G 1985. Relations between Syria-Palestine and Egypt in the 'Hyksos' Period. In J N Tubb (ed.), *Palestine in the Bronze and Iron Ages: Papers in Honour of Olga Tufnell.* Institute of Archaeology, Occasional Publication, 11. London, Institute of Archaeology, 69-87.

Dever, W G 1991. Tell el-Dab'a and Levantine Middle Bronze Age Chronology: A Rejoinder to Manfred Bietak. *Bulletin of the American Schools of Oriental Research* 281, 73-9.

Dever, W G 1992a. The Chronology of Syria-Palestine in the Second Millennium BCE: A Review of Current Issues. *Bulletin of the American Schools of Oriental Research* 288, 1-25.

Dever, W G 1992b. The Chronology of Syria-Palestine in the Second Millennium BC. *Ägypten und Levante* 3, 39-51

el-Sabbahy, A-F 1993. The Military Entry on the Verso of the Rhind Mathematical Papyrus. *Göttinger Miszellen* 133, 97-100.

Gates, M-H 1987. Alalakh and Chronology Again. In P Åström (ed.), *High, Middle or Low? Acts of an International Colloquium on Absolute Chronology held at the University of Gothenburg 20th-22nd August 1987,* Part 2. Gothenburg, Paul Åströms Förlag, 60-86.

Gerstenblith, P 1983. *The Levant at the Beginning of the Middle Bronze Age.* American Schools of Oriental Research Dissertation Series, 5. Winona Lake, IN, Eisenbrauns.

Heniz, M 1992. *Tell Atchana/Alalakh.* Alter Orient und Altes Testament, 41. Kevelaer, Butzon and Bercker; Nuekirchen-Vluyn, Neukirchener Verlag.

Holladay, J S Jr. 1982. *Cities of the Delta,* Part III: *Tell el-Maskhuṭa, Preliminary Report on the Wadi Tumilat Project 1978-1979.* American Research Center in Egypt Reports, 6. California, Malibu, Undena.

Holladay, J S Jr. 1992. The Eastern Nile Delta during the Hyksos and Pre-Hyksos Periods: Towards a Systemic/Socio-Economic Understanding. Paper presented at symposium held at the University of Pennsylvania.

Kaplan, M F 1980. *The Origin and Distribution of Tell el Yahudiyeh Ware.* Studies in Mediterranean Archaeology, 62. Göteborg, Paul Åströms Förlag.

Kempinski, A 1992. The Middle Bronze Age in Northern Israel, Local and External Synchronisms. *Ägypten und Levante* 3, 69-73.

Kitchen, K A 1992. Egypt, History of (Chronology). In D N Freedman (ed.), *The Anchor Bible Dictionary.* New York, Doubleday, 322-31.

du Mesnil du Buisson, R 1948. *Baghouz, l'Ancienne Corsôté; le tell archaïque et la nécropole de l'âge du bronze.* Leiden, E J Brill.

Newberry, P E 1893. *Beni Hasan* I. Archaeological Survey of Egypt 1. London, Egypt Exploration Fund.

Philip, G 1989. *Metal Weapons of the Early and Middle Bronze Ages in Syria-Palestine.* 2 parts. BAR International Series, 526. Oxford, British Archaeological Reports.

Porada, E 1984. The Cylinder Seal from Tell el-Dab'a. *American Journal of Archaeology* 88, 485-8.

Rainey, A 1972. The World of Sinuhe. *Israel Oriental Studies* 2, 369-408.

Tufnell, O 1978. Graves at Tell el-Yehudiyeh: reviewed after a lifetime. In R Moorey and P Parr (eds.), *Archaeology in the Levant: Essays for Kathleen Kenyon.* Warminster, Aris & Phillips, 76-101.

Van Seters, J 1966. *The Hyksos: A New Investigation.* New Haven, CT, Yale University.

Ward, W A 1987. Scarab Typology and Archaeological Context. *American Journal of Archaeology* 91, 507-32.

Weinstein, J M 1975. Egyptian Relations with Palestine in the Middle Kingdom. *Bulletin of the American Schools of Oriental Research* 217, 1-16.

Weinstein, J M 1992. The Chronology of Palestine in the Early Second Millennium BC. *Bulletin of the American Schools of Oriental Research* 288, 27-46.

Williams, B 1975. *Archaeological and Historical Problems of the Second Intermediate Period.* Unpublished Ph.D. Dissertation, University of Chicago.

Wreszinski, W 1935. *Atlas zur altaegyptischen Kulturgeschichte* 2. Leipzig, J C Hinrichs.

Yacoub, F 1983. Excavations at Tell Farasha. *Annales du Service des Antiquités de l'Égypte* 65, 175-6.

EGYPTIAN AND NEAR EASTERN IMPORTS
AT LATE BRONZE AGE MYCENAE*

Eric H Cline

Introduction

The present paper is concerned primarily with the Egyptian and Near Eastern imports (hereafater Orientalia) found in Late Helladic (LH) contexts at Mycenae - from c. 1700 to 1080 BC. Of the 857 Orientalia in good contexts within the LBA Aegean, nearly 10% have been found at Mycenae - more than at any other site, with the exception of Kommos on Crete. These Orientalia include items of faience, ceramic, stone, bronze, glass and ivory.

In all, eighty-two Orientalia have been discovered in good LH I-III contexts at Mycenae: thirty-seven from Syro-Palestine, twenty-nine from Egypt, nine from Mesopotamia, four from Cyprus, and three from Anatolia. It will be noted that these numbers (summarized in **Fig. 1** and in the Appendix) do not match the total number of objects found in the accompanying Catalogue. This is the result of two factors. First, although the Catalogue lists all Orientalia at LBA Mycenae, including raw materials, objects found in contexts too broad for assignation to a specific period (i.e. LH I-III) and those without known provenance or of dubious import-status, only those objects which were imported worked and which have been found in definite LH I-III contexts at Mycenae are considered in this prose section and are listed in **Fig. 1** and in the Appendix.[1] Second, at least one entry in the Catalogue lists multiple objects under a single Catalogue number, e.g. the four or more Egyptian faience plaques found by Tsountas at Mycenae (**26**). It is likely that still more imported objects remain to be found at Mycenae, and it can be safely assumed that the absolute numbers presented here will change in the future.

Faience objects appear to be by far the most common imports, but this finding is undoubtedly skewed by the twenty or more faience vessels from Syro-Palestine found in LH IIIB contexts within the House of Shields (**56-64, 66-8, 70, 74-80**). Other objects of faience found elsewhere at Mycenae in definite LH I-III contexts include cylinder seals, scarabs, plaques and assorted vessels (**14-18, 21, 24-6, 45-6, 50, 53**). The only ceramic items are the nine Canaanite jars (**36-44**), all of which presumably originated in the Syro-Palestine region. There is, in addition, a single terracotta wall-bracket (**81**), in all likelihood imported from Cyprus. Further, there are only three objects of worked bronze (**2, 12, 82**), all probably originating

in the Syro-Palestine area. There are also ten objects of glass, including seven beads, a pendant and a plaque, all probably originating in northern Mesopotamia (**4-11, 27**), and fifteen objects in various types of stone (alabaster, lapis lazuli, diorite, haematite and steatite), imported from various areas in the Eastern Mediterranean (**19, 22-3, 28-35, 48, 51-2, 55, 83-4**). Finally, although all of the ivory found at Mycenae is by necessity to be viewed as imported, only two pieces (**3, 65**) of all those found in LH I-III contexts are thought to have been imported already worked.

No one single type of Egyptian or Near Eastern import predominates at LH I-III Mycenae, and objects of different materials and of functional, ornamental and devotional character have been identified. It must be recognized that less than half of the Orientalia found in LBA contexts at Mycenae may be termed 'functional' items; these are the two stone weights (**83-4**), the terracotta wall-bracket (**81**), the nine Canaanite jars (**36-44**) and possibly the various stone vases and faience bowls. The Canaanite jars appear to be a concrete indication of the exchange of commercial materials between the Aegean and Eastern Mediterranean, for these jars were exchanged more for their contents than for their own intrinsic value. It has been established that such amphorae were utilized as containers for a wide variety of goods, including wine, oils, orpiment, resins, glass beads and probably grain as well.[2] Other non-liquid food items of trade were presumably packed in perishable materials such as straw, wood, or leather, which will not have survived until the present day. The stone vases and faience bowls may have contained 'real' trade items such as fragrant oils or perfume, but seem just as likely to have been imported for their own intrinsic value. Most of the remaining Egyptian and Near Eastern objects found at LH I-III Mycenae are small items, such as seals, scarabs, pins and unusual objects of glass and ivory, scattered over the site both areally and temporally. This situation perhaps supports the hypothesis that the majority of the Orientalia at Mycenae are the 'bric-à-brac' of international trade, remnants derived from the principal trade in metals, wine, oil, grain and textiles.

Looking briefly at the find-spots of these eighty-two Egyptian and Near Eastern imports at Mycenae, one notes that approximately twenty-three tombs contain imported objects, but no single tomb has more than four such imports, and most have only one. There does not seem to be a great difference between the types of imported objects

Origins	I-II	III	IIIA	IIIA-B	IIIB	IIIC	Total
Egypt	5	4	3	1	15	1	29
Syro-Palestine	-	-	2	5	27	3	37
Cyprus	-	2	2	-	-	-	4
Anatolia	2	-	1	-	-	-	3
Mesopotamia	7	-	-	-	2	-	9
Total	14	6	8	6	44	4	82

Fig. 1.   Egyptian and Near Eastern Objects at Mycenae.

found in tombs and those found in houses/buildings at LH I-III Mycenae, although there are far more imports in houses/buildings than in tombs. The 'Citadel House Area' (including the 'South House' to the north, the 'Cult Centre' and the 'Tsountas House' to the south)[3] contains the most imported goods, but the 'House of Shields' is close behind. The concentration of imported artefacts in the 'Citadel House Area', some apparently out of their 'proper' temporal context, may be related to its function as the principal religious area of LH III Mycenae.[4] The concentration of Orientalia in the 'House of Shields' is harder to explain, but the fact that they consist almost entirely of faience vessels may indicate some sort of specialized interest or activity in this house - Wace felt that this house, or its occupants, may have been particularly involved in overseas relations.[5]

The paucity of Anatolian, and specifically of Hittite, artefacts at Mycenae is perhaps not altogether surprising, since only twelve such imports are found in the entire LH/LM I-III Aegean.[6] Moreover, as has been pointed out elsewhere, a parallel situation is found in Anatolia at this time. Although Mycenaean ceramic imports and other remains have been found in quantity along the western and southern coasts of Anatolia, only a single site (Masat) in the inland areas of the Hittite homeland has yielded Mycenaean artefacts. It is clear that little trade occurred between the Hittite homeland and the Mycenaean world during the Late Bronze Age.[7] The few Anatolian objects (**13, 23, 69**) at Mycenae provide additional support for a possible lack of trade between Mycenaeans and Hittites.

Only three, or possibly four, worked objects identifiable as Cypriot have been found at Mycenae (**16, 22, 50, 81**). It should also be noted that one whole and three fragmentary ox-hide ingots, of unworked copper presumably imported from Cyprus, have been found in LH III contexts at Mycenae.[8] Though the numbers are small, the variety of worked imports - scarab, cylinder seal, faience goblet and terracotta wall-bracket - indicates that the old view that the Bronze Age Aegean imported Cypriot copper and little else from this island is outdated.[9] New research has identified numerous Cypriot ceramic vessels in Late Bronze Age contexts elsewhere in the Aegean; so many, in fact, that Cypriot vessels now appear to be the most numerous ceramic imports extant from LBA Aegean contexts.[10] The view of Cypriot-Aegean trade in the Late Bronze Age must thus be updated accordingly, and a fresh appraisal of the situation is called for.[11]

Mesopotamian objects make up fully half of the Orientalia found in LH I contexts at Mycenae - they are the only Orientalia found at LH I Mycenae in contexts both within and outside of Grave Circles A and B. In fact, all but two of the Mesopotamian objects in definite LH I-III contexts at Mycenae are in LH I contexts, and these latter two (a 'star disc' pendant and a nude female plaque, both of blue glass and both in LH IIIB contexts within the 'Cult Centre' at Mycenae) may

have originally arrived during the LH I period as well.[12] As an aside, it may be of some interest, in light of the find-spot of the latter two objects within the 'Cult Centre', that in Near Eastern contexts both the 'star disc' pendant and the nude female plaque had some religious meaning and were usually connected to fertility concepts and to the goddess Ishtar.[13]

All nine Mesopotamian imports are made of blue glass (**4-11, 27**). These findings are apparently consistent with the situation elsewhere in the LBA Aegean. Most of the imports from Mesopotamia in the LBA Aegean are made of blue glass and are found in LH I-II contexts, with the exception of faience cylinder seals found in an LH IIIB context at Boeotian Thebes.[14] Harden originally suggested that the Mycenaeans looked to Mesopotamia, not Egypt, for their supply of blue glass (both raw ingots and worked objects);[15] this suggestion has found recent support from the numerous glass ingots found on the Ulu Burun (Kas) shipwreck.

Surprisingly, imported objects from other areas of the Eastern Mediterranean in LH I-II contexts at Mycenae, and within the Shaft Graves in particular, are not as numerous as has previously been stated.[16] Those which do appear were most likely imported via Crete. The well-known inlaid daggers from these graves may be linked, however, in terms of artistic tradition, craftsmanship and probably influence, to a dagger with an inlaid handle bearing the name of the Hyksos king Apophis and to an inlaid axe and an inlaid dagger of Ahmose found in the tomb of Ahhotpe, mother of Ahmose.[17]

It is surprising that only two Syro-Palestinian objects (**36, 65**) and three Egyptian objects (**29-30, 71**) have been found in definite LH IIIA deposits at Mycenae, considering the quantities of Mycenaean pottery of this period found in these Eastern areas.[18] It may be that the situation at LH IIIA Mycenae has been distorted by the propensity of these objects to remain in circulation, i.e. until the LH IIIB or IIIC periods, or by the relative paucity of such IIIA contexts at Mycenae (apart from tombs).

The substantial increase in Egyptian and Near Eastern artefacts assignable to the LH IIIA-B and IIIB periods at Mycenae is consistent with the abundance of Mycenaean pottery found in the Syro-Palestinian and Egyptian areas during much of these periods. Syro-Palestine as a whole presents a pattern consistent with the continuous importation of LH IIIA and IIIB pottery, except perhaps in the inland regions of northern Syria where LH IIIB ceramics are scarce.[19] Egypt, too, appears to have consistently imported Mycenaean LH IIIA and IIIB pottery throughout most of the 14th and 13th centuries BC. It should be noted that the accumulating evidence from Egypt now indicates that the importation of LH IIIA and IIIB pottery was not unique to Akhenaten, his capital at el-Amarna, or the 'Amarna Period', and suggests rather that such pottery was in use over great areas of Egypt and was imported by a number of Pharaohs, from Amenhotep III to Ramesses II.[20]

Among Late Bronze Age specialists, it is no longer considered accurate to say simply that the LH IIIB period was 'the period of the greatest Mycenaean expansion'.[21] The great expansion in fact seems to have occurred during the LH IIIA2 and IIIB1 periods.[22] However, the majority of the Orientalia at Mycenae have indeed been found in LH IIIB contexts (**Fig. 1**). Thus, on the surface, the LH IIIB period appears to have been the most active in terms of trade or contact between Mycenae and Egypt or the Near East. This observation must bear the caveat that the distribution has probably been distorted by the circulation or heirloom potential of these small imported objects. Some of these Orientalia may actually have arrived amidst the trade and contacts of the LH IIIA period, or even earlier, and then remained in use at Mycenae until some time in the LH IIIB period. The inscribed Amenhotep III/Queen Tiy objects and the glass objects from Mesopotamia in LH IIIB contexts appear to be the best candidates for such a temporal translocation. One must also keep in mind that earlier strata and contexts have generally not been as well preserved at Mycenae as later strata; the situation at Mycenae is heavily weighted in favour of LB IIIB contexts, as these are the best preserved remains at the site. In particular, there is very heavy artefact weighting to phase VII - the period ended by the LH IIIB2 earthquake.[23] Furthermore, our findings may be skewed to some extent since the 'Citadel House Area' is the only part of the Acropolis at Mycenae from which full data for each and every artefact and its depositional context are available.

However, it is of great interest to look at the larger picture at this point in time. The majority of Orientalia in LH/LMI-IIIA1 contexts within the Aegean area have been found on Crete. Importation of worked Orientalia into Crete suddenly ceased, however, during the LM IIIA2 period, while the following LH IIIB period saw a dramatic, nearly ten-fold, increase of Eastern imports into Mainland Greece. Specifically, the vast majority (76%) of Orientalia in LH/LM IIIB contexts within the Aegean area are found on the Greek Mainland (one hundred and sixteen out of one hundred and twenty-six).[24] These figures indicate an overall pattern of importation directed primarily at Crete during the LH/LMI-IIIA periods. The pattern then changes, and importation during the LH/LM IIIB and LH/LM IIIC periods is directed primarily at the Greek Mainland. There is also a corresponding escalation of Mycenaean LH IIIB products sent to the Eastern Mediterranean at this time. Thus, according to the evidence of both the Orientalia found in the LH/LM IIIB Aegean area and the LH/LM IIIB Aegean objects found in the Near East, Mycenaean merchants and vessels had apparently become the principal representatives from the Aegean by this time, and Mainland Greece was apparently the prime destination of the trade routes from Egypt and the Near East. Based on these observations, a link between the destruction of Knossos in early LM IIIA2[25] and a Mycenaean takeover of the Eastern Mediterranean trade routes seems a likely hypothesis to suggest.

It seems, in fact, a distinct possibility that the LM IIIA2 destruction of Knossos was caused by Mycenaeans from the Argolid, perhaps specifically from Mycenae. This is suggested by two observations: (1) much of the LH/LM IIIA2 and IIIB pottery subsequently found in Egypt, Syro-Palestine and Cyprus was made in the Peloponnese on the Greek Mainland specifically for export;[26] and (2) Mycenae and Tiryns together have more than half (55%) of the one hundred and twenty-six Orientalia found in LH/LM IIIB contexts in the Aegean.[27] Boeotian Thebes, with its cache of thirty-eight cylinder seals, represents the only other site in the entire LBA Aegean area to have more than five Orientalia in LH/LM IIIB contexts.

Moreover, the quantity of Amenhotep III/Queen Tiy objects found at Mycenae and the new papyrus fragments from Amarna (Parkinson and Schofield, this volume, **Plate 8**) depicting Mycenaean warriors in Egypt during the LH IIIA2 period again raise the possibility that these Mycenaeans, in their hypothesized destruction of LM IIIA2 Knossos, were aided by Egyptians.[28] Egyptian motivations may have ranged from a desire to eliminate the Minoan 'middle-men' to a desire for a mutual defence treaty with the Mycenaeans against the newly-resurgent Hittite Empire or other foes.[29]

The objects inscribed with the cartouche of either Amenhotep III or Queen Tiy found at Mycenae include one vase (**71**), two scarabs (**17-18**) and at least six plaques (**24-6**). Most of these objects have no obvious functional purpose. Since such plaques had a specific votive function in Egypt and since a number of the plaques (and scarabs) have been found in 'votive' contexts at Mycenae, it has been suggested elsewhere that they were used at Mycenae in a religious or devotional capacity.[30] It has also been suggested that many or all of the Amenhotep III/Queen Tiy objects at Mycenae originally arrived in the LH IIIA1 period, during the actual reign of Amenhotep III.[31] It seems likely that all of these royally-inscribed items arrived together and that this time of arrival corresponds to the period immediately preceding the great expansion in trade and relations between the LH IIIA-B Aegean and the Eastern Mediterranean. This is further supported by the inscribed objects of Amenhotep III/Queen Tiy found in various LH/LM III contexts at five other Aegean sites.[32]

It is problematic whether these inscribed objects of Amenhotep III/Queen Tiy at Mycenae are the extant remains of a Pharaonic gift to woo a potential ally, to establish trade relations or diplomatic ties with a new Aegean power, or merely to maintain and confirm previously existing ties. The probable link of these nine objects to the 'Aegean List' inscribed on the statue-base from Amenhotep III's mortuary temple at Kom el-Hetan (**Plate 6,1**) and to a formal Egyptian embassy sent to

Mycenae has previously been discussed in detail.[33] It is quite possible that they were part of a larger gift, since these small items found at Mycenae hardly appear worthy of a high-level diplomatic exchange.[34] Thus, additional objects found at Mycenae may have originally accompanied these royally-inscribed items. Whether such items suggest more than a phenomenon of expanding contacts remains an interesting question, but the conclusion that Egypt was taking a particular interest in the Aegean during the LH IIIA and IIIB periods seems to be sound.

In contrast to the LH IIIB period, Syro-Palestinian and Egyptian imports found in LH IIIC contexts at Mycenae are rare, as are true Mycenaean IIIC exports to these eastern areas. This is possibly a reflection of the unsettled character of the times in the Aegean and Eastern Mediterranean. One should note, in fact, that all four of the imports found in LH IIIC contexts at Mycenae (**35, 44, 82, 84**) - three from Syro-Palestine and one from Egypt - were in secondary deposits (such as 'wash up against the Cyclopaean Wall') and should be regarded as imports which had arrived at Mycenae earlier, i.e. in the LH IIIA or IIIB periods.[35] It is now clear that Mycenae *was* occupied and reasonably thriving in the LH IIIC period. The noticeable decline in imports during the LH IIIC period might be attributable to the collapse of the international trade routes at this time and to the destruction at most of the major Mycenaean citadels during this period, leading to a new focus on areas separate from the dysfunctional palatial centres.[36] It is also conceivable that the observable decrease in Orientalia in LH IIIC contexts had its origins in an LH IIIB2 earthquake in the Argolid.[37] It is possible that this hypothesized LH IIIB2 earthquake, whose effects may be visible in Mycenae and elsewhere in the Argolid, had a greater impact on these cities and their ability to compete in international markets than has been previously suspected. Certainly, the increase in regional ceramic styles in Greece during the LH IIIB2 period and a possible decline in exports of LH IIIB2 Mycenaean pottery to the Eastern Mediterranean may be indications that the Argolid's influence and mercantile capabilities were severely affected at a point prior to the LH/LM IIIC period.[38]

We may also note an interesting anomaly in the distribution of Orientalia at Mycenae as compared to other major LBA Aegean centres. At Mycenae and its surrounding territory there is a reasonably large number of Egyptian objects but very few Cypriot objects. However, at Tiryns and its environs, only three kilometres away, Cypriot imports are fairly common while Egyptian imports are virtually unknown. Such a distribution pattern may indicate a directional trade, aimed at specific points of entry. It also suggests that there may have been special relationships between specific Aegean sites and individual Eastern Mediterranean areas. It is possible that instead of speaking in sweeping generalizations about trade between the Aegean and the Near East,

we should be speaking in terms of trade between Mycenae and Egypt, Tiryns and Cyprus, and so on.

The distribution pattern noted for the Orientalia imported into the LBA Aegean as a whole also suggests that Mycenae, along with Tiryns, Knossos, Kommos, Kato Zakro and Ialysos, initially received the Orientalia and then redistributed these objects to the surrounding villages and smaller communities. Thus, Mycenae and the other major centres apparently served as 'Gateway Communities'.[39] Such 'Gateway Communities' act as entrances to or from an area, are characterized by long distance trade connections and are located on sites of transportational significance. The ensuing local redistribution, which dispersed the Orientalia from the 'Gateway Communities' to the surrounding villages, can best be described using the 'Central Place' model, which has been used in the past to describe the Mycenaean redistributive system.[40] In this model, a number of autonomous Central Places (generally either palaces or fortified citadels) are responsible for a surrounding territory, which is best described as a polygon with the Central Place at its nucleus. These areas, situated in what are defined as 'Thiessen Polygons', are interlocking but not overlapping, so that the territory of one borders that of others on all sides.[41] Such a model fits well with the distribution pattern of the Orientalia in the LBA Aegean area, for one can visualize a series of circular or polygonal distribution patterns, with a major site such as Mycenae in the centre of each territory. Of course, once in the Aegean area, some of the Orientalia will also have been subsequently reused in gift-exchanges and other high-level communications between the major LBA Aegean centres themselves.

Summary and Conclusions

In summary, an examination of the worked Orientalia found in LH I-III contexts at Mycenae reveals three categories of items: (1) functional trade-related objects; (2) ornamental 'bric-à-brac' from widely-scattered areas of the Eastern Mediterranean; and (3) inscribed Egyptian objects likely to be associated with more formal diplomatic contacts. The distribution pattern suggests that Mycenae, as a major LBA Aegean centre, served as a 'Gateway Community' for the importation of such foreign goods and was the focal point of a deliberate directional trade from Egypt and the Near East. Such trade, while on-going since at least the LH I period, reached a height in the LH IIIB period, just after the reign of Akhenaten - possibly as a result of Egyptian interest and of an Egyptian 'helping hand' in the Mycenaean destruction of LM IIIA2 Knossos.

By way of concluding, we should note that the Orientalia at LBA Mycenae are of interest not only in light of the leading role which Mycenae played in the Aegean during the 14th-11th centuries BC, but also because the ancient Greeks themselves believed that the origins of Mycenae were inextricably linked with Egypt and the Eastern Mediterranean. They not only held that Mycenae was ruled during the Late Bronze Age by the Atreid dynasty, whose ancestor Pelops had migrated from Anatolia, but they also believed that Mycenae was founded by Perseus, who was ostensibly of Egyptian descent - being the great-great-great-grandson of the brothers Danaus and Aegyptus.[42]

Notes

*The following article represents a comprehensive expansion and update of a paper originally presented at the February 1987 *Tell el-Amarna 1887-1987* conference in Chicago (Cline in press). New research and reappraisals conducted during 1988-1993 have significantly added to, and altered, the data presented in the original paper, which dealt only with the imports found in LH III contexts at Mycenae.

I would like to thank M J Cline, E B French, Sp. E Iakovidis and J D Muhly for comments and criticisms made on earlier drafts of this paper. G Cadogan, B D Craig, A B Knapp, P E McGovern, E J Peltenburg, D B O'Connor, D Silverman, L V Watrous and I J Winter kindly provided information on individual objects. I am particularly indebted to Dr E B French, the Ephoria of Nauplion and the Helleno-British excavations at Mycenae for permission to examine firsthand the objects discussed below and for additional permission to republish these objects. The references given for each object in the catalogue are either the primary, most useful, or most up-to-date discussions available; for a comprehensive listing of all references to an object, please refer to the appropriate entry in Cline (1994).

Funding for the initial research was received in the form of grants from the Archaeological Institute of America, the American Schools of Oriental Research and the U.S. Educational Foundation in Greece (Fulbright); this support is most gratefully acknowledged.

1. Also not included or discussed here are objects imported from regions other than Egypt or the Near East. Into this category fall a number of amber objects (Beck et al. 1972; Harding and Hughes-Brock 1974; Harding 1984; Bouzek 1985; Hughes-Brock 1985) and one stone 'winged-axe' mould probably of an Italian origin, the latter found in an LH IIIB context in the House of the Oil Merchant (Stubbings 1954, 297-98; Childe 1960, 575-8, fig. 72:16; Bouzek 1985, 151, fig. 75:1).

2. Amiran 1969, 140-1; Raban 1980; Bass 1986; *idem* 1987; Pulak 1988; Haldane 1993.

3. Taylour 1981, 1-2, plan 2.

4. See Mylonas 1981, 318-9.

5. Wace in Bennet 1953, 6; Killen 1985, 267-9; Knapp 1991, 42.

6. See Cline 1994.

7. Mellaart 1968, 188-9; Muhly 1974, 10; Hooker 1976, 131; Yakar 1976, 126; Mee 1978, 150; Macqueen 1986, 107-8; Mellaart 1986, 76. See now discussions in Cline 1991a; *idem* 1991b.

8. Wace 1953, 6-7, pl. 2a; Buchholz 1958, 36 (no. 35), pl. 5:1-2; Catling 1964, 269-95; Bass 1967, 61 (nos. 52-5);

Cadogan 1972, 9.

9. Catling 1964, 49; *idem* 1980, 14, 16-17; Cadogan 1972, 11-13, Muhly 1982, 254; Portugali and Knapp 1985, 77-8.

10. See now Kilian et al. 1981, 170, 184, fig. 40.5; Kilian 1983, 304; *idem* 1988b, 121, abb. 25 for Cypriot pottery at Tiryns; Watrous 1992 and Shaw 1978-86 for Cypriot pottery at Kommos, Crete; Bass 1986 and Pulak 1988 for Cypriot pottery on the Kas shipwreck. Cypriot vessels have been found elsewhere in the Aegean as well, including Khania on Crete, Aegina and Thera on the Islands, and Trianda and Ialysos on Rhodes. For a full compilation, see Cline 1994.

11. The discovery of over two hundred Cypriot sherds at Marsa Matruh, on the northern coast of Egypt, in the company of several Mycenaean and Minoan sherds and Canaanite jar fragments (White 1985, 10; *idem* 1986, 76-8, figs. 26-34), should be borne in mind during any new discussions of such trade or trade routes.

12. A number of lapis lazuli beads were found in Room 19 (Room with the Idols) of the Cult Centre at Mycenae (Taylour 1969, 92; *idem* 1981, 47-8). The lapis lazuli used in these beads most likely originated in the Badrakhshan region of northern Afghanistan, beyond even Mesopotamia. The beads have not been actively considered in these discussions because it cannot be ascertained at which point during the journey from Afghanistan to Mycenae the raw lapis lazuli was converted into finished beads. For discussions concerning the origin of the lapis lazuli and the routes by which it reached Mesopotamia and points further west, see among others Hermann 1968, Oppenheim 1970, 9-14, and Muhly 1973, *passim,* with references.

13. See e.g. Barag 1970, 189; Oates 1965, 73-4; *idem* 1966, 125. These two objects may well be part of a cache of objects looted from the 'shrine room' next to Room Gamma as suggested by Barag 1970, 190; see also Mylonas 1981, 310-1, pl. 15. One might therefore disagree with Craig (in Barag 1970, 191), who suggested that the religious association(s) of the plaque and the 'star disc' pendant were not understood by the Mycenaeans.

14. Porada 1981.

15. Harden 1981, 40.

16 This finding is in agreement with Vermeule 1975, 18-22; Hooker 1976, 45-54; Dickinson 1977, 53.

17. Cf. Smith 1965, 26, 29, 77, 155, fig. 37; Hankey 1993.

18. A number of lantern-shaped beads, most in faience, have been found in LH III contexts at Mycenae (Wace 1932, 94, 205-6, pl. IX g; Foster 1979, 145, fig. 97; Taylour 1983, 150, fig. 146). These beads have not been included here since their origins/manufacture are so ambiguous. As Taylour 1983, 150, states, this type of bead 'is possibly Syrian but it might equally well be of Mycenaean manufacture. It occurs in Greece, Rhodes, Cyprus, Syria and in Sicily' (see also Wace and Blegen 1939, 142; Wace 1949, 108; McGovern 1985, 77-8, 82 classifies these as Syro-Palestinian 'double-hubbed "wheel" pendants').

19. See now full discussion in Liverani 1986, 407, and Cline 1994.

20. Redford 1983, 482; also Cline 1987, 13-6.

21. Furumark 1944, 262.

22. Cf. Mountjoy 1986, 67; French 1965, 159.

23. See Taylour 1981, 9 on this phase; cf. also Iakovidis 1986.

24. Cline 1994.

25. Hallager 1977, 81-7; Niemeier 1983, 217.

26. Catling et al. 1963; Jones 1986, 542-71; Mommsen et al. 1992.

27. Cline 1994.

28. Cline 1987; Idem 1990; Parkinson and Schofield 1993.

29. Glotz 1925, 211-2, 226; Burn 1930, 99; Cline 1991b.

30. Weinstein 1973, 1xix; Cline 1987, 10-11; *idem* 1990, 200-12. There is also at Mycenae a sherd from an LH IIIB1 stirrup jar, upon which is depicted a dung beetle/scarab (French 1966, 219, 223, 228, pl. 48a). Such a motif may or may not be the result of contact with Egypt, but the sherd does appear to be unique in the Aegean; the motif is not to be found in either Furumark (1972) or Vermeule and Karageorghis (1982). Furthermore, the sherd was found in the Prehistoric Cemetery, Central (Areas III and IV) at Mycenae, in a deposit that might be of a 'votive' nature (French 1966, 217).

31. Cline 1987, 11-13; *idem* 1990.

32. Cline 1987, 11-12, Map 1. There is also now a scarab of Amenhotep III from Panaztepe on the western coast of Anatolia, in a context of LH IIIA pottery; see Erkanal 1986, 258; Mellink 1987, 13; Jaeger and Krauss 1990.

33. See most recently Helck 1979, 96-7; Hankey 1981, 45-6; Muhly 1982, 260-1; Wachsmann 1987, 95-9, 111-4; Cline 1987; *idem* 1990.

34. Detailed descriptions of royal gifts sent elsewhere by Amenhotep III and Akhenaten can be found in the Amarna Letters, i.e. EA 5, 14 and 31; see Moran 1992, updating Knudtzen 1915.

35. See note by French in Tamvaki 1973, 208.

36. The situation regarding imports in the LH IIIC Aegean may well reflect changes in settlement patterns and the like which seem to have occurred in the Aegean during this time; at Perati, for example, there are approximately fifty Egyptian and Near Eastern imports in LH IIIC contexts (Iakovidis 1970; *idem* 1980).

37. Kilian 1980; *idem* 1988a, 134, 151, n. 2, fig. 10; Iakovidis 1986; but *contra* Zangger 1991; Muhly 1992, 11.

38. Sherratt 1980.

39. As defined by Brughardt, Hirth, Hodges and Smith (cf. Smith 1987, 61-2, 65-6, 133-4, 136, 138, with earlier references).

40. Renfrew 1975, 13, 48, figs. 2-3; Cherry 1986, 21, 23, figs. 2.2, 2.4.

41. Cf. Hodder and Orton 1976, 59-60, fig. 4.3.

42. Paus. II.15.4 - II.16.2; Thuc. I.9.2; Pindar, *Olympian Ode* I.24; Apol. II.4.4.

CATALOGUE OF THE ORIENTALIA AT LBA MYCENAE

I. Figurines and Reliefs

a. Figurines

1. Figurine. Frit (Egyptian Blue). NMA no. 4573. Acropolis; in the vicinity of Mylonas' 'House of the High Priest'. LH IIIB2. Egypt. l8th Dynasty. **Plate 6, 2.**

Small blue frit (Egyptian Blue) figurine of squatting or sitting monkey; cartouche in yellow on right shoulder inscribed '3-ḫprw-r' (Aa-kheperu-re), prenomen of Amenhotep II; details on face incised and outlined in black; cheeks are yellow; in fragmentary condition, only head and upper torso extant; most likely, depiction of a Grivet or Green monkey; H: 3.5 cm; W: (body) 1.5 cm, (max) 2.0 cm; Th: 1.3 cm.

Similar figurine in LH IIIA context at Tiryns; cf. Kilian et al 1979: 405, 443, 447, abbs. 30 and 55a-c.

Hall 1901-2; 188, figure 13; Pendlebury 1930b: 55 (no. 85), 118, plate IV; Cline 1987: 21 n. 97, Table 3 no. D1; Lambrou-Phillipson 1990: 343-4 (no. 437), plate 82; Cline 1991c.

b. Statuettes

2. Statuette. Bronze. NMA no. 2631. House on Citadel to NE of Lion Gate; Building M or N. LH IIIB. Syro-Palestine. LB II.

Bronze 'Smiting God' statuette; high conical hat with knob at peak; well-modelled features: squarish face, large ears, short chin; big hands and feet; upper left arm held against side, then bent at elbow with forearm extended straight forward; right arm upraised; left leg forward; feet pegged below; wearing a short kilt; has short dagger over right hip; H: 11.3 cm.

Tsountas 1891: 21-2, plate II: 4-4a; Canby 1969: 142-3; Negbi 1976: 37, 40-1, 168 (no. 1408); Muhly 1980: 153-4; Seeden 1980: 128 (no. 1817), plate 114 (1817); Lambrou-Phillipson 1990: 353 (no. 479), plate 16.

c. Miscellaneous

3. Tusk, carved. Ivory. NMA no. 2916. Chamber Tomb no. 55. LH III A or B (14th-13th centuries BC). Syro-Palestine. LB.

Small carved ivory tusk, covered with decoration: plants and lotus blossoms, wild goats, falcons, etc; possible oil container; 'Egyptianizing' style is reminiscent of time of Amenhotep III; H (pres): 25.5 cm; Dm (base): 7.6 cm.

Poursat 1977b: 94-5 (no. 301), plates XXX-XXXI; Sakellariou 1985: 170, 174-5, plate 73; Lambrou-Phillipson 1990: 350 (no. 466), plate 24.

II.   Jewellery

a.   Beads

4.   Bead. Glass. NMA no. 6534(?). Chamber Tomb no. 516. LH I. Mesopotamia. MB or LB.

Multitubular spacer bead, of blue glass; uncommon decoration: two vertically ribbed oval beads cast in one piece with a flat back and horizontal ribbed borders at top and bottom in front; two holes for threading; L: 2.6 cm; W: 3.5 cm.

Wace 1932: 64-6, 207, figure 25: 5c; Haevernick 1965: 35-40; Barag 1970: 191, 193 n. 210; Cadogan 1976: 19; Harden 1981: 40 n. 36; Barag 1985: 36 n. 70, 38, 46.

5.   Bead. Glass. NMA no. 6534(?). Chamber Tomb no.516. LH I. Mesopotamia. MB or LB.

Multitubular spacer bead, of blue glass; with four tubular parts cast in one piece with a flat back; two holes for threading; broken.

Wace 1932: 64-6, 207, figure 25: 5b; Haevernick 1965: 35-40; Barag 1970: 191, 193; Cadogan 1976: 19; Harden 1981: 40 n. 36; Barag 1985: 36 n. 70, 38, 46.

6.   Bead. Glass, NMA no. 6535. Chamber Tomb no. 516. LH I. Mesopotamia. MB or LB.

Multitubular spacer bead, of blue glass; with four tubular parts cast in one piece with a flat back; two holes for threading; L: 3.0 cm; W: 3.0 cm.

Wace 1932: 64-6, 207, figure 25: 5b; Haevernick 1965: 35-40; Barag 1970: 191, 193; Cadogan 1976: 19; Harden 1981: 40 n. 36; Barag 1985: 36 n. 70, 38, 46.

7.   Bead. Glass. NMA no. 209.1. Shaft Grave 1, Circle A. LH I. Mesopotamia. 16th-13th centuries BC.

Multitubular spacer bead, with four tubular parts, of blue glass.

Karo 1930: 69, no. 209b, plate 150; Wace 1932: 66 n. 1; Haevernick 1960: 49-50; Haevernick 1965: 35-40; Barag 1970: 191, 193; Cadogan 1976: 19; Harden 1981: 40 n. 36; Barag 1985: 36 n. 70, 38, 46.

8.   Bead. Glass. NMA no. 209.2. Shaft Grave 1, Circle A. LH I. Mesopotamia. 16th-13th centuries BC.

Multitubular spacer bead, with four tubular parts, of blue glass.

Karo 1930: 69, no. 209b, plate 150; Wace 1932: 66 n. 1; Haevernick 1960: 49-50; Haevernick 1965: 35-40; Barag 1970: 191, 193; Cadogan 1976: 19; Harden 1981: 40 n. 36; Barag 1985: 36 n. 70, 38, 46.

9.   Bead. Glass. NMA no. 209.3. Shaft Grave 1, Circle A. LH I. Mesopotamia. 16th-13th centuries BC.

Multitubular spacer bead, with four tubular parts, of blue glass.

Karo 1930: 69, no. 209b, plate 150; Wace 1932: 66 n. 1; Haevernick 1960: 49-50; Haevernick 1965: 35-40; Barag 1970: 191, 193; Cadogan 1976: 19; Harden 1981: 40 n. 326; Barag 1985: 36 n. 70, 38, 46.

10.   Bead. Glass. NMA no. 209.4. Shaft Grave 1, Circle A. LH I. Mesopotamia. 16th-13th centuries BC.

Multitubular spacer bead, with four tubular parts, of blue glass.

Karo 1930: 69, no. 209b, plate 150; Wace 1932: 66 n. 1; Haevernick 1960: 49-50; Haevernick 1965: 35-40; Barag 1970: 191, 193; Cadogan 1976: 19; Harden 1981: 40 n. 36; Barag 1985: 36 n. 70, 38, 46.

b.   Pendants

11.   Pendant. Glass. NMA no. 2512. Room Gamma of shrine area of Tsountas House. LH IIIB. Mesopotamia. MB III-LB IIA (16th-13th centuries BC). **Plate 19,1.**

Moulded dark blue glass pendant adorned with eight-pointed star with eight bosses between the rays in high relief; suspension loop with horizontal divisions; H: 6.3 cm.

Tsountas 1886: 78-9; Tsountas 1887: 169, plate 13: 22; Barag 1970: 189-91, figure 100; Harden 1981: 40 n. 36; Barag 1985: 38, 46; McGovern 1985: 30, 35, 77, 82; cf. Grose 1989: 48, figures 20-21.

c.   Pins

12.   Pin. Bronze. NMA no. 2483. Tomb 52. LH IIIA-B. Syro-Palestine. LB?

Bronze roll-top pin; short in the shank, tip hammered flat and rolled tightly into a scroll; L: 18.0 cm.

Tsountas 1888: 157-8, 173, plate 9: 25; Catling 1964: 238; Sakellariou 1985: 131-2, plate 36 (no. 2483).

13.   Pin. Gold. NMA. Shaft Grave IV, Circle A. LH I. Anatolia. LB.

Gold pin, with head in the form of an Argali sheep, which is native to Anatolia.

Evans 1929: 43-5, figure 34b; Higgins 1980: 70-1.

III.   Scarabs, Seals and Plaques

a.   Scarabs

14.   Scarab. Faience. NMA no. 6495.1. Tomb 526. LH III. Egypt. 18th Dynasty.

Faience scarab, white with traces of green glaze; inscription possibly to be read 'nh Hr (Ankh-Hor), 'Horus lives'; L: 2.0 cm; W: 1.5 cm.

Pendlebury 1930b: 56 (no. 95), plate IV; Wace 1932: 93, 198, plate IX (no. 1); Cline 1987: 21 n. 97; Lambrou-Phillipson 1990: 345-6 (no. 450), plate 53.

15. Scarab. Faience. NMA no. 6495.2. Tomb 526. LH III. Egypt. 18th Dynasty.

Faience scarab; white, with traces of green glaze; inscription possibly to be read *s3t-m3't-r'* (Sat-Maat-Re).

Pendlebury 1930b: 56 (no. 96), plate IV; Wace 1932: 93, 198, plate IX (no. 2); Cline 1987: 21 n. 97; Lambrou-Philipson 1990: 346 (no. 451), plate 54.

16. Scarab. Faience. NMA no. 6495.3. Tomb 526. LH III. Cyprus (or local). LC?

Faience scarab, with designs; poor imitation of Egyptian work.

Burton-Brown says it is from North Mesopotamia.

Pendlebury 1930b: 56 (in no. 96); Wace 1932: 93, 199, plate IX (no. 3); Burton-Brown 1978: 161.

17. Scarab. Faience. Mycenae Exc. no. 68-1521. Cult Centre, Room 19 (Room with the Idols). LH IIIB (mid). Egypt. 18th Dynasty.

White faience scarab of Queen Tiy, wife of Amenhotep III; inscribed *ḥmt-nswt Tiy*, 'King's Wife, Tiy'; pierced longitudinally; L: 1.3 cm; W: 1.0 cm; Th: 0.6 cm; Dm (hole): 0.1 cm.

Taylour 1969: 92-3; Cline 1987: 9-10, figure 4, Table 1 no. E; Lambrou-Phillipson 1990: 344 (no. 439), plate 53.

18. Scarab. Faience. NMA no. 2530. Room Gamma of the shrine area of Tsountas House. LH IIIB. Egypt. 18th Dynasty.

Faience scarab of Queen Tiy, wife of Amenhotep III; inscribed *Tiy*, 'Tiy': L: 1.7 cm; W: 1.3 cm.

Tsountas 1887: 169, plate 13: 21-21a; Fimmen 1924: 176, abb. 172; Pendlebury 1930b: 55 (no. 88); Cline 1987: 8-10, figure 3, Table 1 no. D; Lambrou-Phillipson 1990: 344 (no. 438), plate 53.

19. Scarab. Lapis lazuli. NMA. Area beyond NW side of Grave Rho, Circle B. LH IIA. Egypt. 1450 BC (though debated).

Lapis lazuli scarab; possibly Egyptianizing rather than a true import.

Mylonas says it is part of original remains of Grave Rho; Boufides says it dates to 1700-1600 BC (Hyksos).

Mylonas 1966: 107; Boufides 1970: 273-4, figures 1-2; Hankey and Warren 1974: 145; Lambrou-Phillipson 1990: 342-3 (no. 436), plate 53.

b.   Seals

20. Seal. Faience. NMA no. 9095. Chamber Tomb 517. LH I-IIB. Syro-Palestine (Mitanni). 1450 BC.

Cylinder seal of blue faience; intaglio with two men with hats/helmets, a rampant wild goat, and a tree; Mitanni 'Common Style'; H: 2.3 cm; Dm: 0.87 cm; Dm (hole): 0.28 cm.

Found within pit in Chamber Tomb.

Wace 1932: 72-3 (no. 32), 197, figure 28, plate 35; Wace and Porada 1957: 201-3, plate 38b; Buchholz 1967: 157 (no. 52); Sakellarakis 1982: 33 (no. 6); Pini 1983: 115, figure 1:6; Lambrou-Phillipson 1990: 351 (no. 469), plate 13.

21. Seal. Faience. Mycenae Exc. no. 39-170. North Terrace deposit. LH IIIB1. Syro-Palestine (Mitanni). 13th century BC.

White faience cylinder seal, badly worn; had bird design and three human figures, separated by two trees; Mitanni 'Common Style'; H: 2.7 cm; Dm: 1.0 cm.

Perhaps originally from the Shrine of the Palace (Wace); Lambrou-Phillipson gives this NMA no. 1939.

Wace and Porada 1957: 197-204, plates 37a-b, 38a; Buchholz 1967: 157 (no.5l); Pini 1983: 115, figure 1:5; Lambrou-Phillipson 1990: 350-1 (no. 468), plate 13.

22. Seal. Haematite. NMA no. 2447. Chamber Tomb 47. LH IIB-IIIA1. Cyprus (or Crete). LC.

Cylinder seal of haematite, badly damaged; Four human figures in a row; H: 2.25 cm; Dm: 1.1. cm; Dm (hole): 0.6 cm.

Tsountas 1888: 151-4, 179-80, plate 10, no. 38; Buchholz 1967: 156 (no. 49); Pini 1980: 81-2 no. C6, 101-2, Abb. 18; Sakellarakis 1982: 30 (no. 3) with references; Porada 1985: 334-6; Sakellariou 1985: 120, 125, plate 34 (no. 2447); Lambrou-Phillipson 1990: 354 (no. 482), plate 13; Cline 1991a: 138 (no. 8).

23. Seal/Bulla. Steatite. NMA no. 6511. Chamber Tomb 523. LH IIIA2. Anatolia or Syro-Palestine. LB.

Hemispheroid steatite seal/semi-bulla; engraved with linear characters: a narrow edging of marks all around, with symbols/script inside; diametrically perforated; lentoid, planoconvex; Dm: 2.5 cm.

Hogarth 1920: 23; Wace 1932: 36-7, 203-4, plate 20 (no. 16); Sakellariou 1964: 175 (no. 156); Boardman 1966a: 47-8, figure 1; Boardman 1966b: 267; Erlenmeyer 1966: 49-50, 57, Abb. 1-2; Lambrou-Phillipson 1990: 355 (no. 485), plate 62; Cline 1991b: 136 (no. 7).

c.   Plaques

24. Plaque. Faience. Nauplion Mus. nos. 13-887, 13-888. Room M3, Building M (near North Wall of Citadel). LH IIIB2. Egypt. 18th Dynasty.

White faience plaque of Amenhotep III, in two fragments, originally green- or blue-glazed; inscribed *nṯr nfr Nb-m3't-r'*, 'the good god, Neb-Maat-Re', on both obverse and reverse sides; Measurements: 7.3 x 7.5 cm; 6.3 x 6.3 cm.

Mylonas 1963a: 67, figure 67; Mylonas 1963b: 101, figure

76; Hankey 1981: 45-6; Cline 1987: 9-10, figure 8, Table 1 no. B; Lambrou-Phillipson 1990: 345 (no. 447), plate 64; Cline 1990: 200-12.

25. Plaque. Faience. Mycenae Exc. nos. 68-1000, 69-126. Cult Centre, Room 31 (Room with the Fresco). LH IIIB (mid). Egypt. 18th Dynasty. **Plate 6,3.**

Partial white faience plaque of Amenhotep III, originally green-glazed, in two fragments; larger fragment (68-1000) has extant inscription, *nṯr nfr Nb-m3't-r' s[3] r[']* , 'the good god, Neb-Maat-Re, s[on of] R[e]', on both obverse and reverse sides; L: 9.8 cm; W: 11.2 cm; Th: 1.25-1.55 cm; smaller fragment (69-126): obverse with two black vertical lines, reverse completely worn away; L: 5.0 cm: W: 4.0 cm; Th: 1.3 cm.

Larger fragment found within Phase VII of room; smaller fragment found within Phase VIII of same room.

Taylour 1969: 95-6; Hankey 1981: 45-6; Harding 1984: 106; Taylour 1981: 49; Cline 1987: 9-10, figure 9, Table 1 no. C; Lambrou-Phillipson 1990: 345 (no. 448), plate 64; Cline 1990: 200-12.

26. Plaques. Faience. NMA nos. 2566.1-5, 2718, 12582. Area within Citadel, NE of Lion Gate (probably between Buildings M and N). LH IIIB (probable). Egypt. 18th Dynasty.

Seven fragments of white faience plaques, originally blue- or green-glazed; coming from four to seven original plaques, with varying portions of the inscribed prenomen and nomen of Amenhotep III, *nṯr nfr Nb-m3't-r' s3 r' Imn-ḥtp ḥk3 w3st di 'nḫ*, 'the good god, Neb-Maat-Re, son of Re, Amenhotep, Ruler of Thebes, given life', on both obverse and reverse sides; of varying dimensions.

Tsountas 1891: 18, 23-4, 30, plate III: 3-4; Cline 1987: 9-10, figures 6-7, Table 1 no. A; Lambrou-Phillipson 1990: 344-5 (nos. 440-6), plate 63; Cline 1990: 200-12.

27. Plaque. Glass. NMA no. 2511. Room Gamma of shrine area of Tsountas House. LH IIIB. Mesopotamia. MB III-LB IIA (16th-13th centuries BC). **Plate 19,2.**

Fragment of nude female plaque (or pendant); in moulded dark blue glass; head and neck only (Muller says portion of naked body once present); head is standing up in relief from a flat plaque with a rounded top; hair fluted above the brow; on unbroken side the hair frames face and ends in heavy curl on shoulder; possible threading hole at shoulder level; H (pres.): c. 2 cm; W (pres.): c. 2 cm.

Tsountas 1886: 78-9; Barag 1970: 188, 190-1; Harden 1981: 40 n. 36; Barag 1985: 38, 45; McGovern 1985: 30, 35, 77, 82; cf. Grose 1989: 39 (colour plate), 47, 58-9 (nos. 1-3), 397 (drawings).

IV. Vessels and Stands

a. Alabastra

28. Alabastron. Alabaster. NMA no. 3252. Chamber Tomb 81 (prob.). LH III. Egypt. 2nd Intermediate Period or 18th Dynasty.

Baggy alabastron with hole in bottom to make new rim; original rim presumably plugged with separate attachment; converted by Minoans c. MM III-LM I; H (orig.): 26.9 cm; Dm (rim): 6.5 cm (max): 23.5 cm (base, orig.): 10.8 cm.

Found by Tsountas during the 1895 season.

Sakellariou 1985: 266 (no. 3252), plate 130; 3252; Phillips 1991: 842 no. 457.

29. Alabastron. Alabaster. NMA no. 95. Treasury of Atreus; deposit of earth before door. LH IIIA2 (early). Egypt. 18th Dynasty.

Four fragments of a baggy, flat-bottomed alabastron; wide flat lip.

Wace 1921-3: 356; Pendlebury 1930b: 57 (no. 99); Warren 1969: 108, 114; Lambrou-Phillipson 1990: 347 (no. 458).

30. Alabastron. Alabaster. NMA. Tomb of Clytemnestra, within doorway and dromos. LH IIIA2 (late)/B1. Egypt. 18th Dynasty.

Two fragments of a baggy, flat-bottomed alabastron; wide flat lip.

Wace 1921-3: 367; Pendlebury 1930b: 57 (no. 100); Warren 1969: 108, 114; Lambrou-Phillipson 1990: 348 (no. 459).

31. Alabastron. Alabaster. Mycenae Exc. no. 54-565. House of Shields, Ivory Deposit, NE area. LH IIIB (mid). Egypt. 18th Dynasty.

Body fragment of an Egyptian alabastron; broken, burnt; H (pres.): 10.0 cm; W: 8.4 cm; Th: 0.06 cm.

Not found by Warren when looked for in 1965, but found again in 1968.

Unpublished.

32. Alabastron. Alabaster. Nauplion Mus. no. 12356 = Mycenae Exc. no. 53-787. House of Shields, further extension of East wall, surface. LH IIIB (mid). Egypt. 18th Dynasty.

Body fragment from large baggy alabastron; H: 8.8 cm; W: 3.1 cm; Th: 1.5 cm.

Wace 1954a: 237; Wace 1954b: 158; Wace 1956: 116; Warren 1969: 108, 114; Lambrou-Phillipson 1990: 347 (no. 456).

33. Alabastron. Alabaster. Nauplion Mus. no. 12359 = Mycenae Exc. no. 53-162. House of Shields, Ivory Area, in SW section. LH IIIB (mid). Egypt. 18th Dynasty. **Plate 7,1.**

Conical, flat-bottomed 'baggy type' alabastron, in eleven fragments; about one-half of jar left; light grey to ivory, with darker grey markings; fluted grey markings around jar; H: 13.4 cm.

Wace 1954b: 158(?); Warren 1969: 108, 114; Lambrou-

Phillipson 1990: 347 (no. 455).

34. Alabastron. Alabaster. Nauplion Mus. no. 14690 = Mycenae Exc. no. 59-230. Citadel House area, North end of Room II below Megaron. LH IIIB (prob.). Egypt. 18th Dynasty.

Rim fragment from baggy, flat-bottomed alabastron; H: 2.6 cm; W (rim): 3.6 cm; Th (rim): 0.6 cm; Dm (rim): 12.5 cm.

Warren 1969: 108, 114.

35. Alabastron. Alabaster. Mycenae Exc. no. 64-774. Citadel House area. LH IIIC (middle) or Post-Mycenaean. Egypt. 18th Dynasty.

Small body fragment from baggy flat-bottomed alabastron; H (max): 5.6 cm; W (min): 1.5 cm; W (max): 3.2 cm; Th (min): 0.5 cm; Th (max): 1.1 cm.

Context redated since Warren's publication.

Warren 1969: 108, 114; Lambrou-Phillipson 1990: 347 (no. 457).

b.   Amphorae

36. Amphora. Ceramic. Tomb. LH IIIA. Syro-Palestine. LB.

Canaanite jar; no description available.

Found by E. Palailogou.

Kilian 1988a: 127, figure 4.

37. Amphora. Ceramic. NMA no. 2924. Chamber Tomb no. 58. LH IIIA or B. Syro-Palestine. LB II (15th-14th centuries BC).

Canaanite jar; from area of Tyre; brownish clay with greenish-buff surface layer; angular shoulder; three signs incised on one handle; Raban's Type III: Angular, Classic Jar; H: 55.0 cm; Dm: 25.3 cm.

Tsountas 1893: 213-4, figures 1-2; Grace 1956: 81-82, 86, 100, 102-3, plate IX: 5-6, figure 8; Akerstrom 1975: 187, 191, figure 11; Raban 1980: 6, Tables D5: 13; E4: 5; Sakellariou 1985: 179, 184, plate 78; Lambrou-Phillipson 1990: 353 (no. 478), plate 34.

38. Amphora. Ceramic. NMA no. 2925. Chamber Tomb no. 58. LH IIIA or B. Syro-Palestine. LB II (15th-14th centuries BC).

Canaanite jar; from area of Tyre; brownish clay with greenish-buff surface layer; shoulder less steep and less convex than on NMA no. 2924; Raban's Type III: Angular, Classic Jar; H: 48.0 cm.

Tsountas 1893: 213-4, figures 1-2; Grace 1956: 81-2, 86, 102; Akerstrom 1975: 187, 191, figure 12; Raban 1980: 6, Tables D5: 14; E4: 7; Sakellariou 1985: 179, 184; Lambrou-Phillipson 1990: 353 (no. 477), plate 34.

39. Amphora. Ceramic. NMA no. 4569. Chamber Tomb no. 95. LH IIIA or B. Syro-Palestine. LB II (15th-14th centuries BC).

Canaanite jar; from area of Tyre; brownish clay with greenish surface layer; plastic neckridge; shoulder flatter, sharper-edged than other jars; each handle incised with a different mark; Raban's Type III: Angular, Classic Jar; H: 54.0 cm; Dm: 25.7 cm.

Grace 1956: 81-2, 86, 88, 100, 104, plate X: 1, 5, 6, figure 8; Akerstrom 1975: 187, 191, figure 13; Raban 1980: 6, Tables D5: 15, E4: 6; Sakellariou 1985: 271, 273, plate 134; Lambrou-Phillipson 1990: 352-3 (no. 476), plate 35.

40. Amphora. Ceramic. Mycenae Exc. no. 66-518. Citadel House, Room 36, Floor 2. LH IIIB (mid). Syro-Palestine. LB II(?). **Plate 19,3**.

Fragments of one Canaanite jar; shoulder area with handle, plus body fragment with second handle; red clay (grey at core) with very fine grit; red wash surface; carinated with sloping shoulder and tapering lower body; two handles from below carination; H (pres.): 12.5 cm; Dm (shoulder): 26.0 cm; Th: 2.0 cm.

Unpublished, but see Taylour 1981: 40 for description of area and associated finds.

41. Amphora. Ceramic. Mycenae Exc. no. 50-513 = Nauplion Mus. no. 5384. House of the Oil Merchant, among stirrup jars. LH IIIB. Syro-Palestine. LB II. **Plate 19,4.**

Canaanite jar fragments; thin, buff, sandy fabric; large section with rim, neck, gently sloping shoulder and handle; H (pres.): c. 26.0 cm; Dm (shoulder): c. 27.0 cm; Dm (mouth): 18.0 cm.

Akerstrom 1975: 187; Onassoglou 1979: 36; Yannai 1983: 122 n. 71.

42. Amphora. Ceramic. Mycenae Exc. no. 54-601 = Nauplion Mus. no. 11454. South House Annex storeroom (Room l/'Reservoir'). LH IIIB2. Syro-Palestine. LB II. **Plate 7,2.**

Canaanite jar, some fragments of shoulder missing; pale, very hard, buff, sandy clay; surface worn; nearly flat, rather narrow shoulders; fairly short neck; lower body core-shaped, flattened on bottom; deep moulding outside lip; vertical handles below shoulder; red double-axe or butterfly and other design below shoulder; H: c. 50.0 cm.

Bennett 1953: 76-7 (no. 601); Wace 1955a: 179, plate 20b; Wace 1955b: 927, figure 3; Grace 1956: 86-7; Akerstrom 1975: 187-8, 191-2; Lambrou-Phillipson 1990: 352 (no. 475), plate 34.

43. Amphora. Ceramic. Mycenae Exc. no. 60-214. Debris of area to the north of the South House ('Causeway Deposit'). LH IIIB2. Syro-Palestine. LB II.

Canaanite jar, handle; gritty brick-red fabric, coarse, with much chaff; whitish surface wash; straight-sided jar with sloping shoulder; vertical flattened handle; linear sign inscribed on handle after firing; possibly Raban's Type II: Bi-Conical Jar; H (handle): 9.0 cm; W (at top of handle): 4.8 cm.

Wardle 1973: 298 (no. 194), 328, 331, figure 18, plate 59d; Helck 1979: 116.

44. Amphora. Ceramic. Mycenae Exc. no. 64-489. Citadel House, wash up against Cyclopaean Wall. LH IIIC (middle). Syro-Palestine. LB II.

Canaanite jar, lower body only (without base); very heavy reddish buff fabric with much fine sandy grit; pale whitish buff wash; H (pres.): 10.0 cm; Th: 2.0-4.0 cm.

Unpublished.

c.　**Bowls**

45. Bowl/dish. Faience. NMA no. 2719. Area within Citadel, north-east of Lion Gate (between Buildings M and N). LH IIIB (prob.). Egypt. 18th Dynasty.

Fragment of faience bowl/dish; yellow with black design.

Tsountas 1891: 18, 23-4, 30, plate III; Fimmen 1924: 175-6, abb. 171; Hankey 1981: 45-6; Cline 1990: 206.

46. Bowl. Faience. Mycenae Exc. no. 53-320. House of Shields, Ivory Area. LH IIIB (mid). Syro-Palestine (North Syria). LB.

Fragment of base of white faience bowl; very worn; may once have been green; L (max): 2.7 cm; W (max): 4.0 cm.

Peltenburg 1987; Peltenburg 1991: 171.

47. Bowl. Diorite or Gabbro. NMA no. 2778. Acropolis (1886). LH I-III. Egypt (possibly via Crete). Predynastic-Early Dynastic Period.

High-shouldered bowl of gabbro or diorite; grey/black/brown with white massed crystals; rope or coil mouldings carved around edge of rim; high shoulders; three pairs of holes on rim near mouth for addition of separate handles; H: 14.0 cm; Dm (max): 25.0 cm; Dm (rim): 18.1 cm; Dm (base): 11.2 cm.

Probably altered by Minoans before reaching Mainland.

Warren 1969: 107, 114; Lambrou-Phillipson 1990: 348 (no. 460); Phillips 1991: 844 (no. 459).

48. Bowl. Diorite or Gabbro. Mycenae Exc. no. 55-51 = Nauplion Mus. no. 11505. House of the Sphinxes, Room 10, burnt layer. LH IIIB (mid). Egypt (possibly via Crete). Early Dynastic Period/Old Kingdom. **Plate 20,1.**

Rim/body fragment of high-shouldered bowl of diorite or gabbro; grey/white, black, green/black, splodgy; three shallow grooves cut around the flat collar; H (pres.): 6.5 cm; W: 1.2 cm.

Warren says this is a Minoan adaption of an Egyptian vase, with parallels; possibly fallen from upper floor.

Wace 1956: 116, plate 24b; Warren 1969: 107, 114; Lambrou-Phillipson 1990: 340 (no. 429), plate 73; Phillips 1991: 846 (no. 460).

49. Bowl. Porphyrite. NMA no.? Tomb 515 (Pendlebury) or 518 (Warren). LH I-IIIA. Egypt (possibly via Crete). 1st-4th Dynasty.

Rim fragment of bowl, of porphyritic rock, white crystals in black matrix; small, slightly undercut collar; W: 5.5 cm.

Warren says this is unlikely to be a direct import to the Mainland at this date; more likely came via Crete.

Pendlebury 1930b: 53, 57 (no. 97); Wace 1932: 84, 223; Warren 1969: 107, 114; Lambrou-Phillipson 1990: 342 (no. 435).

d.　**Goblets**

50. Goblet. Faience. NMA 2372. Chamber Tomb 49. LH IIIA1. Cyprus. LC 1.

Faience goblet with stylized relief lotus petals; five fragments, including two rim fragments, each with traces of one or two pointed petals in relief; traces of yellow and brown glaze.

Tsountas 1888: 155; Cadogan 1972: 10; Peltenburg 1983: 214, figure 539; Sakellariou 1985: 128, plate 35; Lambrou-Phillipson 1990: 354 (no. 483).

e.　**Jars**

51. Jar. Alabaster. NMA no 829. Shaft Grave V, Circle A. LH I. Egypt (via Crete). 18th Dynasty.

Alabaster jar; originally an 18th Dynasty baggy, flat-bottomed alabastron; modified by MM III-LM I Minoans by being turned upside-down and with addition of spout and gold leaf; wide piriform body; shoulder handles; hollow, footed, moulded base with separate flat plug; holes cut for attachment of separate spout, gold leaf around rim, handles and foot; H: 14.5 cm; Dm (max): 12.3 cm; DM (rim): 6.1 cm; Dm (jar base): 6.0 cm.

Karo 1930: 147, plate 137; Warren 1967: 44 (Q2), plate VII: Q2; Warren 1969: 43, 104, 107-8, 115; Sakellarakis 1976: 177, plate II: 4; Phillips 1991: 839 (no. 455).

52. Jar. Diorite. NMA no 2919. Chamber Tomb 55. LH IIIA or IIIB. Egypt (possibly via Crete). Predynastic.

Heart-shaped jar of diorite; black speckled with white; two horizontal pierced lugs on shoulder; two handles; H: 14.8 cm.

Evans 1928: 31 n 1; Warren 1969: 107, 114; Sakellarakis 1976: 178, plate IV, 8.

f.　**Jugs**

53. Jug. Faience. NMA nos. 123 and 124. Shaft Grave III, Circle A. LH I. Egypt or local. 18th Dynasty (?).

Two fragments of pale-green faience, from a beaked jug; inscribed/painted are two men's heads with banded, horned helmets and top of great shields; Shardana?; L: c. 6.0 cm.

Pendlebury thinks it is Egyptian; Hall unconvinced re-Egypt; Foster thinks it is local Mycenaean.

Karo 1930: 60-1, figure 16, plate 23; Pendlebury 1930b: 53, 56 (no. 90); Foster 1979: 125-6, figure 86, plate 33; Schuchhardt 1979: 207-8, figure 198; Lambrou-Phillipson 1990: 348-9 (no.462), plate 77.

54. Jug (or Ewer). Alabaster. NMA no.3080. Chamber Tomb 68. LH II-III. Egypt, via Crete. 18th Dynasty.

Large jug/ewer; high shoulder, tapering body, flat base, no neck or articulated rim, converted from 18th Dynasty baggy, flat-bottomed alabastron in Minoan Crete, original alabastron turned upside-down, original mouth plugged, hole cut out of the original base to receive the separate neck; new neck and handle each separately made of white limestone; an MM III-LM I export to Mycenae; H: 21.3 cm; Dm (max): 21.2 cm; Dm (rim): 4.9 cm; Dm (base): 9.4 cm.

Warren 1967: 48 (Q5); Warren 1969; 43, 44, 107, 108, 115; Phillips 1991: 840-1 (no. 456).

55. Jug. Stone. NMA no. 4923. Chamber Tomb 102. LH II. Egypt (possibly via Crete). 18th Dynasty.

Stone jug; globular body; cylindrical neck; strap handle passing around neck in two prongs; H: c. 18.0 cm.

MM III-LM I export to Mycenae from Crete; Warren corrects for museum number, Pendlebury corrects for findspot.

Bosanquet 1904: 325-6, plate XIVe; Pendlebury 1930b: 57 (no.98); Warren 1969: 43, 107-8, 115; Lambrou-Phillipson 1990: 346 (no.452), plate 74.

g.   Kylikes

56. Kylix. Faience. NMA no 7505 = Mycenae Exc. no.53-311. House of Shields, Ivory Area. LH IIIB (mid). Syro-Palestine (North Syria). LB.

Fragments of bowl and base of a kylix; white faience with light blue glaze and brown lines; fragmentary, with glaze almost worn off; X pattern along top of rim and below rim, two horizontal lines 2.2 cm below rim, then vertical lines converging towards bottom; dotted lozenge garland; rosette base; Bowl: H (pres.): 7.3 cm; W (rim): 1.3 cm; Base: H (pres.): 4.2 cm; Dm: 9.4 cm.

Wace 1954a: plate 36a; Wace 1956: plate 18 (drawing); Peltenburg 1987; Peltenburg 1991: 171, plate 1d.

57. Kylix. Faience. NMA no. 7506 = Mycenae Exc. no. 53-312. House of Shields, Ivory Area. LH IIIB (mid). Syro-Palestine (North Syria). LB.

Polychrome faience handle, probably from a kylix; cream coloured; yellow, red and blue lozenges bordered by blue and white squares on either side; H (pres.): 6.7 cm; W: 2.1 cm; Th: 0.6 cm.

Wace 1954a: plate 36a; Wace 1956: plate 21a (drawing); Peltenburg 1987; Peltenburg 1991: 171, plate 3 (inset).

58. Kylix. Faience. NMA no 7507 = Mycenae Exc. no.53-314. House of Shields, Ivory Area. LH IIIB (mid). Syro-Palestine (North Syria). LB.

Five fragments (joined) of a white faience kylix (like NMA no 7505); very fragmentary; poor glaze; X design along flat top of rim; decoration of brown lines; petals, two papyri and loop (Nile skiff?); L (pres.): 7.0 cm; W (pres.): 4.1 cm.

Peltenburg 1987; Peltenburg 1991: 171.

59. Kylix. Faience. NMA no 7512 = Mycenae Exc. no. 54-563. House of Shields, north-east area, Section V. LH IIIB (mid). Syro-Palestine (North Syria). LB.

Two fragments of a faience kylix, one from rim (with end of handle); broken, burnt, paint peeling off in places; dark brown/blue decoration; rim fragment has zigzag garland pattern; body fragment has rope pattern; similar to Mycenae Exc. no. 54-416, but not joined; L (rim frag.): 6.0 cm; W: 5.0 cm.

Peltenburg 1987; Peltenburg 1991: 171.

60. Kylix. Faience. NMA no 7513 = Mycenae Exc. no. 54-564. House of Shields, north-east area. LH IIIB (mid). Syro-Palestine (North Syria). LB.

Base fragment of kylix; decoration of lotus blossom, sepals on arcs.

Peltenburg 1987; Peltenburg 1991: 171.

61. Kylix. Faience. NMA no 7515 = Mycenae Exc. no. 55-216. House of Shields, Area 1, Black layer (= North Room). LH IIIB (mid). Egypt. 18th Dynasty (?).

Part of bowl and base of white faience kylix, with green glaze and black paint; tongue pattern design under rim; flower pattern on body (= lotus flower); lotus base, petal garland; Base: H: 5.1 cm; Dm: 8.7 cm; Bowl: Th (lip): 1.3 cm; H (pres.): 6.6 cm.

Bennett 1953: 25, f. 24; Wace 1954a: plate 36a lower left; Wace 1956: 110, plate 19; Wace and Williams 1963: 11, plate 1a; Peltenburg 1987; Lambrou-Phillipson 1990: 349 (no. 463), Peltenburg 1991: 171, plate 1b.

62. Kylix. Faience. Mycenae Exc. no. 53-318. House of Shields, Ivory Area. LH IIIB (mid). Syro-Palestine (North Syria). LB.

Three joined fragments of kylix handle with zoomorphic terminal; white faience, brown lines; may once have been green; four parallel lines the length of the handle; Span: 4.7 cm; Distance from bowl: 2.6 cm.

Peltenburg 1987; Peltenburg 1991: 171.

63. Kylix. Faience. Mycenae Exc. no. 55-401 = Nauplion Mus. no. 12839. House of Shields, Area VIII, Black layer. LH IIIB (mid). Syro-Palestine (North Syria). LB.

Four fragments including one rim piece, of a white faience kylix with green glaze; very broken, worn and friable; decoration in black paint: band around top of lip; largest piece; 5.2 cm x 2.7 cm.

Peltenburg 1987; Peltenburg 1991: 171.

64. Kylix. Faience. Mycenae Exc. no. 55-402 = Nauplion Museum no. 12957. House of Shields, Area I, Black layer. LH IIIB (mid). Syro-Palestine (North Syria). LB.

Four fragments of a white faience kylix; decoration in black paint: row of triangles and row of ovals, separated by double lines; also linked petals, zigzags and lozenges; broken, worn, very friable; largest piece: H: 4.9 cm; W: 9.4 cm; Th: 0.6 cm.

Peltenburg 1987; Peltenburg 1991: 171.

h. Pyxides

65. Pyxis. Ivory. NMA no 9506. Tomb 88. LH IIIA1. Syro-Palestine or Egypt. LB.

Ivory pyxis, in the shape of a ship; made from lower canine of a hippopotamus; L: 20.2 cm; W: 7.9 cm; Th: 3.3 cm.

Sakellarakis 1971: 188-233, figures 1-2, 13 plates 34-5, 39-40, 46-7; Poursat 1977a: 28; Poursat 1977b: 99 (no. 316), plate XXXIII; Krzyszkowska 1988: 233-4.

i. Rhyta

66. Rhyton. Faience. NMA no 7510 = Mycenae Exc. no. 54-416. House of Shields, north-east area, Sections III, IV, V. LH IIIB (mid). Syro-Palestine (North Syria). LB.

Top half of an elongated-ovoid faience rhyton made in three pieces (neck, shoulders, base); neck splayed with a vertical loop handle; bluish glaze with black or dark brown decoration: diagonal bands with spirals bordered on either side by a sort of rope pattern; badly broken and burnt; H (pres.): 14.6 cm; Dm: 12.5 cm; H (neck): 5.5 cm; Dm (lip): 8.0 cm.

Wace 1956: 111, figure 11, plate 20; Peltenburg 1987; Peltenburg 1991: 171.

67. Rhyton. Faience. NMA no 7511 = Mycenae Exc. no. 54-417. House of Shields, north-east area, Section I. LH IIIB (mid). Syro-Palestine (North Syria). LB.

Fragment from the lip of a faience rhyton, slightly splaying; dark brown decoration added; on body, head of a man with arm raised in the attitude of a warrior; on lip: running chevron pattern; broken, burnt; H (pres.): 8.0 cm; W: 7.5 cm.

Wace 1956: plate 17c (drawing); Peltenburg 1987; Peltenburg 1991: 171, plate 2b.

68. Rhyton. Faience. NMA no. 7514 = Mycenae Exc. no. 55-213. House of Shields, Area VIII, north-west corner. LH IIIB (mid). Syro-Palestine (North Syria). LB.

Fragment of white faience, possibly from a rhyton; green surface glaze; decoration in black paint of head of a warrior with helmet, arm raised behind head, above this a band with

lozenge design, dots in centre of each; very worn, chipped, friable; H: 3.3 cm; W: 5.0 cm; Th: 1.3 cm.

Wace 1956: plate 17a-b; Wace and Williams 1963: 11, plate 1d; Peltenburg 1987; Peltenburg 1991: 171, plate 2a.

69. Rhyton. Silver. NMA no. 388. Shaft Grave IV, Circle A. LH I. Anatolia. 16th century BC (probably).

Silver rhyton cast in shape of a stag, with one antler remaining; spout rising from the centre of its back: Weight 2.5 kg; H: 16.2 cm; H (with antlers): 21.7 cm; L: 25.5 cm; W: 9.0 cm.

New tests indicate it is of silver, not of 2/3 silver and 1/3 lead as Schliemann reported; found in a copper vessel in southeast corner of Shaft Grave.

Schliemann 1878: 257, no. 376; Karo 1930: 94, plates 115-6; Schuchhardt 1979: 245-6, 249, n. 247; Stos-Gale 1985: 72; Lambrou-Phillipson 1990: 335 (no. 486), plate 76; Cline 1991a; 134-5 (no.3); Stos-Gale and Macdonald 1991: 271-2, 285.

j. Vases

70. Vase. Faience. NMA no. 223. Shaft Grave II, Circle A. LH 1. Egypt. 18th Dynasty.

Faience vase, pale yellow; squat, knobbed, with four legs and traces of black markings on the rim; H: c. 20.0 cm.

Karo 1930: 71, plate 170; Pendlebury 1930b: 55 (no. 89); Foster 1979: 121-2, figure 85; Lambrou-Phillipson 1990: 348 (no. 461).

71. Vase. Frit (Egyptian Blue). NMA no. 2491. Chamber Tomb 49. LH IIIA. Egypt. 18th Dynasty.

Vase of Egyptian Blue, inscribed ['Imn]-ḥtp ḥk3 w3st, '[Amen]hotep, Ruler of Thebes'; design of lotus leaves in light and dark blue, with white-filled incisions; H: 11.3 cm.

Tsountas 1888: 156, figures 10, 10a; Hall 1901-2: 188-9, Fimmen 1924: 175, abb.170; Pendlebury 1930b: 56 (no. 91); Sakellariou 1985: 127-8, plate 35; Cline 1987: 8, figure 5, Table 1 no. F; Delivorrias 1987: 150-1, illustration 47; Lambrou-Phillipson 1990: 345 (no. 449), plate 75.

72. Vase or Krateriskos. Glass. NMA no. 4530. Acropolis. LH III (probably). Egypt. New Kingdom.

Fragment of glass vase/krateriskos; identical in shape to a common type of Egyptian glass vase; brownish in colour with thread decoration in white; probably originally blue, core-formed.

Marinatos 1927-8: 83; Fossing 1940: 25; Weinberg 1961-2: 279; Harden 1981: 31 and n. 6.

73. Vase. Alabaster. NMA nos. 2657 and 6250. Acropolis. LH I-III (probably). Egypt. Old Kingdom.

Two fragments of an alabaster toilet-vase in the shape of a monkey (mother holding her baby); NMA no. 2657 = body,

104

NMA no.6250 = face; H (approx.): 16.0 cm.

Sakellarakis 1976: 178-9, plate IV, 9; Lambrou-Phillipson 1990; 342 (no. 434), plate 74; Phillips 1991: 378; Cline 1991c: 38.

k.   Vessels

74.   Vessel. Faience. NMA no. 7507 (also) = Mycenae Exc. no. 53-313. House of Shields, Ivory Area. LH IIIB (mid). Syro-Palestine (North Syria). LB.

Fragment of polychrome faience vessel; white, yellow and brown decoration; three grayish parallel lines, horizontal; above them a yellow shell, outlined in brown; L (pres.): 4.7 cm; W (pres.): 3.5 cm.

Peltenburg 1987; Peltenburg 1991: 171.

75.   Vessel. Faience. NMA no. 7508 = Mycenae Exc. no. 53-315. House of Shields, Ivory Area. LH IIIB (mid). Syro-Palestine (North Syria). LB.

Two small white faience fragments from vessel; some glaze; yellow and brown decoration; once possibly blue; bands and petal tips visible on fragments; H (pres.): 4.8 cm; W (pres.): 3.7 cm.

Peltenburg 1987; Peltenburg 1991: 171.

76.   Vessel. Faience. NMA no. 7508 (also) = Mycenae Exc. no. 53-316. House of Shields, Ivory Area. LH IIIB (mid). Syro-Palestine (North Syria). LB.

Fragment of white faience from flat-rimmed vessel; signs of light blue on rim once, possibly also on inside; glaze gone, very worn; H (pres.): 4.7 cm; W (pres.): 4.2 cm; W (rim): 1.3 cm.

Twenty other fragments of various faience vessels are also listed with this Mycenae excavation number, according to Peltenburg. Decoration is dark brown on fragments which have it; one fragment decorated with diagonal stripes; average size: L: 3.5 cm; W: 3.2 cm; Th: 1.2 cm.

Peltenburg 1987; Peltenburg 1991: 171.

77.   Vessel. Faience. NMA no. 7508 (also) = Mycenae Exc. no. 53-317. House of Shields, Ivory Area. LH IIIB (mid). Syro-Palestine (North Syria). LB.

Fragment of white (polychrome) faience, decorated; yellow, light blue, brown decoration; worn edges; glaze good; two parallel horizontal blue bands, above them what appears to be a yellow lion's foot, banded in brown; H (pres.): 2.1 cm; W (pres.): 4.4 cm.

Peltenburg 1987; Peltenburg 1991: 171.

78.   Vessel. Faience. NMA no. 7509 = Mycenae Exc. no. 53-362. House of Shields, Ivory Area, LH IIIB (mid). Syro-Palestine (North Syria). LB.

Five fragments of a white faience vessel; worn at edges, fair glaze; yellow, blue, brown decoration; on one sherd the hind-quarters and tail of a lion in yellow, outlined in brown; on another, the head of a blue bird outlined in brown, with a yellow ground; Lion: L (pres.): 2.3 cm; W (pres.): 2.2 cm; Bird: L (pres.): 2.7 cm; W (pres.): 2.0 cm.

Wace 1956: plate 21b; Wace and Williams 1963: 11, plate 1e; Peltenburg 1987; Peltenburg 1991: 171.

79.   Vessel. Faience. Mycenae Exc. no. 53-319. House of Shields, Ivory Area. LH IIIB (mid). Syro-Palestine (North Syria). LB.

Two fragments of vessel base, of white faience; very worn; H (pres.): 1.4 cm.

Peltenburg 1987; Peltenburg 1991: 171.

80.   Vessel. Faience. Nauplion Mus. no. 12209 = Mycenae Exc. no. 53-366. House of Shields, Central part in red fill. LH IIIB (mid). Syro-Palestine (North Syria). LB. **Plate 20,2**.

Faience handle with ears of an animal head at top; condition good but glaze worn; face of animal broken off; rounded on top, flat beneath; grey core, green outside; pattern along handle, up to animal ears in relief; L (pres.): 6.0 cm; W: 1.1 cm.

Peltenburg 1987.

l.   Wall-brackets

81.   Wall-bracket. Terracotta. NMA no. 2633. Acropolis (probably). LH III(?). Cyprus (Syro-Palestine?). LC.

Terracotta wall-bracket; oblong plate perforated at one extremity with a hole by which it was suspended; lower end forms a scoop-like receptacle.

Stäis 1926: 118 (no. 2633); Leipen 1960: 24; Caubet and Yon 1974: 121 n. 8; Bass, Frey and Pulak 1984: 273, 276.

V.   Weapons and Tools

a.   Armour Scales

82.   Armour scale. Bronze. Mycenae Exc. no. 68-323. Citadel House area. LH IIIC (early). Syro-Palestine. LB. **Plate 20,3**.

Scale of bronze armour; sub-rectangular; top, two sides straight, bottom convex, has rib and groove, 5-6 holes; is from a scale corslet made from several hundred similar scales attached by lacing to a heavy undergarment; L: 5 cm; W: 2 cm.

Widely used in Near East from 16th century on; Helck says possibly Hurrian in origin. Cf. Muhly 1984: 42 n. 15 for recent finds elsewhere in the Mediterranean area.

Catling 1970: 441, 449, figure 1; Karageorghis and Masson 1975: 211-2, figure 4; Helck 1979: 117; Catling 1986: 97.

VI.   Weights and Measures

a.   Weights

83.   Weight. Haematite. Mycenae Exc. no. 60-18. Debris of area to the north of the South House. LH IIIB2. Syro-Pal-estine. LB II?

Haematite weight, sphendenoid shape (biconical with trun-cated ends and flattened on one side); L: 4.6 cm; W (max): 1.9 cm; Weight: 34.5 grams (may be a multiple [3x] of 11.50 gram Hebrew shekel).

Bass 1967: 140, figure 149; Wardle 1973: 298, 337, 340-2, figure 22c; Eran and Edelstein 1977: 56.

84. Weight. Haematite. Mycenae Exc. no. 64-959. Cita-del House. LH IIIC (early). Syro-Palestine. LB II? **Plate 20,4.**

Haematite weight, sphendenoid shape; biconical with trun-cated ends and flattened on one side; ends worn; similar to Mycenae Exc. no. 60-18, but larger and heavier; L: 5.3 cm; Dm (centre, max.): 2.7 cm; Weight (c.): 78.0 grams.

Unpublished.

VII. Raw Material

a. Elephant Tusks

85. Elephant Tusk. Ivory. NMA no. 491. Shaft Grave IV, Circle A. LH. I. Syro-Palestine. LB.

Tip of an ivory elephant tusk, apparently unworked.

Karo 1930: 109; Krzyszkowska 1988: 212, 231, plate 24a.

86. Elephant Tusk. Ivory. NMA no. 899. Shaft Grave V, Circle A. LH I. Syro-Palestine. LB.

Tip of an ivory elephant tusk, apparently unworked; L: 3.7 cm.

Karo 1930: 154-5, figure 73; Krzyszkowska 1988: 231.

87. Elephant Tusk. Mycenae Exc. no. 60-108. Outside entrance to Room 1, Citadel House. LH IIIB2. Syro-Pales-tine. LB. **Plate 20,5.**

Prepared rectangular blank of elephant ivory; L: 11.0 cm; W: 9.3 cm; Th: 0.9 cm.

Wardle 1973: 339-40, figure 23 (no. 60-108); Reese 1985b: 400.

b. Hippopotami Canines/Incisors

88. Hippopotamus Canine. Ivory. Mycenae Exc. no. 62-1058. Room II below Megaron, Citadel House area. LH IIIB. Syro-Palestine (probably). LB. **Plate 20,6.**

One unworked and burnt piece of a large lower Hippopota-mus canine (1/3 complete), distal end, fragmented; L: 16.0 cm; W: 7.0 cm; Th: 4.0 cm; Weight: 253 grams.

Found in 1962 excavations by British; room probably a store-room; Gamma 23, Room II, level xvi, no. 148.

Taylour 1981: 33; Kryszkowska 1984: 124, plate XIIIa; Reese

1985b: 393; Krzyszkowska 1988: 210.

c. Shell

89. Rhyton. Shell, ostrich. NMA no. 552. Shaft Grave IV, Circle A. LH. I. Egypt/Syro-Palestine. 18th Dynasty.

Ostrich eggshell converted into rhyton; faience mouth and underpiece; green discoloration on both egg and mouthpiece because they were originally covered with bronze foil.

One of two from this grave; currently associated: faience mouthpiece NMA no. 567, faience underpiece NMA no. 573.

Karo 1930: 114, 116, 239, plate CXLI; Foster 1979: 130-2, figure 87, plate 41; Sakellarakis 1990: 289, 295, figures 24-9; Lambrou-Phillipson 1990: 349 (no. 464).

90. Rhyton. Shell, ostrich. NMA no. 552.1. Shaft Grave IV, Circle A. LH I. Egypt/Syro-Palestine. 18th Dynasty.

Ostrich eggshell converted into a rhyton, fragments only.

Karo 1930: 239; Foster 1979: 130; Sakellarakis 1990: 289, figure 30.

91. Rhyton. Shell, ostrich. NMA no. 828. Shaft Grave V, Circle A. LH I. Egypt/Syro-Palestine. 18th Dynasty.

Ostrich eggshell converted into rhyton; has faience mouth-piece, gold-covered wooden underpiece, and faience dolphin appliques on shell.

One of two in this grave; currently associated: faience mouth-piece NMA no. 774, gold-covered wooden underpiece NMA no. 651; all added on Crete (Foster).

Karo 1930: 146, 239, plate CXLII; Foster 1979: 130, 132-4, 136-7, figure 88, plate 42; Sakellarakis 1990: 289, 301-3, figures 31-9; Lambrou-Phillipson 1990: 349-50 (no. 465).

92. Rhyton. Shell, ostrich. NMA no. 832. Shaft Grave V, Circle A. LH I. Egypt/Syro-Palestine. 18th Dynasty.
Ostrich eggshell converted into rhyton; covered with bronze and gold foil sheets fastened through pairs of holes in the eggshell; faience mouth and underpiece.

One of two in this grave.

Karo 1930: 147, 239, plate CXLI; Foster 1979: 130, 132, plate 41; Sakellarakis 1990: 289, 295, figures 40, 42; Lambrou-Phillipson 1990: 349 (no. 464).

93. Rhyton. Shell, ostrich. NMA no. 2667. Acropolis. LH III(?). Egypt/Syro-Palestine. 18th Dynasty.

Fragments of ostrich eggshell, probably from a rhyton; per-haps from more than one.

Sakellarakis says these are from two shells; Stäis' NMA no. is incorrect (says it is NMA no. 2267).

Stäis 1926: 119 (no. 2667); Karo 1930: 239 n. 2; Sakellarakis 1990: 289, figures 41, 43.

94. Rhyton. Shell, ostrich. Mycenae Exc. no. 62-952. Room II below Megaron in Citadel House area. LH IIIB (mid). Egypt/Syro-Palestine. 18th Dynasty.

Fragment of an ostrich eggshell, probably from a rhyton; thin shell fragment; polished cream yellow outside, slightly rough surface, off-white inside; L (max.): 2.0 cm; Th: 2.0 cm.

Found in Gamma 23, Trench E, Level xiii, no. 135.

Reese 1985a: 373; Mycenae registration card.

VIII.   Unknown or Disputed Contexts

a.   Vessels and Stands

95. Alabastron. Alabaster. NMA no. 6251. Unknown context. Egypt. 18th Dynasty.

Baggy, flat-bottomed alabastron; fairly narrow base, ovoid body, large mouth; H: 30.0 cm

Warren says this is probably Pendlebury's no. 101; similar ones at Vapheio and Nauplion.

Pendlebury 1930b: 57 (no. 101); Warren 1969: 114; Sakellarakis 1976: 179; Lambrou-Phillipson 1990: 369 (no. 521).

96. Alabastron. Alabaster. NMA. Unrecorded tomb. LH IIIA. Egypt. 18th Dynasty.

Alabaster vase; round shape, flat base, small cylindrical neck; H: 14 cm.

Unpublished, from Tsountas' excavations; restored by Kourachanis.

Lambrou-Phillipson 1990: 333-4 (no. 412).

97. Amphora. Alabaster. NMA no. 3225. Chamber Tomb. LH. Egypt. 18th Dynasty.

Alabaster amphora, with two handles joining the neck; tall, pear-shaped body; rhyton-type neck; ribbed handles; tall spout; small pedestal foot; H: 27.0 cm.

From Tsountas' 1895 excavations; this is not Pendlebury's no. 3225.

Pendelbury 1930b: 57 (no. 102); Warren 1967: 44 (Q3); Warren 1969: 115; Sakellariou 1985: 263, 266, plate 131; Lambrou-Phillipson 1990: 346-7 (no. 454), plate 74.

98. Jug. Stone. NMA no. 6252. Unknown context. Egypt. 18th Dynasty.

Body fragment from stone jug; H (original): 30.8 cm.

Pendlebury mistakenly gives this NMA number to another vase.

Pendlebury 1930b: 57 (no. 98); Warren 1969: 115.

99. Pyxis. Ivory. Nauplion Mus. no. 1090. Unknown findspot. Egypt or Syro-Palestine. LB.

Small ivory neck of a duck pyxis; made from lower canine of a hippopotamus.

Reported as stray find found in 1905; has Nauplion Museum number, but is housed in the Tiryns apotheke.

Krzyszkowska 1988: 234.

100. Vase. Diorite. NMA no. 9739. Unknown context. Egypt (possibly via Crete). 4th-5th Dynasty.

Diorite vase of typical Old Kingdom shape.

Sakellarakis 1976: 179, plate IV, 10.

101. Vessel. Glass. NMA no. 2984. Unrecorded tomb. Egypt. 18th Dynasty.

Two fragments from a blue glass vessel, with traces of wavy lines; the larger fragment measures: H: 4.5 cm, W: 3.0 cm, Th: 0.8 cm; the smaller fragment measures: H: 3.2 cm, W: 2.5 cm; Th: 0.65 cm.

Possibly Egyptian; from Tsountas' 1893 excavations.

Sakellariou 1985: 214-5, plate 99; Lambrou-Phillipson 1990: 333 (within no. 410).

IX.   Dubious or Problematic Imports

a.   Jewellery

102. Bead. Faience. Mycenae Exc. no. 68-1523. Citadel House, Room 19 (Idols), Cult Centre. LH IIIB (mid). Near East(?). LB.

Lantern bead of blue faience; four spokes on either side, plain collars; notched central rib.

The origin of lantern beads is problematic; most likely they were locally manufactured throughout the Aegean and both Eastern and Western Mediterranean.

Unpublished; registration card says Gamma MB, Room 13, Level IV, 30 on plan, within 29 on plan.

103. Diadem. Gold. NMA. Shaft Grave III, Circle A. LH I. Syro-Palestine (Kassite)? LB.

Gold diadem.

Disputed - only the Erlenmeyers suggested this.

Erlenmeyer and Erlenmeyer 1965: 177-8, figures 1-2.

104. Diadem. Gold. NMA. Shaft Grave III, Circle A. LH I. Syro-Palestine (Kassite). LB.

Fragment of possible gold diadem.

Disputed - only the Erlenmeyers suggest this.

Erlenmeyer and Erlenmeyer 1965: 177-8, figures 1-2.

b. Vases and Stands

105. Mortar. Felsite. Mycenae Exc. no. 69-1002. Citadel House. LH III (B?). Syro-Palestine (Cyprus?). LB.

Tripod mortar of igneous rock; black, red and white speckled; shallow, round bowl inside; one surviving leg; H (c.): 10.2 cm; W: 13 x 11 cm.

Probably Cretan or Theran. Cf. Warren 1979 on all of the following mortars.

Unpublished.

106. Mortar. Felsite. Mycenae Exc. no. 66-712. Citadel House. LH III. Syro-Palestine (Cyprus?). LB II.

Tripod mortar of igneous rock; H: 13.7 cm; Dm (rim): 18.0 cm; Th (c.): 2.0 cm.

Probably Cretan or Theran.

Unpublished.

107. Mortar. Felsite. Mycenae no. 66-373/69-445. Citadel House. LH III. Syro-Palestine (Cyprus?). LB II.

Tripod mortar of igneous rock, in two fragments; H: 11.7 cm; Dm (bowl): 20.0 cm.

Probably Cretan or Theran.

Unpublished.

108. Mortar. Felsite. Mycenae Exc. no. 62-20. Citadel House. LH IIIB. Syro-Palestine (Cyprus?). LB II.

Tripod mortar of igneous microdiorite; circular shallow bowl with three squared feet and long spout; H: 11.0 cm; Dm (without spout): 23.0 cm.

Probably Cretan or Theran.

Unpublished.

109. Mortar. Stone. Mycenae Exc. no. 55-255 = Nauplion Mus. no. 11503. House of the Sphinxes, south area. LH IIIB1. Syro-Palestine (Cyprus?). LB.

Hard compact limestone mortar, without feet; shallow basin with square lip; lipped spout; ring base; H: 8.0 cm; Dm: 21.0 cm; Dm (base): 18.0 cm.

Below 'filth from above'; is debated whether local or imported - probably local, since is of limestone; Lambrou-Phillipson gives this as NMA no. 4576.

Wace 1956: 115-6, plate 24a; Buchholz 1963: 54-5, Abb. 3d, 16; Cadogan 1972: 8 (within no. 31); Lambrou-Phillipson 1990: 354 (no. 481), plate 28.

110. Mortar. Stone. Mycenae Exc. no. 68-30. Citadel House area; in corridor to South House Annex (= Room 6). LH IIIB2. Syro-Palestine (Cyprus?). LB.

Three-footed (tripod) hard compact stone mortar; profile over one foot only; pinkish stone with black flecks; shallow bowl with plain rim; broad leg(s) rounded at base; H: 12.7 cm; W (foot): 6.5 cm; Th (min.): 2.6 cm.

Probably Cretan or Theran.

Cadogan 1972: 7-8 (no. 31); Helck 1979: 117; Taylour 1981: 16, 31.

111. Mortar. Stone. Mycenae Exc. no. 62-1341. Citadel House, Room II (= basement?). LH IIIB2. Syro-Palestine (Cyprus?). LB.

Tripod mortar of grey crystalline volcanic stone; thick shallow bowl, three slightly rounded legs; Th (base): 4.0 cm; W (leg): 9.0 cm: L (overall): 20.0 cm.

Probably Cretan or Theran.

Unpublished.

112. Vessel. Glass. NMA no. 2387.8. Tomb 11. LH IIIA. Egypt. 18th Dynasty.

Glass vessel, in four pieces; largest fragment has the following measurements: H: 2 cm; Dm: 6 cm.

Either Egyptian or local Aegean; positive identification still pending.

Sakellariou 1985: 73, plate 11; Lambrou-Phillipson 1990: 333 (no. 411), plate 77.

113. Vessel. Glass. NMA. Tomb. LH IIIA. Egypt. 18th Dynasty.

Vessel of blue glass, with seven horizontal wavy lines on the body; H: 16 cm.

Possibly local Mycenaean; unpublished and reported only in Lambrou-Phillipson 1990; from the excavations of E. Palaiologou; positive identification still pending.

Lambrou-Phillipson 1990: 333 (no. 410), plate 77.

Appendix

Egyptian and Near Eastern Objects in Good LHI-III Contexts
at Mycenae

Date	Object	Material	Origin	Cat..No
LH I	Bead	Glass	Mesopotamia	7
LH I	Bead	Glass	Mesopotamia	8
LH I	Bead	Glass	Mesopotamia	9
LH I	Bead	Glass	Mesopotamia	10
LH I	Bead	Glass	Mesopotamia	4
LH I	Bead	Glass	Mesopotamia	6
LH I	Bead	Glass	Mesopotamia	5
LH IIIB	Pendant	Glass	Mesopotamia	11
LH IIIB	Plaque	Glass	Mesopotamia	27
LH I	Jar	Alabaster	Egypt	51
LH I	Jug	Faience	Egypt	53
LH I	Vase	Faience	Egypt	70
LH II	Jug	Stone	Egypt	55
LH IIA	Scarab	Lapis Lazuli	Egypt	19
LH III	Alabastron	Alabaster	Egypt	28
LH III	Scarab	Faience	Egypt	14
LH III	Scarab	Faience	Egypt	15
LH III	Vase	Glass	Egypt	72
LH IIIA	Vase	Faience	Egypt	71
LH IIIA2	Alabastron	Alabaster	Egypt	29
LH IIIA2	Alabastron	Alabaster	Egypt	30
LH IIIA-B	Jar	Diorite	Egypt	52
LH IIIB	Plaque	Faience	Egypt	25
LH IIIB	Plaques (4)	Faience	Egypt	26
LH IIIB	Bowl	Faience	Egypt	45
LH IIIB	Bowl	Diorite	Egypt	48
LH IIIB	Alabastron	Alabaster	Egypt	33
LH IIIB	Alabastron	Alabaster	Egypt	32
LH IIIB	Alabastron	Alabaster	Egypt	31
LH IIIB	Alabastron	Alabaster	Egypt	34
LH IIIB	Scarab	Faience	Egypt	17
LH IIIB	Scarab	Faience	Egypt	18
LH IIIB2	Plaque	Faience	Egypt	24
LH IIIB2	Figurine	Faience	Egypt	1
LH IIIC	Alabastron	Alabaster	Egypt	35
LH IIIA	Amphora	Ceramic	Syro-Palestine	36
LH IIIA1	Pyxis	Ivory	Syro-Palestine	65
LH IIIA-B	Tusk	Ivory	Syro-Palestine	3
LH IIIA-B	Amphora	Ceramic	Syro-Palestine	39
LH IIIA-B	Amphora	Ceramic	Syro-Palestine	37
LH IIIA-B	Amphora	Ceramic	Syro-Palestine	38
LH IIIA-B	Pin	Bronze	Syro-Palestine	12
LH IIIB	Statuette	Bronze	Syro-Palestine	2
LH IIIB	Amphora	Ceramic	Syro-Palestine	40
LH IIIB	Amphora	Ceramic	Syro-Palestine	41
LH IIIB	Bowl	Faience	Syro-Palestine	46
LH IIIB	Vessel	Faience	Syro-Palestine	76
LH IIIB	Vessel	Faience	Syro-Palestine	78
LH IIIB	Vessel	Faience	Syro-Palestine	75
LH IIIB	Vessel	Faience	Syro-Palestine	74
LH IIIB	Vessel	Faience	Syro-Palestine	80
LH IIIB	Vessel	Faience	Syro-Palestine	79
LH IIIB	Vessel	aience	Syro-Palestine	77
LH IIIB	Rhyton	Faience	Syro-Palestine	67
LH IIIB	Rhyton	Faience	Syro-Palestine	66
LH IIIB	Rhyton	Faience	Syro-Palestine	68
LH IIIB	Kylix	Faience	Syro-Palestine	56
LH IIIB	Kylix	Faience	Syro-Palestine	58

LH IIIB	Kylix	Faience	Syro-Palestine	59
LH IIIB	Kylix	Faience	Syro-Palestine	64
LH IIIB	Kylix	Faience	Syro-Palestine	63
LH IIIB	Kylix	Faience	Syro-Palestine	60
LH IIIB	Kylix	Faience	Syro-Palestine	57
LH IIIB	Kylix	Faience	Syro-Palestine	62
LH IIIB	Kylix	Faience	Syro-Palestine	61
LH IIIB1	Seal	Faience	Syro-Palestine	21
LH IIIB2	Amphora	Ceramic	Syro-Palestine	42
LH IIIB2	Amphora	Ceramic	Syro-Palestine	43
LH IIIB2	Weight	Haematite	Syro-Palestine	83
LH IIIC	Weight	Haematite	Syro-Palestine	84
LH IIIC	Armour scale	Bronze	Syro-Palestine	82
LH IIIC	Amphora	Ceramic	Syro-Palestine	44
LH III	Scarab	Faience	Cyprus	16
LH III	Wall-Bracket	Terracotta	Cyprus	81
LH IIB-IIIA1	Seal	Haematite	Cyprus	22
LH IIIA1	Goblet	Faience	Cyprus	50
LH I	Rhyton	Silver	Anatolia	69
LH I	Pin	Gold	Anatolia	13
LH IIIA2	Semi-bulla	Steatite	Anatolia	23

References

Akerstrom, A 1975. More Canaanite Jars from Greece. *Opuscula Atheniensia* 11, 185-92.

Amiran, R 1969. *Ancient Pottery of the Holy Land.* Jerusalem, Masada Press Ltd.

Barag, D 1970. Mesopotamian Core-Formed Glass Vessels (1500-500 B.C.). In A L Oppenheim, R H Brill, D Barag and A von Saldern (eds.), *Glass and Glassmaking in Ancient Mesopotamia,* Corning, NY, The Corning Museum of Glass, 129-99.

Barag, D 1985. *Catalogue of Western Asiatic Glass in the British Museum* I. Jerusalem, The Magnes Press.

Bass, G F 1967. *Cape Gelidonya: A Bronze Age Shipwreck.* Transactions of the American Philosophical Society, 57, pt. 8. Philadelphia, The American Philosophical Society.

Bass, G F 1973. Cape Gelidonya and Bronze Age Maritime Trade. In H A Hoffner, Jr (ed.), *Orient and Occident,* Neukirchener, Verlag Butzon and Bercker Kevelaer, 29-38.

Bass, G F 1986. A Bronze Age Shipwreck at Ulu Burun (Kas), 1984 Campaign. *American Journal of Archaeology* 90, 269-96.

Bass, G F 1987. Oldest Known Shipwreck Reveals Splendors of the Bronze Age. *National Geographic* 172/6, 693-733.

Bass, G F, Frey, D A and Pulak, C 1984. A Late Bronze Age Shipwreck at Kas, Turkey. *International Journal of Nautical Archaeology* 13.4, 271-9.

Beck, C W, Southard, G C and Adams, A B 1972. Analysis and Provenience of Minoan and Mycenaean Amber, IV, I, Mycenae. *Greek, Roman, and Byzantine Studies* 13, 359-85.

Bennett, E L (ed.) 1953. *The Mycenae Tablets II.* Philadelphia, The American Philosophical Society.

Boardman, J 1966a. Hittite and Related Hieroglyphic Seals from Greece. *Kadmos* 5, 47-8.

Boardman, J 1966b. Review of *CMS I* (Sakellariou). *Gnomon* 38, 264-7.

Bosanquet, R C 1904. Some 'Late Minoan' Vases Found in Greece. *Journal of Hellenic Studies* 24, 317-29.

Boufides, N 1970. A Scarab from Grave Circle B of Mycenae. *Athens Annals of Archaeology* 3, 273-4.

Bouzek, J 1985. *The Aegean, Anatolia and Europe, Cultural Interrelations in the Second Millennium B.C.,* SIMA 29. Göteborg, Paul Åströms Förlag.

Buchholz, H-G 1958. Keftiubarren und Erzhandel im Zweiten vorchristlichen Jahrtausand. *Prähistorische Zeitschrift* 36, 1-40.

Buchholz, H-G 1963. Steinerne Dreifussschalen des Ägäischen Kulturkreises und Ihre Beziehungen zum Östen. *Jahrbuch des Deutschen Archäologischen Instituts* 78, 1-77.

Buchholz, H-G 1967. XII. The Cylinder Seal. In G F Bass (ed.), *Cape Gelidonya, A Bronze Age Shipwreck.* Transactions of the American Philosophical Society, 57, pt. 8. Philadelphia, The American Philosophical Society, 148-59.

Burn, A R 1930. *Minoans, Philistines, and Greeks.* New York, Kegan Paul.

Burton-Brown, T 1978. *Second Millennium Archaeology.* Oxfordshire, T. Burton-Brown.

Cadogan, G 1972. Cypriot Objects in the Bronze Age Aegean and Their Importance. In *Acts of the First International Congress of Cypriot Studies* 1, 5-13. Nicosia, Dept of Antiquites, Cyprus.

Cadogan, G 1976. Some Faience, Blue Frit and Glass

from Fifteenth Century Knossos. *Temple University Aegean Symposium* 1, 18-19.

Canby, J V 1969. Some Hittite Figurines in the Aegean. *Hesperia* 38, 141-9.

Catling, H W 1964. *Cypriot Bronzework in the Mycenaean World*. Oxford, University Press.

Catling, H W 1970. A Bronze Plate from a Scale-Corslet found at Mycenae. *Archäologischer Anzeiger* 1970, 441-9.

Catling, H W 1980. *Cyprus and the West 1600-1050 BC*. Sheffield, University of Sheffield Press.

Catling, H W 1986. Cypriot Bronzework - East or West? In V Karageorghis (ed.), *Acts of the International Archaeological Symposium: 'Cyprus Between the Orient and the Occident'*. Nicosia, Department of Antiquities, Cyprus, 91-9.

Catling, H W, Richards, E E and Blin-Stoyle, A E 1963. Correlations betwen composition and provenance of Mycenaean and Minoan pottery. *Annual of the British School of Archaeology at Athens* 58, 94-115.

Caubet, A and Yon, M 1974. Deux Appliques Murales Chypro-Geometriques au Louvre. *Report of the Department of Antiquities, Cyprus* 1974, 112-31.

Cherry, J F 1986. Polities and palaces, some problems in Minoan state formation. In C Renfrew and J F Cherry (eds.), *Peer polity interaction and sociopolitical change*. Cambridge, University Press, 19-45.

Cherry, J F and Davis, J L 1982. The Cyclades and the Greek Mainland in LCI, The Evidence of the Pottery. *American Journal of Archaeology* 86, 333-41.

Childe, V G 1960. An Italian Axe-Mould from Mycenae. *Civilta del Ferro*, 575-8. Documenti e Studi 6. Bologna.

Cline, E H 1987. Amenhotep III and the Aegean, A Reassessment of Egypto-Aegean Relations in the 14th Century BC. *Orientalia* 56/1, 1-36.

Cline, E H 1990. An Unpublished Amenhotep III Faience Plaque from Mycenae. *Journal of the American Oriental Society*, 110/2, 200-12.

Cline, E H 1991a. Hittite Objects in the Bronze Age Aegean. *Anatolian Studies* 41, 133-43.

Cline, E H 1991b. A possible Hittite Embargo Against the Mycenaeans. *Historia* XL, 1-9.

Cline, E H 1991c. Monkey Business in the Bronze Age Aegean: The Amenhotep II Figurines at Mycenae and Tiryns. *Annual of the British School of Archaeology at Athens* 86, 29-42.

Cline, E H 1994. *Sailing the Wine-Dark Sea: International Trade and the Late Bronze Age Aegean*. Bar International Series 591. Oxford, Tempus Reparatum.

Cline, E H in press. International Trade in the Amarna Period: Egyptian and Near Eastern Imports at LH III Mycenae. In G D Young and B J Beitzel (eds.), *Tell el-Amarna, 1887-1987*. Winona Lake, IN, Eisenbrauns.

Delivorrias, A (ed.) 1987. *Greece and the Sea*. Amsterdam, De Nieuwe Kerk.

Dickinson, O T P K 1977. *The Origins of Mycenaean Civilisation*, Göteborg, Paul Åströms Förlag.

Eran, A and Edelstein, G 1977. The Weights. In S Ben-Arieh and G Edelstein (eds.), *Akko, Tombs Near the Persian Garden. 'Atiqot* 12. Jerusalem, 52-62.

Erkanal, A 1986. Panaztepe Kazisiniu 1985 Yili Sonuçlari. *VIII. Kazi Sonuçlari Toplantisi I (26-30 May 1986)*, 258.

Erlenmeyer, H 1966. Über ein Schriftsiegel aus einem Kammergrab in Mykene. *Kadmos* 5, 49-57.

Erlenmeyer, M-L and Erlenmeyer, H 1965. Kassitische Goldarbeiten aus dem Schachtgrab III in Mykene? *Kadmos* 3, 177-8.

Evans, A J 1928. *Palace of Minos II*. London, MacMillan and Co.

Evans, A J 1929. *The Shaft Graves and Bee-Hive Tombs of Mycenae and Their Interrelations*. London, MacMillan and Co.

Fimmen, D 1924. *Die Kretisch-Mykenishe Kultur*. Leipzig, B G Teubner.

Fossing, P 1940. *Glass Vessels Before Glass-Blowing*, Copenhagen, Ejnar Munksgaard.

Foster, K P 1979. *Aegean Faience of the Bronze Age*. New Haven, Yale University Press.

French, E B 1965. Late Helladic IIIA2 Pottery from Mycenae. *Annual of the British School of Archaeology at Athens* 60, 159-202.

French, E B 1966. A Group of Late Helladic IIIB1 Pottery from Mycenae. *Annual of the British School of Archaeology at Athens* 61, 216-38.

Furumark, A 1944. The Mycenaean IIIC Pottery and its Relation to Cypriote Fabrics. *Opuscula Archaeologica* III, 194-265.

Furumark, A 1972a. *Mycenaean Pottery I, Analysis and Classification* (reprint). Stockholm, Swedish Institute in Athens.

Furumark, A 1972b. *Mycenaean Pottery II: Chronology* (reprint). Stockholm, Swedish Institute in Athens.

Glotz, G 1925. *The Aegean Civilisation*. New York, Kegan Paul.

Grace, V R 1956. The Canaanite Jar. In S S Weinberg (ed.), *The Aegean and the Near East*, Locust Valley, New York, J J Augustin, 80-109.

Grose, D F 1989. *Early Ancient Glass. The Toledo Museum of Art, Core-formed, Rod-formed, and Cast Vessels and Objects from the Late Bronze Age to the Early Roman Empire, 1600 B.C. to A.D. 50*. New York, Hudson Hills Press.

Haevernick, T E 1960. Beiträge zur Geschichte des antiken Glases, III, Mykenisches Glas. *Jahrbuch des Romisch-Germanischen Zentralmuseums Mainz* 7, 36-50.

Haevernick, T E 1965. Beiträge zur Geschichte des antiken Glases, XIII, Nuzi-Perlen. *Jahrbuch des Romisch-Germanischen Zentralmuseums Mainz* 12: 35-40.

Haldane, C 1993. Direct evidence for organic cargoes in the Late Bronze Age. *World Archaeology* 24/3, 348-60.

Hall, H R 1901-2. Keftiu and the Peoples of the Sea. *Annual of the British School of Archaeology at Athens* 8, 157-89.

Hallager, E 1977. *The Mycenaean Palace at Knossos.* Stockholm, Medelhavsmuseet.

Hankey, V 1981. The Aegean Interest in El Amarna. *Journal of Mediterranean Anthropology and Archaeology* 1, 38-49.

Hankey, V 1993. A Theban 'Battle Axe'. *Minerva* 4/3, 13-14.

Hankey, V and Warren, P 1974. The Absolute Chronology of the Aegean Late Bronze Age. *Bulletin of the Institute of Classical Studies* 21, 142-52.

Harden, D B 1981. *Catalogue of Greek and Roman Glass in the British Museum I.* London, Trustees of the British Museum.

Harding, A F 1984. *The Mycenaeans and Europe.* London, Academic Press.

Harding, A G and Hughes-Brock, H 1974. Amber in the Mycenaean World. *Annual of the British School of Archaeology at Athens* 69, 145-72.

Helck, W 1979. *Die Beziehungen Ägyptens und Vorderasiens zur Ägäis bis ins 7 Jahrhundert v Chr.* Darmstadt, Wissenschaftliche Buchgessellschaft.

Hermann, G 1968. Lapis Lazuli, The Early Phases of its Trade. *Iraq* 30, 21-57.

Higgins, R 1980. *Greek and Roman Jewellery.* Berkeley, University of California Press.

Hodder, I and Orton, C 1976. *Spatial Analysis in Archaeology.* Cambridge, University Press.

Hogarth, D G 1920. *Hittite Seals, with Particular Reference to the Ashmolean Collection.* Oxford, Clarendon Press.

Hooker, J T 1976. *Mycenaean Greece.* London, Routledge and Kegan Paul.

Hughes-Brock, H 1985. Amber and the Mycenaeans. *Journal of Baltic Studies* 26/3, 257-67.

Iakovidis, S E 1970. *Perati, To Nekrotapheion.* Athens, Athens Archaeological Society.

Iakovidis, S E 1980. *Excavations of the Necropolis at Perati.* Occasional Paper 8. Los Angeles, University of California, Institute of Archaeology.

Iakovidis, S E 1986. Destruction Horizons at Late Bronze Age Mycenae. In *Philia Epi eis Georgion E. Mylonan,* v.A. Athens, Athens Archaeological Society, 233-60.

Jaeger, B and Krauss, R 1990. Zwei Skarabäen aus der mykenischen Fundstelle Panaztepe. *Mitteilungen der Deutschen Orient-Gasellschaft zu Berlin* 122, 153-56.

Jones, R E 1986. *Greek and Cypriot Pottery.* Fitch Laboratory Occasional Paper 1. Athens, The British School at Athens.

Karageorghis, V and Masson, E 1975. A propos de la découverte d'ecailles d'armure en Bronze à Gastria-Alaas (Chypre). *Archäologischer Anzeiger,* Heft 2, 209-22.

Karo, G 1930. *Die Schachtgraber von Mykenai.* Munich, F Bruckmann.

Kilian, K 1980. Zum ende der Mykenischen epoche in der Argolis. *Jahrbuch des Romisch-Germanischen Zentralmuseums Mainz* 27, 166-95.

Kilian, K 1983. Ausgrabungen in Tiryns 1981. *Archäologischer Anzeiger,* 277-328.

Kilian, K 1988a. Mycenaeans Up to Date, Trends and Changes in Recent Research. In E B French and K A Wardle (eds.), *Problems in Greek Prehistory.* Bristol, Bristol Classical Press, 115-52.

Kilian, K 1988b. Ausgrabungen in Tiryns 1982/83. *Archäologischer Anzeiger,* 105-51.

Kilian, K, Podzuweit, C and Haevernick, T 1979. Ausgrabungen in Tiryns 1977. *Archäologischer Anzeiger,* 379-458.

Kilian, K, Podzuweit, C and Weisshaar, H-J 1981. Ausgrabungen in Tiryns 1978, 1979. *Archäologischer Anzeiger,* 149-256.

Killen, J T 1985. The Linear B Tablets and the Mycenaean Economy. In A M Davies and Y Duhoux (eds.), *Linear B: A 1984 Survey.* Louvain, Université de Liège, 241-305.

Knapp, A B 1991. Spice, Drugs, Grain and Grog, Organic Goods in Bronze Age East Mediterranean Trade. In N H Gale (ed.), *Bronze Age Trade in the Aegean,* 21-68. Jonsered, Paul Åströms Förlag, 21-68.

Knudtzon, J A 1915. *Die El-Amarna Tafeln.* Leipzig, J C Hinrichs.

Krzyszkowska, O 1984. Ivory from Hippopotamus Tusk in the Aegean Bronze Age. *Antiquity* LVIII, 123-5.

Krzyszkowska, O 1988. Ivory in the Aegean Bronze Age, Elephant Tusk or Hippopotamus Ivory? *Annual of the British School of Archaeology at Athens* 83, 209-34.

Lambrou-Phillipson, C 1990. *Hellenorientalia, The Near Eastern Presence in the Bronze Age Aegean ca. 3000-1100 B.C. plus Orientalia: A Catalogue of Egyptian, Mesopotamian, Mitannian, Syro-Palestinian, Cypriot and Asia Minor Objects from the Bronze Age Aegean.* Göteborg, Paul Åströms Förlag.

Leipen, N 1960. A Bronze Wall-Bracket. *Annual of the Royal Ontario Museum* 1960, 21-6.

Liverani, M 1986. La Ceramica e I Testi, Commercio Miceneo e Politica Orientale. In M Marazzi, S Tusa and L Vagnetti (eds.), *Traffici Micenei Nel Mediterraneo,Problemi storici e documentazion archeologica.* Taranto, Instituto per la storia e l'archeologia della Magno Grecia, 405-12.

Macqueen, J G 1986. *The Hittites and Their Contemporaries in Asia Minor,* London, Thames and Hudson.

McGovern, P E 1985. *Late Bronze Palestinian Pen-*

dants, *Innovation in a Cosmopolitan Age*. JSOT/ ASOR Monograph 1. Sheffield, Sheffield University Press.

Marinatos, S 1927-28. Isterominoikos Laxeutos Taphos en Kaptero Kritis. *Deltion* XI, 68-90.

Mee, C 1978. Aegean Trade and Settlement in Anatolia in the Second Millennium BC. *Anatolian Studies* 28, 121-56.

Mellaart, J 1968. Anatolian Trade with Europe and Anatolian Geography and Culture Provinces in the Late Bronze Age. *Anatolian Studies* 18, 187-202.

Mellaart, J 1986. Hatti, Arzawa and Ahhiyawa: A Review of the Present Stalemate in Historical and Geographical Studies. In *Philia Epi eis Georgion E. Mylonan*, v.A. Athens, Athens Archaeological Society, 74-85.

Mellink, M J 1987. Archaeology in Anatolia. *American Journal of Archaeology* 91, 1-30.

Mommsen, H, Beier, T, Diehl, U and Podzuweit, C 1992. Provenance Determination of Mycenaean Sherds Found in Tell el Amarna by Neutron Activation Analysis. *Journal of Archaeological Science* 19, 295-302.

Moran, W L 1992. *The Amarna Letters*. Baltimore, Johns Hopkins University Press.

Mountjoy, P A 1986. *Mycenaean Decorated Pottery*. SIMA 73. Göteborg, Paul Åströms Förlag.

Muhly, J D 1973. *Copper and Tin*. New Haven, Transactions of the Connecticut Academy of Arts and Sciences.

Muhly, J D 1974. The Hittites and the Aegean World. *Expedition* 16/2, 3-10.

Muhly, J D 1980. Bronze Figurines and Near Eastern Metalwork. *Israel Exploration Journal* 30, 148-61.

Muhly, J D 1982. The Nature of Trade in the LBA Mediterranean: The Organization of the Metals' Trade and the Role of Cyprus. In J D Muhly, R Maddin and V Karageorghis (eds.), *Early Metallurgy in Cyprus, 4000-500 B.C.* Nicosia, Dept of Antiquities, Cyprus, 251-66.

Muhly, J D 1984. The Role of the Sea Peoples in Cyprus During the LC III Period. In V Karageorghis and J D Muhly (eds.), *Cyprus at the Close of the Late Bronze Age*. Nicosia, Dept of Antiquites, Cyprus, 39-55.

Muhly, J D 1992. The Crisis Years in the Mediterranean World: Transition or Cultural Disintigration? In W A Ward and M S Joukowsky (eds.), *The Crisis Years, The 12th Century B.C.* Dubuque, Iowa, Kendall/Hunt Publishing Co, 10-26.

Mylonas, G E 1963a. Mycenae. *Ergon* 1963, 64-74.

Mylonas, G E 1963b. Anaskaphi Mycenon. *Praktika* 1963, 99-106, figs. 74-9.

Mylonas, G E 1966. *Mycenae and the Mycenaean Age*. Princeton, Princeton University Press.

Mylonas, G E 1981. The Cult Centre at Mycenae. *Proceedings of the British Academy* 67, 307-20.

Negbi, O 1976. *Canaanite Gods in Metal*. Tel Aviv, Tel Aviv University, Institute of Archaeology.

Niemeier, W-D 1983. The Character of the Knossian Palace Society in the Second Half of the 15th Century B.C. - Mycenaean or Minoan? In O H Krzyszkowska and L Nixon (eds.), *Minoan Society. Proceedings of the Cambridge Colloquium 1981*. Bristol, Bristol Classical Press, 217-36.

Oates, D 1965. The Excavations at Tell Al Rimah, 1964. *Iraq* 27, 620-80.

Oates, D 1966. The Excavations at Tell Al Rimah, 1965. *Iraq* 28, 122-39.

Onassoglou, A 1979. Enas Neos Mykinaikos Thalamoeidis Taphos sto Koukaki. *Deltion* 34, 15-42, 268-9.

Oppenheim, A L 1970. The Cuneiform Texts. In A L Oppenheim, R H Brill, D Barag and A von Saldern (eds.), *Glass and Glassmaking in Ancient Mesopotamia*. Corning Museum of Glass, NY, 2-86.

Parkinson, R and Schofield, L 1993. Akhenaten's Army? *Egyptian Archaeology* 3, 34-5.

Peltenburg, E J 1983. Appendix I. Glazed Vessels from Hala Sultan Tekke, 1972-79. In P Åström et al. (eds.), *Hala Sultan Tekke* 8. Göteborg, Paul Åströms Förlag, 214-18.

Peltenburg, E J 1987. The Oriental Character of Faience Vessels from the House of Shields, Mycenae. Paper presented at the Sixth International Congress of Aegean Prehistorians. Athens, September 1987.

Peltenburg, E J 1991. Greeting Gifts and Luxury Faience, A Context for Orientalising Trends in Mycenaean Greece. In N H Gale (ed.), *Bronze Age Trade in the Aegean*. Jonsered, Paul Åströms Förlag, 162-79.

Pendlebury, J D S 1930a. Egypt and the Aegean in the Late Bronze Age. *Journal of Egyptian Archaeology* 16, 75-92.

Pendlebury, J D S 1930b. *Aegyptiaca, A Catalogue of Egyptian Objects in the Aegean Area*. Cambridge, University Press.

Petruso, K M 1984. Prolegomena to Late Cypriot Weight Metrology. *American Journal of Archaeology* 88, 293-304.

Phillips, J 1991. *The Impact and Implications of the Egyptian and Egyptianizing Objects found in Bronze Age Crete ca. 3000 - ca. 1100 B.C.* Ph.D. Dissertation. Toronto, University of Toronto.

Pini, I 1980. Kypro-Ägäische Rollsiegel. *Jahrbuch des Deutschen Archäologischen Instituts* 95, 77-108.

Pini, I 1983. Mitanni-Rollsiegel des 'Common Style' aus Griechenland. *Prähistoriche Zeitschrift* 58, 114-26.

Porada, E 1981. The Cylinder Seals Found at Thebes in Boeotia. *Archiv für Orientforschung* 28, 1-70, 77.

Porada, E 1985. The Cylinder Seal from Chamber Tomb 47 at Mycenae. In A Sakellariou (ed.), *Les tombes a chambre de Mycénes*. Paris, Diffusion de Boccard, 334-6.

Portugali, Y and Knapp, A B 1985. Appendix: Catalog of Cypriote Objects in the Aegean and of Aegean Objects in Cyprus During the MC III-LC I Era. In A B Knapp and T Stech (eds.), *Prehistoric Production and Exchange: The Aegean and Eastern Mediterranean*. Los Angeles, UCLA Institute of Archaeology, 70-8.

Poursat, J-C 1977a. *Les Ivoires Mycéniens*. Paris, Diffusion de Boccard.

Poursat, J-C 1977b. *Catalogue des Ivoires Mycéniens du Musée National D'Athènes*. Paris, Diffusion de Boccard.

Pulak, C 1988. The Bronze Age Shipwreck at Ulu Burun, Turkey, 1985 Campaign. *American Journal of Archaeology* 92, 1-37.

Raban, A 1980. *The Commercial Jar in the Ancient Near East, Its Evidence for Interconnections Amongst the Biblical Lands*. Ph.D. Dissertation. Jerusalem, Hebrew University.

Redford, D B 1983. Review of Helck 1979. *Journal of the American Oriental Society* 103, 482.

Reese, D S 1985a. Appendix VIII(B), The Kition Ostrich Eggshells. In V Karageorghis (ed.), *Excavations at Kition V, pt. 2*. Nicosia, Department of Antiquities, 371-82.

Reese, D S 1985b. Appendix VIII(D), Hippopotamus and Elephant Teeth from Kition. In V Karagoerghis (ed.), *Excavations at Kition V, pt. 2*. Nicosia, Department of Antiquities, 391-409.

Renfrew, C 1975. Trade as Action at a Distance, Questions of Integration and Communication. In J A Sabloff and C C Lamberg-Karlovsky (eds.), *Ancient Civilisation and Trade*. Albuquerque, University of New Mexico Press, 3-59.

Sakellarakis, J A 1971. Elephantinon Ploion ek Mykinon. *Archaiologike Ephemeris* 1971, 188-233.

Sakellarakis, J A 1976. Mycenaean Stone Vases. *Studi Micenei ed Egeo-Anatolici* 17, 173-87.

Sakellarakis, J A 1982. *Corpus der minoischen und mykenischen Siegel: Band I. Supplementum. Athen Nationalmuseum*. Berlin, Begr. Mann Verlag.

Sakellarakis, J A 1990. The Fashioning of Ostrich-Egg Rhyta in the Creto-Mycenaean Aegean. In D A Hardy and A C Renfrew (eds.), *Thera and the Aegean World III. v.1*. London, The Thera Foundation, 285-308.

Sakellariou, A 1964. *Die Minoischen und Mykenischen Siegel des Nationalmuseums in Athens. (CMS I)*. Berlin, Gebr. Mann.

Sakellariou, A 1985. *Les tombes a chambre de Mycénes*. Paris, Diffusion de Boccard.

Schliemann, H 1878. *Mycenae*. Leipzig, F.A. Brockhaus.

Schuchhardt, C 1979. *Schliemann's Discoveries of the Ancient World*. Translated by E Sellers. New York, Avenel Books.

Seeden, H 1980. *The Standing Armed Figurines in the Levant*. Prähistoriche Bronzefünde, Abt. 1, Band 1. Munich, C. H. Beck'sche.

Shaw, J P 1978-86. Excavations at Kommos (Crete). *Hesperia*, 47-55.

Sherratt, E S 1980. Regional Variation in the Pottery of Late Helladic IIIB. *Annual of the British School of Archaeology at Athens* 75, 175-202.

Smith, T R 1987. *Mycenaean Trade and Interaction in the West Central Mediterranean 1600-1000 B.C.* BAR International Series 371. Oxford, British Archaeological Reports.

Smith, W S 1965. *Interconnections in the Ancient Near East*. New Haven, Yale University Press.

Stäis, V 1926. *Mycenaean Collection of the National Museum. v. II*. Athens, Hestia.

Stos-Gale, Z A 1985. A Puzzle of the Bronze Age Silver-Lead on Cyprus. In *Proceedings of the Fifth Cypriote Congress*. Nicosia, Dept of Antiquites, Cyprus, 67-72.

Stos-Gale, Z A and Macdonald, C F 1991. Sources of Metals and Trade in the Bronze Age Aegean. In N H Gale (ed.), *Bronze Age Trade in the Aegean*. Jonsered, Paul Åströms Förlag, 249-88.

Stubbings, F H 1954. Mycenae 1939-1953. Part VIII. A Winged-Axe Mould. *Annual of the British School of Archaeology at Athens* 49, 297-98.

Tamvaki, A 1973. Some Unusual Mycenaean Terracottas from the Citadel House Area, 1954-69. *Annual of the British School of Archaeology at Athens* 68, 207-65.

Taylour, Lord W D 1969. Mycenae, 1968. *Antiquity* 43, 91-7.

Taylour, Lord W D 1981. *Well-Built Mycenae I*. Warminster, Aris and Phillips, Ltd.

Taylour, Lord W D 1983. *The Mycenaeans*. London, Thames and Hudson.

Tsountas, C 1886. Anaskaphai Mykinon tou 1886. *Praktika* 1886, 59-79.

Tsountas, C 1887. Archaeotites ek Mykenon. *Archaiologike Ephemeris* 1887, 155-72, pls. 10-13.

Tsountas, C 1888. Anaskaphai Taphon en Mykenais. *Archaiologike Ephemeris* 1888, 119-80.

Tsountas, C 1891. Ek Mykenon. *Archaiologike Ephemeris* 1891, 1-44, pls. 1-3.

Tsountas, C 1893. *Mykenai kai Mykenaios Politismos*. Athens.

Vermeule, E T 1975. *The Art of the Shaft Graves of Mycenae*. Norman, Oklahoma, University of Oklahoma Press.

Vermeule, E T and Karageorghis, V 1982. *Mycenaean Pictorial Vase Painting*. Cambridge, MA, Harvard University Press.

Wace, A J B 1921-23. Excavations at Mycenae. *Annual of the British School of Archaeology at Athens* 25.

Wace, A J B 1932. *Chamber Tombs at Mycenae*. Archaeologia 82. Oxford, The Society of Antiquaries.

Wace, A J B 1949. *Mycenae: An Archaeological His-*

tory and Guide. Princeton, University Press.

Wace, A J B 1953. Mycenae 1939-1952, Pt. I, Preliminary Report on the Excavations of 1952. *Annual of the British School of Archaeology at Athens* 48, 3-18.

Wace, A J B 1954a. Mycenae 1939-1953, Pt. I, Preliminary Report on the Excavations of 1953. *Annual of the British School of Archaeology at Athens* 49, 231-43.

Wace, A J B 1954b. Excavations in 1954. *Fasti Archaeologici* 9, 158-9.

Wace, A J B 1955a. Mycenae 1939-1954, Pt. I, Preliminary Report on the Excavations of 1954. *Annual of the British School of Archaeology at Athens* 50, 175-89.

Wace, A J B 1955b. Noble Stone Vases and Geometric Pottery, A Season's Finds from Mycenae. *Illustrated London News*, 21 May, 1955, 927-9.

Wace, A J B 1956. Mycenae 1939-1955, Pt. I, Preliminary Report on the Excavations of 1955. *Annual of the British School of Archaeology at Athens* 51, 103-22.

Wace, A J B and Blegen, C W 1939. Pottery as Evidence for Trade and Colonisation in the Aegean Bronze Age. *Klio* 32, 131-47.

Wace, A J B and Porada, E 1957. Mycenae 1939-1955, 1957, Pt. II, A Faience Cylinder. *Annual of the British School of Archaeology at Athens* 52, 197-204.

Wace, H and Williams, C K 1963. *Mycenae Guide*. 3rd Edition. Connecticut, Meriden Gravure Co.

Wachsmann, S 1987. *Aegeans in the Theban Tombs*. Leuven, Uitgeverij Peeters.

Wardle, K A 1973. A Group of Late Helladic IIIB2 Pottery from within the Citadel at Mycenae. *Annual of the British School of Archaeology at Athens* 68, 297-348.

Warren, P M 1967. Minoan Stone Vases as Evidence for Minoan Foreign Connexions in the Aegean Late Bronze Age. *Proceedings of the Prehistoric Society* 33, 37-56.

Warren, P M 1969. *Minoan Stone Vases*. Cambridge, University Press.

Watrous, L V 1992. *Kommos III, The Late Bronze Age Pottery*. Princeton, Princeton University Press.

Weinberg, G D 1961-62. Two Glass Vessels in the Heraclion Museum. *Kretika Chronika* 15-16, 226-9.

Weinstein, J M 1973. *Foundation Deposits in Ancient Egypt*. Unpublished Ph.D. Dissertation. Philadelphia, University of Pennsylvania.

White, D 1985. Excavations of Mersa Matruh, Summer 1985. *Newsletter of the American Research Center in Egypt* 130, 3-17.

White, D 1986. Excavations on Bate's Island, Marsa Matruh, 1985. *Journal of the American Research Center in Egypt* 23, 51-84.

Yakar, J 1976. Hittite Involvement in Western Anatolia. *Anatolian Studies* 26, 117-28.

Yannai, A 1983. *Studies on Trade Between the Levant and the Aegean in the 14th to 12th Centuries B.C.* D.Phil. Thesis. Oxford, Oxford University.

Zangger, E 1991. Tiryns Unterstadt. In E Pernicka and G Wagner (eds.), *Archaeometry '90. International Symposium on Archaeometry, Heidelberg. April 1991*. Basel, Birkhäuser Verlag, 831-40.

STIRRUP JARS AT EL-AMARNA[1]

Vronwy Hankey

In 1890-91, Petrie found 1341 Mycenaean sherds at El-Amarna (1894,15-8). Among them he recognised the false-necked jar, now known as the stirrup jar, anfora a staffa, bügelkanne, vase à étrier, *pseudostomos amphoreus*. It was given its name before the automobile influenced verbal invention (what would it have been called if found for the first time in 1994?). *Ka-ra-re-we* has been identified as the name for stirrup jars in Linear B (Ventris and Chadwick 1959, 328). They were first made during Middle Minoan III, probably in development from Middle Minoan oval-mouthed storage amphorae. Mycenaean potters took up the shape in LH IIA (Mountjoy 1986, 30), and from then until after the end of the Bronze Age it was a hall-mark of Mycenaean and Aegean activity and influence in every area reached by them or their products (Leonard et al. 1993, 105-7; Hankey 1993).

Methods of making the pot and applying the false neck have been elucidated by xeroradiography and illustrated by working potters (Leonard et al. 1993, especially 120). Most of the stirrup jars from El-Amarna have a false neck, partly hollow or solid, thrown in one with the body (**8**, below). In some cases a globular pot was thrown to which a hollow or solid false neck was applied (**6**). The large coarse ware jar (**9**) may have been thrown in one piece with a narrow neck and rim to which the disk was attached. Furumark identified seven main types and twenty-two shapes of 'false-necked jar' (his preferred name for the pot) made between LH IIA and the end of LH IIIC (1941, 610-6).

Fine Decorated Ware

Six shapes in fine ware, dating to LH IIIA2 and /or early IIIB, have been identified at El-Amarna - FS 166, 170, 171, 171/173, 178, 182. Except for FS 170, they are between 10.00 and 18.00 cm. high, made in fine clay, with a smooth almost shiny slip. All have a combination of fine and broad bands round the body, a motif on the shoulder area, and usually a small reserved plain triangle at the join of disk and handle (**8**). They date to LH IIIA2 and / or early IIIB. Nos. **3** and **5** are complete, the others are reconstructed from sherds.

1. FS 166. Piriform. H. c.18.0. Mountjoy 1986, 77, fig. 91. LH IIIA2. **Fig. 1.**
Shape based mainly on EMC/JE 57255 (TA 31/32, 605, 606 from Q 41.7) and bases in most collections. FM 19 multiple stem, angular, on the shoulder.

Other motifs on the shoulder of FS 166 include FM 18 Mycenaean flower, FM 45 U pattern, FM 64 foliate band.

FM 166, similar to those from El-Amarna, was also found at Saqqara in the tomb chapel of Horemheb, in surface débris and Shaft I in the outer court, reused in the time of Ramesses II (Martin 1991, 91; Hankey and Aston 1995). More importantly, a complete example was found in the burial chamber of the tomb of Aper-El (north-east Saqqara) with a small piriform jar FS 45 and other Mycenaean pottery (as well as Cypriot wares). The excavator, A Zivie, concluded that Aper-El died when Amenophis III was still alive and that his son, Houy, an official in Akhenaten's administration, placed him 'sous la protection explicite du dieu Aton' in perhaps year 10 of Akhenaten (Zivie 1990, 135, 144-5, 165-6, pls. 89-90). This is the first time that Aegean pottery of LH IIIA2 has been found in a narrowly dated *grand* context in Egypt, reinforcing the chronological link between Egypt and the Aegean during the reigns of Amenophis III and Akhenaten (Warren and Hankey 1989, 148-53). The narrow base and tall piriform profile presents FS 166 as elegant rather than practical. It was easily knocked over, and this may be why the more stable globular FS171 took its place (see below).

2. FS 170. Large globular. H. c. 20.0. Mountjoy 1986, 77, fig. 92. LH IIIA2.
Identification tentative and based on UCL 1072. Max. D. c. 18.0, D. base 7.0. **Fig. 2.**
Motifs on the shoulder include FM 19 multiple stem, or 64 foliate band together with FM 60 N pattern.

The large fine ware stirrup jar, decorated with deep broad wavy line from Sedment/Sidmant tomb 59 (FS 172: 6), matches this in-between category (Kemp and Merrilees 1990, 246-9, fig. 76) (see below).

3. FS 171. Globular. H. 10.0-15.0. Mountjoy 1986, 77-9, fig. 93. LH IIIA2. **Fig. 3.**
EMC/JE 66472 (TA 36/37, 164). H. 12.6, max. D. 12.7, base 3.6, disk 3.4, spout 2.5. Complete, mended. Dirty buff clay with dark and light grits, same coloured shiny slip, decoration in shiny dark red, cracked in places. FM 45 U pattern in three rows on the shoulder, zone of FM 64 foliate band. Mountjoy does not think it was made in the Argolid (personal communication). Pendlebury et al. 1953, 41, pl. 78, 9; Parkinson and Schofield 1993.

Hankey wrongly dated this pot to LH IIIB1, because of its decorated zone, which anticipates the narrow zone on many stirrup jars of LH IIIB 1 (1973). The type was the model for small imitations in Egyptian faience (see below).

4. FS 171, with decoration on the shoulder but no decorated zone below the shoulder. H. c.11.0. Mountjoy 1986, 77-9, fig. 93. LH IIIA2, continuing into IIIB and LH IIIC. **Figs. 4, 5.**

Recognised among shoulder sherds. Motifs on the shoulder as for FS 166; Petrie 1894, pattern nos. 55-9, 63-9, 71-6.

5. FS 171, with bands round the body and no decoration on the shoulder. LH IIIA2 and IIIB1. **Plate 21.**
UCD 50 is complete. H. 10.0, D. 10.2, D. base 3.4, disk 2.6. 'Tell el-Amarna, Petrie' is written on the base. It looks like Argolid manufacture. Petrie did not record any whole pots.

6. FS 171/173. Mountjoy 1986, 105-6, figs. 127-29. LH IIIBI. **Fig. 6, Plate 22.**
Restoration based on AKMUB 295,15. Upper part only. H. extant 6.5, max. D. 11.0, disk 3.2, spout 2.0, narrow handle. The conical disk suggests that this might belong to FS 173 rather than 171. FM 73, lozenge (Kaiser 1976, 91, pl. 27, 1-3; Warren and Hankey 1989, 149-50, fig. 8).

Note that the globular stirrup jar, a sturdy and quickly made shape, had a long life and did not disappear until after the end of the Bronze Age, when it was superseded by the lekythos (Cook 1981).

7. FS 178. Squat. H. 8-12.0. Mountjoy 1986, 79-81, fig. 94. LH IIIA2. **Fig.7.**
Based on a body sherd, EMC/JE 48100 (inside in pencil 'from house dug by Petrie', no other marking). Max. D. 14.0. This shape, 'slightly squat with a distinct shoulder', was for Pendlebury the most common type of stirrup jar at El-Amarna, but sherds from the shoulder are easily confused with those of FS 171.

8. FS 182. Conical. H .10-12.0. Mountjoy 1986, 106-8, fig. 131. Based on UCL 725 + 742. Max. D. c. 16.0. **Fig. 8.**
The flat shoulder, thin false neck, curved FM 19 multiple stem on the shoulder, and the loop enclosing base of the false neck and the spout date this fragment to LH IIIB 1. It could possibly belong to the rare square-sided stirrup jar FS 184. Warren and Hankey 1989, 149-50, fig. 9.

Coarse Ware

9. FS 164. H. 30-60.0. LH and LM IIIA2 and B. A tall ovoid jar, plain and decorated, used for transporting and storing olive oil. **Fig. 10.**
Identification is based on two sherds, one from the lower body, and part of the shoulder and handle incised (after firing) with a cross ? (MCAC / TA 71, 55 = TA 36/37, 222 b, a, from the Northern Harem). Max. D. c. 24.0. Pink to brown clay, grey in the core, thick light buff slip, decoration in dark brown, FM 53 deep wavy line above two broad bands, diagonal stripes on round handle, loop at base. Pendlebury et al. 1953, 237-8, pl. 109, 4; Bourriau 1981, 124-5, no. 248. Bell identified sherds from a similar jar in a tomb at Deir El-Medina (Bell 1982, 150-3).

Oil in Egypt

Egypt's oil-producing plants did not include the olive, which, with almonds (not necessarily as plants), made its début in Egypt at El-Amarna (Manniche 1989, 17). It is tempting to suggest that both arrived either through the efforts of an agricultural adviser to an Egyptian mission sent to the Aegean late in the reign of Amenophis III (Hankey 1981; Cline 1987), or with the Aegean mercenaries who seem to have been present

at Akhetaten (Parkinson and Schofield 1993; and this volume). Olive oil must have been a welcome addition to oils from the moringa tree, castor-oil plant and sesame seeds (Manniche 1989, 48, 122-3, 142-3, 147). Apart from its virtue as a food, the olive provided a supreme luxury in a world which had no soap and no perfumes based on alcohol. Olive leaves were used in the funeral ceremony for Tutankhamun - in a bouquet, in garlands round the heads of the cobra and vulture on the crown in his outer coffin, on his shroud, and on the wrappings of protective ritual statues (Manniche 1989, 19, 128-9; Reeves 1990, 83, 106-7). Were these leaves carefully picked from young trees in a royal garden or brought from abroad?

Stirrup Jars and the Oil Trade

Many coarse-ware stirrup jars found in the Aegean area and elsewhere in contexts of, or contemporary with, LH IIIA2 (late) and LH/LMIIIB were made in Crete for exporting Cretan olive oil (Haskell 1981, 234-7; 1990; Hallager 1987; Watrous 1990, 178-80; Dickinson 1994, 252, 254, with references). Pot **9**, with its deep wavy line (shorthand for the tentacles of an octopus) is probably Cretan (Kanta 1980, 276-8, fig. 104, 3; Hankey 1979, 149). It could have arrived in the baggage of an envoy returning from a mission to the Aegean, or with a free-lance Aegean unwilling to face service in Egypt without olive oil for his food. It and the jar from Deir el-Medina were perhaps part of Aegean trade with the east in which Cyprus was the first call and Egypt last in the line. This possibility could be supported by the sign on the handle. Hirschfeld's study of similar signs, made after firing, on coarse-ware stirrup jars concludes that they are related to a Cypriot system of marking pottery in the LH and LM IIIB period (1993). Coarse-ware pottery has not always been carefully kept during excavations in Egypt, but current and future work will surely add to this list of two, and may help to decide whether Egypt too was a partner in the trade in Aegean oil, and by what route it arrived (Hallager 1987; Watrous 1990, 173-83).

The Small Jars

The small stirrup jars of LH IIIA2 and B seem inadequate as containers for wine, and are unsuitable for water, which in warm climates was best carried in an unslipped porous vessel. In general, no LH or LM pottery is totally water-tight, but slipped pots are less porous than unslipped ware. The stirrup jars at El-Amarna are thought to have been used mainly for perfumed oil. The stirrup and disk made it possible for slippery fingers to hold the pot securely while pouring the valuable liquid drop by drop from its narrow side-spout (Cook 1981, pl. 32).

The appeal of the small stirrup jar is reflected in imitations in Egyptian faience, which usually have a decorated zone of Aegean type at or near the maximum diameter. These were modelled on the stirrup jar with a

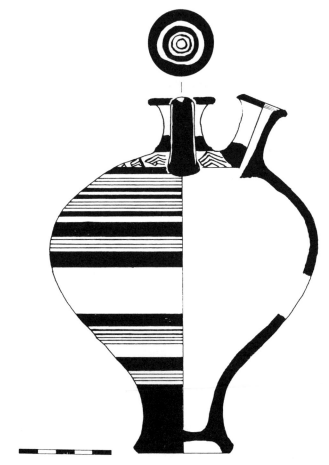

Fig. 1.   FS 166. Piriform stirrup jar.

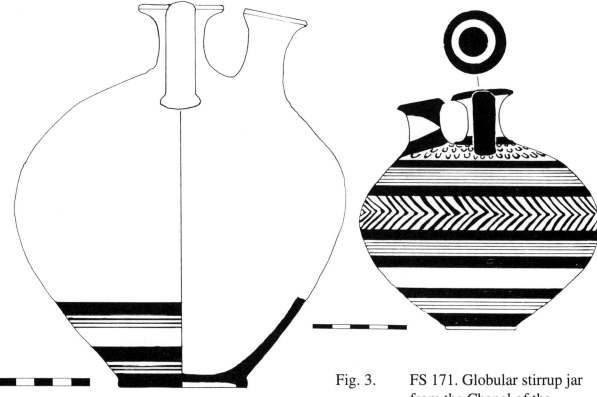

Fig. 2.   FS 170. Large fine ware stirrup jar.

Fig. 3.   FS 171. Globular stirrup jar
from the Chapel of the
King's Statue. EMC/JE 66472.

Fig. 4.   FS 171. Globular stirrup jar with shoulder pattern (see fig. 5).

Fig. 5.   Patterns from shoulder area of stirrup jars.

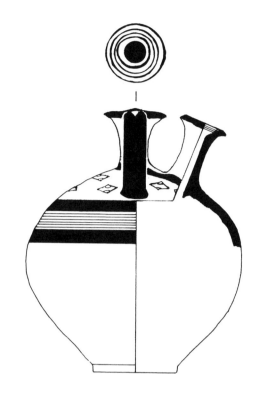
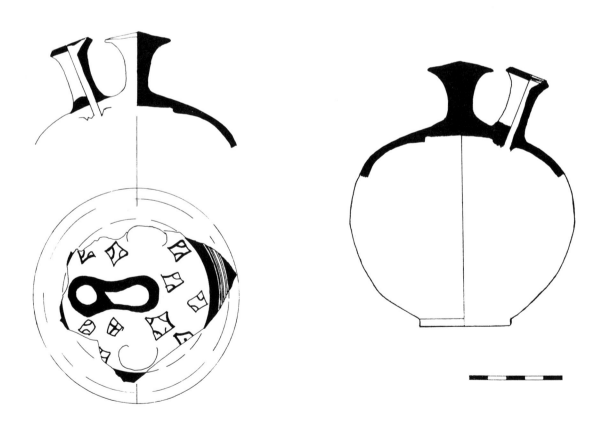

Fig. 6.   FS 171 or 173. AKMUB 295,15.

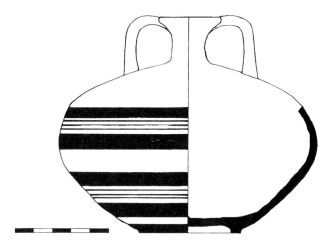

Fig. 7.   FS 178. Squat stirrup jar.

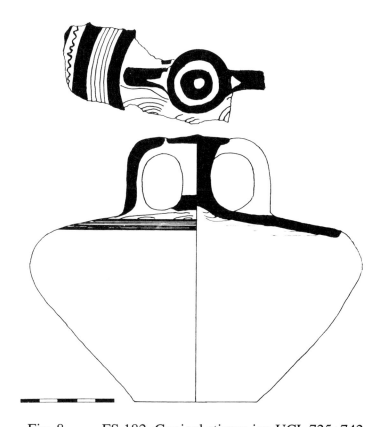

Fig. 8.   FS 182. Conical stirrup jar. UCL 725+742.

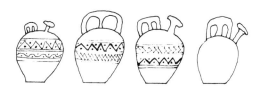

Fig. 9.   Stirrup jars in the tomb of Ramesses III, Valley of the Kings, Thebes (sketch).

Fig. 10.   FS 164. Large stirrup jar for storage and transport. MCAC TA 71,55.

body zone, like the one found in the Chapel of the King's Statue (**3**). The following examples illustrate this: BM EA 35413, height 6.7 cm, provenance unknown - blue, decorated with a zigzag pattern (**Plate 23**); Lachish (Israel) - a fragment from a green globular jar decorated in black with foliate band and a zone of small circles, found in the make-up of the floor in Room E of Fosse Temple III, rebuilt during the reign of Amenophis III (Tufnell et al. 1940, pl. 23, 63); Gurob - complete, globular, plain blue, from tomb group 217 (Brunton and Engelbach 1927, 12, pl. 25, 4 = AMO 1921.1310); Soleb (Nubia) - complete, squat to globular, blue-green decorated in black with a zone of foliate band, from tomb 17, possibly of the time of Amenophis III (Giorgini 1971, 199, 210-1, fig. 395; see also Bourriau 1981, 138, provenance unknown; Bell 1983). These were made for use, others are unserviceable substitutes reminiscent of wooden vessels painted to imitate stone found in the tomb of Yuya and Thuya, no. 46, in the Valley of the Kings. BM EA 4656, in calcite, height 5 cm, provenance unknown, was made in two pieces (**Plate 24**). A calcite jar from a tomb group at Gurob dated by Petrie to the time of Seti II was only partly hollowed out (Petrie 1891, 18, pl. 19, 27 = AMO 1890. 997).

An In-between Size

FS 170 falls between FS 164 and the small fine ware pots. It brings to mind George III's goose (too much for one, not enough for two). It seems too large for the bath or dining room, not strong enough for the storeroom. Perhaps it was specially made to order for grand customers or for wholesalers, who then re-sold perfumed oil in smaller, more profitable quantities. A special order or purpose is implied by an incised sign on the handle of a few jars of FS 170.

The Stirrup Jars of Ramesses III

The tomb of Ramesses III (Valley of the Kings, no. 11) contains the only wall-painting in Egypt which shows stirrup jars (**Fig. 9**). On the right side of the entrance corridor, in room 6 (more like a large cupboard than a room) the walls are decorated with treasured commodities, such as leopard skins, elephant-tusks, bundles of wood, copper ingots, clay and metal vessels - green jugs, red storage jars with white and dark blue clay sealings, a cup of Vaphio shape, a tall ewer, and stirrup jars. These are quite large, one green, one blue (faience), and seven dark pink (clay). The large storage jars (often referred to as Canaanite) and the stirrup jars have similar body zones of zigags with dots or crosshatching. On the back wall (difficult to see from the barred entrance) a female figure appears to have replaced the 'stirrup'. Is the representation fanciful or can we assume that faience and clay stirrup jars were made in Egypt long after Aegean imports decreased sometime in LH IIIB? Were they symbols of wealth taken from the past to adorn a king's funeral, like the vessels on the walls of the treasury in the temple of Ramesses III at Medinet Habu?

Conclusion

Stirrup jars were not the only small containers for oil used at El-Amarna. The most popular shape was the vertical flask FS189, decorated with concentric circles and a formal motif on the panels below the handles - an elegant and distinctive variation on the lentoid flask common in the Levant and Egypt (Mountjoy 1986, 80, fig. 95; Hankey 1973; 1981; 1993, 112). We can, however, be certain that the stirrup jar (**3**) found in the Chapel of the King's Statue was one of many fashionable imported containers of olive oil used in the palaces, grand houses and places of cult. Some of these found their way as empties to modest houses until their broken fragments landed on the rubbish heaps of Akhetaten, or lurked unnoticed in dark corners. By imitating this singular pot in clay, calcite and faience the discerning Egyptians paid the Aegean world a compliment which we can still appreciate.

Notes

1. A brief account of the typology of Aegean pottery at El-Amarna will appear in the volume dedicated to the memory of Martha Bell (ed. J Phillips, in preparation). For permission to study and publish pieces used for this paper I warmly thank Dyfri Williams (Greek and Roman Department), Vivian Davies (Egyptian Department) of the British Museum; Barbara Adams, Curator of the Petrie Museum, UCL; Mohammad Saleh, Director of the Egyptian Museum, Cairo; Wilfred Geominy at the Akademisches Kunstmuseum der Universität Bonn; Alan Peatfield at University College Dublin; Anthony Snodgrass at the Museum of Classical Archaeology, Cambridge; Helen Whitehouse at the Ashmolean Museum, Oxford. I also thank Henry Hankey, Geoffrey Martin, Penelope Mountjoy, Louise Schofield for help in drawing, advice and access to information. Finally, I remember with affection and gratitude the kindness and wisdom of the late Reynold Higgins during his years in the Greek and Roman Department.

Abbreviations

FM   Furumark Motif, in Furumark 1941, 236 - 424.
FS   Furumark Shape, in Furumark 1941, 583 - 643.
LH   Late Helladic
LM   Late Minoan

Museums

AMO   Ashmolean Museum, Oxford.
AKMUB   Akademisches Kunstmuseum der
         Universität Bonn.
BM   British Museum, London.
EMC/JE   Egyptian Museum, Cairo -
         Journal d'Entrée.
MCAC   Museum of Classical Archaeology,
         Cambridge.
UCD   University College, Dublin.
UCL   Petrie Museum, University College London.

Measurements are in centimetres, D. = Diameter, H. = Height, Max. = Maximum. The year of excavation and find number, written on the sherd, are given in parentheses following the museum number, e.g. (TA 1936/37, 151 or 36/37. 151 or 36/151).

References

Bell, M R 1982. Preliminary Report on the Mycenaean Pottery from Deir El-Medina (1979-1980). *Annales du Service des Antiquités de l'Égypte* 68, 143-63.

Bell, M R 1983. Egyptian Imitations of Aegean Vases. *Göttinger Miszellen* 63, 13-24.

Bourriau, J 1981. *Umm el -Ga'ab: Pottery from the Nile Valley before the Arab Conquest.* Cambridge, Fitzwilliam Museum.

Brunton, G and Englebach, R 1927. *Gurob.* London, British School of Archaeology in Egypt.

Cline, E 1987. Amenhotep and the Aegean: A Reassessment of Egypto-Aegean Relations in the 14th Century BC. *Orientalia* 56, fasc. 1, 1-36.

Cook, K 1981. The Purpose of the Stirrup Vase. *BSA* 76, 167.

Dickinson, O 1994. *The Aegean Bronze Age.* Cambridge, Cambridge University Press.

Furumark, A 1941. *The Mycenaean Pottery: Analysis and Classification.* Stockholm, Kungl. Vitterhets Historie och Antikvitets Akademien.

Giorgini, M S 1971. *Soleb* II. *Les Nécropoles.* Firenze, Sansoni.

Hallager, E 1987. The Inscribed Stirrup Jars: Implications for Late Minoan IIIB Crete. *AJA* 91, 173-90.

Hankey, V 1973. The Aegean Deposit at El Amarna. In V Karageorghis (ed.), *The Mycenaeans in the Eastern Mediterranean.* Nicosia, Department of Antiquities, Cyprus, 128-36.

Hankey, V 1979. Crete, Cyprus and the South-eastern Mediterranean, 1400 - 1200 BC. In V Karageorghis (ed.), *The Relations between Cyprus and Crete, ca. 2000-500 BC.* Nicosia, Department of Antiquities, Cyprus, 144-57.

Hankey, V 1981. The Aegean Interest at El-Amarna. *Journal of Mediterranean Anthropology and Archaeology* 1, 38-49.

Hankey, V 1993. Pottery as evidence for Trade:1. From the Mouth of the Orontes to the Egyptian Border. 2. Egypt. In C W and P C Zerner (eds.), *Wace and Blegen: Pottery as Evidence for Trade in the Bronze Age.* Amsterdam, J C Gieben, 101-15.

Hankey, V and Aston, D 1995. Mycenaean Pottery from Saqqara. In J Carter and S Morris (eds.), *The Age of Homer.* Texas University Press, promised this year.

Haskell, H W 1981. Coarse-ware Stirrup-jars at Mycenae. *BSA* 76, 225-38.

Haskell, H W 1990. Late Bronze Age Trade: transport stirrup jars. *AJA* 94, 298.

Hirschfeld, N 1993. Incised marks (post firing) on Aegean Wares. In C W and P C Zerner (eds.), *Wace and Blegen: Pottery as Evidence for Trade in the Aegean Bronze Age.* Amsterdam, J C Gieben, 311-8.

Kaiser, B 1976. *Corpus Vasorum Antiquorum Deutschland* 40. Bonn 2. München, C H Beck.

Kanta, A 1980. *The Late Minoan III Period in Crete: A Survey of Sites, Pottery and their Distribution.* Göteborg, Paul Åströms Förlag.

Kemp, B J and Merrillees, R M 1980. *Minoan Pottery in Second Millenium Egypt.* Mainz am Rhein, Phillip von Zabern.

Kitchen, K A 1987. The Basics of Egyptian Chronology in Relation to the Bronze Age. In P. Åström (ed.), *High, Middle or Low?. Acts of an International Colloquium on Absolute Chronology held at the University of Gothenburg (20th - 22nd August 1987)*, Part 1. Gothenborg, Paul Åströms Förlag, 37-55.

Leonard, A, Hughes, M, Middleton, A and Schofield, L 1993. The Making of Aegean stirrup jars: technique, tradition and trade. *BSA* 88, 105-24.

Manniche, L 1989. *An Ancient Egyptian Herbal.* London, British Museum Publications.

Martin, G T 1991. *The Hidden Tombs of Memphis.* London, Thames and Hudson.

Mountjoy, P M 1986. *Mycenaean Decorated Pottery: A Guide to Recognition.* Göteborg, Paul Åströms Förlag.

Parkinson, R and Schofield, L 1993. Akhenaten's Army? *Egyptian Archaeology* 3, 34-5.

Pendlebury, J D S, et al. 1953. *The City of Akhenaten* III. London, Egypt Exploration Society.

Petrie, W M F 1891. *Illahun, Kahun and Gurob.* London, David Nult.

Petrie, W M F 1894 . *Tell El Amarna.* London, Methuen and Co.

Reeves, N 1990. *The Complete Tutankhamun.* London, Thames and Hudson.

Tufnell, O, Inge, C H and Harding, L 1940. *Lachish* II: *The Fosse Temple.* Oxford, Oxford University Press.

Ventris M and Chadwick, J 1959. *Documents in Mycenaean Greek.* Cambridge, Cambridge University Press.

Warren, P M and Hankey, V 1989. *Aegean Bronze Age Chronology.* Bristol, Bristol Classical Press.

Watrous, L V 1992. *Kommos* III: *The Late Bronze Age Pottery.* Princeton, Princeton University Press.

Zivie, A 1990 *Découverte à Saqqarah: Le vizir oublié.* Paris, Éditions du Seuil.

IMAGES OF MYCENAEANS
A RECENTLY ACQUIRED PAINTED
PAPYRUS FROM EL-AMARNA[1]

Richard Parkinson and Louise Schofield

A matter of weeks before the colloquium 'Egypt, the Aegean and the Levant' took place, the Egyptian Department of the British Museum made a remarkable new acquisition. As this was of direct relevance to the question of contacts between Egypt and the Aegean in the second millennium BC, a preliminary paper was prepared and added to the colloquium programme. What follows is an account of the object before it reached the Museum and a brief report on the study we were able to make before the colloquium.

In December 1936, shortly before the end of the season, Pendlebury wrote from el-Amarna, describing his recent excavations of House R 43.2: 'finds in this building included a complete Mycenaean vase (the second complete example to be found on the site) and a number of fragments of papyrus - still awaiting proper treatment'. The fragments were discovered on 1st December according to the Dig Diary (both letter and Diary are now in the archives of the Egypt Exploration Society).

The building R 43.2 lies on the edge of the official zone of the city and the southern residential area. In an inner hall the remains of a wooden shrine with images were found, with a painted inscription mentioning a 'great statue which the king caused to be made'. The same fragment names Akhenaten, so he is clearly the 'king'; the great statue was presumably of Akhenaten or possibly of Amenhotep III (whose name occurs on some small objects from the building).[2] The building seems to have been a 'chapel of the King's Statue'.[3] This find-spot suggests a date in the Amarna period (c. 1340 BC).

As the exact position of the papyrus find was unrecorded and as the nature of the cult in the chapel is uncertain, it would be rash to interpret the papyri exclusively in terms of this context. It is also possible that the fragments could have been blown into the chapel from another area of the site.[4]

In Pendlebury and Fairman's *City of Akhenaten* III, 141, there is only a brief reference to the fragments, and without any number. This brevity is explained by a letter from Fairman to the Egypt Exploration Society dated 5th January 1954:

> 'Are Pendlebury's notes of the last season at Amarna (1936-37) accessible and available?...The reason is that I am working on some papyrus fragments found in that season, which could not be published in COA

III because they were temporarily lost: though pitiful fragments, they are most unusual, and I want to publish them in JEA, but really need Pendlebury's field notes, for they obviously have a special connection with the building in which they were found.'

Thus by 1954 they were being studied by Professor Fairman, but remained unpublished at his death (1982). In 1992 a set of the fragments appeared at Christie's; these were mounted in two glass frames and comprised a number of pieces of painted papyrus and two of painted leather.[5] They were acquired by the British Museum in June 1992 after consultation with the Egypt Exploration Society.

The School of Archaeology, Classics and Oriental Studies at the University of Liverpool had in their keeping a small white cardboard box, with the label: 'R 43.2 Papyrus Fragments 30.xi.36'. This contained two painted fragments of papyrus, some darker, thinner fragments with traces of (illegible) writing, and one very small leather fragment. In the weeks following the colloquium these were presented to the British Museum by the Egypt Exploration Society; we are very grateful to the Society and to Dr Chris Mee for facilitating this process. Although the date on the box differs from that recorded in the Dig Diary, this is probably the result of hasty recording (there were only two days to excavate the whole chapel complex).

The original find seems to have contained the remains of at least three different manuscripts, which probably could not be differentiated when they were excavated. It seems that all the fragments came to England in the cardboard box, and that Fairman mounted the larger pieces between glass, but left some of the smaller, less significant fragments in the box. The fragments have now been registered as three items:

EA 74100	A painted papyrus.
EA 74101	Two substantial fragments of painted leather, one with a flying heraldic falcon, another with a feather (rishi-like) pattern.
EA 74102	Small papyrus fragments with illegible traces of signs in black ink.

The painted papyrus is the best preserved, and also the most startling. Fairman had reassembled the fragments as a naval battle,[6] but was clearly sufficiently dissatisfied with this to refrain from publication. Preliminary study in the Department of Egyptian Antiquities showed that this was a misarrangement. A subsequent detailed examination enabled a more extensive reassembly than had at first been thought possible. This process was greatly aided by the work of Bridget Leach (Conservation Department of the British Museum). All of the fragments with painting have now been positioned with reasonable certainty, and their present arrangement is seen in **Plate 8**. Two substantial scenes survive relatively intact and a third is much more fragmentary.

The first (11 x 6.5cm), on the right, shows that the original papyrus included scenes of battle. Libyan archers are depicted attacking a fallen Egyptian in a rocky landscape. The reassembly of this scene was unproblematic apart from the tree (the vertical position of which is uncertain) and one unplaced fragment which is blank. The second scene (10.3 x 10.47cm), in the middle, shows running troops and an archer shooting an arrow. The reassembly of this area posed severe problems, since the fragments were smaller than those of the first scene and appeared to consist of unjoined heads, bodies and legs. After a preliminary rearrangement, it was realised that two crucial additional joins could be made - firstly joining a helmeted head to a body, secondly the fragments of an area behind the archer's head.[7] The fragmentary third scene, on the left, also shows running foot soldiers; there are few direct joins but the reassembly is confirmed by the fibre patterns.

Given the focus of the colloquium, the presentation concentrated not on the striking Egyptological implications of the battle-scene but on the unusual features exhibited by some of the running troops. Helmets worn by two of the figures bear a remarkable similarity to the boar's tusk helmets of the Mycenaeans - a similarity which had presumably been noted by Fairman.[8] The colour and vertical demarcations of the helmets are particularly relevant. Since the colloquium additional features have become apparent. A join made two days before the colloquium showed that one of the helmeted figures also wore a cropped ox-hide tunic and subsequent research has revealed Aegean parallels for such a garment.

This important new acquisition, arriving in the Museum in such a timely fashion on the eve of the colloquium, is thus another part of the jigsaw of evidence for the relations between Egypt and the Aegean in the second millennium BC. Its find-spot at Tell el-Amarna places it at the centre of this controversy; the quantities of Mycenaean pottery found at the site have long provoked debate (for the stirrup jar from the same context as the battle-scene see Hankey, this volume, **Fig. 3**). An historical interpretation of the possibly Mycenaean features is advanced by L. Schofield and R. Parkinson, 'Of helmets and heretics: a possible Egyptian representation of Mycenaean warriors on a papyrus from el-Amarna', *BSA* 89 (1994) 157-70.[9]

Notes

1. A great debt of gratitude is owed by both authors to Vivian Davies for his unfailing encouragement at every stage of our work.

2. J D S Pendlebury, *The City of Akhenaten*: III, *The Central City and the Official Quarters* (MEES 44, 1951), 140-1. The small objects are a faience ring (36/79), and a pen-case with the cartouche 'Amenhotep' (36/163); ibid. 141, pl. lxxix, 9. See also B J Kemp, *Ancient Egypt: Anatomy of a Civilization* (London and New York, 1989), 283-5; B J Kemp and S Garfi, *A Survey of the Ancient City of el-'Amarna* (London, EES, 1993), 63, map sheet 5.

3. Kemp and Garfi (n. 2), 63; see also B J Kemp, *Amarna Reports* IV (London, EES, 1987), 123, no. 16.

4. Kemp and Garfi (n. 2), 61.

5. The Christie's catalogue includes a brief description and photograph of one of the frames: *Fine Antiquities: London, Wednesday, 8 July 1992 at 10.30 a.m.* (London 1992), 102.

6. A J Spencer, pers. com. The arrangement is shown in the photograph in the Christie's catalogue (n. 5); the description there is derived in part from Fairman's notes.

7. The second join was made shortly after the colloquium.

8. It is mentioned in the entry in the Christie's catalogue (n. 5), which drew on Fairman's notes.

9. A brief account of the papyrus was initially published in *Egyptian Archaeology* 3 (1993), 34-5. A monograph is planned to provide a full publication of this and other manuscripts from el-Amarna in the British Museum and the Ashmolean Museum, Oxford.

THE ORIGIN OF EGYPTIAN COPPER
LEAD-ISOTOPE ANALYSIS OF METALS FROM EL-AMARNA

Zofia Stos-Gale, Noel Gale and Judy Houghton

Introduction

Our interest in the origin of copper used for the manufacture of bronzes at El-Amarna was primarily aroused by the long-term project, carried out at Oxford since the early 1980s, the aim of which is the reconstruction of the patterns of trade in metals in the Bronze Age Mediterranean. The Amarna letters provide written evidence, unique for this period, of the importation to the town of copper from Alashia, which generally seems to be identified with the whole, or part, of Cyprus (see for example Muhly 1982 and references within). The depiction of ox-hide ingots in some of the tombs at Amarna provides some additional support for this theory, though Bass regards the ingots as brought by Syrians (Bass 1967, 66). Our research at Oxford is based on lead-isotope analyses of ancient artefacts and their comparison with the characteristic 'fingerprints' of ore deposits. The successful identification of ore sources used in the Bronze Age depends on a systematic lead-isotope analysis of ore deposits, with parallel surveys of traces of ancient mining and smelting of ores. Such work has been carried out in the last decade mostly in the Eastern Mediterranean and Anatolia, resulting in a data base of several thousand lead-isotope analyses of ores and copper, lead and silver artefacts from archaeological sites (Gale and Stos-Gale 1992; Wagner et al. 1989 and references within).

To date, the question of the sources of copper used by the ancient Egyptians remains an enigma. Lead-isotope analyses of ancient Egyptian silver and lead (Stos-Gale and Gale 1980) have demonstrated that, in spite of there being many lead ore deposits in the Eastern Desert, the metal did not originate from these deposits. On the other hand, some of the lead and silver objects dated to the Middle and New Kingdoms were made from ores that could have come from the Lavrion mines in Attica. So far, there are no published lead-isotope analyses of copper-based artefacts from Egypt dating to the period before the first millennium BC. As a preliminary attempt to fill this gap, and also to test the extent of imports of copper to Egypt from the Aegean and Cyprus in the Late Bronze Age, we obtained samples from seventeen copper-based artefacts from El-Amarna held in the collections of the Ashmolean Museum, Oxford. The analysed artefacts, together with information about their archaeological context, are listed in **Table 1**.

Copper Deposits in Egypt and Sinai.

Prior to the assessment of the results of the lead-isotope analyses of the Amarna bronzes, we will briefly consider the availability of copper in Egypt from the geological point of view. The majority of the mineral deposits of Egypt are situated in the Eastern Desert, along the coast of the Red Sea. Gold is the most important mineral occurring in this region and much has been written about its exploitation in ancient and modern times. However, some lead, tin and copper also occur there, together with iron, zinc, talc, tungsten and phosphates (El Shazly 1957). It seems that copper mineralisations in the Eastern Desert are of little significance and there are no reports known to us of ancient copper slags in this region.

Contrary to the scarcity of evidence for the ancient exploitation of copper in the Eastern Desert, Sinai has often been quoted as an ancient source. A E Thomas wrote in 1909, 'As far as is known, the chief ancient copper workings from which the Egyptians obtained ore for their bronze implements are in the south of the Sinai Peninsula, and Absciel and Hammamid in the Eastern Desert.' However, further on he states that 'Careful study of the copper mines, taken with the estimate of the amount of bronze the ancients had at their disposal, has led many to the conclusion that the mines of Sinai could not have supplied the Egyptians with all their copper...'

Neither of these statements has ever been verified. From the geological reports it seems that copper is well attested in Sinai together with ancient slag-heaps of unknown date. Thomas (1909, 182) mentions copper slag in Wadi Nasba, which contains 18% of copper; such high copper content would be expected in a slag from Bronze Age copper-smelting. Additionally, copper prills were found in this slag under microscopic examination (El Shazly et al. 1955). It has been suggested that copper ore in the form of malachite was mined in antiquity in Maghara, Gebel Um Rinna and Serabit El Khadim. El Shazly et al. (1955) list a further seven sites with 'important copper mineralisations', which contain other copper minerals: Suweira, Bathat um Rebei, Abu El Nimran, Feiran, Regeita, Rahaba and Samra. The excavations at Timna in the Wadi Arabah by Rothenberg et al. (1988 and 1989) and those of the team from Bochum in Feinan (Hauptmann and Roden 1988) have proved that there was quite consid-

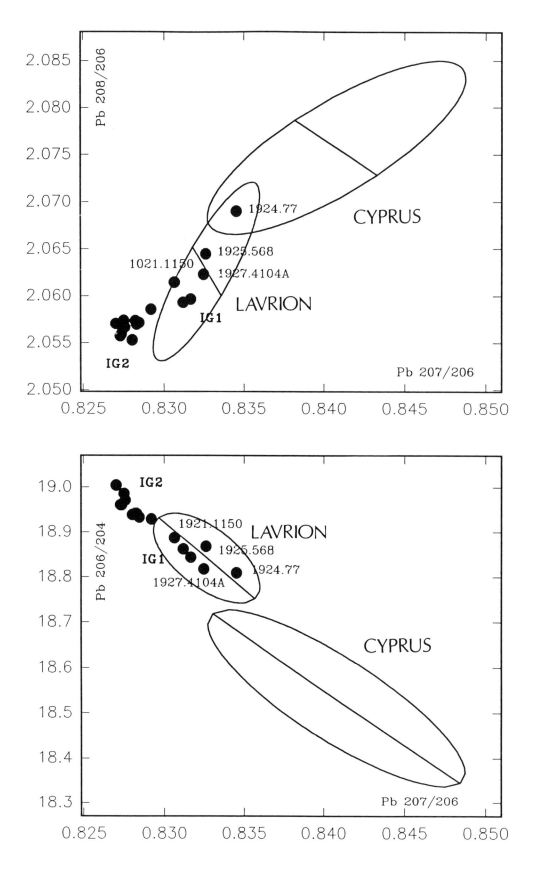

Fig. 1.   Lead-isotope compositions of bronzes from El-Amarna (groups IG1 and IG2) compared with the 95% confidence ellipses calculated around a number of data points for ores from Lavrion and Cyprus.

Table 1.   List of analysed artefacts from El-Amarna

Mus. No.	Find Spot	Description
1890.305	Purchased at site	Small knife
1921.1129	Main city, Street A	Axe with binding
1921.1131	Not known	Hoe
1921.1132	House N 50.30	Awl
1921.1150	Not known	Stud
1924.77	House Q 46.33?	Knife (dagger)
1924.81	Not known	Small chisel
1924.82	Not known	Awl/chisel
1924.84	House O 46.33	Tongs with hands
1925.413	Not known	Hook (?bent awl)
1925.568	Not known	Small silver ingot
1927.4104A	Great Temple, sanctuary	Situla fragments
1927.4104B	Great Temple, sanctuary	Situla fragments
1931.487	Mycenaean house T 36.36	Knife
1933.1209	Not known	Horse bit
1934.267	Police barracks R 42.10	Small knife
1935.595	Great Palace, pav. O 42.1	Chisel

Table 2.   Lead-isotope analyses

Mus. No.	208 Pb/206 Pb	207 Pb/206 Pb	206 Pb/204 Pb	LI Origin
1890.305	2.05733	.82822	18.941	IG2
1921.1129	2.05573	.82728	18.961	IG2
1921.1131	2.05667	.82758	18.971	IG2
1921.1132	2.05932	.83119	18.862	IG1: Lavrion
1921.1150	2.06143	.83065	18.887	IG1: Lavrion
1924.77	2.06900	.83453	18.809	IG1: Lavrion
1924.81	2.05703	.82702	19.004	IG2
1924.82	2.05698	.82828	18.940	IG2
1924.84	2.05529	.82802	18.939	IG2
1925.413	2.05595	.82736	18.961	IG2
1925.568	2.06446	.83260	18.868	IG1: Lavrion
1927.4104A	2.06229	.83246	18.818	IG1: Lavrion
1927.4104B	2.09906	.85888	18.148	Timna
1931.487	2.05714	.82844	18.933	IG2
1933.1209	2.05857	.82920	18.929	IG2
1934.267	2.05738	.82750	18.986	IG2
1935.595	2.05964	.83166	18.844	IG1: Lavrion

erable copper production in these locations in the Bronze Age. Furthermore, an ancient copper mine was recently reported in the Wadi Tar in the south-east of the Sinai Peninsula by Ilani and Rosenfeld (1994).

All this information seems to suggest that the ancient Egyptians had plenty of copper minerals available in the Sinai and that the majority of the metal artefacts excavated in Egypt could well have been made ultimately from ores which came from this area. However, so far, the only available lead-isotope analyses of copper ores from near the Sinai are those of minerals and slags from Timna (Gale et al. 1989) and Feinan (Hauptman et al. 1992); in consequence, much remains to be done in this respect. The question remains: why would Egypt import copper from Cyprus (assuming that Alasia *is* Cyprus) when supplies were present within the borders of Egypt?

Sources of Copper in the Bronze Age Eastern Mediterranean

There is no doubt that, in the second half of the Late Bronze Age, Cyprus was producing a quantity of ox-hide ingots which were then traded to places as far away as Mycenae and Sardinia (Gale 1991). On the other hand, the earliest ox-hide ingots found in the Aegean, those from LMI contexts at Ayia Triadha and Kato Zakro, are, alone amongst all others so far analysed, of unknown origin, possibly from the Middle East (Gale and Stos-Gale 1986). Lead-isotope research into the sources of metals used in the Bronze Age Aegean has somewhat undermined theories about the metals- trade derived from imported pottery at various sites (Stos-Gale and Gale 1992; Stos-Gale 1994). The full implications of our study and the archaeological assessment of the results are to a large extent still awaiting publication, but it is already clear that in the Late Bronze Age the major source of lead, copper and silver in the Minoan/Mycenaean world was on its doorstep - at Lavrion in Attica. Practically all Late Bronze Age lead and silver analysed (about 460 samples) is consistent with its origin being the Lavrion mines. Out of nearly 450 copper-based artefacts, 51% have lead-isotope compositions consistent with this deposit, and 20% with Cyprus (this figure includes 20 samples of ox-hide ingots and their fragments). About 9% of the metal has a high probability of originating from Northern Anatolian copper deposits and 20% shows lead-isotope compositions which do not match any of the ore deposits analysed so far.

Lead-Isotope Analyses of Bronzes from El-Amarna

The results of lead-isotope analyses of the bronzes from El-Amarna are summarised in **Table 2**. One of the objects (fragment of a situla No. 1927.4104 B) has a distinctly different lead-isotope composition from all the others. This composition is fully consistent with one of the groups of ores from Timna analysed at Oxford (Gale et al. 1981). It should be mentioned here, though,

that as far as we know at present the lead-isotope compositions of ores from Timna and Feinan are very similar and perhaps indistinguishable. The composition of the situla is consistent at present with samples from Timna, not Feinan, but one cannot exclude the possibility that more analyses of Feinan copper might also result in the same lead-isotope ratios. One has to note, however, that, on the field-evidence (Hauptmann et al. 1992), the copper mines in Feinan were mostly active in the Early Bronze Age and in the Iron Age (as these periods are defined at Feinan).

The other objects analysed have lead-isotope compositions falling into two groups (see **Fig. 1**). The first group (IG1) numbers six objects (1921.1132, 1921.1150, 1924.77, 1925.568, 1927.4104A and 1935.595). Their lead-isotope ratios are consistent with the samples of lead and copper ores and litharge from Lavrion in Attica. The elemental analyses (NAA and XRF) have proved that one of these objects is in fact a small silver ingot with about 3% of copper, 0.5% of gold and about 0.2% of lead. All the others are high-tin bronzes.

The artefacts falling into the second lead-isotope group (IG 2) cluster very closely together: eleven objects have lead-isotope compositions falling within 0.2-0.4% range of their lead-isotope ratios. It seems highly likely, therefore, that all these metals originate from the same mineralisation. There is no ore deposit known at present which is characterised by such lead-isotope ratios. There are no ores of this composition in the Aegean or in Cyprus. Lead-isotope ratios of seven samples of copper ores from Ergani Maden in south-east Turkey analysed in Mainz (Seeliger et al. 1985) are the only ore samples which isotopically fall in the near vicinity of this group, but not a single sample of these ores shows a lead-isotope composition identical to the bronzes from El-Amarna. It seems that at present it is not possible to identify the geographical source of this metal. Lead-isotope analyses of copper ores from Sinai might solve this puzzle.

All the analysed bronzes from El-Amarna have a uniformly low lead content (below 0.3%); it seems reasonably certain, therefore, that lead was not added to copper during the production of the bronze. The only alloying components are copper and tin. Bronze Age tin was most probably smelted from cassiterite, which is usually characterised by a very low content of impurities, lead in particular. It is, therefore, most likely that the lead-isotope compositions of the El-Amarna bronzes resemble those of the copper deposits from which the copper came. The lead-isotope compositions of the artefacts indicate that the metals were not made by mixing and re-melting fragments of copper of different origin. A mixture of metal from two different sources should have lead-isotope compositions plotting on straight lines between the samples of ores from these deposits. There are no known ore deposits (or groups of ancient copper artefacts) which have lead-isotope compositions lower than those in group IG2; this group, therefore, could not have been achieved by mixing metal of different origins. With some exercise of the imagination, one could say that the IG1 group might have been made by mixing copper from Timna with that of IG2. However, it seems quite unlikely that such mixing would result in a group of objects with such a small range of lead-isotope ratios (one would expect to find at least some cases falling in the 208/206 range between values 2.07 and 2.12) and additionally fitting exactly the Lavrion range.

The question of mixing and re-melting of objects is often mentioned by archaeologists as an argument against the reliability of lead-isotope provenance studies of ancient metals. The large number of analyses of artefacts from Bronze Age sites in the Mediterranean shows no signs of extensive mixing of metals in this period. One of the main reasons for this picture might be the fact that the metal artefacts made in this period (with the exception of ox-hide ingots) are mostly quite small, and obviously melting a large amount of metal was not an easy task. All crucibles excavated at sites are relatively small and, therefore, could only have been used to re-melt correspondingly small objects. The coherent patterns of lead-isotope compositions of metals from one site and one period might also reflect the fact that, at any given time, certain geographical areas have relied on a limited number of copper and lead/silver sources. The situation gets complicated if a large number of artefacts spanning a long period of time from a busy trading site are analysed (see for example Pernicka et al. 1990 or Stos-Gale and Gale 1993), where metals were coming from several different sources. In such cases, some artefacts show lead-isotope compositions which can be interpreted either as matching an ore deposit or as resulting from mixing of metal from different sources. However, this is not the case with the seventeen artefacts from El-Amarna - here it seems reasonably certain that groups IG1 and IG2 represent lead-isotope compositions characteristic of specific ore sources.

Chemical Composition of Metals from El-Amarna
Drilled samples of the artefacts were analysed using instrumental Neutron Activation Analysis; the lead content of the drillings was checked by ED XRF and the ingot 1925.568 was also analysed by XRF to confirm its silver content. The data is listed in **Table 3**; it is not possible to determine the lead and bismuth content using NAA, but the semiquantitative XRF analyses have shown the lead content to be below 0.3% in all samples. The identity of the artefact No. 1925.568 as a silver ingot was revealed by the chemical analyses - previously it was believed to be a 'bronze ingot'

The comparison of the elemental composition of the samples of copper-based metal artefacts from El-Amarna shows that nearly all of them contain a high proportion of tin: only one object, a small knife

(1890.305), seems to have much less of this component. The arsenic content is fairly uniform ranging from 0.2%-0.5%, iron from 0.1%-0.3%, nickel from 0.02% to 0.07%. All these elements, as well as cobalt and antimony, occur in the El-Amarna bronzes in concentrations typical for Late Bronze Age bronzes from the Mediterranean and Anatolia.

However, the comparison of the gold and silver content in the two isotopic groups of bronzes (one consistent with an origin from copper minerals obtained at Lavrion, the other of unknown source) gives rather surprising results. The mean value of the gold content in ten bronzes of identical lead-isotope composition of group IG2 is 204.4 ppm, whilst the mean value of gold content of four bronzes falling in the middle of the Lavrion lead-isotope 'field' and designated IG1 (see **Fig. 1**) is only 17.4 ppm. One object, accepted at present as consistent with the Lavrion ores (1924.77), has a much higher gold and silver content than the other four (297 ppm and 284.5 ppm respectively), and its lead-isotope 208/206 ratio is somewhat higher. It clearly stands out from the other artefacts forming this group.

The very high gold content in the artefacts forming group IG2 is most unusual. The gold content in the copper ores from Greece, Turkey and Cyprus (excluding the Devil's Mud deposits, which are not a source of copper and were not anciently exploited) is only rarely a few parts per million (ppm). Usually, the concentration of gold in copper minerals is below 1 ppm. For example, the highest gold content in ores from Ergani Maden, which have lead-isotope composition closest to the bronzes from El-Amarna, is 0.86 ppm (Seeliger et al. 1985, 653, Table 3). This ore sample contained 10% of Cu; in consequence, the maximum gold content in copper smelted from such ore would be about 9 ppm - a far cry from 200 ppm! Amongst the ox-hide ingots analysed at Oxford using NAA, the highest gold content is 49.5 ppm (ingot F from Ayia Triadha) and the ingots made of Cypriot copper have a gold content ranging from just a few to about 30 ppm. Clearly, the high gold content in the Amarna bronzes must be of some significance. There are several possibilities which are worth examining:

1. *The tin added to copper to produce bronze had a high gold content*
Tin and gold often occur in the same localities. Amin (1955, Table 1, p. 211) lists 43 occurrences of gold in the Eastern Desert, from which, in the proceeding 45 years, 143,061 tonnes of gold were mined. In the same table, he mentions seven occurrences of tin where 78 tonnes of tin were produced in seven years. Indeed, there are deposits in the Eastern desert where tin and gold occur side by side. Of particular interest here is the deposit of Abu Dabbab, where tin and gold are found in alluvial deposits formed by weathering and erosion (Amin 1955, 222). If tin was being recovered by the ancient Egyptians by panning, then it is quite likely

that a few grains of gold could have found its way in to the metal. For example, for 200 ppm of gold to be found in bronze with 10% of tin it would be enough to have 2 g of gold in 1 kg of pure tin.

2. *The copper source IG2 contains high gold*
If this copper source was also in the Eastern Desert, or even if only the ore from another locality was smelted there, then the grains of gold might perhaps have been present in some of the minerals or the quartz used as a flux (gold occurs in quartz veins). There are no lead-isotope analyses of copper minerals from the Eastern Desert. However, for one of the mineralisations, in Umm Samiuki, a small number of copper ores occur together with galena. The lead-isotope ratios of the galena from Umm Samiuki are quite different from any of the artefacts from El-Amarna (208/206 ratio is in the range 2.14). The same can be said for all other lead-isotope analyses of samples from lead/zinc occurrences in the Eastern Desert. There are no reports known to us of gold concentrations in the copper ores in Sinai. The gold content in the Timna and Feinan ores is in the range of a few ppm at the most.

3. *A small amount of gold was added to the bronze*
At a glance this suggestion might sound impractical, but some strange alloys have been found amongst other Egyptian metals. For example, in the collections of the Ashmolean Museum there are two small implements (a pin E.1237 and a square tipped object E.378) from Protodynastic times, which consist of an alloy of copper, silver and gold (Cu 83% and 91% respectively, the gold in both cases about 4%) (Stos-Gale, unpublished XRF analyses). These unusual compositions suggest that a small amount of alluvial gold/electrum was added to copper. It is rather difficult to imagine why, unless the electrum was mistaken for tin, or this was one of the early experiments with alloying metals which were at hand. The 1:1 and 3:1 silver/gold ratio is not unusual amongst Egyptian silver artefacts (Gale and Stos-Gale 1981).

Comparison of the Lead-Isotope Composition of the Metals from El-Amarna with other Eastern Mediterranean Metals
As a result of the lead-isotope and chemical analyses of the Mediterranean Bronze Age artefacts within the framework of the British Academy project (Gale and Stos-Gale 1992), we have at present at Oxford several hundreds of analyses of artefacts which await publication, in most cases as a collaborative effort with a number of Greek, English and American archaeologists. It is hoped that in these publications the full assessment of the archaeological features of the artefacts mentioned here will be given. At present we would like only, with the kind permission of our collaborators, to mention their compatibility with the metals from El-Amarna.

The metal artefacts from El-Amarna forming group IG1 are isotopically indistinguishable from over two hundred Bronze Age copper-based artefacts from the Aegean. It was mentioned earlier that copper, lead and silver from Lavrion were extensively used by the Minoans and Mycenaeans. More interesting is the fact that throughout the Aegean, in the Near East and even as far as Troy, there are copper-based Bronze Age artefacts (mainly, but not exclusively, dated to the Late Bronze Age) which have lead-isotope compositions consistent with the Amarna group IG2.

Amongst a roughly comparable number of copper-based artefacts from Crete and the Mainland so far analysed (c. three hundred from each region), twenty-seven objects from Crete and five from the Argolid match the IG 2 group within the range of analytical error. Nine metal items are from Knossos: four fragments and an axe from the Unexplored Mansion, two vessels from Zapher Papoura, a double axe from House B and a large vessel from the South House. Two double axes from Phaistos and one from Palaikastro also match this group. Five artefacts from the excavations in West Crete: a LMII axe from Neroukourou, a LMIIIA sword from Pighi, two fragments from Chania and a LMIIIB chisel from Samonas. The number of items of the same lead-isotope composition in the Argolid is smaller: from Tsoungiza there are two small items, a blade and a chisel, from Mycenae a LHIIIB cauldron handle, from Vapheio a sickle and from Nichoria a LHIIIA fragment.

The lead-isotope database for Anatolian and Near Eastern metal artefacts is still quite small. Amongst the items analysed we found two small items from Mersin (a pin and an arrowhead), three weapons from Ugarit and (surprisingly) a flat axe from Troy dated to EBII matching the lead-isotope compositions of group IG2.

The majority of the samples of artefacts mentioned above have been analysed for their trace elemental composition by NAA (unpublished data at the Isotrace Laboratory, Oxford). Nearly all of them are tin-bronzes, and their trace elemental compositions of arsenic, cobalt, nickel, antimony and iron seem to resemble closely those of the El-Amarna bronzes. However, the highest gold content is 21 ppm (average below 10 ppm) and the silver content is also on average much lower than in the Egyptian bronzes.

Conclusions
Lead-isotope analyses of seventeen artefacts from El-Amarna cannot provide any conclusive information about the range of metal sources used during this period in Egypt. The choice of artefacts for analyses was based chiefly on their suitability for sampling and the number selected is tiny in comparison with the large quantity of metal which must have been circulating in Late Bronze Age Egypt. The fact that none of the artefacts has lead-isotope compositions consistent with copper ores from Cyprus does not prove that no Cyp-

Table 3. Chemical composition of the artefacts from El-Amarna

Mus.No.	Au ppm	As ppm	Sb ppm	Te ppm	Ag ppm	Sn %	Cu %	Zn ppm	Co ppm	Ni ppm	Fe ppm
1890.305	66.267	2150.9	92.7	119.5	51.9	2.74	96	nd	52.4	268.2	2602.3
1921.1129	87.4	4327.8	271.1	52.3	111.9	8.53	91	nd	81.5	697.5	1237.8
1921.1131	11.433	3305.4	126.4	226.8	66.1	12.71	87	nd	58.6	303.5	1104.6
1921.1132	7.829	3146.2	190.7	81.2	110.9	10.45	89	nd	430.0	646.8	1250.5
1921.1150	5.752	2299.9	177.6	106.2	38.1	15.16	84	nd	93.2	307.7	nd
1924.77	297.453	1152.0	43.9	32.4	284.5	11.43	88	nd	44.1	213.4	1079.3
1924.81	60.669	4895.8	386.8	nd	214.8	6.25	93	nd	40.4	791.5	1753.5
1924.82	102.510	4905.6	255.3	48.8	132.7	6.94	93	38.6	57.0	258.5	1668.4
1924.84	970.344	3863.2	245.7	nd	717.2	7.51	92	nd	76.3	456.2	1891.7
1925.413	29.556	5287.6	359.8	55.0	341.0	8.78	90	nd	78.2	487.0	nd
1925.568	5723.518	367.2	nd	200	96%	nd	3	nd	nd	nd	nd
1927.4104A	6.167	2613.9	148.9	72.1	33.5	10.63	89	nd	48.8	219.7	2776.4
1927.4104B	5.032	2155.9	74.3	55.2	26.4	11.23	88	17.1	109.2	195.5	2447.3
1931.487	128.548	3281.2	198.7	72.4	123.5	9.21	90	nd	121.9	386.1	2274.3
1933.1209	279.363	4933.5	220.0	55.0	296.1	7.68	91	nd	76.4	841.0	nd
1934.267	307.714	5359.2	383.2	86.2	366.1	9.34	90	40.6	82.7	537.9	1537.0
1935.595	50.470	2205.6	228.1	nd	112.7	12.91	87	nd	52.8	383.0	3233.4

riot copper was coming to El-Amarna; only a much more comprehensive programme of analyses can prove or disprove this point.

On the other hand, even these seventeen analyses can lead to a number of interesting conclusions. The lead-isotope analyses show that there was a small flow of metal between Egypt and the Aegean. The presence of copper and silver from the deposit in Attica, which was extensively used by the Mycenaeans and Minoans (if we still agree to call them that in the second half of the 2nd millenium BC), comprises new evidence for Aegean contacts with Egypt.

Perhaps even more interesting would be the presence in the Aegean of metal of the isotope group called in this article IG2. We have to be cautious here, because the high gold content of the bronzes from El-Amarna strongly differentiates them from the bronzes of the same lead-isotope compositions excavated in the Aegean and at Ugarit. Since we do not know of a copper deposit from which metal of such composition could have originated, one cannot exclude the possibility that in fact there are two such deposits of the same range of lead-isotope ratios but distinctly different gold content. Keeping that in mind, we can now consider the other option: namely that both the Aegean and Egyptian bronzes are made of copper from the same deposit. On the present evidence, metal of this origin dominates the bronzes from El-Amarna (59% of artefacts fall into this group), while it is quite rare in the Aegean (fewer than 1% of Late Bronze Age bronzes are consistent with this lead-isotype composition). It seems possible, therefore, that the copper deposit from which the copper originated was within the 'Egyptian' domain. This 'Egyptian' metal is found not only on Crete, where it would complement many other artefacts known to be imported from Egypt, but also in the Argolid, mainly in LHIII contexts.

If this metal really came to the Aegean from Egypt, how can one explain the much higher gold content of bronzes from El-Amarna compared with that of bronzes from the Aegean and Ugarit? If we look again at the cases made previously for this unusual composition, two points may be valid: either the tin added to this copper in Egypt was from the Eastern Desert and that added outside Egypt was of a different origin with a much lower gold content, or the Egyptians were indeed adding a small amount of gold to their copper alloys. It must be emphasized here that neither the bronzes consistent with the Lavrion ores nor those from the Aegean consistent with 'Egyptian' copper have any stylistic features which would make them stand out amongst the assemblages in which they were found. As far as we know, there are no other published trace elemental analyses of Egyptian bronzes, so at present there is no comparative material for a closer consideration of this possibility. There is evidently vast potential in a new programme of analytical work on Egyptian metallurgy.

Acknowledgements
We are very grateful to Dr Helen Whitehouse of the Ashmolean Museum for her help with obtaining the samples of the artefacts, to the Hon. Vronwy Hankey for valuable comments, and to the British Academy and SBAC SERC for the funding of this project.

References
Amin, M S 1955. Geological features of some mineral deposits in Egypt. *Bull. de l'Institut du Desert d'Egypte* 5, 209-39.

Bass, G F 1967. *Cape Gelidonya: a Bronze Age Shipwreck.* Transactions of the American Phil. Soc. 57, Part 8. Philadelphia.

El Shazly, E M, Abdel Naser, S and Shukri, B 1955. Contributions to the mineralogy of the copper deposits in Sinai. *Geological Survey of Egypt.* Paper No.1. Ministry of Commerce and Industry and Mineral Resources Department. Le Caire, Imprimerie Française.

El Shazly, E M 1957. Classification of Egyptian mineral deposits. *The Egyptian Journal of Geology* I, No. 1, 1-20.

Gale, N H and Stos-Gale, Z A 1981. Ancient Egyptian Silver. *Journal of Egyptian Archaeology* 67, 103-15.

Gale, N H and Stos-Gale, Z A 1986. Oxhide ingots in Crete and Cyprus and the Bronze Age metals trade. *Annual of the British School at Athens* 81, 81-100.

Gale, N H, Bachmann, H G, Rothenberg, B, Stos-Gale, Z A and Tylecote, R F 1988. The adventitious production of iron in the smelting of copper in Timna, W. Arabah. In B Rothenberg (ed.), *Ancient Metallurgy in Timna.* London, Thames and Hudson, 182-91.

Gale, N H and Stos-Gale, Z A 1991. Lead isotope studies in the Aegean. In M Pollard (ed.), *Advances in Science Based Archaeology.* London, Royal Society/British Academy Special Publication, 63-108.

Gale, N H 1991. Copper oxhide ingots: their origin and their place in the Bronze Age metals trade in the Mediterranean. In N H Gale (ed.), *Bronze Age Trade in the Mediterranean.* Studies in Mediterranean Archaeology, XC. Jonsered, Paul Åströms Forlag, 197-239.

Hauptmann, A and Roden, C 1988. Archäometallurgische Untersuchungen zur Kupferverhuttung der Frühen Bronzezeit in Fenan, Wadi Arabah, Jordanien. *Jahrbuch des Römisch-Germanischen Zentralmuseums Mainz* 35, 510-6.

Hauptmann, A, Begemann, F, Heitkemper, E, Pernicka, E, Schmitt Strecker, S 1992. Early Copper Produced at Feinan, Wadi Araba, Jordan: the Composition of Ores and Copper. *Archaeomaterials* 6, 1-33.

Ilani, S and Rosenfeld, A 1994. Ore source of arsenic copper tools from Israel during Chalcolithic and Early Bronze ages. *Terra Nova* 6, 177-9.

Muhly, J D 1982. The Nature of Trade in the LBA Eastern Mediterranean: The Organisation of the Metal Trade and the Role of Cyprus. In J D Muhly, R Maddin and V Karageorghis (eds.), *Early Metallurgy in Cyprus 4000-500 B.C.* Nicosia, 251-70.

Pernicka, E, Begemann, F, Schmitt-Strecker, S and Grimanis, A P 1990. On the Composition and Provenance of Metal Artefacts from Poliochni on Lemnos. *Oxford Journal of Archaeology* 9 (3), 263-98.

Rothenberg, B (ed.) 1988. *Ancient Metallurgy in Timna.* London, Thames and Hudson.

Rothenberg, B (ed.) 1989. *The Egyptian Mining Temple at Timna.* London, Institute for Archeo-Metallurgical Studies.

Seeliger, T, Pernicka, E, Wagner, G A, Begemann, F, Schmitt Strecker, S, Eibner, C and Baranyi, I 1985. Archäometallurgisch Untersuchungen in Nord-und Ostanatolien. *Jahrbuch des Römisch-Germanischen Zentralmuseums Mainz* 32, 597-659.

Stos-Gale, Z A and Gale, N H 1980. Sources of galena, lead and silver in Predynastic Egypt. *Actes du XXème Symposium International d'Archeometrie. Revue d'Archeometrie* 5/III, 285-95.

Stos-Gale, Z A and Gale, N H 1992. New light on the provenance of the copper oxhide ingots found on Sardinia. In R H Tycot and T K Andrews (eds.), *Sardinia in the Mediterranean: a Footprint in the Sea.* Studies in Sardinian Archaeology presented to Miriam Balmuth. Sheffield Academic Press, 317-46

Stos-Gale, Z A 1993. Lead isotope provenance studies - do they really work? *Archaeologia Polona* 31 (PL ISSN 0066-5924), 149-80.

Stos-Gale, Z A and Gale, N H 1993. The origin of metals excavated on Cyprus. Chapter 3 in B Knapp and J Cherry (eds), *Provenance studies and Bronze Age Cyprus: Production exchange and Politico-Economic change.* Madison, Prehistory Press. In press.

Thomas, A E 1909. The mineral industry of Egypt. *The Cairo Scientific Journal* III, No. 35, 181-5.

Wagner, G A, Oztunali, O and Eibner, C 1989. Early copper in Anatolia. Archaeometallurgical field evidence. In A Hauptman, E Pernicka and G A Wagner (eds), *Old World Archaeometallurgy.* Der Anschnitt, Beiheft 7. Bochum, Deutschen Bergbau-Museums, 299-306.

Wagner, G A, Begemann, F, Eibner, C, Lutz, J, Oztunali, O, Pernicka, E and Schmitt-Strecker, S 1989b. Archäometallurgische Untersuchungen an Rohstoffquellen des Frühen Kupfers Ostanatoliens. *Jahrbuch des Römisch-Germanischen Zentral-museums Mainz* 36, 637-86.

AN AEGEAN PRESENCE IN EGYPTO-CANAAN

Jonathan N Tubb

In 1986, at a conference entitled 'The Bronzeworking Centres of Western Asia', held at the British Museum, the writer presented a paper, 'The Role of the Sea Peoples in the Bronze Production Centres of the Levant during the latter part of the Late Bronze Age', which was subsequently published in the conference proceedings (Tubb 1988a), and which seems to have initiated something of a controversy. The paper had two main aspects - firstly, that towards the very end of the Late Bronze Age, corresponding with the final phase of the Egyptian Empire in Canaan, the populations of those cities directly controlled by the Egyptians might well have included a Sea Peoples element, and secondly, that there appeared to be a correlation between those sites, admittedly few in number, which provided evidence for bronze production, and those Egyptian-controlled sites where some evidence for a Sea Peoples presence could be adduced

These aspects were further developed into what was, in reality, a suggestion rather than a hypothesis, namely, that the role of such Sea Peoples might not always have been necessarily military, as has often been presumed, but might instead have been related to specialized technological or industrial processes such as bronze production. It is not, however, this last, and indeed originally cautiously stated idea, that has caused consternation, but rather the original suggestion that Sea Peoples might have been present in Canaan generally, and in the Jordan Valley specifically, at the end of the Late Bronze Age, prior to the reign of Rameses III.

Ora Negbi has recently devoted a whole article to the issue, in which she not only dismisses the notion of a Sea Peoples involvement in the bronze industry on the grounds of insufficient evidence, but also goes to some considerable lengths to deny the very presence of Sea Peoples in the Jordan Valley at the end of the Late Bronze Age (1991).

As far as the bronze industry is concerned, her criticism is, in part, fair. The evidence for a relationship between bronze production and the Sea Peoples is, indeed, slight, but enough surely to justify what was intended to be little more than a suggestion for consideration. Negbi's more sweeping denial of a Sea Peoples presence in the Jordan Valley at the end of the Late Bronze Age is, however, unacceptable, especially given the somewhat idiosyncratic nature of her reasoning, which ultimately leads her to the conclusion that there most probably were foreigners present in the region,

but that these should be seen as representatives of the 'Land Peoples' rather than 'Sea Peoples'! Now, this is clearly not an appropriate place to argue semantic niceties. Suffice it to say that here (in accordance with the generally accepted practice), the term 'Sea Peoples' is taken to include those of their number who arrived in the Levant by means of some overland route.

Negbi's arguments, although flawed, do at least highlight one of the most important problems in dealing with the Sea Peoples, and that is the question of definition. How can a Sea Peoples presence in the Jordan Valley (or anywhere else in the Levant for that matter) be detected and defined? What are the criteria to be established? Unfortunately, the answers to both of these questions are, at best, elusive, given the generally ambiguous nature of the interpretation of any potentially associable artefacts. Only with the Philistines has it been possible (with certain reservations) to match the people with a distinctive class of artefact, the pottery, but even the effect of this connection has been reduced somewhat in recent years by the realization that the distinctive Philistine style did not develop until some fifty years or so after their settlement on the coastal plain (see especially Mazar 1985, 119-24).

With regard to groups of Sea Peoples that might have been present in the Levant prior to the 8th year of Rameses III, the difficulties of identification are even more severe, so much so that the rationale for seeking their presence may be called into question. This rationale, however, is provided by a combination of the Egyptians' tight control of Canaan in the Late New Kingdom (Weinstein 1981) together with the long-standing association of the Egyptians with the Sea Peoples, extending back at least as far as the 14th century BC (see Barnett 1975, 359-78; Dothan, M 1989, 63-4; Tubb 1988a, 263-4, n.13). In such circumstances, it would certainly be reasonable to assume the presence of groups of Sea Peoples within the populations of Egyptian-controlled cities in Canaan, either as military personnel or perhaps as industrial specialists.

Again, the question arises as to what classes of artefact should be sought in order to demonstrate the existence of such groups? Clearly, the presence or absence at sites of Philistine pottery, or its Mycenaean IIIC1 prototypes, cannot be seen as relevant: not only had this pottery not yet been developed but, more importantly, it cannot be assumed that all groups of the Sea Peoples would necessarily have developed the same style of pottery as the Philistines undeniably did.[1] All other classes of ceramic evidence tend to be ambiguous. Exotic wares, alien to the local tradition, can always be explained as imports, and not as indicative of an alien population. Similarly, the occurrence of local imitations of imported wares, even in relatively high proportions, need not imply the presence of foreign potters attempting to copy the traditions of their homeland, but may simply be the result of local potters responding to the demand for aesthetically pleasing imports. There is no means of distinguishing between these two possibilities, and so the occurrence, for example, of imitation Mycenaean IIIB simple-style stirrup jars in 13th century contexts at sites such as Beth Shan or Tell Fara cannot be used as evidence to support a pre-Philistine, Sea Peoples presence at these sites.

One of the fundamental difficulties in relation to any discussion of the Sea Peoples is the vexed question of their origins. Fortunately, the consensus seems, mercifully, to have shifted away from the more bizarre locations, arrived at purely on the grounds of name similarity, and, on the basis of sounder archaeological and textual investigations, has settled instead on the more reasonable, if more generalized, suggested homelands of the Aegean and southern and south-western Anatolia (see, for example, Sandars 1978, 197-202, noting, however, her inclination to bring the Sherden from North Syria). In any event, the localization of the Sea Peoples' homeland(s) may be of limited value in relation to the chronological and functional contexts that are being sought. For the intention is to identify those Sea Peoples who might have been serving in the Egyptian employ during the 19th and 20th Dynasties, and not those Sea Peoples who became settled following the invasions of Rameses III's reign. In these circumstances, pottery can be all but excluded from the assessment anyway, since there is no good reason why Sea Peoples serving with the Egyptians in Canaan should have included potters; certainly if their role was primarily military or, as suggested above, perhaps technological. Soldiers or industrial workers would surely have adopted whatever pots came to hand - Egyptian in Egypt or Canaanite in Canaan.

Metal artefacts might be expected to provide a more reliable indicator of cultural intrusion, but here again the evidence is nearly always ambiguous. An Aegean-style dagger might well have been the long-cherished weapon of a Sherden warrior, but it could equally have been a prized luxury import. It is possibly for this reason that when in 1968 James Pritchard suggested, on the basis of a high proportion of Aegean-style metal artefacts found in the cemetery at Tell es-Sa'idiyeh, that a Sea Peoples element might have been present in the population (1968, 99-112), the idea attracted very little attention. It is, however, a suggestion that can now be revived and substantiated on the basis of the results of the writer's renewed excavations at the site since 1985.

Tell es-Sa'idiyeh, which lies approximately 1.8 km

east of the River Jordan, on the south side of the Wadi Kufrinjeh, consists of a large double mound, the base area of which covers about 15 hectares **(Plate 25, 1-2)**. The Upper Tell, to the east, rises to some 40 metres above plain level, and this is adjoined on the western side by the low, bench-like projection of the Lower Tell. Pritchard's work at the site between 1964 and 1967 revealed, on the Upper Tell, remains of the Roman, Hellenistic and Persian periods and a series of important Iron Age city-phases dating between the 9th and 7th centuries BC. The most remarkable discovery, however, was of a beautifully constructed, stone-built staircase, cut into the north slope, a structure which Pritchard assumed to be part of Sa'idiyeh's water-supply system and which he tentatively dated to the 12th century BC (see Pritchard 1985 - the final report of the University of Pennsylvania expedition's work on the Upper Tell).

On the north side of the Lower Tell, Pritchard discovered part of what was clearly an extensive cemetery, cut into a deep silt layer overlying the eroded remains of Early Bronze Age occupation. The Pennsylvania team excavated 45 graves, dating to the 13th-12th centuries BC, some of which were extremely rich, containing, in particular, bronze weapons, utensils, vessels and ornaments thought by Pritchard to be of Aegean origin and hence indicative of a Sea Peoples element within the population (see Pritchard 1980 for the final report on the cemetery, and 1968 for his interpretations).

Renewed excavations at Tell es-Sa'idiyeh, conducted by the writer since 1985 on behalf of the British Museum, have continued to explore the site both in depth, continuing areas begun by the Pennsylvania expedition, and in extent, expanding these areas and initiating new ones (see composite site plan, **Fig. 1**).[2]

On the Upper Tell, excavations have exposed a sizeable area of the Iron Age city-level of the 9th-8th centuries BC, Stratum VII, the lowermost reached by the Americans. An important phase, with evidence for industrial specialization, principally textile preparation and weaving, Stratum VII represents an intensive occupation with a city wall, a well laid out grid of intersecting streets and alleyways, and densely packed buildings occupying the entire surface area of the mound (at least to judge from the situation on the north and west sides).

Excavations below Stratum VII have revealed, by contrast, a series of sparsely occupied phases (Strata VIII - XIB), apparently unwalled and nucleated towards the centre of the mound. The lowest of these phases, XIB, which was seen to be a somewhat ephemeral occupation, consisting of little more than hearths, pits and potholes, and which can be interpreted as a 'pre-construction' phase for the small temple of Stratum XIA (Tubb 1988b, 38), was found to have been sited on top of a dense deposit of destruction debris, about 1.5 metres deep and composed of burnt mud-brick, ashes and charred timber, within the abandoned and heavily weathered ruins of what was clearly an extensive and

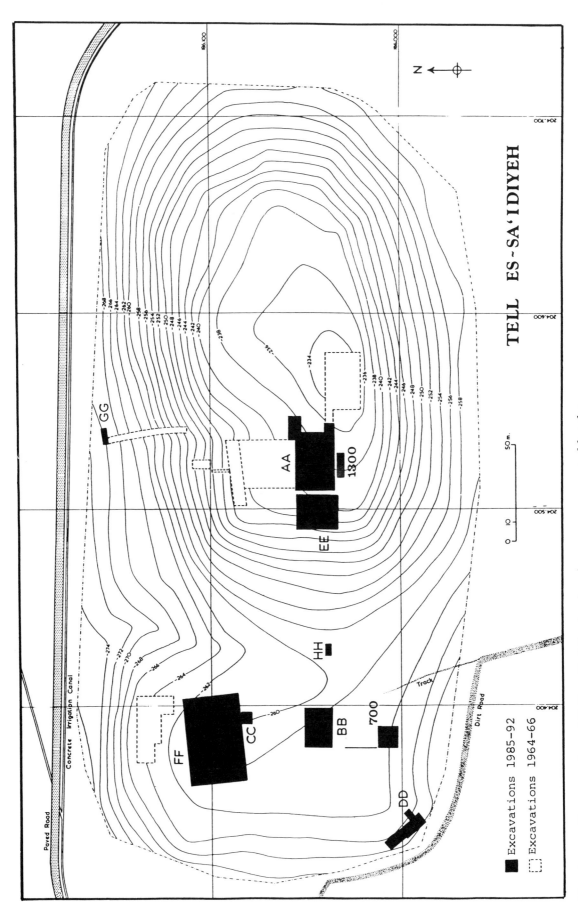

Fig. 1.   Contour plan of Tell es-Sa'idiyeh, showing areas excavated by the
Pennsylvania expedition (dotted) in relation to those of the on-going
British Museum project (solid).

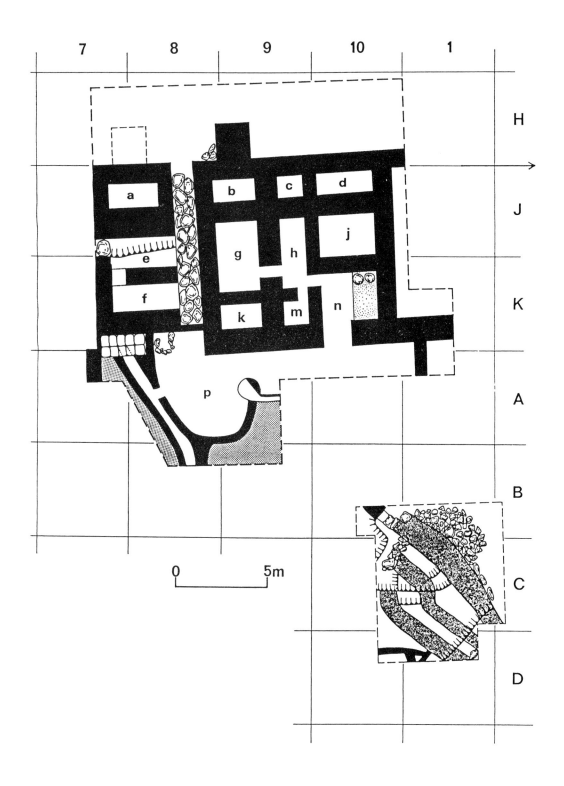

Fig. 2.　　Tell es-Sa'idiyeh: plan of the 12th Century BC 'Western Palace'.

impressive architectural complex.

Excavations in 1987-92 were directed towards the clearance of the destruction debris and the isolation of the architecture of Stratum XII. Towards the centre of the Tell, a substantial public building has been partially excavated which, on the basis of its plan and construction method, provides a further example of a so-called 'Egyptian Governor's Residency' (see Oren 1984). Most closely similar to the buildings at Tell Sera and Tell Fara (S), the Sa'idiyeh residency shows typically Egyptian constructional features such as the use of deep brick foundations and the provision of a drainage/insulation channel between external walls (**Plate 26,1**).

On the western side of the Upper Tell, a second public or administrative building, showing similar use of Egyptian construction techniques, has been found, situated immediately behind a 4 metre thick casemate city wall. The 'Western Palace', as it has been loosely termed, consists of suites of rooms, courtyards and cisterns disposed either side of a narrow passageway, which gives access to the outside by means of a small postern gate (**Fig. 2**). The most interesting features of the building are two interconnecting bathrooms or possibly cisterns, and a thickly plastered, semi-circular pool provided with an elaborate system of inlet and outflow channels. The pool was found to contain a large number of handle-less Egyptian-style store-jars, indicating that its function was not related to bathing, but was concerned instead with the water-cooled storage of some commercial commodity, perhaps wine.

Feeding the pool, and perhaps the 'Western Palace' in general, was an unusual type of aqueduct, consisting of two parallel, thickly-plastered passageways, rising in a gently-stepped gradient towards the north side of the Tell (see Tubb and Dorrell 1993, figs. 10-12).

The aqueduct forms the link between the Stratum XII architecture excavated by the British Museum expedition and what was surely the most impressive feature discovered by the Pennsylvania team, the great stone-built staircase cut into the northern slope of the Tell.

Although the work was not completed in 1967, Pritchard considered this magnificent structure to be part of the city's water-supply system (see Pritchard 1985, 57-9 and figs. 105-16). This conclusion was fully substantiated in 1987 when the staircase was re-excavated and the work continued beyond the point reached by the Americans (**Plates 26,2** and **27,1**). Having descended the mound, the staircase was found to turn through a right angle at the bottom and to continue down in a series of much steeper steps. At a depth of approximately 8 metres below plain level, the two side containing-walls were seen to incurve and meet to form an enclosed, semicircular pool which, to judge from the quantity of stone removed from its base, would almost certainly have been covered. Water, from an underground spring, was fed into the pool by means of a small conduit in the south wall, and a similar conduit, placed at a lower level in the north wall, provided an

outflow to prevent stagnation.

As recorded by Pritchard, the upper part of the staircase was provided with a mud-brick wall running along its centre, a device not only to support a covering necessary for concealment but also to create a separation for two-directional traffic.

The uppermost part of the staircase was found to have been lost through erosion, and with it has also been lost the possibility of a direct stratigraphic relationship. At the base of the pool, however, were found sherds of Egyptian-style store-jars similar to those from the Stratum XII Western Palace. The attribution of the staircase to Stratum XII is, however, more plausibly demonstrated by the nature and orientation of the aqueduct found to the north-east of the Western Palace pool. Not only does the aqueduct reflect the twin passageway arrangement of the staircase, but extrapolation of the line of the aqueduct to the north-east produces a precise coincidence with the projected top of the staircase. It is, therefore, suggested that not only does the staircase belong to Stratum XII but that it was also linked directly to the aqueduct and hence to the water-installations of the Western Palace.

The city of Stratum XII was destroyed in an intense conflagration, the dense, associated debris sealing a valuable corpus of finds, examination of which has established a date for this event at around 1150 BC. Interestingly, the majority of the finds consisted of large utilitarian pottery vessels - cooking pots, store-jars and kraters - and large, frequently broken, stone objects - bowls, mortars and incense burners. Very few small or intrinsically valuable items were encountered, and this observation, together with the absence of evidence for conflict, and also the rather unusual way in which many of the doorways of the residency and palace had been blocked with stones from the outside, strongly suggest that the destruction was wrought by the inhabitants themselves as part of a planned withdrawal.

A further dimension can be added to the city of Stratum XII by consideration of the excavations undertaken between 1985 and 1989 on the Lower Tell, where part of the contemporary cemetery has been revealed.

As mentioned previously, this cemetery had already been investigated by the Pennsylvania expedition in the 1960s, in a limited exposure on the north side of the Lower Tell. In 1985, a new area (BB on the site plan, **Fig. 1**) was initiated, situated towards the centre of the mound. The initial intention in establishing this new excavation area was primarily to provide a field for the examination of the Early Bronze Age remains, into which the cemetery was known to have been cut from the results already produced and published by Pritchard. As the 1985 season progressed, however, it became apparent that the intensity of burial in this more centrally situated area was very much greater than on the northern side of the mound; to such an extent, indeed, that the cutting in of graves here had, in fact, all but obliterated the third millennium occupation. Area BB became, therefore, between 1985 and 1989, the focus of a large-scale cemetery excavation and yielded some 420 burials.

Of the graves which contained datable finds or which could be phased on the basis of internal stratigraphic relationships, a small number (less than 5%) can be assigned to the Persian Period, represented by Stratum III on the Upper Tell (see Pritchard 1985, 60-8). The majority, however, belong to a quite restricted period, dating to the late 13th - mid-12th centuries BC, contemporary, in other words, with Stratum XII on the Upper Tell. Many of the graves have been grossly disrupted through the effects of intensive and repeated use of the same area, but despite this it has been possible to assemble a sizeable corpus of burial types (for outline details, see the 'Inventories of Graves' in Tubb 1988b, 73-80; 1990, 38-42; Tubb and Dorrell 1991, 84-6 and 1993, 68-72).

The burials show considerable variation with regard to grave construction, disposition of the deceased, burial practice and grave-goods, suggestive indeed of a mixed population. Most of the graves consist of simple, sub-rectangular pits, many of which have made use of structural elements from the underlying Early Bronze Age architecture - courtyard or foundation stones used as markers, or fragments of walling or individual mud-bricks used as kerbs or linings. Several graves were more elaborately constructed from newly-made mud-brick slabs, set into neatly dug rectangular pits, and roofed over with the same material. From the evidence of differential erosion, it is clear that these were intended to be partially visible above ground level, being more in the nature of tombs rather than graves.

Generally, the burial practice was single and primary. A few examples of double or multiple burials have been found and, similarly, a small number of secondary burials have been encountered. Quite a common finding, however, is what may be described as a 'derived secondary' practice, arising from the extreme intensity of usage of the same cemetery area over a period of time. In cases where the digging of a grave had intruded upon a previous burial, in order to show some degree of respect for the earlier interment, the skull, and frequently one or two of the long bones, had been carefully retrieved and re-deposited in the new grave.

In terms of grave-goods, the Sa'idiyeh cemetery is quite rich, arguing for an affluent and sophisticated society. The graves have produced fine assemblages of pottery, metalwork, stone vessels, ivory and jewellery, many of which show strong Egyptian influence or are indeed purely Egyptian (**Plate 9,1**). Not only are many of the grave-goods Egyptian in character, however, but so too are some of the somewhat unusual burial practices. In several instances, for example, a pottery, or more usually a bronze, bowl had been placed over the face of the individual, and examples have also been found in which the genitals had similarly been covered with a bowl. In the most bizarre case of this latter prac-

tice, the deceased had been buried face down, and three fishes had been placed over the back of the head. A bronze bowl had been placed over the genitals and, when this vessel was emptied of earth, it was found to contain an exquisite ivory cosmetic box in the form of a fish (**Plate 9,2**).

Ritual 'killing' of funerary gifts was found to have occurred in many of the graves. Daggers in particular but also javelins and even arrowheads had been bent almost double before deposition. This practice was not, however, confined solely to metal weapons: many of the pottery vessels included in the burials had had a tiny piece taken out of the rim.

The majority of the bronze objects found in the graves (vessels, weapons, pins and other items of jewellery) were found to be covered in textile remains, preserved by mineralization through the corrosion of the metal. Examination of these materials has demonstrated that, in every case so far examined, they consist of Egyptian linen.[3] In some instances, the evidence would suggest that the objects had been wrapped in cloth and deposited separately, but in others it is clear that they had been incorporated into a tight binding around the body (**Plate 27,2**). Even when bronzes had not been included amongst the grave offerings, the process of binding is often suggested by the posture of the deceased - shoulders tightly drawn up, arms drawn across the chest or feet crossed over at the ankles. The Egyptian character of these bound burials hardly needs pointing out. Even more remarkable, however, has been the discovery in a few cases of a black resinous material covering the bones, a finding which implies that some attempt at mummification was being made (see also Pritchard's Tombs 117 and 119 for this practice [1980, 20-3]).

The strongly Egyptian character of both the cemetery and the architecture of Stratum XII on the Upper Tell (though not the water-system)[4] indicates, beyond all reasonable doubt, that Sa'idiyeh, like Beth Shan, Gaza or Tell Fara, was a site under Egyptian control during the final phase of the New Kingdom empire in Canaan under the Pharaohs of the 20th Dynasty. It is unfortunate, of course, that corroborative evidence for this statement cannot be adduced from the Egyptian textual sources. Topographic texts covering the reigns of Rameses III and his immediate successors have not yet been forthcoming, and even the Great Harris Papyrus, which documents in some considerable detail the offerings made by the Pharaoh to the various temple estates, contains no specific references to towns or cities in Canaan (Breasted 1906, 87-206).

There are, it is true, references to several sites in north Jordan in various texts of the 19th Dynasty, but here it is important to emphasize that the excavations have produced no evidence to suggest that Sa'idiyeh was a city of any great significance until the latter half of the 13th century. None of the graves excavated to date can be placed any earlier than the last half of the 13th century and by far the highest proportion should be dated early in the 12th century, contemporary, that is, with the phase of usage of the large public buildings of Stratum XII on the Upper Tell. It should further be noted that no surface finds have been collected on either the Upper or the Lower Tell which can be dated to the earlier phases of the Late Bronze Age. This suggests that, if these periods are present at all, they are represented by small, rather insignificant settlements, nucleated within the heart of the Upper Tell. Negative though the evidence is, therefore, it is not surprising that Sa'idiyeh cannot be identified in Egyptian texts of the 19th Dynasty, since all of the evidence leads to the conclusion that the city was not founded or substantially developed until quite late in the reign of Rameses II, or perhaps even not until the beginning of the 20th Dynasty, for which, in both cases, topographical texts are not available.

The reasons for the establishment of an Egyptian centre at Sa'idiyeh during this final phase of the empire are almost certainly related to the site's location. For Tell es-Sa'idiyeh is situated very close to the River Jordan, immediately east of a wide and extremely shallow ford. The river would have presented, therefore, no barrier to communication between east and west, and in these terms, Sa'idiyeh can be seen as an eastern extension of Egypt's network of administrative centres in Canaan. Its function was probably quite specific. For, despite its strong fortifications, complete with concealed water system, it would seem unlikely that Sa'idiyeh's role was strategic in a strictly military sense. It seems more reasonable to suggest that its importance was primarily economic, serving as a trading entrepôt or taxation centre.

In this capacity, the location of the site was ideal, for not only does Sa'idiyeh lie at the heart of the most extensive alluvial fan east of the Jordan, commanding some of the richest and most fertile agricultural land in the country, but it also had immediate access to the equally important hinterland to the east. The valley of the Kufrinjeh, the western end of which skirts Sa'idiyeh to the north, leads back to the area that divides, very roughly, the hill country of Gilead, renowned for its vines, and the well-watered plateau south of Bashan, noted for its cattle.

That such commodities as wine, olive oil, agricultural produce and cattle were in great demand in Egypt is certainly clear from the temple lists in papyrus Harris, and these lists do refer to produce received from 'Syria', that is, in the wider sense, including Palestine.

Sa'idiyeh has yet another considerable advantage. It lies at the narrowest neck of the Valley, at a point where the *Ghor* is no more than 4 km wide. Moreover, the main fan of the Kufrinjeh gives reasonable footing across the marl in wet weather, as does the subsidiary fan extending across the flood plain from the Kufrinjeh's descent to the edge of the marl. An east-west route across the Jordan at Sa'idiyeh would have had a number of clear advantages, for not only would it involve the shortest valley crossing, but it would also avoid the badlands topography further south (which is virtually impassable in wet weather). This factor would have been of particular value, of course, if the crossing involved animals. Camels, and especially laden camels, are helpless on a slippery surface and are quite unable, or unwilling, to enter a stream from a muddy bank.

Altogether, then, it would seem most likely that the Egyptians were attracted to Sa'idiyeh because of its geographical setting. The ford west of the site provided easy access to the much-needed commodities of the east central Jordan Valley and its hinterland, and the development of Sa'idiyeh as a major commercial centre would, therefore, have made sound economic sense to the 20th Dynasty Pharaohs, struggling to maintain their failing empire.

To return now to the question of Sea Peoples in the Jordan Valley. Given the overwhelming evidence for direct Egyptian control of Sa'idiyeh during the late 13th - 12th centuries, it would certainly not be out of place to suggest that a group of such people might have been present within the population, serving the Egyptians in some capacity. Substantiation for this idea cannot, however, be sought from the ceramic corpus, for although it does indeed include a high proportion of imitation Mycenaean IIIB vessels, this class of evidence must, for the reasons of ambiguity stated previously, be disregarded. For similar reasons, a Sea Peoples presence cannot be adduced on the basis of the Aegean-style bronzes cited by Pritchard (1968,108-9).

The evidence for a Sea Peoples presence at Tell es-Sa'idiyeh derives instead from an aspect of the material culture, the nature of which is unambiguous, and which is traditionally so conservative that it demands recognition as an ethnic indicator - burial custom. For, in addition to the pit and built graves, the Sa'idiyeh cemetery has been found to contain a large number of double-pithos burials. These burials, completely alien to the Canaanite tradition, consist of two large store-jars with their necks removed, joined shoulder to shoulder to form, in effect, a pottery coffin, which was then set into a pit (**Plates 28,1-2** and **29,1**). The deceased, always a single individual, extended on the back, was placed inside, and grave-goods were either placed with the body or were arranged around the outside of the 'coffin' (occasionally in both places). Altogether, 27 double-pithos burials have been found at Sa'idiyeh to date (1993). In addition, 52 jar burials containing the remains of infants have been excavated. In these cases, a single store-jar was used, again the neck having been removed in order to allow for insertion of the deceased, and closure was effected by means of a stone or a large sherd (**Plate 29,2**). One further, clearly related, burial type, of which two examples have been discovered, deserves mention: in this case, the head only of the deceased was contained within a similarly adapted store-jar, the remainder of the body having been covered with a 'shroud' of large store-jar sherds.

Generally, the grave-goods from the double-pithos and jar burials are comparable with those from the rest of the cemetery and, if any preference at all can be detected, it would seem to be for Egyptian items - scarabs, jewellery, bronze knives and delicately carved ivory boxes **(Plate 30,1)**. Two of the double-pithos burials contained long-tanged daggers which show an interesting feature, not previously recorded. The two blades, one of which had been ritually 'killed' by bending, revealed, on cleaning, delicately executed incised geometric decorations, extending along the mid-ribs of both faces **(Plate 30,2)**. The only parallel found so far for this unusual decorative treatment comes from a poorly documented, effectively undated, dagger-blade from Olympia (Avila 1982, pl. 48,1003).

The large number of double-pithos and jar burials at Sa'idiyeh is surely significant, for elsewhere in Palestine these burial types are extremely rare. A single double-pithos burial from Kfar Yehoshua in the Jezreel Valley was published by Druks (1966, 213-20), and this example is closely comparable to those from Sa'idiyeh, both in terms of the overall configuration of the burial and in the nature of the grave-goods. It has been dated by the excavator to the late 13th century.

A double-pithos burial, but without associated finds, was excavated in the 12th-11th century cemetery at Azor, where, in addition to this finding, a number of other fascinating funerary practices were recorded, including mud-brick built tombs and a cremation burial (see Dothan, T and M 1992, 114-5).

Some sixty double-pithos burials are reported to have been found at Tel Zeror, all apparently in poor condition, and again without associated finds. According to the excavator, these burials date to the Late Bronze Age, Iron Age and Hellenistic period, but it is not clear on what basis these unquantified attributions are made (Ohata 1970, 73-4).

At Tell Farah (N) a somewhat disrupted jar (double-pithos?) burial was found on the Tell and dated by the excavators to the late 13th century BC (de Vaux and Steve 1948, 573-4).

The most recent discoveries of double-pithos and jar burials have been made at Tel Nami on the coast of Israel. So far, these have only been recorded in brief preliminary reports but are said to date to the 13th century and to contain rich assemblages of grave-goods, including many Egyptian items (Artzy 1993, 10).

The presence of significant numbers of double-pithos burials in the cemetery at Sa'idiyeh must surely indicate the presence of a sizeable alien element within the population. That this element was composed of a group of the Sea Peoples is indicated by the origin of this burial type. For, if it is seen to have been rare in Palestine, the double-pithos burial was, by contrast, one of the most ubiquitous burial types of Hittite Anatolia in the Late Bronze Age. Closely similar burials (although accompanied by purely local grave-goods) have been found, for example, at Alishar (Von der Osten 1937,

84-108) and Yanarlar (Emre 1978 - see especially pp. 123-37 for a discussion of the occurrences of double-pithos and jar burials throughout the Hittite empire), and further west at Sardis, where the double-pithos burial tradition can be traced back to the third millennium (Hanfmann 1983, 17-18 and fig. 14). If, as is now widely accepted, some of the groups of the Sea Peoples originated in this region, then the occurrence of double-pithos burials at Sa'idiyeh can only serve to demonstrate the presence of such people at the site during the late 13th-12th centuries BC. It would seem likely, too, that the other instances of double-pithos and jar burials in Palestine recorded above should also be attributed to groups of Sea Peoples.

It is possible, as suggested by Gonen (1992, 30), that these people arrived in Palestine by means of an overland route following the collapse of the Hittite empire at the end of the 13th century (and might, in these terms, have been Hittite refugees rather than Sea Peoples). Whilst a gradual infiltration of this sort could well account for some of the isolated occurrences of double-pithos and jar burials, it cannot possibly explain the situation at Sa'idiyeh. For here, the high proportion of such burial types in the cemetery of what was clearly a strongly controlled Egyptian city implies a much longer-standing relationship between the aliens and the Egyptians. It would seem more reasonable to suggest in this case that the Sea Peoples formed a previously-integrated component of the Egyptian contingent that was responsible for the development of the site as a commercial centre in the latter part of the 13th century.

The identity of the Sea Peoples group at Sa'idiyeh cannot, of course, be established. Of the possible candidates, the most likely, in the writer's opinion, would be the Sherden (see the extended note in Tubb 1988a, note 13, which cites the relevant Egyptian textual sources), an opinion now also shared by Moshe Dothan (1989, 64), and although the process of identification of Sea Peoples origins based on name similarity has been dismissed above it is perhaps worth pointing out that the equation of Sherden with Sardinia is far less satisfactory than it would be with Sardis!

Notes

1. One of the most significant developments in Philistine archaeology in the last ten years has been the recognition at a number of sites of an initial phase of Philistine settlement, during which Mycenaean IIIC1 pottery was locally produced. Trude Dothan, on the basis of her work at Tel Miqne-Ekron, has identified a 'simple monochrome' style of Mycenaean IIIC1 pottery, which she attributes to the arrival at the site of Sea People settlers, early in the reign of Rameses III (before year 8) (1989, 6). A second monochrome 'elaborate' style is said to develop following the settlement of the Philistines after year 8 of Rameses III, the pottery based in part on the previous 'simple style' and in part on new ideas brought from the Aegean (ibid, 67). The true Philistine bichrome ware appears, according to Dothan, almost simultaneously with this 'elaborate style', in other words, quite early in the reign of

Rameses III (ibid, 7). A less compressed, and perhaps more realistic, chronology is offered by Mazar (1985, 119-20), who sees the monochrome Mycenaean IIIC1 ware (simple and elaborate) as having been produced by the Philistines following their settlement after the 8th year of Rameses III. The bichrome 'Philistine' pottery was not produced, according to Mazar, for another forty or so years, perhaps in the time of Rameses V or VI, towards the middle of the 12th century.

2. The results of the current British Museum expedition's excavations at Tell es-Sa'idiyeh have been fully published in preliminary form: see Tubb 1988, 1990; Tubb and Dorrell 1991, 1993 and 1994. A more popular account of the first four seasons appears as chapter 4 in Tubb and Chapman 1990.

3. The examinations were undertaken by Miss Elizabeth Crowfoot and the writer would wish to express his gratitude to her for providing this information.

4. It is interesting to note that the Sa'idiyeh water-system is neither Egyptian nor Canaanite in style, but instead finds its closest parallels in the external, slope-cut systems at Mycenae and Tiryns (see R L Miller's Appendix E in Tubb 1988, 84-8 and associated references). There is, however, a more local parallel to the Sa'idiyeh system which is often overlooked. At Megiddo, there was found a fragment of a descending passageway on the west side of the Tell, which pre-dates the well-known rock-cut system. This passageway (Gallery 629) was almost certainly linked to the spring cave (1007), presenting in effect a system almost identical to that at Sa'idiyeh (see Lamon 1935, 10-12). The passageway lay beneath the 'inset-offset' city wall, which, despite Yadin's attempts to redate (1960, 62-8), was correctly assigned by the excavators to the Solomonic period. The passageway was dated by the excavators to the 12th century BC, a time during which Megiddo too was under Egyptian control.

References

Artzy, M 1993. Nami: Eight Years Later. *C.M.S. News.* University of Haifa, Center for Maritime Studies 20, 9-12.

Avila, R A J 1983. *Bronzene Lanzen - und Pfeilspitzen der Griechischen Spätbronzezeit.* Prähistorische Bronzefunde V,1. Munich, C H Beck.

Barnett, R D 1975. 'The Sea Peoples.' In *The Cambridge Ancient History,* II, Part 2, Third Edition. Cambridge, Cambridge University Press, 359-78.

Breasted, J H 1906. *Ancient Records of Egypt: Historical Documents,* Vol. IV. *The Twentieth to the Twenty-sixth Dynasties.* Chicago, University of Chicago.

Dothan, M 1989. Archaeological Evidence for Movements of the Early 'Sea Peoples' in Canaan. In S Gitin and W G Dever (eds.), *Recent Excavations in Israel: Studies in Iron Age Archaeology.* Annual of the American Schools of Oriental Research, 49. Winona Lake, ASOR, 54-70.

Dothan, T 1989. The Arrival of the Sea Peoples: Cultural Diversity in Early Iron Age Canaan. In S Gitin and W G Dever (eds.), *Recent Excavations in Israel: Studies in Iron Age Archaeology.* Annual of the American Schools of Oriental Research, 49. Winona Lake, ASOR, 1-14.

Dothan, T and M 1992. *People of the Sea: The Search for the Philistines.* New York, Macmillan.

Druks, A 1966. A 'Hittite' Burial near Kfar Yehoshua. *Bulletin of the Israel Exploration Society* 30, 213-20 (Hebrew).

Emre, K 1978. *Yanarlar: A Hittite Cemetery near Afyon.* Ankara, Turkish Historical Association.

Gonen, R 1992. *Burial Patterns and Cultural Diversity in Late Bronze Age Canaan.* American Schools of Oriental Research, Dissertation Series, 7. Winona Lake, ASOR.

Hanfmann, G M A 1983. *Sardis, from Prehistoric to Roman times: Results of the Archaeological Exploration of Sardis 1958-1975.* Cambridge, MA, Harvard University Press.

Lamon, R S 1935. *The Megiddo Water System.* Oriental Institute Publications XXXII. Chicago, University of Chicago.

Mazar, A 1985. *Excavations at Tell Qasile, Part Two: The Philistine Sanctuary: Various Finds, the Pottery, Conclusions, Appendixes.* QEDEM 20. Jerusalem, Hebrew University.

Negbi, O 1991. Were there Sea Peoples in the Central Jordan Valley at the Transition from the Bronze Age to the Iron Age? *Tel Aviv* 18, 205-43.

Ohata, K 1970. *Tel Zeror* 3. Tokyo, Society for Near Eastern Studies in Japan.

Oren, E D 1984. 'Governors' Residencies' in Canaan under the New Kingdom: A Case Study of Egyptian Administration. *The Journal of the Society for the Study of Egyptian Antiquities* 14, 37-56.

Osten, H H von der 1937. *The Alishar Hüyük: Seasons of 1930-32,* Part II. Oriental Institute Publications, XXIX. Chicago, University of Chicago.

Pritchard, J B 1968. New Evidence on the Role of the Sea Peoples in Canaan at the Beginning of the Iron Age. In W A Ward (ed.), *The Role of the Phoenicians in the Interaction of Mediterranean Civilizations.* Beirut, American University of Beirut, 99-112.

Pritchard, J B 1980. *The Cemetery at Tell es-Sa'idiyeh, Jordan.* University Museum Monograph, 41. Philadelphia, University Museum, University of Pennsylvania.

Pritchard, J B 1985. *Tell es-Sa'idiyeh: Excavations on the Tell, 1964-1966.* University Monograph, 60. Philadelphia, University Museum, University of Pennsylvania.

Sandars, N K 1978. *The Sea Peoples: Warriors of the Ancient Mediterranean.* London, Thames and Hudson.

Tubb, J N 1988a. The Role of the Sea Peoples in the Bronze Industry of Palestine/Transjordan in the Late Bronze - Early Iron Age Transition. In J E Curtis (ed.), *Bronzeworking Centres of Western Asia.* London, Kegan Paul, 251-70.

Tubb, J N 1988b. Tell es-Sa'idiyeh: Preliminary Report on the First Three Seasons of Renewed Excavations. *Levant* 20, 23-89.

Tubb, J N 1990. Preliminary Report on the Fourth Season of Excavations at Tell es-Sa'idiyeh in the Jordan Valley. *Levant* 22, 21-42.

Tubb, J N and Dorrell, P G 1991. Tell es-Sa'idiyeh: Interim Report on the Fifth (1990) Season of Excavations. *Levant* 23, 67-86.

Tubb, J N and Dorrell, P G 1993. Tell es-Sa'idiyeh: Interim Report on the Sixth Season of Excavations. *Palestine Exploration Quarterly* 125, 50-74.

Tubb, J N and Dorrell P G 1994. Tell es-Sa'idiyeh 1993: Interim Report on the Seventh Season of Excavations. *Palestine Exploration Quarterly* 126, 52-67.

de Vaux, R and Steve, A M 1948. La Seconde Campagne de Fouilles à Tell Far'ah, Près Naplouse: Rapport Préliminaire. *Revue Biblique* 55, 544-80.

Weinstein, J M 1981. The Egyptian Empire in Palestine: A Reassessment. *Bulletin of the American Schools of Oriental Research* 241, 1-28.

Yadin, Y 1960. New Light on Solomon's Megiddo. *Biblical Archaeologist* 23, 62-8.

ANCIENT EGYPTIAN TIMBER IMPORTS
AN ANALYSIS OF WOODEN COFFINS
IN THE BRITISH MUSEUM

W Vivian Davies

Introduction

In recent years the Department of Egyptian Antiquities at the British Museum has begun a long-term programme of scientific analysis of its collection of wooden objects, with the aim of advancing knowledge in an area of ancient technology which has been relatively neglected in the past.[1] It is widely accepted that Egypt, lacking native wood suitable for large-scale constructional and various other prestige purposes, traded for conifer-timber from the Levant, the major imported species, it is often stated, being cedar, cypress, juniper, fir and pine.[2] An important goal of the project is to confirm the identity of these woods and at the same time to determine the nature and extent of their use. Some analyses have already been included in Museum catalogues devoted to certain categories of object.[3] Published here are the preliminary results deriving from a sample of the Museum's large coffin-collection.[4] Coffins are the ideal source-material for such research in that they are sizeable, complex, often closely datable and survive in large quantitites from most periods of Egyptian history.

The thirty-six coffins (some of them fragmentary) in this first sample date from the Old Kingdom (Sixth Dynasty) to the late Second Intermediate Period/early Eighteenth Dynasty. They come from four sites: Assiut, Beni Hasan, Bersheh and Thebes. They are listed below by site and then chronologically. The documentation provided consists in each case of museum number, name and title(s) of owner, if known, details of provenance, maximun dimensions (length, width and height) of the intact or near-intact coffins, date, material and selective bibliography. Following this brief catalogue, a provisional assessment of the results is offered and some broader implications considered.

Catalogue
Assiut[5]

1. EA 46629. *Ḥtp-nb (.i). imy-r ḫnty-š pr-' 3 sḥd ḥmw-nṯr ḥwt-k3 Ppy smr w'ty*, 'overseer of the tenants of the Great House, inspector of the priests of the *ka*-temple of Pepy,[6] sole companion'. Hogarth Tomb 56. Dynasty 6. 186. 5 x 60.5 x 59.5 cm. *Tamarix* sp. (tamarisk). Taylor 1989, 15, fig. 5; Magee 1989, Vol. ii, 44, C2; Lapp 1993, 121, para. 272, and 294, S41. **Plate 31,1.**

2. EA 46634. *Ḥwit* (female). *rḫt-nswt ḥm[t]-nṯr Ḥwt-Ḥr*, 'she who is known to the King, priestess of Hathor'. Dynasty 6. 175 x 59 x 51 cm. *Ficus sycomorus* (syca-

more fig). PM iv, 268; Magee 1989, Vol. ii, 44-5, C3; Lapp 1993, 121, para. 272, and 296-7, S61.

3. EA 46632. *Sn-k3w. smr*, 'companion'. Late Old Kingdom. 143 x 52.3 x 48.2 cm. *Ficus sycomorus* (sycamore fig). PM iv, 268; Magee 1989, Vol. ii, 48, C8.

4. EA 46633. *Ḫnnw. ḥk3 ḥwt ḫry-tp nswt smr w'ty n mrwt*, 'chief of an estate, royal chamberlain, beloved sole companion'. Late Old Kingdom. 150.2 x 50.5 x 43.5 cm. *Ficus sycomorus* (sycamore fig). PM iv, 268; Magee 1989, Vol. ii, 46, C5; Lapp 1993, 121-2, para. 274, and 296, S56.

5. EA 46637. *K3i(t) Idni(t)* (female). *ḫkrt-nswt w'tt ḥm(t)-nṯr Ḥwt-Ḥr*, 'sole ornament of the King, priestess of Hathor'. Late Old Kingdom. 79.5 x 38 x 32.5 cm. *Ficus sycomorus* (sycamore fig). Magee 1989, Vol. ii, 46, C6.

6. EA 46647. *Wrt* (female). Herakleopolitan Period. Fragmentary. *Ficus sycomorus* (sycamore fig) with dowels of *Ficus sycomorus*. Magee 1989, Vol. ii, 55-6, C18.

7. EA 46630. *Nfrw*. Hogarth Tomb 10A. Late Dynasty 11. 188 x 42 x 45.5 cm. *Ziziphus* sp. (sidder). PM iv, 268; Magee 1989, Vol. ii, 77-8, C59; Lapp 1993, 294-5, S42.

8. EA 46631. *'nḫ.f.* Early Dynasty 12. 183.5 x 41.2 x 49.3 cm. *Tamarix* sp. (tamarisk). PM iv, 268; Andrews 1984, 27, no. 25; Lapp 1993, 292-3, S21.

9. EA 29575. *Ḥty*. Purchased. Early Dynasty 12. 197 x 46 x 54 cm. *Ficus sycomorus* (sycamore fig). PM iv, 268; Magee 1989, Vol. ii, 87-8, C77.

10. EA 29576. *Ḥni*. Purchased. Early Dynasty 12. 184 x 43 x 50.5 cm. *Ficus sycomorus* (sycamore fig). PM iv, 268; Magee 1989, Vol. ii, 94-5, C87; Lapp 1993, 296-7, S52.

11. EA 46644. *Ini-it.f* (female). Early Dynasty 12. Fragmentary. *Cedrus* sp. (cedar). Seipel 1989, 95, no. 61, a-b; Magee 1989, Vol. ii, 113, C111.

12. EA 46642. Name lost. Early Dynasty 12. Fragmentary. *Ficus sycomorus* (sycamore fig). Magee 1989, Vol. ii, 103-4, C98.

13. EA 46654. *Msḥti.* End of Dynasty 12/Dynasty 13. Fragmentary. *Ficus sycomorus* (sycamore fig) with one dowel also of *Ficus sycomorus* and other dowels, tenons and pegs of *Ziziphus spina-christi* (sidder). Magee 1989, Vol. ii, 120, C120.

14. EA 46646. Name lost. Middle Kingdom. Fragmentary. *Ficus sycomorus* (sycamore fig) with dowels of *Tamarix* (tamarisk).

15. EA 47594. Name lost. Middle Kingdom. Fragmentary. *Tamarix* sp. (tamarisk).

16. EA 47607. Name lost. Middle Kingdom. Fragmentary. *Ficus sycomorus* (sycamore fig).

Beni Hasan
17. EA 41571. *Sbk-ḥtpi.* Outer coffin. Purchased. Garstang Grave 723. Late Dynasty 11/early Dynasty 12. 206 x 62.8 x 85 cm. *Ficus sycomorus* (sycamore fig). Garstang 1907, 168, fig. 170; PM iv, 187 (wrongly under 'Bersheh'); Guide 1924, 45-6; Ruffle 1977, 204-5, fig. 153; Willems 1988, 22 (BH2L), 63-4, n. 27, and 65; Lapp 1993, 280-1, BH17a. **Plate 10,2.**

18. EA 41572. *Sbk-ḥtpi* (as above). Inner coffin. Purchased. Garstang Grave 723. Late Dynasty 11/early Dynasty 12. 186 x 41 x 44.8 cm. *Cedrus* sp. (cedar). Bibliography as last, save for Garstang 1907, 138, 168, fig. 170, and 237, fig. 231; PM iv 162 and 187; Willems 1988, 22 (BH1L), 63-4, n. 27, and 65; Lapp 1993, 280-1, BH17b. **Plate 10,1.**

19. EA 32051. *Ḥnw* (female). Garstang Grave 834 (?). Dynasty 12/13. 187.5 x 45 x 52.2 cm. *Cedrus* sp. (cedar). Lapp 1993, 61, para. 155ff., 278-9, BH11, pl. 9, b; Quirke and Spencer 1992, 104, fig. 82.

Bersheh
20. EA 30839. *Gw3. wr swnw,* 'chief of physicians'. Outer coffin. Purchased. Probably from Tomb 12/G. Mid to late Dynasty 12. 261.7 x 93 x 123.8 cm. *Cedrus* sp. (cedar). PM iv, 187; Willems 1988, 21 (B2L), 69, 72, n. 65, 75-7; Taylor 1989, 19, fig. 8; Lapp 1993, 77, 90-1, 276-7, B21a, pl. 18.

21. EA 30840. *Gw3* (as above). Inner coffin. Purchased. Probably from Tomb 12/G. Mid to late Dynasty 12. 224 x 60 x 65 cm. *Cedrus* sp. (cedar). PM iv, 187; Willems 1988, 21 (B1L), 69, 72, n. 65, 75-7; Taylor 1989, 18, fig. 6; Lapp 1993, 77, 90-1, 276-7, B21b.

22. EA 30841. *Sni. imy-r pr* and *wr swnw,* 'overseer of the house' and 'chief of physicians'. Outer coffin. Purchased. Probably from Tomb 11. Mid to late Dynasty 12. 262 x 89 x 107.5 cm. *Cedrus* sp. (cedar). PM iv, 187; Willems 1988, 21 (B4L), 69, 72, n. 65, 75-7, n. 87; Lapp 1993, 77 and 276-7, B19a.

23. EA 30842. *Sni* (as above). Inner coffin. Purchased. Probably from Tomb 11. Mid to late Dynasty 12. 215.5 x 61 x 62.5 cm. *Cedrus* sp. (cedar). PM iv, 187; Willems 1988, 21 (B3L), 69, 72, n. 65, 75-7, n. 87; Taylor 1989, 19, fig. 7; Lapp 1993, 77 and 276-7, B19b.

24. EA 55315. *Spi. imy-r ms',* 'army commander'. Purchased. Probably Tomb 14/E. Mid to late Dynasty 12. 212.5 x 53.5 x 67.5 cm. *Cedrus* sp (cedar). PM iv, 184 and 187; Andrews 1984, 41, fig. 42; Willems 1988, 21 (B5L), 69, 75-7, n. 82; Taylor 1989, 23, fig. 13; Lapp 1993, 77, 91, 276-7, B17. **Plate 31,2.**

25. EA 34259. *S3t-ipi* (female). *nbt pr,* 'mistress of the house'. Purchased. Probably from Tomb 17/C. Dynasty 12. 231.5 x 83.5 x 102 cm. *Ficus sycomorus* (sycamore fig). PM iv, 183; Willems 1988, 35 (B5); Lapp 1993, 77 and 276-7, B12.

26. EA 35285. *Nḫt-'nh.* Purchased. Dynasty 12. 213.2 x 60.2 x 62 cm. *Cedrus* sp (cedar). PM iv, 187; Willems 1988, 35 (B6); Seipel 1989, 96, no. 62; Lapp 1993, 77 and 276-7, B10.

Thebes
27. EA 6654. *Im3w. ḥtmy-bity smr w'ty,* 'seal-bearer of the king, sole companion'. Purchased. Late Dynasty 11. 214 x 69 x 76.5 cm. *Cedrus* sp. (cedar). PM i (2), 827; Willems 1988, 33 (T1L), 110 and 115; Lapp 1993, 163ff. and 308-9, T4.

28. EA 6655. *Mntw-htp.* Purchased. First half of Dynasty 12. 198.2 x 55.2 x 74.3 cm. *Cedrus* sp. (cedar). PM i (2), 827; Willems 1988, 33 (T2L), 115, n. 268, and 116, n. 269; Lapp 1993, 167ff., 308-9, T13, pl. 37.

29. EA 29570. *Sbk-ḥtp. imy-r t3* (?), 'overseer of the land' (?). Purchased. Dynasty 12. 216.3 x 54.2 x 59.5 cm. *Cedrus* sp. (cedar). PM i (2), 827; Willems 1988, 33 (T3L), and 115-6, n. 268; Lapp 1993, 167ff. and 310-11, T29.

30. EA 12270. *Imn-htp. ḥm-ntr,* 'priest'. Purchased. Late Dynasty 12/Dynasty 13. 202 x 46.5 x 56.5 cm. *Ficus sycomorus* (sycamore fig). PM i (2), 827; Andrews 1984, 42, fig. 43; Willems 1988, 39 (T18), and 115; Lapp 1993, 169 ff. and 308-9, T7.

31. EA 29997. *Hrw-nfr. ḥtmy-bity s3-nswt smsw imy-r ms' wr,* 'seal-bearer of the King, eldest son of the King, commander-in-chief'. Purchased. Second Intermediate Period, Dynasty 17 (?). Fragmentary. *Ficus sycomorus* (sycamore fig) with dowels of *Tamarix* (tamarisk). PM i (2), 657; Willems 1988, 33 (T5L), and 117; Parkinson and Quirke 1992, 37-51, pls. ii-iv.

32. EA 6652. *Ini-it.f. nswt-bity,* 'King of Upper and Lower Egypt'. Purchased. Second Intermediate Period,

Dynasty 17. 192.5 x 60.5 x 48 cm. *Ficus sycomorus* (sycamore fig). Winlock 1924, 229-30, pl. xiv; Handbook 1938, 32, pl. x; PM i (2), 602; Andrews 1984, 43, fig. 44; Raven 1989, 83; Taylor 1989, 26, fig. 19; Quirke 1990, 25, n. 3; Quirke and Spencer 1992, 105, fig. 83; Quirke 1994. **Plate 32,1.**

33. EA 6653. Anonymous. Purchased. Second Intermediate Period, Dynasty 17. 186 x 53 x 43 cm. *Ficus sycomorus* (sycamore fig). Guide 1898, 35-6; Guide 1904, 68-9; Guide 1924, 48; Handbook 1938, 32.

34. EA 52950. Anonymous. Purchased. Second Intermediate Period, Dynasty 17. 193.7 x 47 x 49 cm. *Ficus sycomorus* (sycamore fig). Guide 1924, 47; Handbook 1938, 32. **Plate 32,2.**

35. EA 52951. Anonymous. Purchased. Second Intermediate Period, Dynasty 17. 191 x 46 x 59.5 cm. *Ficus sycomorus* (sycomore fig). Guide 1924, 47; Handbook 1938, 32. **Plate 32,3.**

36. EA 54350. *T3-iwy* (female). Dra Abu el-Naga, Birabi. Intrusive burial in Tomb 41. Early Dynasty 18. 195 x 50.5 x 72.5 cm. *Ficus sycomorus* (sycamore fig). Guide 1924, 47; PM i (2), 827; Handbook 1938, 33; Niwinski 1988, 10, fig. 7, and 11, n. 21; Reeves and Taylor 1992, 100, with fig.

Assessment

Of the thirty-six coffins analysed, twenty-four are made of native wood - twenty of sycamore fig, three of tamarisk, and one of sidder - and twelve of foreign wood, in each case cedar. Where it has been possible to analyse dowels and such parts, they have all been found to be made of native wood - sycamore fig (**6 and 13**), tamarisk (**14 and 31**) and sidder (**13**). The Sixth Dynasty coffins of tamarisk (**1**) and sycamore fig (**2**) and the one Middle Kingdom example of sidder (**7**) are now the earliest documented examples of the use of these woods for full-length coffins, though we can expect future analyses to yield earlier examples, certainly of the first two. The use of sidder for such a purpose is rare[7] and, interestingly, the same appears to be true of another stock native wood, acacia, which is not represented in the BM sample.[8] All the BM cedar coffins date to the Middle Kingdom, but there was evidently a long tradition of such usage of the wood, as it has already been identified in coffins of the Old Kingdom (Fourth and Sixth Dynasties).[9] In general these results fully confirm a pattern that had already begun to emerge from other coffin analyses: that sycamore fig was the most widely used of the native woods, that native woods were preferred for parts such as dowels, pegs etc, and that cedar was predominant among the imported timbers.[10]

The superior qualities of a coniferous softwood like cedar as compared to the native hardwood species are well documented: long straight lengths of timber, ease of working, durability, immunity from rot and resistance to insects and an attractive colour and fragrance.[11] Its practical advantages are evident from comparison of coffins made from the different species, for example, nos **17-18** (interestingly, two coffins belonging to the same man, each of a different wood) and **1** and **24** (**Plates 10, 1-2,** and **31, 1-2**). The long straight planks of the cedar coffins, easily fitted together and thus economical of time and material, contrast strikingly with the uneven structure of the native specimens, with their crooked planks, holes and other irregularities. The sidder coffin (**7**) is a classic patchwork construction,[12] formed by joining together a large number of pieces of different shape and size (over a dozen to make one side alone). An additional advantage of cedar is that its planks produce a relatively smooth unbroken surface, eminently suitable for decoration, whether by carving in relief or by painting. The difficulties of carving in a flawed and intractable surface are well exemplified by **1 (Plate 31,1)**, made of tamarisk, which illustrates why it was not often attempted. More usually, native woods were covered with a thick layer of plaster, which served as a ground for painted decoration and at the same time concealed the underlying flaws (**Plate 10,2**). Outside the areas of decoration, the surfaces of cedar coffins were either covered with a very thin wash or left completely exposed to reveal the wood's attractive colour and texture (**Plates 10,1 and 31,2**). The prestige value of owning such a coffin is underlined by those cases where a coffin made of native wood was disguised to make it look like cedar or some other conifer, either by painting or veneering.[13]

Other conifers such as cypress and juniper had similar properties to cedar[14] but on present data appear to have been considerably less popular. To the small list in Lucas and Harris[15] may be added only three examples of cypress: two full-size coffins of the Middle Kingdom[16] and one coffin-lid of the Late Period.[17] Examples of fir and pine are even sparser: to date, only one coffin of the Late Period made of fir[18] and one coffin-lid of the Third Intermediate Period made of pine.[19] This compares with a total of about forty coffins, covering a range of dates, identified as being made of cedar.[20] To this long list of coffins may be added a further sizeable and impressive object, one of the funerary boats of King Sesostris III of the late Twelfth Dynasty, also now known to be made of cedar,[21] representing, it has been suggested, 'a kingly display of wealth and power.'[22]

From a regional perspective, it is noticeable how Assiut stands apart from the rest. Of the sixteen coffins from Assiut (**1-16**), almost all are made of native wood; indeed, only one (**11**) is made of cedar. This contrasts strikingly with, for example, the results from Bersheh (**20-26**), which of the other sites is the best represented with contemporary analysed material. Six of the seven from Bersheh are made of cedar and to this number can be added five other coffins together with a canopic box now in Boston,[23] and two coffins and a canopic box in Cairo.[24] We know that these Bersheh coffins belonged to the elite of the region, those in Cairo to a nomarch, those in Boston probably to a nomarch and his wife, and those in the BM to high officials of the provincial court.[25] Much detailed work remains to be done on the Assiut material in general, but to judge from the limited prosopographical evidence, the overall quality of decoration of the coffins and the nature and the quantity of the associated burial equipment, their owners were certainly people of some standing. The apparent scarcity, or lack of use, of foreign timber may not then in this case be simply a matter of relative status. Were there perhaps special economic factors affecting the availability of foreign timber at Assiut? Or was it a case of a strong local craft tradition (running, perhaps, in parallel with what we know to have been a conservative and distinctively local tradition of coffin-decoration)?[26] Such speculation is probably premature. There are indications from different categories of object[27] and from other coffins[28] - yet to be tested but which appear from visual inspection to be made of some conifer - that foreign timber may have been more prevalent at Assiut than is suggested by the BM sample. It is certainly too early to draw any conclusions. We need first to be sure that we have a truly representative picture, and this can only be achieved by increasing the number of analyses from the sites concerned, while at the same time extending the research to include material from other areas.[29]

Also worthy of note is the temporal variation revealed by the results from the Theban coffins. Three of the four Middle Kingdom examples (**27-9**) are made of cedar.[30] A further Theban example in Brooklyn,[31] of the same period, has recently been identified as cypress.[32] In contrast, all the coffins of the Second Intermediate Period/early Eighteenth Dynasty (**31-6**), most of them of the distinctive 'rishi'-type (**Plate 32,1-3**), corresponding in date to the Hyksos Period and its immediate aftermath, are made of native wood, namely sycamore fig (as are two further examples of the same date in Boston and Prague respectively).[33] This group includes two royal coffins (**31-2**), one, finely gilded, belonging to a king (**Plate 32,1**), the other, now fragmentary, belonging to a king's eldest son - people, it need hardly be said, of the highest status, whom one would have expected in normal circumstances to have had coffins made of cedar or some other prestige wood. But these were not, of course, normal circumstances. During the later Second Intermediate Period the Theban Kingdom was in political and economic isolation, cut off from the northern trading routes and the sources of fine timber by the Hyksos Kingdom based at Avaris (Tell el-Dab'a) in the Delta. It is a reasonable inference that the use of local wood for these coffins was the result of this reduced economic situation. Admittedly, this is not a new observation[34] but now for the first time it has a secure scientific basis. Significantly, following the so-called wars of liberation at the end of the Seventeenth and beginning of the Eighteenth Dynasties, Theban royal coffins, some on a very substantial scale, begin again to be made of conifer wood.[35]

The predominance of cedar and implications for lexicography

Many terms referring to different varieties of foreign wood are attested in Egyptian texts but, frustratingly, none are certainly identified, though there has been much debate. Particularly at issue has been the meaning of the term 's (ash). The textual evidence indicates that ash-wood was used for a variety of constructional and prestige purposes and was the most popular and highly prized of the foreign timbers. For example, in the second stela of King Kamose, last ruler of Dynasty 17, which gives an account of a successful Theban attack on the Hyksos capital, the King boasts of capturing a large number of Hyksos boats made of new ash-wood and of not leaving a plank of them behind.[36] Following Loret,[37] ash has generally been taken as referring to 'fir' (Abies cilicica) or 'pine' (Pinus pinea or halepensis) or as a generic term for both, while an associated term, mrw, has been understood as referring to cedar.[38] The question has recently been re-opened by Meiggs,[39] who points to weaknesses in Loret's evidence and makes out a balanced case for returning to the older translation of ash as 'cedar', though his view has yet to find general favour.[40] It would take much more space than is available here, indeed a substantial monograph, to consider in detail all the evidence bearing on this issue. Suffice it to say for the present that the material record, which to date has not played a full enough part in the debate, looks to be very much on Meiggs's side. There is a growing body of reliable evidence, derived from scientific analysis, and now substantially enhanced by the BM data, that cedar was the imported wood *par excellence* for the Egyptians. I list here major sets of analyses (other than those of the BM coffins), published and unpublished,[41] carried out since the identifications collected in Lucas and Harris (some of which, it should be said, are very old and in need of retesting).[42] They amount in total to over one thousand individual wood identifications,[43] from source-material of varied type, covering the entire span of ancient Egyptian history, from the Predynastic to the Graeco-Roman Periods.

(1) British Museum. Stelae. Seventeenth Dynasty - Graeco-Roman Period. Bierbrier 1987. Sycamore fig 72; cedar 3; fig 1; tamarisk 1.

(2) British Museum. Axe-hafts and accoutrements. First Intermediate Period/Middle Kingdom - Roman Period. Davies 1987. Acacia 4; sidder 3; tamarisk 2; plum 2; cedar 1; fig 1.

(3) British Museum. Mummy-labels. Roman Period.

	Total	PD	ED	OK	FIP	MK	SIP	NK	TIP	LP	GR	UD
Native	530											
Acacia	53	2		3	2	2 10		23	2		7	2
Balanites	2								1	1		
Carob	15							12			3	
Date Palm	2							2				
Fig	7			1		3	1		1	1		
Maerua	4							2			2	
Olive	5										5	
Persea	1					1						
Sidder	35			1		5		4	1	1	23	
Sycamore Fig	230	1		4	4	27	10	20	53	43 7	58	3
Tamarisk	158	15		2	1	15	2	31	30	·4 1	54	3
Willow	18							1			17	
Foreign	180											
African Rosewood	1										1	
Ash	1							1				
Beech	2										2	
Box	7			1		1		1			4	
Cedar	88	7	1	3	1	1 32	1	5	3	1	33	
Cypress	7			1		2				1	3	
Ebony *Dalbergia melanoxylon*	2							2				
Ebony *Diospyros* sp.	1							1				
Elm	2							1			1	
Fir	9										9	
Juniper	16		1					6			9	
Morus	1										1	
Pear	1										1	
Pine	37								1		36	
Pistachio	1							1				
Plum	2					1	1					
Pomegranate	1									1		
Spruce	1											1

Table 1.   Wood identifications post-Lucas and Harris (1962)

Unpublished. Tamarisk 46; pine 35; cedar 32; sycamore fig 25; sidder 23; willow 17; juniper 9; fir 8; acacia 5; olive 5; box 4; carob 3; beech 2; cypress 2; maerua *(Maerua crassifolia)* 2; African rosewood *(Pterocarpus* sp.) 1; elm 1; pear 1.

(4) British Museum. Statues and statuettes. Old Kingdom and New Kingdom. Some published in Penny 1993, 125-6, pls. 114-5, 143-5, pl. 131, and 280 and 281-2; and Davies 1993. Sycamore fig 3; juniper 2; cedar 1; tamarisk 1.

(5) Berkley, Lowie Museum. Coffins and miscellaneous. First Intermediate Period - Third Intermediate Period. Podzorski et al. 1985, 122-4. Acacia 2; sycamore fig 2; ebony *(Diospyros* sp.*)* 1; persea 1; sidder 1; tamarisk 1.

(6) Berlin, Schweinfurth Collection. Miscellaneous. Predynastic - Late Period. Germer 1988, 55-6. Cedar 3; sycamore fig 3; tamarisk 2; acacia 1; cypress 1; date palm 1; juniper 1.

(7) Berlin and Munich, Egyptian Museums. Miscellaneous. First Intermediate Period - Late Period.Grosser, Grünewald and Kreissl in Schoske, Germer and Kreissl 1992, 116 and 259. Tamarisk 11; acacia 4; juniper 4; sycamore fig 4; ebony *(Dalbergia melanoxylon)* 2; maerua 2; sidder 2; box 1; cedar 1; pistachio 1.

(8) Boston, Museum of Fine Arts. Coffins and canopic box. Old Kingdom - Third Intermediate Period. D'Auria et al., 1988, 76, 105, 109-11, 131, 173-4. Cedar 8; sycamore fig 2; acacia 1.

(9) Bremen, Übersee-Museum. Coffins and miscellaneous. Middle Kingdom - Ptolemaic Period. Grosser in Martin 1991, 26, 37, 43, 45, 53, 95, 136, 140, 144. Sycamore fig 6; tamarisk 2; acacia 1; cypress 1.

(10) Cairo, Egyptian Museum. Coffin reused for Ramesses II. Originally probably late Dynasty 18. Normand in Balout and Roubet 1985, 326-9. Cedar with dowels of ash and brace of tamarisk.

(11) Czechoslovakia, various collections. Coffins. New Kingdom - Graeco-Roman Period. Březinová and Hurda 1976, 139-42; Verner 1982. Sycamore fig 21; tamarisk 4; cedar 2; date palm 1.

(12) Freiburg, Museum für Völkerkunde. Coffin. Late Period. Grosser in Gerhards 1990, 21-3. Sycamore fig with dowels of tamarisk.

(13) Hannover, Kestner-Museum. Coffin. Ptolemaic Period. Fischer in Drenkhahn and Germer 1991, 39-42 and 51. Sycamore fig with dowels of tamarisk.

(14) Hierakonpolis. Miscellaneous. Predynastic Period. Hadidi in Hoffman 1982, 107-9. Tamarisk 3; acacia 1; sycamore fig 1.

(15) Hildesheim, Pelizaeus-Museum. Funerary furniture and models. Old Kingdom - Middle Kingdom. Grosser in Martin-Pardey 1991, *passim.* Sycamore fig 10; cedar 6; tamarisk 4; box 1; sidder 1.

(16) Hildesheim, Pelizaeus-Museum. Coffins. Old Kingdom - Graeco-Roman Period. Grosser, results mostly unpublished. Meiggs 1982, 409; Eggebrecht et al. 1986, 98-9, no. 39. Sycamore fig 17; tamarisk 6; cedar 5; acacia 1; cypress 1; pine 1; pomegranate 1; sidder 1.

(17) Kew, Royal Botanic Gardens. Coffin fragments. Graeco-Roman Period. Recent (1978) identifications cited in Killen 1980, 7. Cypress 1; fir 1; sycamore fig 1.

(18) Maadi. Miscellaneous. Predynastic Period. Rizkana and Seeher 1989, 24-5, 31 and 134-5 (Kroll). Tamarisk 12; cedar 7.

(19) Munich, Egyptian Museum. Cradle for mummified ox. Ptolemaic Period. Grosser in Boessneck 1987, 49-54. Sycamore fig with dowels of tamarisk.

(20) Munich, Institut für Holzforschung. Over 400 wood samples from 240 objects. No details or dates given. Grosser, Grünewald and Kreissl in Schoske, Kreissl and Germer 1992, 258-9, Table 7. Sycamore fig 138; tamarisk 106; acacia (all species) 44; cedar 44; sidder 13; juniper 10; fig 8; ebony *(Dalbergia melanoxylon)* 5; box 4; olive 4; persea 3; pine 3; beech 2; cypress 2; moringa 2; willow 2; dom palm 1; fir 1; pomegranate 1; yew 1.

(21) Oxford, Ashmolean Museum. Coffins and miscellaneous. Old Kingdom - New Kingdom and undated. Western in Meiggs 1982, 404. Tamarisk 7; acacia 4; sycamore fig 2; elm 1; fig 1; sidder 1; spruce 1.

(22) Paris, Louvre. Toilet objects. Middle Kingdom and New Kingdom. Vandier d'Abbadie 1972, ll, n. 1, and *passim.* Acacia 20; carob 12; tamarisk 8; sycamore fig 3; cedar 2; willow 1; also 'karité nilotica' 1 and 'ébène' (not further specified) 22.

(23) Paris, Louvre. Statues and statuettes. Middle Kingdom. Delange 1987, 7 and *passim.* Acacia 5; tamarisk 4; fig 3; box 1; cedar 1; sidder 1; also conifer 2; 'grenadille d'Afrique, dite "ébène"' 2; and 'karité' 1.

(24) Paris, Louvre. False doors. Old Kingdom. Ziegler 1990, 25, 104, no. 16, 176, no. 28, 240, no. 44. Acacia 3.

(25) Pittsburgh, Carnegie Museum of Natural History. Boat of Sesostris III. Dynasty 12. Patch 1990, 24-5, no. 15; Patch and Haldane 1990, 32ff. Cedar.

(26) Saqqara. Coffins. Late New Kingdom - Third Intermediate Period. Fundter in Raven 1991,11-13. Sycamore fig 37, with dowels and tongues of tamarisk.

(27) Toronto, Royal Ontario Museum. Funerary bed. Roman Period. Needler 1963, 1 and 31, n. 2. Pine and *Morus* sp.

(28) Turin, Egyptian Museum. Coffins. Twelfth Dynasty-Third Int. Period. Donadoni Roveri 1989, 42, 63-4 and 69. Acacia 2; balanites 2; cedar 2; fig 1.

The results, including the latest BM data but omitting those under (20) above,[44] are summarised in Table 1, where the totals for each wood are given and the identifications arranged chronologically. It can be seen that the overall picture is broadly in accord with the pattern established by the coffin analyses. Cedar, which is attested at every period, easily emerges as the leading foreign timber (representing nearly 50% of the total and almost 70% of Pharaonic cases). Indeed it is exceeded in overall frequency only by the stock native woods, sycamore fig and tamarisk. Even when the identifications listed in Lucas and Harris (1962) are added, the picture remains largely unchanged. Cedar was the most significant of the imported timbers, followed, during the Pharaonic period, by juniper and cypress; by comparison, occurrences of fir and pine are few and sporadic before the post-Pharaonic period. Caution is, of course, in order. There are still huge gaps in the evidence and these results need to be supplemented and confirmed by many more analyses. If they are at all representative, however, it is difficult to see how *ash* could mean 'fir' or 'pine'; more logically, from the present material data, the term should refer essentially to 'cedar', though it might also on occasion have had a generic usage covering a group of similar timbers.

Conclusion

This brief paper has, I believe, amply demonstrated the great scholarly potential of the scientific identification of wood, especially when such work forms part of a planned and integrated project rather than being simply random and opportunistic as has tended to be the case in the past. Though still at an early stage, the British Museum project has already advanced knowledge of relative wood use and of wood technology in general, raised questions as to the extent and significance of geographical and temporal variation, particularly with regard to their bearing on social and economic issues, confirmed what appears to be the clear pre-eminence of cedar among imported timbers, and contributed important new evidence to what should in due course be the solution of certain lexicographical problems. Further progress may be expected. It is intended to continue the BM programme to cover not only the remaining coffins but also other datable wooden objects, and it is hoped to extend the project to other museum collections. The growing database should allow future research to proceed from a position of considerably greater strength and confidence than has previously been possible. Wood has survived from Egypt in much greater quantity and in far better condition than from any other part of the ancient world. It is a uniquely rich scholarly resource, which we have barely begun to exploit.

Notes

1. The project has been carried out with the support and collaboration of the Jodrell Laboratory, Royal Botanic Gardens, Kew, and the Department of Scientific Research at the British Museum (see further n. 4 below).

2. Lucas and Harris 1962, 429-48 and 467-8;Helck 1971, 374-9; Dixon 1974, 206-7; Śliwa 1975, 12ff.; Muller 1977, 1263-9; Killen 1980, 1-6; Meiggs 1982, 60-8 and 405-9; Germer 1985, 6-13; Taylor 1989, 14-5; Hepper 1990, 44-6; Grosser, Grünewald and Kreissl in Schoske, Kreissl and Germer 1992, 253-4; for a dissenting voice, Nibbi 1994 a and b.

3. Bierbrier 1987, *passim*; Gale in Davies 1987, 128; see also Penny 1993, 125-6, 143-4, 280 and 281-2, and Davies 1993. Another set of analyses has been carried out in connection with the preparation of a catalogue of mummy-labels of the Roman Period, yet to be published; these results are summarised in the list of analyses, page 149 (3).

4. Mostly identified by Rowena Gale, formerly of the Jodrell Laboratory, Kew, with supplementary analyses by Caroline Cartwright of the British Museum. I am most grateful to both for their willing co-operation, without which this paper would not have been possible. I have also benefited from the advice and assistance of Drs. Renée Friedman, Dilwyn Jones, Diana Magee, Stephen Quirke, Donald Spanel and John Taylor.

5. All but two of these Assiut coffins come from the 1906-7 excavations of Hogarth, which are still to be published. A preliminary treatment of the work is contained in Ryan 1988, which is being prepared for press. Several more Assiut coffins and coffin-fragments in the BM remain to be analysed.

6. This title is noteworthy in that it provides evidence for the existence of a royal *ka*-chapel at Assiut in Dynasty 6 (see, most recently, on these chapels Brovarski in Silverman 1994, 16). Note that the name of the owner of this coffin is read as *Ny-ibw-htp* by Kanawati 1992, 275, n. 1777.

7. For two other examples, both much later, see Podzorski et al. 1985, 124, and Hildesheim, Pelizaeus-Museum 3099, unpublished, the former Third Intermediate Period, the latter

probably Late Period.

8. Again only two other examples, one First Intermediate Period, the other (part of a lid) Third Intermediate Period; see D'Auria et al. 1988, 105, no. 38, and Donadoni Roveri 1989, 63.

9. D'Auria et al. 1988, 76-7, no. 6, Dynasty 4; Eggebrecht et al. 1986, 98-9, no. 53, Dynasty 6.

10. Lucas and Harris 1962, 429ff.; Březinová and Hurda 1976, 139-42; Meiggs 1982, 409; Podzorski et al. 1985, 122-4; Boessneck 1987, 53-4; D'Auria et al. 1988, *passim*; Gerhards 1990, 21-3; Drenkhahn and Germer 1991, 39-42 and 51; Martin 1991, 53 and 136; Raven 1991, 8ff.

11. Meiggs 1982, 405; Penny 1993, 143; Moorey 1994, 348.

12. Lucas and Harris 1962, 452; Dixon 1974, 209.

13. Painting: D'Auria et al. 1988, 99, no. 31; Robins 1990, 60 and 81, no. 34, and examples cited by Willems 1988, 118, n. 3. Veneer: D'Auria 1988, 105, no. 38, and Hayes 1953, 315-6 (= Willems 1988, 166, fig. 15).

14. Meiggs 1982, 405; Moorey 1994, 348.

15. 1962, 430.

16. Martin 1991, 26, and James 1974, 37, no. 85, this latter recently analysed by Caroline Cartwright (see further n. 32).

17. Hildesheim, Pelizaeus-Museum 1591, unpublished, identified by Grosser.

18. Lucas 1962, 430.

19. Hildesheim, Pelizaeus-Museum 1902b, unpublished, identified by Grosser.

20. In addition to the BM coffins: Lucas and Harris 1962, 430, at least ten, Middle Kingdom, Third Intermediate and Late Periods; D'Auria et al. 1988, 76, 110, one Old Kingdom, five Middle Kingdom; Březinová and Hurda 1976, 139-42, one 18th Dynasty, one Graeco-Roman Period; Balout and Roubet 1985, 326-9, coffin reused for King Ramesses II, originally probably late 18th Dynasty; Eggebrecht et al. 1986, 98-9, Old Kingdom; Hildesheim, Pelizaeus-Museum 3060, 3063, 1275/6 and 4750, unpublished, identified by Grosser, four Middle Kingdom; Donadoni Roveri 1989, 42 and 63-4, one Middle Kingdom, one Third Intermediate Period; Schoske, Germer and Kreissl 1992, 116, no. 45, one Third Intermediate Period.

21. Patch 1990, 24-5, no. 15; Patch and Haldane 1990, 32ff; Haldane in Arnold 1992, 103 and 108. Other Egyptian boats await analysis. Beams from what seem to have been real freight boats of early Dynasty 12 were made of local wood, 'probably a species of acacia' (Arnold 1992, 92, n. 194; Haldane in Arnold 1992, 102ff.). Though a few of its associated parts have been identified, the main timbers of the famous Cheops boat, often stated to be of cedar, have yet to be analysed (Lucas and Harris 1962, 498-9; Meiggs 1982, 408; Lipke 1984, 24-5).

22. Haldane in Arnold 1992, 108.

23. D'Auria et al. 1988, 109-11.

24. Engelbach 1931, 144; Lucas and Harris 1962, 430, with nn. 7 and 7a, referring in the case of the coffins to Cairo, CG 28091 and 28092 (Willems 1988, 20, B9C-11C, and 74-5; Lapp 1993, 77 and 274, B1a and b, pl. 13, b).

25. Willems 1988, 68-9.

26. Willems 1988, 102; Magee 1989, Vol. i, 30-2 and 66; Lapp 1993, 132-5. In view of the special sacred status of the sycamore fig tree *(nht)*, the possibility of a religious factor in the use of its wood should also not be discounted (see Grosser in Boessneck 1987, 53; Baum 1988, 23, 37, and 273-4; Niwinski 1988, 57).

27. Martin-Pardey 1991, 6/69-70, 6/73, 6/76-7, 6/80, 6/83-4, 6/89-90, funerary models made of a mixture of different woods, mostly sycamore fig and cedar, in some cases very likely off-cuts from coffins.

28. See, for example, Lapp 1993, pls. 24 (S36a), a-b, 27, (S65), a-c, 29 (S18), a-c.

29. Only a very small number of contemporary coffins from other sites has yet been analysed: one from Abu Sir, made of cypress, Middle Kingdom (Martin 1991, 26); one from Dahshur, of cedar, Dynasty 12 (Germer 1988, 55); one from Naga ed-Der, of sycamore fig, First Intermediate Period (Podzorski et al. 1985, 122 and 124); one from Qau el-Kebir, of cedar, Dynasty 12 (Donadoni Roveri 1989, 42); and one from Sheikh Farag, of acacia veneered with cedar, First Intermediate Period (D'Auria et al. 1988, 105, no. 38).

30. The fourth (**30**), made of sycamore fig, is a good example of an 'off-the-shelf' coffin, made not to order but for stock. Originally, a blank space had been left at the end of the lines of inscription, into which were later inserted, clearly in a different hand, the name and title of the owner.

31. James, 1974, 37, no. 85, name changed for princess Mayet (reign of Mentuhotep II), mid-Dynasty 11.

32. By Caroline Cartwright, from samples kindly provided by Dr Donald Spanel and Won Yee Ng of the Brooklyn Museum. Two braces and a dowel from this coffin were also analysed and found to be made of sycamore fig and tamarisk respectively, again confirming that native woods were considered more suitable for such parts (see above).

33. D'Auria et al. 1988, 131, no. 64; Verner 1982, 317 (P 626).

34. Winlock 1947, 101-2; Hayes 1959, 29; 1973, 66.

35. Winlock 1924, 251, n. 5, with pl. xvi, and 275; Daressy 1909, 1, pls.i-ii, 3, pls. iii-iv; 8 and 10, pls. viii-ix; Winlock 1932, 16, 19, 70-1, pls. xviii-xxvi; Taylor 1989, 28-30.

36. Habachi 1972, 37; Smith and Smith 1976, 60.

37. 1916, 33-51.

38. Lucas and Harris 1962, 319-20; Helck 1971, 374-7; Janssen 1975, 375; Charpentier 1981, 176-9, no. 268, and 342-3, no. 536; Germer 1985, 6-8; Manniche 1989, 64; Traunecker 1989, 95, n. 36, and 102.

39. 1982, 405-9.

40. Germer 1986 (but see now Grosser, Grünewald and Kreissl in Schoske, Kreissl and Germer 1992, 260, n. 6); Nibbi 1994 a and b.

41. The list results from a fairly rapid search through the literature and is highly unlikely to be exhaustive. I am most grateful to Drs. Arne Eggebrecht and Bettina Schmitz for supplying the Hildesheim coffin results (16) and for permission to publish them. The scientific identifications were carried out by Prof. Dietger Grosser of the Institut für Holzforschung, Munich.

42. 1962, 429-48; the Tutankhamun material is further discussed by Germer 1989 and Hepper 1990.

43. Note that when several dowels from one coffin are made of the same wood they count in this list as representing a single identification of that wood.

44. Omitted because the relation between sample(s) and object is unclear in this case and it is also uncertain to what extent these data incorporate results already included elsewhere, for example, under (6), (9), (12), (15), (16) and (19). The identification of various exotic African woods (*Dalbergia retusa*, Zingana and African mahogany), quoted in Śliwa 1975, 17, came to my attention too late for inclusion. For recent analysis of wooden objects of the Coptic Period, see Rutschowscaya 1986.

References

Andrews C, 1984. *Egyptian Mummies*. London, British Museum Publications.

Arnold D, 1992. *The South Cemeteries of Lisht,* Vol. III. *The Pyramid Complex of Senwosret I.* New York, The Metropolitan Museum of Art.

Balout L and Roubet C (eds.), 1985. *La momie de Ramsès II. Contribution scientifique à l'Égyptologie.* Paris, Editions Recherche sur les Civilisations.

Baum N, 1988. *Arbres et Arbustes de l'Egypte Ancienne. La liste de la tombe thébaine d'Ineni (no. 81).* Orientalia Lovaniensia Analecta, 31. Leuven. Peeters.

Bierbrier M L, 1987. *Hieroglyphic Texts from Egyptian Stelae etc.* Part II. London, British Museum Publications.

Boessneck J (ed.), 1987. *Die Münchner Ochsenmumie.* Hildesheimer Ägyptologische Beiträge 25. Hildesheim, Gerstenberg Verlag.

Březinová D and Hurda B, 1976. Xylotomic Examination of Timber from Ancient Egyptian Coffins.

Zeitschrift für Ägyptische Sprache und Altertumskunde 103, 139-42.

Charpentier G, 1981. *Receuil de Matérieux Épigraphiques Relatifs à la Botanique de l'Égypte Antique.* Paris, Trismégiste.

Daressy G, 1909. *Catalogue Général des Antiquités Égyptiennes du Musée du Caire, Nos. 61001-61044. Cercueils des Cachettes Royals.* Cairo, Institut Français d'Archéologie Orientale.

D'Auria S, Lacovara P and Roehrig C H, 1988. *Mummies and Magic. The Funerary Arts of Ancient Egypt.* Boston, Museum of Fine Arts.

Davies W V, 1987. *Catalogue of Egyptian Antiquities in the British Museum, VII, Tools and Weapons I. Axes.* London, British Museum Publications.

Davies W V, 1993. Wooden Bes Figure. *British Museum Magazine* 14, 28.

Delange E, 1987. *Musée du Louvre. Catalogue des statues égyptiennes du Moyen Empire, 2060-1560 avant J.-C.* Paris, Réunion des musées nationaux.

Dixon D M, 1974. Timber in Ancient Egypt. *Commonwealth Forestry Review* 157, 204-9.

Donadoni Roveri A M, 1989. *Dal Museo al Museo. Passato e Futuro del Museo Egizio di Torino.* Turin, Umberto Allemandi.

Drenkhan R and Germer R (eds.), 1991. *Mumie und Computer, ein multidisziplinäres Forschungsprojekt in Hannover.* Hannover, Kestner-Museum, Th. Schäfer Druckerei.

Eggebrecht A, Schmitz B, Schulz R and Seidel M, 1986. *Das Alte Reich. Ägypten im Zeitalter der Pyramiden.* Katalog-Handbuch, Pelizaeus-Museum, Hildesheim. Mainz am Rhein, Verlag Philipp von Zabern.

Engelbach R, 1931. Ancient Egyptian Woods. *Annales du Service des Antiquités de l'Égypte* 31, 144.

Garstang J, 1907. *The Burial Customs of Ancient Egypt, as illustrated by Tombs of the Middle Kingdom, being a Report of Excavations made in the Necropolis of Beni Hasan during 1902-3-4.* London, Archibald Constable and Co Ltd.

Gerhards E, 1990. *Ägyptischer Mummiensarg. Analysen, Konservierung, Restaurierung.* Freiburg. Museum für Völkerkunde, Druckerei Weber.

Germer R, 1985. *Flora des pharaonischen Ägypten.* Deutsches Archäologisches Institut Abteilung Kairo, Sonderschrift 14. Mainz am Rhein, Verlag Philipp von Zabern.

Germer R, 1986. Zeder. In W Helck and W Westendorf (eds.), *Lexikon der Ägyptologie* VI. Wiesbaden, Otto Harrassowitz, 1357-8.

Germer R, 1988. *Katalog der altägyptischen Pflanzenreste der Berliner Museen.* Ägyptologische Abhandlungen, 47. Wiesbaden, Otto Harrassowitz.

Germer R, 1989. *Die Pflanzenmaterialien aus dem Grab des Tutanchamun.* Hildesheimer Ägyptologische Beiträge, 28. Hildesheim, Gerstenberg Verlag.

Guide 1898. E A Wallis Budge. *British Museum. A Guide to the First and Second Egyptian Rooms. Mummies, Mummy-Cases and other Objects connected with the Funeral Rites of the Ancient Egyptians.* London, Trustees of the British Museum.

Guide 1904. E A Wallis Budge and H R Hall. *British Museum. A Guide to the First and Second Egyptian Rooms. Predynastic Antiquities, Mummies, Mummy-Cases, and other Objects connected with the Funeral Rites of the Ancient Egyptians.* Second Edition. London, Trustees of the British Museum.

Guide 1924. E A Wallis Budge and H R Hall. *British Museum. A Guide to the First, Second and Third Egyptian Rooms. Predynastic Human Remains, Mummies, Wooden Sarcophagi, Coffins and Cartonnage Mummy Cases, Chests and Coffers, and other Objects connected with the Funerary Rites of the Ancient Egyptians.* London, Trustees of the British Museum.

Habachi L, 1972. *The Second Stela of Kamose and his struggle against the Hyksos ruler and his capital.* Abhandlungen des Deutschen Archäologischen Instituts Kairo, Ägyptologische Reihe, 8. Glückstadt, Verlag J J Augustin.

Handbook 1938. I E S Edwards. *A Handbook to the Egyptian Mummies and Coffins exhibited in the British Museum.* London, The British Museum.

Hayes W C, 1953. *The Scepter of Egypt. A Background for the Study of Egyptian Antiquities in the Metropolitan Museum of Art.* Part I. *From the Earliest Times to the End of the Middle Kingdom.* New York, Harper and Brothers.

Hayes W C, 1959. *The Scepter of Egypt. A Background for the Study of the Egyptian Antiquities in the Metropolitan Museum of Art.* Part II. *The Hyksos Period and the New Kingdom (1675-1080 BC).* Cambridge, Harvard University Press.

Hayes W C, 1973. Egypt from the Death of Ammenemes III to Seqenenre II. In I E S Edwards, C J Gadd, N L Hammond and E Sollberger (eds.), *The Cambridge Ancient History,* Third Edition, Vol. II, Part I, *History of the Middle East and the Aegean Region c.1800-1380 BC.* Cambridge University Press, 42-76.

Helck W, 1971. *Die Beziehungen Ägyptens zu Vorderasien im 3. und 2. Jahrtausend v. Chr. 2,* verbesserte Auflage. Wiesbaden, Otto Harrassowitz.

Hepper F N, 1990. *Pharaoh's Flowers. The Botanical Treasures of Tutankhamun.* London, HMSO.

Hoffman M A (ed.), 1982. *The Predynastic of Hierakonpolis - An Interim Report.* Egyptian Studies Association. Publication no. 1. Oxford, Alden Press.

James T G H, 1974. *Corpus of Hieroglyphic Inscriptions in the Brooklyn Museum, I. From Dynasty I to the End of Dynasty XVIII.* New York, The Brooklyn Museum.

Janssen J J, 1975. *Commodity Prices from the Ramessid Period. An Economic Study of the Village of Necropolis Workmen at Thebes.* Leiden, E J Brill.

Kanawati N, 1992. *Akhmim in the Old Kingdom,* Part I. *Chronology and Administration.* Sydney, Macquarie University, The Australian Centre for Egyptology.

Killen G, 1980. *Ancient Egyptian Furniture,* Vol I, *4000-1300 BC.* Warminster, Aris and Phillips Ltd.

Lapp G, 1993. *Typologie der Särge und Sargkammern von der 6. bis 13. Dynastie.* Studien zur Archäologie und Geschichte Altägyptens, 7. Heidelberg, Heidelberges Orientverlag.

Lipke P, 1984. *The Royal Ship of Cheops. A retrospective account of the discovery, restoration and reconstruction. Based on interviews with Hag Ahmed Youssef Moustafa.* National Maritime Museum, Greenwich, Archaeological Series No 9. BAR International Series 225.

Loret V, 1916. *Quelques notes sur l'arbre ÂCH. Annales du Service des Antiquités de l'Égypte* 16, 33-51.

Lucas A and Harris J R, 1962. *Ancient Egyptian Materials and Industries.* Fourth Edition, revised and enlarged. London, Edward Arnold Ltd.

Magee D, 1989. *Asyut to the end of the Middle Kingdom: a historial and cultural study,* 3 Vols. Unpublished D. Phil. Thesis, University of Oxford.

Manniche L, 1989. *An Ancient Egyptian Herbal.* London, British Museum Publications.

Martin K, 1991. *Corpus Antiquitatum Aegyptiacarum. Übersee-Museum Bremen,* Lieferung 1. *Die altägyptischen Denkmäler,* Teil I. Mainz am Rhein, Verlag Philipp von Zabern.

Martin-Pardey E, 1991. *Corpus Antiquitatum Aegyptiacarum. Pelizaeus-Museum Hildesheim,* Lieferung 6. *Grabbeigaben, Nachträge und Ergänzungen.* Mainz am Rhein, Verlag Philipp von Zabern.

Meiggs R, 1982. *Trees and Timber in the Ancient Mediterranean World.* Oxford, Clarendon Press.

Moorey P R S, 1994. *Ancient Mesopotamian Materials and Industries. The Archaeological Evidence.* Oxford, Clarendon Press.

Müller C, 1977. Holz und Holzverarbeitung. In W Helck and W Westendorf (eds.), *Lexikon der Ägyptologie,* II. Wiesbaden, Otto Harrassowitz, 1264-9.

Needler W, 1963. *An Egyptian Funerary Bed of the Roman Period in the Royal Ontario Museum.* Art and Archaeology Division, Occasional Paper, 6. University of Toronto, Royal Ontario Museum.

Nibbi A, 1994a. Some remarks on the Cedars of Lebanon. *Discussions in Egyptology* 28, 35-52.

Nibbi A, 1994b. The Byblos Question Again. *Discussions in Egyptology* 30, 115-41.

Niwinski A, 1988. *21st Dynasty Coffins from Thebes. Chronological and Typological Studies.* Mainz am Rhein, Verlag Philipp von Zabern.

Parkinson R and Quirke S, 1992. The Coffin of Prince

Herunefer and the Early History of the Book of the Dead. In A B Lloyd (ed.), *Studies in Pharaonic Religion and Society in Honour of J Gwyn Griffiths*. London, The Egypt Exploration Society, 37-51.

Patch D C, 1990. *Reflections of Greatness. Ancient Egypt at the Carnegie Museum of Natural History*. Pittsburgh, The Carnegie Museum of Natural History.

Patch D C and Haldane C W, 1990. *The Pharaoh's Boat at The Carnegie*. Pittsburgh, The Carnegie Museum of Natural History.

Penny N, 1993. *The Materials of Sculpture*. New Haven and London, Yale University Press.

PM i (2). The late Bertha Porter and Rosalind L B Moss, assisted by Ethel W Burney, *Topographical Bibliography of Ancient Egyptian Hieroglyphic Texts, Reliefs and Paintings, I. The Theban Necropolis*, Part 2. *Royal Tombs and Smaller Cemeteries*. Second Edition. Revised and augmented. Oxford, Clarendon Press, 1964.

PM iv. Bertha Porter and Rosalind L B Moss, *Topographical Bibliography of Ancient Egyptian Hieroglyphic Texts, Reliefs and Paintings, IV. Lower and Middle Egypt (Delta and Cairo to Asyut)*. Oxford, Clarendon Press, 1934.

Podzorski P V, Rem N C and Knudsen J A, 1985. Identification of some Egyptian wood artifacts in the Lowie Museum of Anthropology. *MASCA Journal* 3 (no. 4), 122-4.

Quirke S, 1990. *The Administration of Egypt in the Late Middle Kingdom. The Hieratic Documents*. New Malden, S I A Publishing.

Quirke S and Spencer J (eds.), 1992. *The British Museum Book of Ancient Egypt*. London, British Museum Press.

Quirke S, 1994. Richisarg eines Königs Intef. In *Pharaonen und Fremde. Dynastien im Dunkel*. Sonderaustellung des Historischen Museums der Stadt Wien, 275.

Raven M J, 1989. The Antef Diadem Reconsidered. *Oudheidkundige Mededelingen uit het Rijksmuseum van Oudheden* 68, 77-86.

Raven M, 1991. *The Tomb of Iurudef. A Memphite Official in the Reign of Ramesses II*. Leiden, National Museum of Antiquities, and London, Egypt Exploration Society.

Reeves N and Taylor J H, 1992. *Howard Carter Before Tutankhamun*. London, British Museum Press.

Rizkana I and Seeher J, 1989. *Maadi* III. *The Non-Lithic Small Finds and the Structural Remains of the Predynastic Settlement*. Deutsches Archäologisches Institut Abteilung Kairo, Archäologische Veröffentlichungen, 80. Mainz am Rhein, Verlag Philipp von Zabern.

Robins G (ed.), 1990. *Beyond the Pyramids. Egyptian Regional Art from the Museo Egizio, Turin*. Atlanta, Emory University Museum of Art and Archaeology.

Ruffle J, 1977. *Heritage of the Pharaohs. An Introduction to Egyptian Archaeology*. Oxford, Phaidon.

Rutschowscaya M-H, 1986. *Musée du Louvre. Catalogue des bois de l'Egypt copte*. Paris, Réunion des musées nationaux.

Ryan D P, 1988. *The Archaeological Excavations of David George Hogarth at Asyut, Egypt, 1906/1907*. Unpublished manuscript.

Schoske S, Kreissl B and Germer R, 1992. *'Ankh' - Blumen für das Leben. Pflanzen im alten Ägypten*. Schriften aus der ägyptischen Sammlung, 6. Munich, Staatliche Sammlung Ägyptischer Kunst.

Seipel W, 1989. *Ägypten. Götter, Gräber und die Kunst: 4000 Jahre Jenseitsglaube*. Linz, Landesmuseum.

Silverman D P (ed.), 1994. *For His Ka. Essays Offered in Memory of Klaus Baer*. Studies in Ancient Oriental Civilization, 55. Chicago, The Oriental Institute of the University of Chicago.

Śliwa J, 1975. *Studies in Ancient Egyptian Handicraft. Woodworking*. Cracow, Nakladen Uniwersytetu Jagiellonskiego.

Smith H S and Smith A, 1976. A Reconsideration of the Kamose Texts. *Zeitschrift für Ägyptische Sprache und Altertumskunde* 103, 48-76.

Taylor J H, 1989. *Egyptian Coffins*. Aylesbury, Shire Publications.

Traunecker C, 1989. Le "Château de l'Or" de Thoutmosis III et les magasins nord du temple d'Amon. *Sociétés urbaines en Égypte et au Soudan. Cahiers de Recherches de l'Institut de Papyrologie et d'Egyptologie de Lille* 11, 89-111.

Vandier d'Abbadie J, 1972. *Musée du Louvre. Catalogue des objets de toilette égyptiens*. Paris, Éditions des musées nationaux.

Verner M, 1982. *Corpus Antiquitatum Aegyptiacarum. Altägyptische Särge in den Museen und Sammlungen der Tschechoslowakei*. Prague, Univerzita Karlova.

Willems H, 1988. *Chests of Life. A Study of the Typology and Conceptual Development of Middle Kingdom Standard Class Coffins*. Leiden, Ex Oriente Lux.

Winlock H E, 1924. The Tombs of the Kings of the Seventeenth Dynasty at Thebes. *Journal of Egyptian Archaeology* 10, 217-77.

Winlock H E, 1932. *The Tomb of Queen Meryet-Amun at Thebes*. New York, The Metropolitan Museum of Art Egyptian Expedition, Vol. VI.

Winlock H E, 1947. *The Rise and Fall of the Middle Kingdom in Thebes*. New York, The Macmillan Company.

Ziegler C, 1990. *Musée du Louvre. Catalogue des stèles, peintures et reliefs égyptiens de l'Ancien Empire et de la Première Période Intermédiaire vers 2686-2040 avant J.-C.* Paris, Réunion des musées nationaux.

PLATE 1 (Bietak)

1. Bull-leaper against the background of a maze-pattern (wall-plaster of lime, fragment F4: 22.5×17×0.6 cm). Reconstruction by Lyla Pinch-Brock.

2. Maze-pattern with a blue rectangle (wall-plaster, fragment F24: 16×13.3×0.7–1.3 cm).

PLATE 2 (Bietak)

1. Bull-leaper (wall-plaster, fragment F5: 22.5×19×1.2 cm).

2. Exhausted and defeated bull with a taureador in front teasing him and a second one grasping the bull's head and resting his chin on the animal's forehead—at the end of a bull-game? (wall-plaster, fragment F3: 17.5×10×1.3 cm).

PLATE 3 (Bietak)

1. Acrobat performing beside a palm tree (wall-plaster, fragment F7:
21×17.3×0.8 cm).

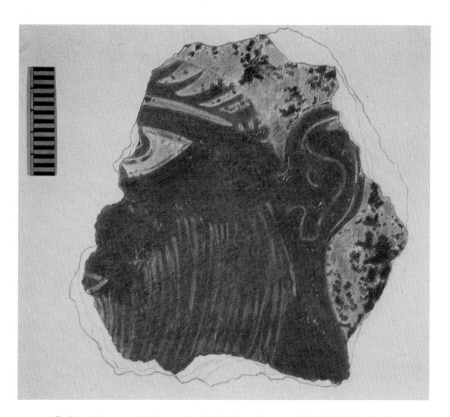

2. Bearded man, probably a priest (wall-plaster, fragment F6: 17.5×14.4×6 cm).
Drawing by Lyla Pinch-Brock.

PLATE 4   (Bietak)

1. Fleeing antelopes attacked by dog in a river landscape (wall-plaster, fragment F33: 39.5×27×1.2 cm).

2. Hind-legs of a leopard in flying gallop over reed (wall-plaster, fragment F18: 13.1×9.8×1.3 cm).

3. Part of wings of a griffin (wall-plaster, fragment F15: 6.3×4.9×0.7 cm).

4. Griffin from Xeste 3 at Thera, courtesy of the Thera Foundation, after Doumas 1992.

PLATE 5 (Maguire)

1. Sherds of WP PLS, Tell el-Dab'a.

2. Sherds of WP CLS, Tell el-Dab'a.

3. WP V, Tell el-Dab'a.

4. Plain Ware, Tell el-Dab'a.

5. Sherds of Base Ring, 'Ezbet Helmi.

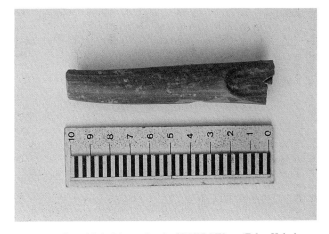

6. Handle (with incision at base) of RLWM Ware, 'Ezbet Helmi.

PLATE 6 (Cline)

1. Statue-base of Amenhotep III, with Aegean name-rings. Thebes, Kom el-Hetan, 18th Dynasty.

2. Monkey-figurine of Egyptian blue, inscribed with prenomen of Amenhotep II. 18th Dynasty, Cline Catalogue no. 1.

3. *Above and below right* Faience plaque inscribed on both sides with titles and prenomen of Amenhotep III. 18th Dynasty, Cline Catalogue no. 25.

PLATE 7 (Cline)

1. Egyptian alabastron. 18th Dynasty, Cline Catalogue no. 33.

2. Canaanite amphora. Syro-Palestine, LB II, Cline Catalogue no. 42.

PLATE 8 (Parkinson and Schofield)

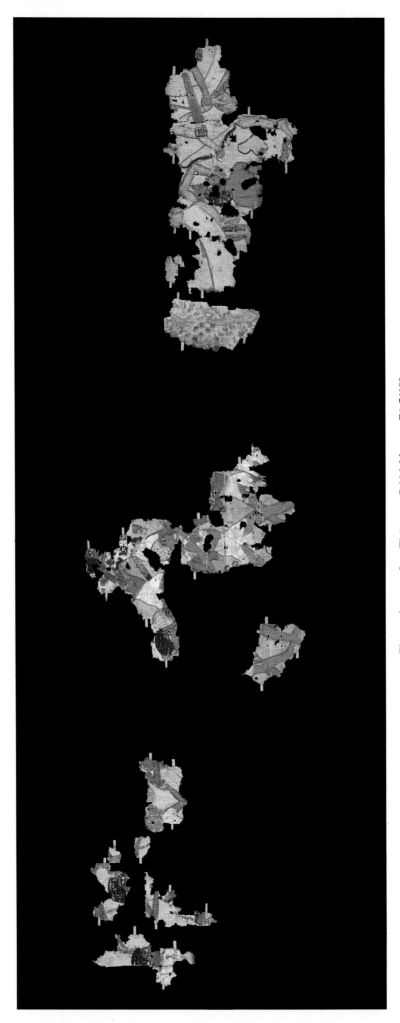

Illustrated papyrus from El-Amarna. British Museum, EA 74100.

PLATE 9 (Tubb)

1. Tell es-Sa'idiyeh. Bronze wine-set from Grave 32, a burial of the early 12th century BC.

2. Tell es-Sa'idiyeh. Ivory cosmetic box and bronze bowl from Grave 232,
a late 13th century BC burial.

PLATE 10 (Davies)

1. Inner coffin of *Sbk-ḥtpi,* from Beni Hasan. Late 11th/early 12th Dynasty, made of cedar. British Museum, EA 41572.

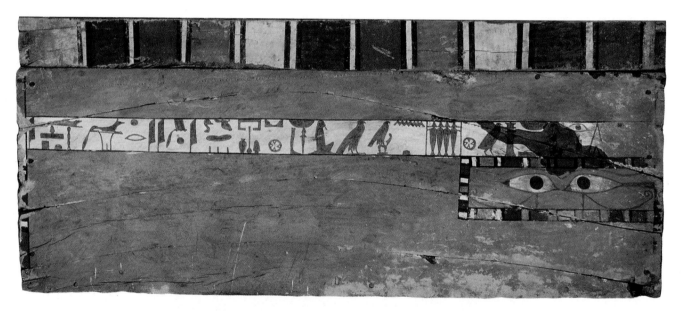

2. Outer coffin of *Sbk-ḥtpi,* from Beni Hasan. Late 11th/early 12th Dynasty, made of sycamore fig. British Museum, EA 41571.

PLATE 11 (Warren)

1. Terracotta sistrum from Arkhanes, Phourni, Funerary Building 9. Height approx. 10 cm, *c.* 2000 BC.

2. Terracotta plaque from Mallia, Quartier Mu. Height 6.9 cm, Middle Minoan II, 1700 BC.

3–5. Egyptian alabaster *Gravidenflasche* from Katsamba, front and side views. Height 14.2 cm, 18th Dynasty.

PLATE 12 (Warren)

1.

2.

3.

4.

1–4. Statuette of User in Chephren diorite from Knossos, showing front (1), side (2–3) and rear (4) views.
Maximum height approx. 14 cm, Middle Kingdom.

PLATE 13 (Warren)

1. Carinated bowl of Chephren diorite from Knossos.
Height approx. 4.3 cm, 4th–6th Dynasties.

2. Carinated bowl of obsidian from Knossos.
Height approx. 4.65 cm, Middle Minoan.

4. Inscription of Tuthmosis III on
same amphora, scale 6/7.

3. Egyptian alabaster amphora inscribed with cartouches of Tuthmosis III
(1479–1425 BC), from Katsamba Tomb B. Height 29.8 cm.

PLATE 14 (Bietak)

1. Golden pendant from palace tomb F/I-p/17-no. 14
(str. d/1, *c.* 1750 BC).

2. Dagger with tangential spirals from palace tomb F/I-m/18-no. 3
(str. d/l, *c.* 1750 BC).

PLATE 15 (Bietak)

1. Platform construction H/I in the Hyksos citadel, viewed from the east.

2. Platform construction H/I in the Hyksos citadel, viewed from the south.

PLATE 16   (Bietak)

1. Excavation area north of platform H/I. Two strata of garden remains with tree-pits and probably vineyard pits set in 'pergola' system; in the foreground, the fortification wall.

2. Excavation area north of platform H/I, detail.

PLATE 17 (Bietak)

1. Wall-plaster fragments *in situ* above a limestone statue of a lion, area H/I.

2. Wall-plaster fragments *in situ*, area H/I.

PLATE 18 (Morgan)

1. Syrian cylinder seal (impression), 18th–17th century BC, (?) Aleppo workshop, after Collon 1994.

2. Bull-sports panel. Wall-painting from the Court of the
Stone Spout, Knossos, after Immerwahr 1990.

PLATE 19 (Cline)

1. Glass pendant. Mesopotamia, 16th–13th
centuries BC, Cline Catalogue no. 11.

2. Head from glass plaque. Mesopotamia, 16th–13th
centuries BC, Cline Catalogue no. 27.

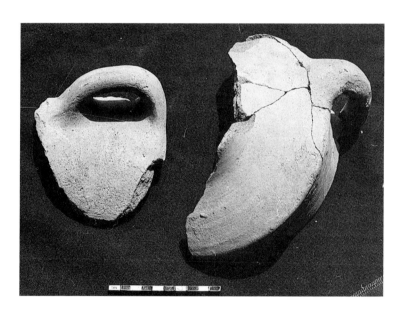

3. Fragments of Canaanite amphora. Syro-Palestine, (?)LB II,
Cline Catalogue no. 40.

4. Fragments of Canaanite amphora. Syro-Palestine, LB II,
Cline Catalogue no. 41.

PLATE 20 (Cline)

1. Bowl-fragment of diorite or gabbro. Egypt, Early Dynastic/Old Kingdom,
Cline Catalogue no. 48.

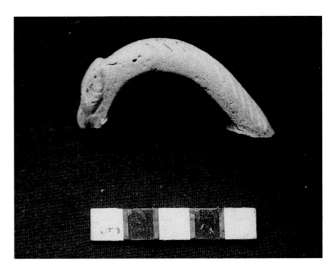

2. Handle of faience vessel. Syro-Palestine, LB,
Cline Catalogue no. 80.

3. Bronze armour-scale. Syro-Palestine, LB,
Cline Catalogue no. 82.

4. Haematite weight. Syro-Palestine, (?)LB II,
Cline Catalogue no. 84.

5. Blank of elephant ivory. Syro-Palestine, LB,
Cline Catalogue no. 87.

6. Piece of hippopotamus canine. Probably Syro-Palestine, LB,
Cline Catalogue no. 88.

PLATE 21 (Hankey)

Stirrup jar, FS 171. UCD 50.

PLATE 22   (Hankey)

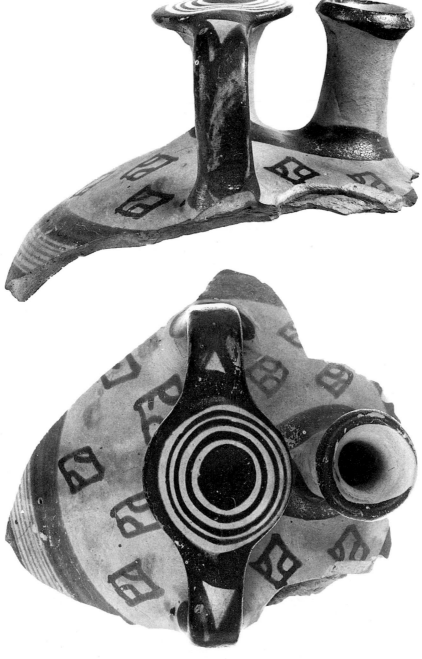

Stirrup jar, FS 171 or 173. AKMUB 295, 15.

PLATE 23 (Hankey)

Faience stirrup jar. British Museum EA 35413.

PLATE 24 (Hankey)

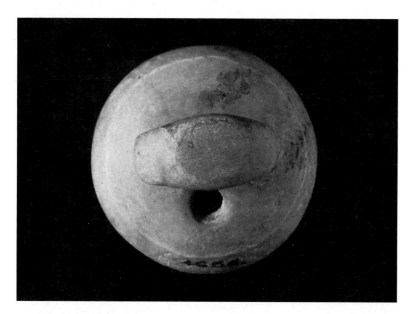

Calcite stirrup jar. British Museum EA 4656.

PLATE 25 (Tubb)

1. View of Tell es-Saʻidiyeh from the north, with the Wadi Kufrinjeh
in the foreground.

2. View of Tell es-Saʻidiyeh from the east, with the hills of Samaria
in the background.

PLATE 26 (Tubb)

1. Overhead view of the 12th century BC 'Egyptian Governor's Residency' at Tell es-Sa'idiyeh.

2. Tell es-Sa'idiyeh, water system staircase after its 1987 're-excavation'.

PLATE 27 (Tubb)

1. Overhead view of the lower part of the water system at Tell es-Saʻidiyeh,
showing the spring-fed pool chamber.

2. Tell es-Saʻidiyeh, Grave 251, showing a bronze javelin which had been incorporated
into a linen binding around the deceased.

PLATE 28   (Tubb)

1. Tell es-Saʻidiyeh, Grave 76, a 12th century BC Double-Pithos burial.

2. Tell es-Saʻidiyeh, Grave 364A, a Double-Pithos burial of the late 13th century BC, showing a straight-sided 'ration-bowl' in position over the pelvis.

PLATE 29 (Tubb)

1. Tell es-Sa'idiyeh, Double-Pithos burial 364B (late 13th century BC) with anthropomorphic pilgrim flask against left leg and imitation Mycenaean pyxis near to left shoulder.

2. Tell es-Sa'idiyeh, Grave 63, a jar burial of the 12th century BC which contained the remains of an infant.

PLATE 30 (Tubb)

1. Tell es-Sa'idiyeh, finely decorated ivory pyxis from Double-Pithos burial 204 (late 13th century BC). Enlarged by approx. 1.5.

2. Tell es-Sa'idiyeh, two dagger blades from Double-Pithos burials showing intricate incised decorations along their mid-ribs. Enlarged by approx. 2.

PLATE 31 (Davies)

1. Coffin of *Ḥtp-nb.í.* From Assiut, 6th Dynasty, made of tamarisk. British Museum, EA 46629.

2. Coffin of *Spí.* From Bersheh, mid- to late 12th Dynasty, made of cedar. British Museum, EA 55315.

PLATE 32 (Davies)

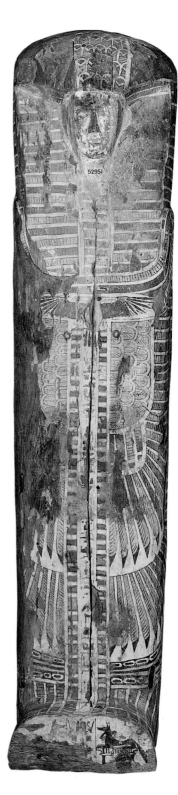

1. Rishi-coffin of King *'Iní-ít.f.* From Thebes, 17th Dynasty, made of sycamore fig. British Museum, EA 6652.

2. Rishi-coffin, owner anonymous. From Thebes, 17th Dynasty, made of sycamore fig. British Museum, EA 52950.

3. Rishi-coffin, owner anonymous. From Thebes, 17th Dynasty, made of sycamore fig. British Museum, EA 52951.